Verdun 1916

Verdun 1916

The Renaissance
of the Fortress

J.E. Kaufmann and H.W. Kaufmann

Pen & Sword
MILITARY

First published in Great Britain in 2016 by
Pen & Sword Military
an imprint of
Pen & Sword Books Ltd
47 Church Street
Barnsley
South Yorkshire
S70 2AS

ISBN 978 1 47382 702 8

A CIP catalogue record for this book is available from the British Library

Typeset in Ehrhardt by
Mac Style Ltd, Bridlington, East Yorkshire
Printed and bound in the UK by CPI Group (UK) Ltd, Croydon, CR0
4YY

Pen & Sword Books Ltd incorporates the imprints of Pen & Sword
Archaeology, Atlas, Aviation, Battleground, Discovery, Family History,
History, Maritime, Military, Naval, Politics, Railways, Select, Social History,
Transport, True Crime, and Claymore Press,
Frontline Books, Leo Cooper, Praetorian Press, Remember When, Seaforth
Publishing and Wharncliffe.

For a complete list of Pen & Sword titles please contact
PEN & SWORD BOOKS LIMITED
47 Church Street, Barnsley, South Yorkshire, S70 2AS, England
E-mail: enquiries@pen-and-sword.co.uk
Website: www.pen-and-sword.co.uk

Contents

Acknowledgements

We would like to thank the following people for their help with this project: Bernard Bour and Patrick Corbon on French army tactics; Clayton Donnell for use of photos and loan of books; Christine Holstein for additional details on the battle; Tom Idzikowski for information on the Russian forts; Patrice Lang for information on the French army; Bernard Lowry for use of photos and other items; Marcus Massing for information about Verdun's fortifications; Frank Philippart for use of photos and information; Marc Romanch for photos from the archives and information on artillery; Lee Unterborn for Internet searches; General David Zabecki for information on artillery. In addition, we thank the members of SiteO who helped us and hopefully have not forgotten anyone. Also, we would like to thank our editor, Rupert Harding, for tolerating the delay with the project and helping with contacts.

Note to Reader
In the text, all German and Austrian units are *italicized* to avoid confusion. Like most books of this size, the number of illustrations has been limited. It is strongly recommended that the reader use additional maps and plans that may be found in other books such as the volume *West Point Atlas of Military History* related to the First World War. There are also numerous Internet sites with good campaign and battle maps. The reader can find additional plans and illustrations of the French forts at Verdun and the battlefield in relatively inexpensive books such as *Verdun 1916* by William Martin (Osprey), *The Fortifications of Verdun 1874–1917* by Clayton Donnell (Osprey) and *Fort Douaumont* and *Fort Vaux* by Christina Holstein (Pen & Sword). Some older books found in many libraries, including Pétain's *Verdun*, include detailed maps.

Preface

'Nothing except a battle lost can be half as melancholy as a battle won'
The Duke of Wellington at Waterloo, June 1815

Since the Battle of Verdun, a hundred years ago, an extraordinary number of books has been written on this long and gruesome engagement. The accounts cover many different points of view of the battle, relate individual experiences or present the conflict in a detached way disregarding the terrible experiences the soldiers endured. The last approach was particularly favoured by some of the generals who sat far behind the lines, moving their units like the pieces of a chess game. Although the numbers presented are shocking enough, they alone cannot give the proper perspective on a battle that is best described as hell on earth. To get an accurate picture of how Verdun brought together the horrors of combat, it would be advisable to read individual accounts and even some good historical fiction.

In the present volume, we have chosen to take the more objective approach, without, however, leaving out the horrifying aspects of this engagement. We examine the background, strategy and events of this great battle, although this has already been done. Not all historians will agree or draw the same conclusions. Primary sources, just like secondary ones, whether they come from individual accounts or official documents, must be subject to scrutiny and are not necessarily reliable. The contents of key primary sources such as reports, official documents, individual accounts and especially newspapers are not always dependable since they are often written with the intent of twisting the truth or bending it to the author's point of view. They may glorify an event, cover up mistakes or be written by someone with a limited view of events. The historian must take these and other sources, including secondary ones, and attempt to recreate the events as best he can. As a result, there are many different versions of a single battle or action.

One of the best examples of the difficulties historians face is the famous Schlieffen Plan, which shaped Germany's strategy in the First World War. In this case, the problem is that there is no actual and detailed pre-1914 documentation of the plan. After the war, General Wilhelm Gröner shed some light on the plan in his memoirs in which he claimed that Helmuth von Moltke the Younger had modified the plan formulated by Alfred von Schlieffen. In *Supplying War*, military historian Martin van Creveld points out that, assuming that he and some other prominent figures are correct, the operation would have failed because Schlieffen had not taken into account the logistical needs of a modern army. He seemed to think that twentieth-century

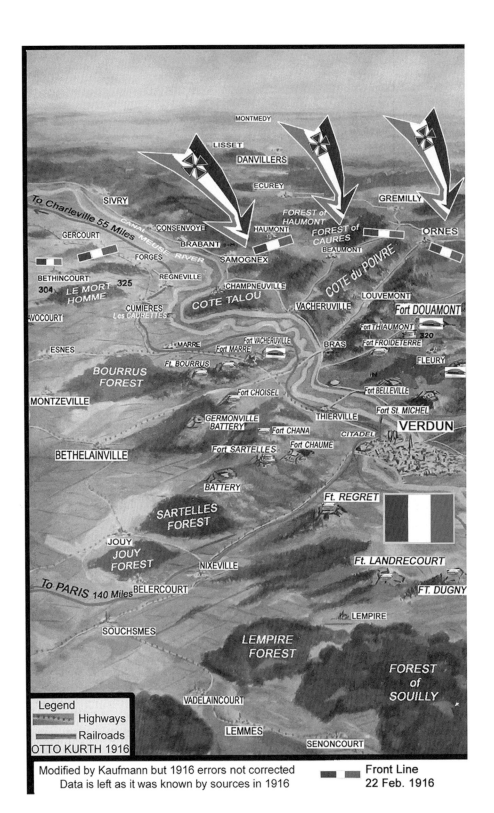

MONTMEDY

LISSET

DANVILLERS

ECUREY

SIVRY

GREMILLY

To Charleville 55 Miles

CANAL MEUSE RIVER

CONSENVOYE

FOREST of HAUMONT

GERCOURT

HAUMONT

FOREST of CAURES

ORNES

BRABANT

BEAUMONT

FORGES

SAMOGNEX

BETHINCOURT

REGNEVILLE

CHAMPNEUVILLE

COTE du POIVRE

304 LE MORT HOMME 325

COTE TALOU

LOUVEMONT

CUMIERES

VACHERUVILLE

Les CAURETTES

Fort DOUAMONT

AVOCOURT

Fort THIAUMONT

320

MARRE

Fort VACHERUVILLE

BRAS

Fort FROIDETERRE

ESNES

Fort MARRE

FLEURY

Ft. BOURRUS

BOURRUS FOREST

Fort BELLEVILLE

MONTZEVILLE

Fort CHOISEL

Fort St. MICHEL

GERMONVILLE BATTERY

THIERVILLE

Fort CHANA

VERDUN

CITADEL

BETHELAINVILLE

Fort SARTELLES

Fort CHAUME

BATTERY

Ft. REGRET

SARTELLES FOREST

JOUY

JOUY FOREST

NIXEVILLE

Ft. LANDRECOURT

To PARIS 140 Miles

BELERCOURT

FT. DUGNY

LEMPIRE

SOUCHSMES

LEMPIRE FOREST

FOREST of SOUILLY

VADELAINCOURT

LEMMES

SENONCOURT

Legend

Highways

Railroads

OTTO KURTH 1916

Modified by Kaufmann but 1916 errors not corrected
Data is left as it was known by sources in 1916

Front Line
22 Feb. 1916

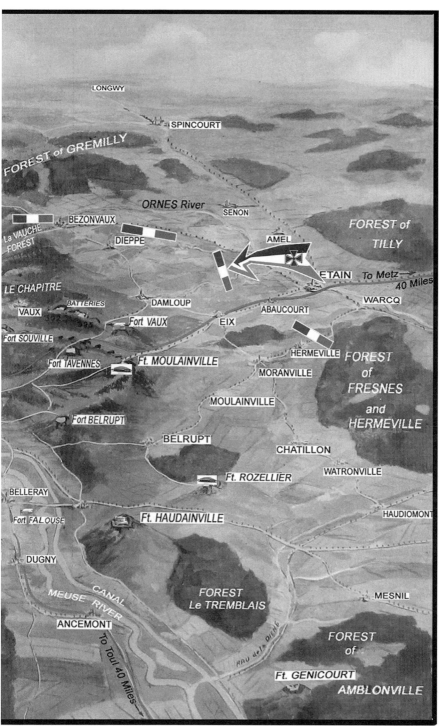

LONGWY

SPINCOURT

FOREST of GREMILLY

ORNES River

SENON

BEZONVAUX

La VAUCHE FOREST

DIEPPE

AMEL

FOREST of TILLY

LE CHAPITRE

ETAIN   To Metz→
40 Miles

BATTERIES

DAMLOUP

ABAUCOURT

WARCQ

VAUX

Fort VAUX

EIX

Fort SOUVILLE

HERMEVILLE   FOREST
of
FRESNES
and
HERMEVILLE

Fort TAVENNES   Ft. MOULAINVILLE

MORANVILLE

Fort BELRUPT

MOULAINVILLE

BELRUPT

CHATILLON

Ft. ROZELLIER

WATRONVILLE

BELLERAY

Fort FALOUSE

Ft. HAUDAINVILLE

HAUDIOMONT

DUGNY

CANAL
MEUSE RIVER

FOREST
Le TREMBLAIS

MESNIL

ANCEMONT

To Toul 40 Miles→

RAU de la DIEUE

FOREST
of

Ft. GENICOURT

AMBLONVILLE

Positions of forts and batteries are exaggerated by the artist
to highlight their signficance and some positions and locations omitted

armies could still live off the land the way they had done in the age of Napoleon despite the fact that they were far bigger in size. In the autumn of 1914, only an abundant harvest, prosperous Belgian merchants and supplies abandoned by the Belgian army actually kept the German invasion force from starving. Even so, many of the German army dray horses, which had pulled supply the wagons and moved the field artillery, did not survive. This was 'modern' warfare and the much-maligned Moltke realized it before 1914. Like his uncle, Helmuth von Moltke the Elder, the Younger saw the need to develop Germany's heavy artillery to make it capable of destroying modern forts built after the 1880s. Thus, due to contradictory historical evidence, many historians have been forced to re-evaluate Schlieffen's genius, and reconsider the alleged short-comings of Moltke the Younger.[1] Likewise, General Falkenhayn's reasoning for launching the Battle of Verdun may seem clear and obvious based mainly on his post-war writings, but it is likely that he was motivated by the need to justify his actions. After all, Erich von Falkenhayn was a rational and skilled general, yet, outwardly at least, his strategy at Verdun appears absurd. The Battle of Verdun and the naval Battle of Jutland were the climax as well as the anti-climax of the First World War and best exemplify the futility of the conflict. Here, when the two main antagonists met in 1916, their armies had finally reached the point of true modernization from their troops' equipment to more massive and up-to-date weapons. Both sides also adjusted their tactics as the conflict degenerated into a gigantic battle of the trenches. Forts regained their importance after being considered obsolete after 1914.

Most of the weapons commonly associated with the First World War, except the tank, appeared on the battlefield at Verdun. Air warfare came of age over the skies of Verdun. Some of the best and worst generals on the Western Front got involved there as well. The battle in terms of win and loss devolved into a giant stalemate in which neither side achieved a major success but in which thousands of men were slaughtered. The Battle of Verdun did not dramatically change the course of the war, which continued to drag on in the West for over a year. Both sides would have been better off without the events that took place in 1916 on the Western Front.

According to some historians and pseudo-historians, this great battle began in 1914 and ended in 1918 simply based on events that took place between those four years. However, the Battle of Verdun did not last the entire war, but was rather one action or campaign among many in the four-year conflict. Generally, when fighting ceases for weeks or months a battle is considered to be over, unless it is a siege where little action may occur for extended periods. Verdun was not a siege and nor was it a long battle that lasted for most of the war except in the eyes of people trying to rewrite history. The ten-month Battle of Verdun essentially was one of the longest and most horrific battles of the war, but compared to some of the other battles it produced fewer casualties.

The Germans gained some ground in the opening weeks of the battle. However, when it was concluded at the end of the year, they were pushed back almost to their starting point. The French boasted that they had prevented the Germans from breaking their line and saved their central front. That would have been a significant triumph if the German commander, General Erich von Falkenhayn, had actually intended to take Verdun. The evidence indicates that he gave no orders with regard to breaking through the French line and taking Verdun. According to popular belief, he had planned a battle of attrition and his aim had been to create a killing ground. His only stated objectives consisted of taking and holding the Meuse Heights on the right bank of the river. By late 1916, as the battle wound down, many soldiers lay dead, but the French army had not been 'Bled White' and neither side could legitimately claim it had won a great victory.

Prologue

In the morning of 21 February 1916, the Poilus glumly huddled over their breakfasts, trying to get warm before they started their daily chores in the muddy trenches of the Verdun sector. It was miserably cold and it had snowed overnight; the leaden clouds overhead promised more snow in the near future. Most of the soldiers expected little action that day. During the last year, this sector of the front had been relatively quiet after all.

Suddenly, at about 7.15 am, an unearthly roar rent the air and shells started raining on the hapless French soldiers from the direction of the German lines. The entire Verdun sector was engulfed in fire, smoke and dust. As shells of various calibres ploughed into the ground, great plumes of mud and rocks spewed into the air. Trees were reduced to matchsticks. In some places, the soggy earth revetments gave way, sliding into trenches and dugouts and burying the soldiers alive. In other places, the shells smashed men and trenches to pieces sending bits of human flesh, splintered logs and shattered guns and equipment flying through the air to land pell-mell in the deep craters left by other exploding shells. Telephone wires were destroyed, cutting off the units in the field from their commanders. The ferocious shelling went on for hours. The shock waves were so intense that they were felt as far as Lac Noir, 160km away in the Vosges, where General Passaga remarked in his journal, 'I clearly perceive across the floor of my shelter an incessant drumroll punctuated by rapid box-like hits.'

The only positive aspect for the French on that fateful day was the performance of the fortifications they had erected around Verdun. Of the eleven fortified positions that were actually targeted that day, not one was crippled and put out of action. The worst their crews could complain of was the noise, the shaking, the plaster and dust falling from the ceilings, one or two pierced walls in peripheral positions, a busted parapet or minor damage to the surface superstructure. If Fort Douaumont fell into German hands a few days later, it was because, like most of its sister forts in the Verdun Fortress, it had been stripped of its artillery and its garrison had been reduced to a skeleton crew. In addition, Douaumont and most of its sister forts had been readied for demolition because the French High Command had little faith in their ability to withstand an attack.

The bombardment finally ceased in the late afternoon and an eerie silence descended over the battlefield. The surviving French infantrymen and chasseurs rallied as best they could and braced themselves for the assault they knew was coming. Many of their officers and comrades lay dead; others were so shell-shocked they lay on the ground in a stupor, unable to move a muscle.

The shock troops were the first German soldiers to cross no-man's-land to the obliterated French trenches that afternoon. In addition to their usual array of

Map showing the major rail lines and fortified areas in France, 1907.

weapons, some of them carried a terrifying new weapon, the flamethrower, to spew jets of fire on any enemy soldiers hiding in the last points of resistance – not that they expected to encounter much opposition. After all, their artillery had done its job thoroughly – they thought – if the churned ground and charred remains of the woods were anything to go by. To their surprise, they did not get very far into enemy territory before they ran into lively resistance in some places, especially in Caures Woods where Major Driant's chasseurs had been preparing for such an event for weeks. The unrelenting fighting went on until dusk when both sides hunkered down for the night. The Germans had made some headway, but failed to gain a resounding victory. The occasional snow flurries that had hampered the combatants during the late afternoon intensified, dusting the charred, wounded land, the dead and the dying. Thus ended the first day of battle at Verdun, a presage of worse things to come. This book examines the war aims, the strategy and the tactics that led up to this, the start of the longest battle of the First World War, and reconsiders the months of intense fighting around the French fortifications that followed.

Chapter One

The Road to Verdun

'The First World War had causes but no objectives'

Correlli Barnett, *The Swordbearers*
(Bloomington, IN: Indiana University Press, 1975)

'Victory will come to the side that outlasts the other'

General Ferdinand Foch's order issued
during the Battle of the Marne in September 1914

Beginning of War and Mobilization

Proclaimed as the war to end all wars, the First World War failed to achieve that goal. The main players had no objectives other than to crush the enemy, take their capital and end the war in short order. German pre-war planning proved just as bad as that of the French in bringing victory. The Prussian-dominated General Staff had produced a single strategic plan formulated by General Alfred von Schlieffen who assumed that France must be part of any major conflict. By 1905, this plan called for the mobilization of the bulk of the German army on the Western Front. Schlieffen based his strategy on the premise that the army must knock out France quickly before concentrating on the lumbering Russian bear.[1] France, on the other hand, had only one major antagonist, which allowed it to concentrate its forces in the northeast. In July 1914, Austria-Hungary went to war with Serbia, which caused Russia to mobilize to protect its Slavic brothers. The Germans, in turn, considering Russian mobilization an act of war, began massing its troops. The German single war plan – beat the French – drew France into the conflict even though that nation had nothing to do with what should have been a localized problem in the Balkans.

Germany faced a dilemma. The terms of the Entente required France to join a war if another member of the alliance was attacked; however, in this case Russia was initiating hostilities. Unfortunately, Schlieffen's plan created a rigid mobilization and war plan difficult to change. Once the forces began to assemble, Moltke the Younger, commander of the German army in 1914, would need weeks to redeploy the bulk of the army to the Eastern Front if France remained neutral. The Germans were not greatly concerned about a Russian attack because they had failed to notice the improvements the Tsar had instituted after the disastrous Russo-Japanese War, which had exposed many weaknesses not only within the armed forces but also in the country's infrastructure. Instead, the Germans were afraid that if they moved their army to the East, the French, who were still seething after their humiliating defeat in the Franco-Prussian War, might seize the opportunity for a retaliatory strike. The German diplomats strove to dissuade the French from joining the Russians. On Friday, 31 July 1914 at 7.00 pm, Baron von Schoen, the German ambassador in Paris, received a dispatch from the German Chancellor, Theobald von Bethmann Hollweg, instructing him as follows:

> Russia has ordered mobilisation of her entire army and fleet … in spite of our still pending mediation, and although we ourselves have taken no measures of mobilisation. We have therefore declared the threatening state of war, which is bound to be followed by mobilisation, unless Russia stops within 12 hours all measures of war against us and Austria. Mobilisation inevitably implies war. Please ask French Government whether it intends to remain neutral in a Russo-German war. Reply must follow within 18 hours. Wire at once time when question was put. Utmost speed necessary.
>
> If contrary to expectation, French Government declares that it will remain neutral, Your Excellency will please declare to the French Government that we must demand as a guarantee of neutrality the handing over of the fortresses of Toul and Verdun, which we should occupy and hand back on the conclusion of the war with Russia.
>
> Reply to this last question must be here before four o'clock on Saturday afternoon.
>
> (signed) Bethmann Hollweg

The French had until 1.00 pm on Saturday, 1 August to reply and confirm that they would not join with Russia. In the unlikely event that the French opted for neutrality, von Schoen's instructions directed him to present them with the demand that they evacuate the fortified sites of Toul and Verdun, and giving them three hours to comply (by 4.00 pm on Saturday). The time limit and the stipulation made it apparent that the Germans did not anticipate or even want the French to comply. No one could expect the French to accept the humiliation of handing over their strongest fortress, Verdun, and opening the road to Paris. The Germans had war-gamed their Schlieffen Plan for years and counted on this becoming a knockout blow against France. The plan prevented the army from getting bogged down in the heavy French fortifications between Verdun and Toul by launching a surprise assault on neutral Belgium to outflank French fortifications.[2]

The French mobilized and the German onslaught against Belgium that quickly followed did not come as a total surprise. General Joffre, commander of the French armies, wanted to advance into Belgium before the Germans did, but he was ordered to keep his troops well away from the frontier. Soldiers in field grey (*feld grau*) and spiked leather helmets (the pickelhaube) swarmed into Belgium on 4 August and isolated the forts of Liège that barred the main line of communications.[3] Heavy artillery, including Austrian manned Skoda 305mm and German 420mm weapons pounded the forts into submission after infantry assaults failed to take them. Shortly afterwards Namur suffered a similar fate, but this time the Germans let the big guns do most of the work instead of sacrificing their infantry.

Thus, after the war broke out in the summer of 1914, two factors arose that would eventually affect General Erich von Falkenhayn's strategy in 1916.[4] The first was Great Britain's involvement in the war, which caused Falkenhayn to turn his efforts to forcing the British out of the war in order to assure ultimate victory for Germany. An offensive against Verdun combined with a campaign of unrestricted U-boat warfare, he believed, would achieve this objective. In 1916, however, the German leadership denied his request for a submarine campaign, partially because this type of warfare had failed in 1915 and had already had a negative impact on the USA as a result of the sinking of the British liner *Lusitania*. The second factor that influenced Falkenhayn was Verdun, which occupied a salient created in the course of German advances in 1914, but to which, the general believed, the French would cling at all costs. An important factor that did not influence the general's planning was that Joffre, under the mistaken impression that the French forts were as weak as the Belgian forts and would be as easily smashed with big guns, had disarmed its forts. The process, initiated by General Joffre in the late summer of 1915, consisted of stripping the forts of artillery and ammunition to fill shortages in the French field army. Thus weakened, Verdun became the target of the 1916 German offensive even though it was only a shell of its former self.

Alfred von Schlieffen had clearly identified France as the primary enemy and claimed that there was no guarantee that the Russians would actually join France in the next war. Regardless of Russia's decision, Germany had to concentrate its military resources against one enemy and pull off a quick and decisive victory. By the end of the first decade of the century, neither Schlieffen nor his successor, Moltke the Younger, realized that Russia was no longer the crippled bear of the Russo-Japanese War. It was generally assumed that France would participate in any European conflict involving Germany. Schlieffen had little enthusiasm for building additional fortifications, preferring instead to expand the railroad system. His aim was to avoid getting the German army bogged down in the new line of French fortresses and to deal France a crushing blow by outflanking its armies. The Franco-German frontier with its strong belt of fortifications stretching from Verdun to Belfort presented little room for manoeuvre. To create the needed space, he proposed invading the Low Countries.[5] The three Belgian fortresses of Liège, Namur and Antwerp were something of a conundrum. The first two lie on the main line of advance and logistical support for an assault on France through Belgium. The answer was to produce heavy artillery able to reduce the forts. Since the French had not defended its frontier with Belgium as heavily as the one with Germany, a rapid advance would allow the Germans to manoeuvre around its main fortifications. Although the occupation of Luxembourg was part of the plan, invading that Duchy alone would merely serve to open an additional railway line to the front since its border with France was very short and did not offer any strategic advantage. The Ardennes of southern Belgium offered the manoeuvre room the Germans needed, but lacked the rail and road routes found in the part of Belgium north of the Meuse (Maas) that were necessary to maintain the

French Casualties in 1915

Most histories of the First World War ignore operations on the Western Front in 1915 since they did not break the stalemate. Most of the attention focuses on Gallipoli, U-boat warfare, Italy's entry into war and secondary activities outside Europe. In some respects, 1915 was as important year on all fronts. The Gorlice-Tarnów Offensive not only inflicted huge losses on the Russians, but it also drove them a few hundred kilometres back from their borders. Both sides experimented with new weapons and methods in the West. Joffre launched his costly 'nibbling' operations which enabled the French army to learn how to fight a trench war, but at a tremendous cost in lives.

The British opened an attack at Neuve Chapelle with a short bombardment from which they drew the wrong conclusions when the incorrect type of shells failed to breach enemy obstacles. As a result, the Allies adopted bombardments of long duration that tore up the battlefield and alerted the Germans to an impending infantry attack. This method led to unproductive offensives which resulted in massive numbers of casualties. There are significant discrepancies regarding the number of casualties, and these can vary by up to 100,000 men or more, but 1915 may have been the bloodiest year for France.

Table 1: War Casualties, 1914–18

Nation	Mobilized	Deaths (All Fronts)	Deaths of Those That Served	Wounded (All Fronts)	Total Losses*
France	8.4 million	1.36 million	16%	4.27 million	73%
British Empire	8.9 million	0.9 million (0.7 British)	10% (13% British)	2.1 million	36%
Russia	12 million	1.7 million	14%	5 million	76%
Germany	11 million	1.8–2 million	16–17%	4.2 million	65%
Turkey	2.85 million	0.33 million	12%	0.4 million	34%

* Includes dead, wounded and prisoners of total number mobilized.

French casualties totalled 5,630,000, not including prisoners, or just over 67 per cent of the men mobilized during the war (73 per cent when including prisoners). Robert Doughty, a specialist in French military history, estimates that France suffered over 50 per cent of its casualties of the entire war during the first fifteen months of the conflict.* The next year, 1916, losses dropped to 20 per cent of its wartime casualties. In 1914, French losses numbered about 400,000 and in 1915, they rose to 500,000 on the Western Front or almost a million men lost in the major battles (The Frontier, the Marne, etc.). Doughty's numbers include

---

* Robert Doughty, *Pyrrhic Victory: French Strategy and Operations in the Great War* (Cambridge, MA: Belknap Press, 2005).

losses in typical trench fighting as well as smaller engagements during the Race to the Sea, engagements in Alsace and Lorraine, along the Meuse, at the St Mihiel Salient, in the Argonne and others that brought the total number of losses closer to 3 million if one includes prisoners. In 1915, Joffre's largely unsuccessful secondary efforts in the Argonne and the St Mihiel Salient alone cost the French another 65,000 men. The French lost another 550,000 men in 1916 before the numbers dropped until 1918. On the Western Front, 1915 passed in almost constant fighting even when neither side was attacking or counter-attacking and even though most advances amounted to a few hundred metres at most.

large forces required to outflank the French.[6] One German pre-war exercise consisted of advancing through Belgium and then attempting to turn the French fortified line at Verdun, which was the linchpin. Whether the Germans penetrated behind it or took it outright, theoretically, the move would compromise the entire French fortified line, leaving the road to Paris open. Once Germany eliminated France, supposedly by day forty, the bulk of the German army would be able to shift to the East theoretically before Russia could become a threat.

The French strategists were not to be outdone by the Germans. In 1913, General Joffre formulated Plan XVII.[7] Even though they knew of German plans to invade Belgium, French military intelligence officers incorrectly assumed that the Germans would remain south of the Meuse and advance through the Ardennes. Joffre's plan placed the concentration area of the 5th Army as far on his left as Mézières where it could meet a German advance through southern (eastern) Belgium. He seemed unconcerned, however, about a German advance north of the Meuse apparently believing that the Belgians could handle the situation. Plan XVII called for an advance into central Germany through Lorraine. Considering the fact that there was a fortified German belt between Thionville and Metz, the plan was faulty because the French relied heavily on their light 75mm guns and had a paucity of heavy and modern siege artillery that would have made it possible to eliminate the German fortresses. In addition, the French soldiers, dressed in uniforms more suited for a parade ground than a battlefield, were expected to carry the day by charging against machine guns bolstered solely by elan and the will to win.

Field Marshal Franz Conrad von Hötzendorf, reputed to be Austria's 'master strategist', planned on a two-front war. His mobilization scheme called for putting armies on the Serbian and the Russian border with a large reserve ready to move to the aid of either. He failed to consider, however, that the Austrian railways were incapable of handling such a movement without disrupting the nation's infrastructure. He also had a plan for mobilizing on the Italian border since he did not trust Italy to honour its alliance and considered launching a pre-emptive war prior to 1914. Germany had to support its ally's operations in the East and Austria's failures soon became a major drain on German military resources.

In 1914, the mobilized forces were the largest ever to take the field up to that point in history, however, command and control remained mired in the past. The telegraph and telephone linked almost all forts, but their use was limited for the field armies, especially during an advance. Some generals still preferred to use written communication delivered by couriers instead of field telephones and radios. Considering the size of the forces, it was no longer possible for generals to lead from the front or take up a key position overlooking the battlefield from where they could issue orders since the battlefields spanned great distances. Joffre, Moltke and Conrad commanded from far behind the lines and were, in fact, armchair generals who moved armies into battle from their headquarters knowing little of the conditions at the front. The army corps, generally consisting of two or more divisions with some smaller support units, provided their commanders with effective control because the new large armies had too many division-size forces for one general and his headquarters staff to direct and manage. The division, the largest combat formation, had become necessary to group numerous regiments. By 1915, as each side massed several armies on most fronts, the immense forces required a more complex command system between the combat elements and the commander-in-chief. These higher level commands took the titles of army group, group of armies or something equivalent. The enormous national armies also required massive logistical support, which Schlieffen seemed to have overlooked. When the war began, railroads and horsepower were the prime movers of logistics. In many cases, troops had to march a hundred or more miles from the railhead to the front. By 1916, however, motorization became an increasingly significant factor.[8]

Tactical doctrine played a significant role in the opening battles. Infantry was still considered the key factor not only by the French, but also by the Germans and the Austrians. In some of the first engagements of the war, French, German, Austrian as well as Russian infantrymen charged, bayonets fixed, in large, closely packed groups to the tune of marches played by military bands. Until 1915, the only difference between the various factions was that the French presented the easiest targets in their bright-red trousers and blue jackets. Before long, the belligerents learned that this type of assault was no longer practical. The French, convinced that the Germans outnumbered them significantly, continued to count on elan to win. The Germans, on the other hand, firmly believed that their own superiority would overwhelm the enemy.[9] Some generals did not come to terms with the idea that the infantry would play second fiddle to the artillery until the Battle of Verdun. After the first inconclusive battles of 1914 and the bloody but fruitless engagements of 1915 in the West, the belligerents were forced to come up with new types of strategy and tactics.[10]

Elusive Victory

The French, Germans, Russians and Austrians were convinced that they had go quickly on the offensive in order to win the war in spite of the fact that a few of their prominent military leaders had predicted that the next conflict would be a long one. As the Germans raced through Belgium to outflank and crush the French armies,

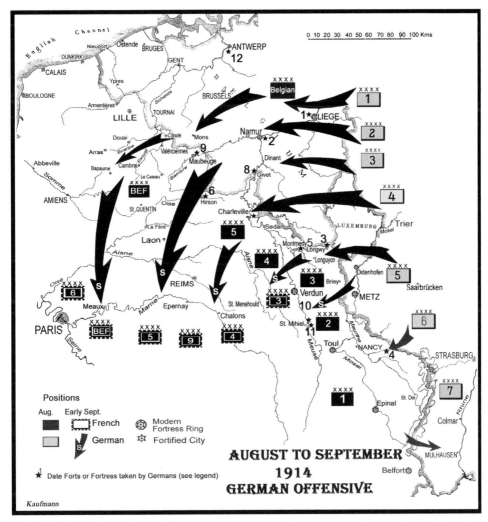

1 - (4 Aug.) Aug.16 - Last Liege fort Surrenders	7 - Aug 29 - Fort Ayvelles Captured (Evacuated Aug. 25)
2 - (20 Aug.) Aug. 25 - Fortress Namur Surrenders	8 - (Aug. 27) Sept. 1 - Ft. Charlemont Surrenders
3 - (21 Aug.) Aug. 26 - Fortress Longwy Surrenders	9 - (Aug. 29) Sept. 7 Fortress Maubeuge Surrenders
4 - (24 Aug.) Aug. 27 - Fort Manovniller Surrenders	10 - Sept 7 - Ft. Troyon Repels Assault
5 - Aug. 27 - Fortress Montmedy Evacuated	11 - Sept 25 - Ft. Camp des Romains Captured
6 - Aug. 28 - Fort Hirson Evacuated	12 - (Aug. 17) - Last fort of Antwerp Surrenders
Note: (Date Battle Begins)	

Opening moves and failure of forts.

French divisions launched an assault into Lorraine and Alsace.[11] Alas, elan was not enough to carry the day for the brightly clad French troops charging into German machine-gun fire. Meanwhile, Belgian soldiers delayed the Germans storming through their country by destroying railroads. The forts of Liège, located at a key choke point, resisted longer than anticipated.[12] Although Moltke planned logistical

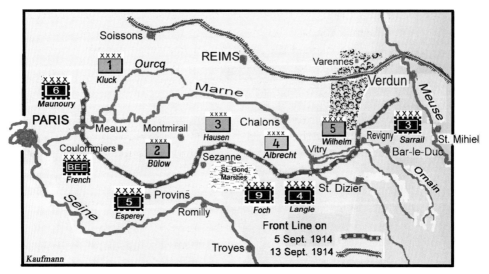

German defeat and retreat from the Marne.

support better than Schlieffen, his efforts fell short of the needs of a massive force committed to such an ambitious strategy.[13] In September 1914, the French checked the German offensive at the Marne forcing them to pull back and take up defensive positions along the Aisne. The Germans dug in taking advantage of the 150m-high ridge of Chemin des Dames, which rose above the river.[14] Here, both sides had their first taste of trench warfare as the Germans created a defensive position with two to three lines of trenches, which, however, were neither as deep nor as extensive as those dug later in the war. General Erich von Falkenhayn replaced Moltke at this time.

The French launched a surprise attack across the Aisne in mid-September, bombarding and taking a large section of the heavily defended first line of trenches. Both sides suffered heavy losses. At the end of October, the Germans launched a counter-attack to drive the French from the lost trench line. Their howitzers were effective in a barrage against trenches. By contrast, the French artillery, which consisted mostly of the famous '75' direct-fire cannons and lacked howitzers, inflicted little damage on entrenched troops. In a second assault in January, the Germans recaptured the remainder of the line on the Aisne. Both sides soon learned the ineffectiveness of frontal assaults in trench warfare.

In August and early September, before the Battle of the Marne, the Germans eliminated the French border forts from Fortress Maubeuge to Fort Manonviller during the so-called Battle of the Frontiers.[15] In late September 1914, as they retreated from the Marne and created a defensive position, the Germans pulled their heavy artillery back into Belgium to reduce Fortress Antwerp and its potential threat to its right flank.

In the East, the Russians mobilized and went on the offensive sooner than anticipated. Two Russian armies, part of the Northwest Front (army group), launched an attack into East Prussia. On 23 August, Paul von Hindenburg, recalled from retirement, and Erich von Ludendorff, the victor of Liège, took command in the East.[16] They formed the best command team of the German army during the war. In late August, they handed the Russians a major defeat at a place they called Tannenberg. This symbolic gesture was meant to restore German pride and avenge the crushing fifteenth-century defeat of the Teutonic Knights near a location of the same name.[17]

After a painfully slow mobilization, General Conrad was anxious to get the Austro-Hungarian forces involved on the Galician Front. He realized that the Germans were committed to winning a decisive victory in the West while staying on the defensive in

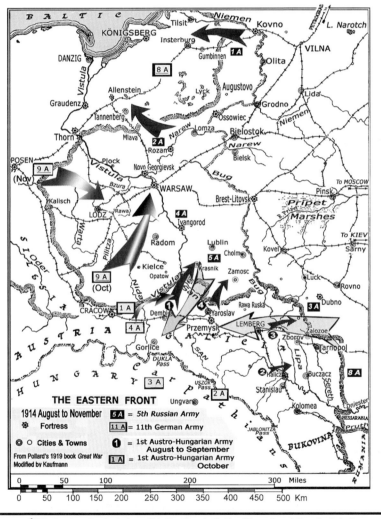

THE EASTERN FRONT
1914 August to November

5 A = 5th Russian Army
11 A = 11th German Army
1 = 1st Austro-Hungarian Army August to September
1 A = 1st Austro-Hungarian Army October

⊚ Fortress
◎ ○ Cities & Towns
From Pollard's 1919 book *Great War* Modified by Kaufmann

0   50   100   200   300 Miles
0 50 100 150 200 250 300 350 400 450 500 Km

↘ Russian offensive in August into East Prussia (Battle of Tannenberg & Masurian Lakes)
↗ Austro-Hungarian offensive late August
↙ Russian offensive of Southwest Army Group in September (Rout of Austro-Hungarian Army)
↘ German 9th Army and Austrian Offensive in October (Battle of Warsaw & Vistula)
↘ German 9th Army Offensive in November (Battle of Lodz)

the East. Like most of his contemporary military leaders, he believed that a successful offensive would lead to a quick victory. As a result, he was eager to engage the Russians before they could attack. Encouraged by faulty intelligence regarding the size and deployment of the Russian forces and expecting the Germans in East Prussia to form a northern pincer, he directed a northward assault out of Galicia towards Lublin. Meanwhile, Conrad's invasion of Serbia floundered. Despite superior armaments, the Austrians suffered a humiliating defeat at the hands of the Serbs. The Austrians struggled with a railway system not up to German standards, causing many delays in bringing up reinforcements and supplies. On 19 August, more than one week before the German victory of Tannenberg, Conrad ordered his *1st* and *4th armies* to attack north towards Lublin and the *3rd Army* to conduct an 'active' defence on the Gniła Lipa River.[18] At the end of the month, General Nikolai Ivanov's Russian Southwest Front had a two-to-one advantage as it went on the offensive. Conrad had won a few

minor victories, but the Russians defeated his overextended forces on 28 August at the Złota Lipa initiating a retreat that by 11 September had turned into a rout with three Austrian armies smashed by mid-September.[19] The crushing Austrian defeat was worse than what the Russians suffered at Tannenberg days earlier. Instead of stopping at the San River, the Austrians fled to the Dunajec River, a tributary of the Vistula. Conrad, unable to halt the advancing Russians, pleaded for the Germans to help. Hindenburg, who had just won a victory over the Russian 2nd Army at Tannenberg, was still engaged with the Russian 1st Army during the second week of September. As the Austrians reformed along the Dunajec on 26 September, the new German *9th Army* under Hindenburg formed up north of Cracow.[20] A large Austrian garrison remained at the fortress of Przemyśl to prepare for a siege, but all of Galicia was lost to the Russians who also advanced to the Carpathian mountain passes.

Finally, the victorious Russian armies sputtered to a halt along the muddy roads of Galicia as they too outran their logistical support. However, they had eliminated 300,000 Austro–Hungarian troops and tied up another 100,000 in the siege of Przemyśl. The Austrian army had already lost 100,000 men in the attack on Serbia. To bolster the Austrian Front, Hindenburg created the *9th Army* and put the Austrian forces under direct German command because he had no confidence in their senior officers.[21] Hindenburg's October offensive fizzled out as his troops trudged along the muddy roads and the soggy fields of Poland before engaging the Russians who had already withdrawn to the Vistula in preparation for their own offensive.[22] An Austrian relief force reached Przemyśl on 9 October, breaking the siege that had begun on 25 September during the Austrian rout.[23] Meanwhile, Conrad, ignoring German advice, the weather conditions and the state of his own troops, launched another assault and lost 40,000 additional men. Despite the fact that his army had returned to its starting line on 24 October after suffering 100,000 casualties, Hindenburg was undeterred. On 2 November, General August von Mackensen took command of the *9th Army*, which moved northward and launched a new attack in the vicinity of Łódź on 11 November.[24] Meanwhile, the Russian forces once again pushed the Austrians back and put the Przemyśl fortress under siege on 8 November.[25] The armies in the East continued to manoeuvre and clash instead of getting mired in stalemates or trench warfare like those on the Western Front.[26]

Winter brought a respite from the fighting on the Eastern Front as the Russians reached the height of their success when their raiding forces reached the Carpathian passes and threatened to enter the Hungarian Plain. Russian armies also loomed over Cracow and East Prussia. The situation looked grim for the Germans whose victory at Tannenberg had been ephemeral due to poor supply lines, rough terrain and a larger than expected Russian force that had prevented them from advancing out of East Prussia in late September. In October, the Germans advanced into Russian Poland but they failed to take the fortresses of Ivangorod (Polish Dęblin) and Warsaw or to breach the Vistula. Only a renewed attack in November finally took Łódź on 6 December. Winter hindered operations, but Conrad prepared for an offensive into the Carpathians to relieve Przemyśl in January 1915. This operation was a dismal

Table 2: Major Campaigns and Battles, 1914–16

Western Front	Dates	Eastern Front	Dates	Other Fronts	Dates
1914					
1st Marne	5–10 September	Tannenberg	26–31 August		
		Rava Ruska*	3–11 September		
1st Aisne	23–8 September	1st Masurian Lakes	7–14 September		
1st Artois	27 September–10 October	Przemyśl – 1st siege	25 September–11 October		
1st Ypres	19 October–22 November	1st Warsaw and Vistula	19–30 October		
		Łódź	11 November–6 December		
1st Champagne	20 December–17 March	Przemyśl – 2nd siege	Begins 6 November		
1915					
(1st Champagne)	Ends 17 March	Przemyśl falls	27 March		
Neuve Chapelle	10–13 March				
2nd Ypres	22 April–25 May			Gallipoli	25 April–9 January
2nd Artois	9 May–18 June	Gorlice–Tarnów	2 May–22 June		
Aubers Ridge	9–10 May	Germans advance to Riga and Pinsk	June–30 September	1st Isonzo	23 June–7 July
				2nd Isonzo	18 July–3 August
				Fall of Serbia	October–November
3rd Artois/Loos	21 September–14 October			3rd Isonzo	18 October–3 November
2nd Champagne	25 September–6 November			4th Isonzo	10 November–2 December
				Kut – siege	9 December–29 April
1916					
Verdun	21 February–18 December	Lake Naroch	18 March–14 April	5th Isonzo	9–17 March
		Brusilov Offensive	4 June–18 October	Jutland (naval)	31 May–1 June
Somme	1 July–18 November			6th–9th Isonzo	4 August–4 November

* Rava Ruska was part of the series of battles in the Galician Campaign that resulted in the collapse of the Austrian Front and led to rout and the siege of Przemyśl.

fiasco as many of his soldiers froze to death without achieving much. Both sides continued to blunder and stumble on the Eastern Front.[27] The Russian troops began receiving their first shipments of barbed wire in December, which allowed them to improve their defensive positions while they waited for ammunition.

Meanwhile, on the Western Front, after the costly Battle of the Aisne, the 'Race to the Sea' (the English Channel) began on 18 September. Joffre and Falkenhayn sent their forces northward trying to outflank each other. Neither side succeeded. The 26,000 railway troops who continued to restore the Belgian railways had returned less than 600km to service at that point. The Germans had to shift their armies from the left in Alsace and Lorraine to the right wing, but the railroad situation in Belgium hindered their movements. The French, on the other hand, operating on interior lines with an excellent railway system, rapidly moved divisions and corps from their right flank to their left flank.

None of the belligerents had prepared for a long conflict. The German soldiers were ordered to conserve ammunition since stocks had begun to run low. Joffre faced a similar problem. The first artillery barrages at the onset of trench warfare consumed more ammunition than had been used during the entire duration of past wars. Thus, during the Race to the Sea, Falkenhayn ordered his *5th Army* to engage the French 3rd Army in the vicinity of Verdun in order to tie down some of the French forces. As a result, the Germans succeeded in creating a bridgehead over the Meuse at St Mihiel at the end of September while some of their troops advanced in the Argonne near Varennes threatening to isolate Verdun.

On 19 October, Falkenhayn launched the 1st Battle of Ypres, his first major offensive. He had planned to mass his forces in order to break the line in the vicinity of Ypres and drive on the Channel ports. The battle consisted of a series of encounters with costly German frontal assaults and British counter-attacks. The engagement ended in late November when winter set in. One massed charge of units consisting mostly of enthusiastic but poorly trained German youth concluded, according to the grossly exaggerated claims of propaganda, as 'a heroic slaughter'.[28] The Germans were not the only ones to suffer heavy losses. Casualties whittled down the British professional army to the point that conscripts had to replace its professionals during the next year.

Before long, Falkenhayn realized that a breakthrough in the West would be impossible and that he needed to develop new methods. The stalemate endured while trenches were dug from the North Sea to the Swiss border. General Joffre, still convinced that he could deliver a knockout blow, decided that he must also maintain pressure on the enemy by conducting smaller offensive actions, which he called 'nibbling'. He justified these costly attacks by saying that they kept the enemy from diverting forces to the Eastern Front. In early December 1914, Joffre launched a new campaign with the 1st Battle of Champagne. The campaign had a slow start due to winter weather and a Christmas truce, but it continued into the next year and had gathered pace by February. The French gained very little and suffered heavy casualties before it ended in March 1915.[29]

The first months of the war in 1914 failed to bring the anticipated victory and a speedy end to the war. At the end of the year there was little to celebrate since

A War of Resources

During the First World War, the belligerents and the neutral nations depended for the most part on imports of certain products ranging from foodstuffs to minerals to maintain their economy and military strength. Any long-lived conflict placed demands on production and often required substitutes, a problem that had not faced the most industrialized nations during the wars of the nineteenth century. The loss of Alsace and much of Lorraine after the Franco–Prussian War denied the French access to many mineral resources in Lorraine.[30] Since the large iron deposits, especially in the Briey Basin, were not discovered until late in the nineteenth century, the French military had not made plans to defend the part of this region that remained in their own territory. Apparently, there was no concern about the economic impact of the loss of this region until it happened.

In a 1916 French senator Henri Bérenger wrote, 'There is no reason to be astonished that Germany, from the very beginning of the war, has sought ... possession of the Basin of Briey, which represented 90% of our iron ore production'.* He added that this was the key to the war since the area lay at an equal distance between the French fortress of Verdun and the German fortress of Metz. Before 1914, Germany's annual production of iron had been 28 million tons, 21 million of which came from their section of the Briey Basin. France's production amounted to 22 million tons, 15 million of which came from their own part of the Briey Basin. After August 1914, France was forced to import iron from Great Britain and the USA, while Germany's production was supplemented by 15 million tons from the French part of Briey and 6 million from the Luxembourg Basin increasing its annual production from 28 million to 49 million tons. Bérenger quoted a memorandum sent to the German chancellor Bethmann Hollweg, which stated that the Briey Basin furnished 60–80 per cent of all appliances made of iron and steel at that time.

Senator Bérenger was convinced that the Germans launched the offensive against Verdun in 1916 to secure ownership of this region before they sat at the peace table. 'Once masters of Verdun the Germans will be able to believe themselves masters of the indefinite continuation of the war', he wrote in the article 'The Iron Key to War and Peace'. However, General von Falkenhayn never mentioned iron production as one of his reasons for the Verdun Offensive. Bérenger, nonetheless, was not the only one to see iron and steel as key factors in the war. In an article published at the end of 1916, George Weiss opined:

> Germany's remarkable resistance to the combined assaults of England, France, Russia and later on Italy, Serbia, and Roumania, these six powers possessing numerical as well as financial superiority, lies in its resources of iron and steel. Krupps, the armorer of Germany, and Skoda works of

---

* Henri Bérenger, 'The Iron Key to War and Peace', *Current History*, No. 4 (July 1916).

Austria, have been the backbone of the powerful Teutonic military strength. The long days of preparation on the part of the Allies, the stalling for time when they would take the offensive, was due to their unpreparedness in the matter of steel.[*]

As can be expected, French production of heavy artillery and other military equipment – even helmets – slowed and was delayed by the iron shortages. Surprisingly though, despite acquiring additional resources, Germany suffered from a similar problem in part because the mobilization took many men out of industry and the economy. According to Weiss, the Germans had planned even before the war to reduce France's ability to produce steel. However, this strategy does not appear in Schlieffen's plans, which seemed to focus on winning a quick war rather than acquiring iron deposits. The impact of these resources was largely ignored until it started to affect the economy in 1915.

The conquest of Belgium and the Briey Basin also augmented Germany's supply of coal, a commodity in high demand by the iron and steel industry as well as the civilian population. After the loss of the Briey Basin, France had to rely on Great Britain and the USA to make up the shortfall. For the Germans, a major consideration for dropping the Netherlands from the Schlieffen Plan was to keep them as a trade outlet in case the war did not turn out to be as brief as planned. The need for resources did not become a serious consideration until shortages were felt.

Even if the resources were available, all sides would have had problems with the delivery of the war materiel because the heavy traffic of troop trains and supply trains caused delays. During the offensives, trains carrying ammunition often had to take precedence over those transporting foodstuffs for the troops. The First World War had suddenly become an economic war for which neither side had adequately prepared. Even in the early months of the war many nations began to experience a shortage of ammunition partially because pre-war estimates for ammunition stockpiles were barely adequate for a short war and the ability to produce sufficient quantities was limited by the natural resources, manpower and the time needed to expand the industrial sites.

---

[*] George Weiss, 'What the War has Done for Steel', *The FORUM*, Vol. LVII (January 1917– June 1917), New York: Forum Publishing Co., 1917.

losses had been staggering. The tally for the Germans and French was approximately 1 million casualties each. The Austrians lost even more men and the Russians possibly as many as 2 million. No other war since the end of the Napoleonic Wars in Europe had resulted in such massive losses, and this conflict had only just begun. In addition, all sides had underestimated the amount of ammunition their artillery would need since they had anticipated a short conflict. As a result, all the belligerents had to ramp up ammunition production so the war could continue. None of them was prepared for trench warfare, but there was no other way to protect troops from the massive artillery barrages and machine guns. The various armies proceeded to dig in within sight of each other, separated by a no-man's-land between the opposing trenches that was only several hundred metres wide and sometimes much less. From this point on, soldiers would have to advance or defend keeping their heads close to the ground. Fighting in a standing position invited certain death but not everyone realized it until late 1916. Although General Falkenhayn was convinced that the French soldiers were more experienced in trench warfare than his own were, in actuality their pre-war training had emphasized the offensive. Trench warfare was also adopted in Russia, but, since the area to be covered was much larger, continuous lines were impractical and fortresses continued to play a more significant role.

The table on p. 12 details the major actions on the Western Front from 1914–16 and a few of the other significant encounters in Europe. There is some confusion with the numbering and naming of battles, so this list attempts to match the text. The dates vary according to the sources used.

The Road to Verdun, 1915

At the close of 1914, the Austro-Hungarian army had suffered approximately 1 million casualties and struggled to hold on while over 100,000 of its troops remained encircled at Przemyśl. Austrian General Oskar Potiorek, who had been defeated twice in Serbia, finally took Belgrade on 1 December 1914 and was hailed a hero until he lost the city on 15 December.[31]

After a failed offensive in the 1st Battle of Ypres in late November 1914, the German troops completed a continuous trench line in the West. General Falkenhayn, who believed that the best way to end the war was to force the enemy to the negotiating table, ordered his subordinates not to give up any ground thus eliminating any flexibility and ability to manoeuvre. He also scraped together new reserves for operations in the West, but his proposals met with a great deal of resistance, including from Chancellor Bethmann Hollweg who embraced the view that victory was essential and achievable. The opposition, led by the Hindenburg/Ludendorff team, demanded priority in the East and plotted to bring down the new and young chief-of-staff. The Kaiser, Falkenhayn's main supporter, asked him to give priority to the Eastern Front. An important factor in this decision was the need to prop up the Austrians, who still had over 100,000 men under siege at Przemyśl. The Austrian dilemma may well have been the deciding factor in Germany's war policies.

In 1915, Falkenhayn sent his reserve of four new corps to the East. Hindenburg received a little over half of Germany's divisions to pursue offensives intended to knock Russia out of the war. Falkenhayn, nonetheless, remained convinced that a quick victory in the East would remain as unattainable as in the West because his troops would be sucked into Russia's vastness. Austria's failures had depleted Conrad's armies forcing Falkenhayn to rely on reservists and new recruits. Despite the fact that he despised Conrad, Falkenhayn had to prop him up to give Germany a bargaining position in peace negotiations. Falkenhayn also realized that the Italians were wavering in their neutrality and that there was a distinct possibility that Rumania would take advantage of the Russian victories to seize Transylvania from Austria. To prevent these two nations from joining the war, he urged the Hapsburg Empire to cede some territory in the Trento region to Italy and parts of Transylvania to Rumania. However, the Austrian emperor refused to cooperate, leaving Falkenhayn with additional problems in the East.

Hindenburg opened his 1915 campaign on 7 February with the 2nd Battle of the Masurian Lakes after ordering Mackensen to launch a diversionary assault towards Warsaw during a snowstorm on 4 February 1915. Hindenburg's victory, according to the Germans, eliminated an additional 100,000 Russians. The Austrians, on the other hand, had not been able to resupply Przemyśl after October 1914 and the force that had relieved them during that month used some of their dwindling supplies. The Austrian army continued to lose Slavic troops (Czechs, Poles and others) who persistently surrendered or simply joined the Russians. Even the Slavic population of Galicia could not be trusted. Conrad's attempted relief of the fortress during the winter had failed as many of his ill-equipped soldiers froze to death in the Carpathians. In March 1915, when the fortress of Przemyśl surrendered, the Austrians lost over 100,000 men. Hindenburg had to shift German forces towards Galicia to keep his Austrian ally from collapsing. On 2 May, Mackensen, at the head of the German *11th Army*, which had moved into position east of Cracow, and several Austrian armies in support, opened the Gorlice-Tarnów Offensive. Falkenhayn did not inform Conrad and the other Austrian generals of the plans for the operation until shortly before it began. This was the turning point campaign on the Eastern Front.

On the Western Front, before his offensive in Champagne in December 1914, when the Germans were within 65 miles of Paris, Joseph Joffre wrote:

> The best and largest portion of the German army was on our soil, with its line of battle jutting out a mere five days' march from the heart of France. This situation made it clear to every Frenchman that our task consisted of defeating this enemy, and driving him out of our country.
>
> My views, on this matter remained unchanged during the whole time I was directing operations.*

Joffre's goal was to eliminate the Noyon Salient by launching major offensives in Champagne and Artois to create a double envelopment. The offensive began on 22 December 1914 and lasted until 17 March 1915 with French forces concentrated for a breakthrough in Champagne just east of where they had been defeated in the 1st Battle of the Aisne. The attack in the vicinity of the Suippes River cost Joffre at least 90,000 men – as many as 146,000 according to some sources – but gained only

---

* Joseph Joffre, Colonel T. Bentley Mott (trans.) and Colonel S.J. Lowe (trans.), *The Personal Memoirs of Joffre*, 2 vols (New York: Harper & Brothers Publishers, 1932), Vol. 2, p. 327.

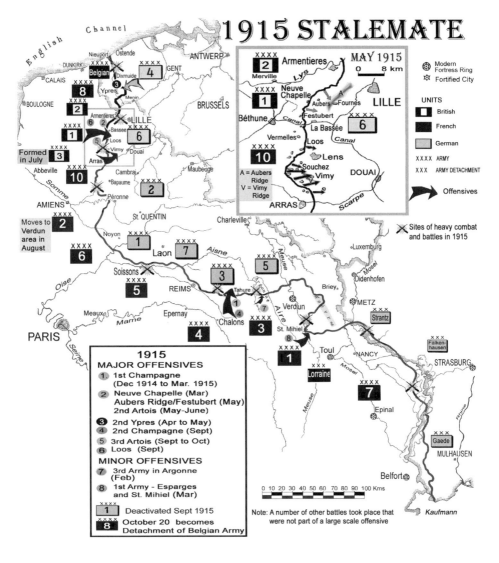

a few hundred metres of territory. In mid–March 1915, the British attacked north of the Noyon Salient, taking the village of Neuve Chapelle before grinding to a halt. After a short but massive artillery barrage, they advanced all of 2km, but despite their initial success they failed to take the Aubers Ridge.[32] They lost 13,000 men to enemy counter-attacks while the Germans lost 14,000. Joffre's strategy was good, but the tactics employed in trench warfare that year made it impossible to succeed.

Falkenhayn launched the 2nd Battle of Ypres on 22 April, but the month-long contest ended in another German defeat. The Germans opened the action with the release of chlorine gas from canisters.[33] The French colonial troops, who lacked gas protection, panicked and broke. The Canadians on their flank held and closed the gap left by their ally before the Germans could take advantage of the situation. Falkenhayn did not have enough troops to exploit the gap because the battle was merely a diversion to cover the withdrawal of several divisions headed for the East. The Germans' modest gains failed to eliminate the Allied salient at Ypres. The battle cost the Allies 60,000 men, many in the British counter-attacks, and the Germans 35,000.

During May and June, Joffre continued to nibble away at the Germans by launching attacks in Artois. In September, the British had some success again at Loos. Joffre's final major offensives in 1915 were the battles of 3rd Artois and 2nd Champagne during the months of September and October which resulted in additional heavy casualties for the French. The Allies achieved little with their tactics beyond wearing down their own armies. General Pétain, among others, concluded that this was becoming a war of attrition.

War on the East Front and in the Balkans

The entry of the Turks into the war in 1914 opened new fronts. In the Middle East, the British abandoned the Sinai, but repulsed a Turkish army of several regiments

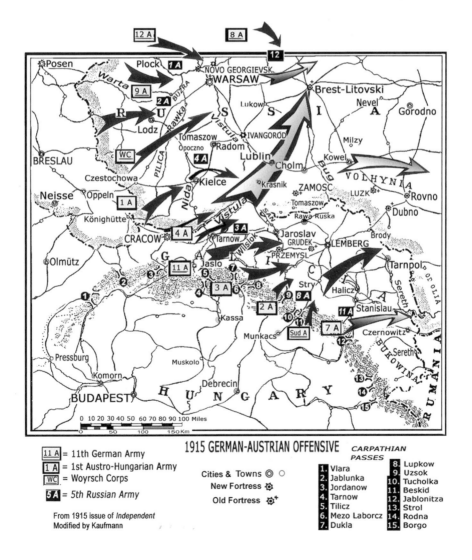

1915 GERMAN-AUSTRIAN OFFENSIVE

Legend	
11 A = 11th German Army	
1 A = 1st Austro-Hungarian Army	
WC = Woyrsch Corps	
5 A = 5th Russian Army	

Cities & Towns ◎ ○
New Fortress ✪
Old Fortress ✪⁺

CARPATHIAN PASSES

1. Vlara
2. Jablunka
3. Jordanow
4. Tarnow
5. Tilicz
6. Mezo Laborcz
7. Dukla
8. Lupkow
9. Uzsok
10. Tucholka
11. Beskid
12. Jablonitza
13. Strol
14. Rodna
15. Borgo

From 1915 issue of *Independent*
Modified by Kaufmann

at the Suez Canal in February 1915. In April 1915, the world's attention turned to the Dardanelles where an Allied invasion force landed at Gallipoli hoping to knock the Turks out of the war. The Allied command bungled the operation and the Turks pinned down the invaders for most of the year until they were evacuated in December 1915. The Allies lost 200,000 men. Initially, this operation seemed to offer the possibility of breaking the stalemate, removing the Turks from the war, and opening a supply route to Russia. Also in 1915, a British force tried to advance from the Arabian Gulf through Mesopotamia in an attempt to take Baghdad, but it was trapped in Kut in December 1915 and forced to surrender in 1916. Joffre did not pay much attention to the fronts opened by France's allies since his priority was the defence of his own country and the 'advantages offered by [secondary operations] were almost wholly theoretical …'.[*]

Joffre's offensives in the West in 1915 failed to divert German troops from the Russian campaign before or during the Gorlice-Tarnów Offensive. Hindenburg's winter campaign in early 1915 was equally fruitless. In February, German troops out of East Prussia failed to breach the Russian fortresses on the Niemen and Narew river lines. The Russians relied heavily on these scattered fortresses on the Eastern Front to bolster their defences. In the Second Battle of the Masurian Lakes two German armies inflicted heavy losses on a Russian army, but were stopped at the Augustów Forest. Austrian forces supported by some German divisions failed to relieve Przemyśl, the garrison of which, its resources expended, surrendered.[34]

The Russians failed to create a decent position on the Galician Front between Tarnów and Gorlice. According to Norman Stone, they prepared 'not much more than a thin, ill-connected trench with a strand or two of barbed wire before it; and communications to the rear often ran over open ground'.[**] It took the Russians many days to move divisions into position because their railway system lacked the efficiency of the French and German railroads. In addition, almost half of their transport space was dedicated to horse feed for their numerous cavalry divisions. Availability of ammunition was also a problem at this time because Russian factories were unable to produce sufficient supplies. The Russian industry could not even produce enough rifles to equip all the soldiers. Despite the overall weakness of the Austro-Hungarian army, these factors gave the Germans the advantage.

Only the Gorlice-Tarnów Offensive spearheaded by General von Mackensen's *11th Army* in May 1915 offered a chance for the Germans to break the deadlock in the East. It was the last spectacular victory for the German army under the leadership of Falkenhayn. The battle opened with a 4-hour hurricane bombardment with 476 field guns and 159 medium and light guns on the morning of 2 May. German artillery fired 700,000 rounds along a 48km (30-mile) front between Gorlice and Tarnów.[35] The artillery virtually obliterated the Russian trench line, sowing panic among the troops before German infantry surged forward at about 6.00 am and created an 8km gap in the Russian lines. Within two days, a breakthrough at Gorlice

*   Joffre, *The Personal Memoirs of Joffre*, Vol. 2, p. 327.
**   Norman Stone, *The Eastern Front 1914–1917* (New York: Penguin, 1998).

turned into a pursuit. After the first week, the Russians lost over 200,000 men. The Russian formations south of Przemyśl retreated to avoid encirclement. Only 40,000 men of the Russian 3rd Army's original 250,000 remained by 10 May. The German/Austrian armies advanced about 150km by 14 May. On 16 May, the Germans crossed the San River at over a dozen points, rendering the Russian position untenable. The trapped Russian troops were forced to abandon Fortress Przemyśl because its position, even if rehabilitated, offered no advantages.

General Mackensen renewed the offensive on 24 May. Between 2 and 31 May, the Russians lost as many as 412,000 men. The German victory was as great as the Russians' triumph had been the previous autumn on the same ground.[36] On 3 June, a British liaison officer reported that the Russian 3rd Army was a 'harmless mob' that allowed German and Austrian troops to retake the fortress at Przemyśl unopposed. Mackensen's troops returned to the offensive on 13 June. A few days later, Austrian troops engaged the Russians at Lemberg, taking the city on 22 June, while Mackensen drove Brusilov's 8th Army from Rava Ruska. The Kaiser rewarded General Mackensen with a field marshal's baton as his troops advanced between the Vistula and the Bug rivers bagging over 150,000 prisoners by 30 June. Mackensen's troops took the old fortress of Zamość, between Lublin and Lemberg. The collapse of the Galician Front forced the Russians to abandon the Polish salient finally giving Falkenhayn and Hindenburg an excellent chance to defeat them. Trench warfare did not dominate this battlefield, which was the most fluid in Europe, especially since German eastward advances widened the front. The Russians, even though overwhelmed, often resisted tenaciously.

Falkenhayn approved Hindenburg's plan to encircle Brest-Litovsk as the German armies in East Prussia joined the general offensive. On 5 July, a Russian counter-offensive held Mackensen's forces in check for a week. On 6 July, the German *9th Army* moved against the centre of the Polish salient towards Warsaw and launched a gas attack that failed. The *12th Army* thrust southward from East Prussia on 13 July and advanced about 8km towards the Narew in four days, eliminating 70,000 Russian troops. On 15 July, German troops attacked eastward from East Prussia towards Riga as Mackensen's forces advanced north into the Polish salient, taking Radom on 18 July. On 21 July, they besieged the fortress of Ivangorod while other German troops crossed the Vistula. In the north, the *12th Army* overran Różan and established bridgeheads over the Narew in the face of fierce Russian counter-attacks between 23 and 30 July. During the last week of July, the Russians began evacuating Fortress Warsaw and Riga.

In early August 1915, Falkenhayn, who was responsible for army operations on all fronts, halted further advances. The Gorlice-Tarnów Offensive had raised the hopes of the Central Powers because it represented their greatest victory. A serious problem for Falkenhayn after he had taken command in 1914 had been creating a reserve and distributing the newly formed divisions effectively. He struggled to maintain a proper balance of forces, but, by his own account, he often seemed to face crises resulting from the need to shift his divisions or corps from one front to the other. In late 1915, despite Hindenburg's success, which took a heavy toll on the Russians and allowed deep advances, Falkenhayn saw no indication that the Tsar wanted to negotiate an end to the war. Thus, he decided to stop the eastern offensives in September and sent an army to help the Austrians knock Serbia out of the war. Although Hindenburg did not agree with him, Falkenhayn realized that the onset of the autumn rains would reduce the Russian dirt roads to mud. At the same time, the German engineers would have to convert the Russian broad-gauge railways to standard gauge if they were to support the advancing army.[37]

The Wild Card – Italy

With the belligerents locked in a stalemate on the Western Front and before the Gorlice Offensive routed Russian forces in Galicia, Italy joined the war on the side of the Entente on 23 May 1915. On 14 May, Conrad, anticipating Italy's entry into the war, dispatched troops to the Southern Front, including a corps from Galicia that arrived just in time. The Italians, wooed into joining the Entente, were encouraged to strike at Austria to relieve pressure on the Russians. After some success on their Alpine border, they launched their main offensive on 23 June at the Isonzo Front, where they suffered heavy losses. This was to be the first of many defeats on the Isonzo Front for the Italians. General Luigi Cadorna, Chief of the General Staff, was one of the worst Allied generals. He boasted that he would break through on the Isonzo and march on Vienna and Budapest, but nothing came of his bravado. The 2nd Battle of the Isonzo (18 July–3 August) reached a climax with 42,000 Italian and 45,000 Austrians casualties and small gains for the Italians.[38] Before the end of 1915, the 3rd and 4th battles of Isonzo brought a total of 275,000 casualties for Italy and 165,000 for Austria. This was the only front in the war where the Austrian and Slavic troops fought with equal commitment since there was a history of conflict between them and the Italians.

In late summer, Field Marshal Mackensen, at the head of *11th Army*, left the Russian Front for Serbia where he launched an offensive on 6 October and soon took Belgrade. Bulgaria, seeing a golden opportunity, joined forces with the Central Powers on 11 October 1915, rendering the Serbian position untenable. The Allies tried to enter Serbia from Salonika, Greece, but failed. By December, Austro-German forces had occupied all of Serbia. The remnants of the Serbian army joined the Allies in Greece. Falkenhayn was finally able to open a rail link to Turkey and eliminate one major front for the Austrians allowing them to concentrate their troops on the Italian and Russian fronts.

Late in the year, Falkenhayn formulated a new strategy for 1916. By the beginning of 1916, Germany had reached its high water mark of the war even though Russia did not surrender until the end of 1917. The French had suffered immense losses in their 1915 offensives. German/Austrian forces had advanced deep into Russia, Serbia was eliminated, the Allies were about to abandon the Gallipoli Campaign, the British stood on the verge of defeat in Mesopotamia, a rail link to the Turks was open and the Italians had taken huge losses in exchange for small gains. Rumania continued to waver and remained neutral for almost another year. However, Falkenhayn was not convinced that another major offensive in the East would bring Russia down.

He also thought that the German forces were stretched to the point that there were insufficient divisions available to exploit any breakthrough in the West. He decided to strike a decisive blow in the West to cripple the French army and force the British to seek an end to the war. Like Joffre, he believed that victory in the West was the only pathway to a negotiated peace. To achieve this goal, he thought, he must launch a major offensive against either Belfort or Verdun in a battle in which the goal was not to achieve a breakthrough and initiate a campaign of manoeuvre, but simply to kill.

1915 – Seeking New Methods and Alternatives

As the prospect of a brief war evaporated in 1915, the combatants sought alternative pathways to victory. After several unproductive operations, none of which achieved a knockout blow, and the sacrifice of hundreds of thousands of infantrymen Joffre finally concluded that artillery should be the dominant arm. In August, he began to disarm many of the French forts to beef up his own field artillery.

All the belligerents had calculated their munitions needs based on past conflicts. As a result, their artillery expended most of their ordnance by October 1914. During 1915, the industrial complexes of all the major belligerents had to expand ammunition production to prevent further shortages and they had to develop new weapons and equipment for the war effort.[39] The French lacked heavy artillery and mortars, a requirement for trench warfare. Joffre, who had pushed for the manufacture of howitzers even before the war, strove to correct the situation. Falkenhayn decided that the German 77mm gun lacked the efficiency and great range of the French '75' and ordered German industry to develop a similar gun, but this did not reach the battlefield until late 1916.[40] Germany also had to face the problem posed by an embargo that cut off its imports. The Germans had to find alternatives for production of explosives, but they were unable to compensate for shortages in food production. They had to rely on neutrals like the Netherlands to provide it with limited amounts of imports.

As war casualties escalated rapidly for all the warring nations, it became necessary to improve individual protection. One of the first and most successful innovations was the metal helmet, which was adopted by the French, the British and the Germans. Through most of 1915, the French soldiers wore a steel skullcap under their kepi, but in May, the steel Mle 1915 Adrian helmet went into production. It was designed to protect the wearer from shrapnel and other flying objects but not from bullets. By the end of 1915, there were enough helmets to equip most of the French army.[41] The British and the Germans followed the French lead. That same year, John Brodie designed the Mark I Helmet (or Brodie Helmet), which weighed a bit more than the Adrian helmet but provided about the same protection. The Germans replaced the leather pickelhaube, with which they had begun the war, with the *Stahlhelm* (steel helmet). While the British helmet looked like a medieval foot soldier's pan-shaped headgear, the *Stahlhelm* resembled the late medieval sallet. All these helmets, with slight modifications, were used in the Second World War. The German design offered the greatest protection – especially to the neck. It was tested in late 1915 and issued to *Stosstruppen* (storm troops or *Sturmtruppen*). In 1916, it began to appear in the remainder of the army.[42]

German Trench Mortar

Austrian 305 mm Morser

**Fixed Flamethrowers
in action**

GERMAN
WEAPONS

Stick Grenades

Portable Flamethrower

170 mm minewerfer

Assortment of German weapons from early trench mortar to Austrian 305mm Mörser (on loan with crews). Also, examples of German grenades.

Other developments included body armour, similar to a breastplate, moveable shields that could be pushed along the ground, various types of optical equipment, such as periscopes for observation from the trenches, and standard manufactured grenades. The *Stosstruppen* units, created in 1915, were the first to test the new helmets, flamethrowers, infantry gun and other equipment. They also developed a new attack procedure, which consisted of advancing waves of soldiers with machine guns and light artillery. The storm-troop units that formed in 1916 actually applied these new tactics to the battlefield.[43]

The Balancing Act

In 1914, Falkenhayn could not quickly replenish his depleted divisions in northern France because the railheads behind his right wing were five days' march behind the front. Failure to maintain adequate logistical support during and after deep penetrations in enemy territory created a shortage of munitions on all fronts. Railroads as well as horse-pulled wagons were key to logistical support for most of the war. The Germans had to deal with the great distance separating their two main fronts. The Allies, on the other hand, had the advantage of deploying along interior lines thanks to the French rail network, which allowed them to shift their forces rapidly.

After 1st Ypres, Falkenhayn switched to the defensive in the West because he had to send six infantry divisions to the East, which stripped him of reserves. He ordered the creation of belts of several lines of trenches to be held by a minimum number of men while the excess troops formed a reserve. Falkenhayn eventually realized that it was unrealistic to order his troops not to give up any ground. During the initial engagements, troops in the first trench line suffered heavy casualties. As a result, he ordered only a few troops to remain in the first line until the enemy infantry actually advanced. Even with the newly formed divisions, he was unable to meet the demands of the two-front war. In April 1915, the structure of the German infantry division changed from two infantry brigades, each with two infantry regiments of three battalions (twelve infantry battalions per division). Falkenhayn removed one brigade headquarters and one of its regiments, and reassigned the remaining regiment to the other brigade giving the division three infantry regiments, totalling nine battalions. The fourth regiment and the brigade headquarters often went to form a new three-regiment division. The French infantry divisions underwent a similar change, but it was not until late 1916 that about forty divisions had converted from two brigades of four regiments to three regiments (without a brigade headquarters) in the closing stages of the Battle of Verdun. Most of the remaining French divisions converted in 1917. Both French and German armies had to stretch their resources in manpower as casualties mounted.

Falkenhayn launched 2nd Ypres in 1915, his only offensive in the West that year, as a diversion to cover the movement of units from the Western Front to the Eastern Front. He claimed he used poison gas to compensate for a shortage of troops. However, despite achieving some early success with this new weapon, he did not have enough troops to exploit the situation. Joffre had his own difficulties in maintaining his

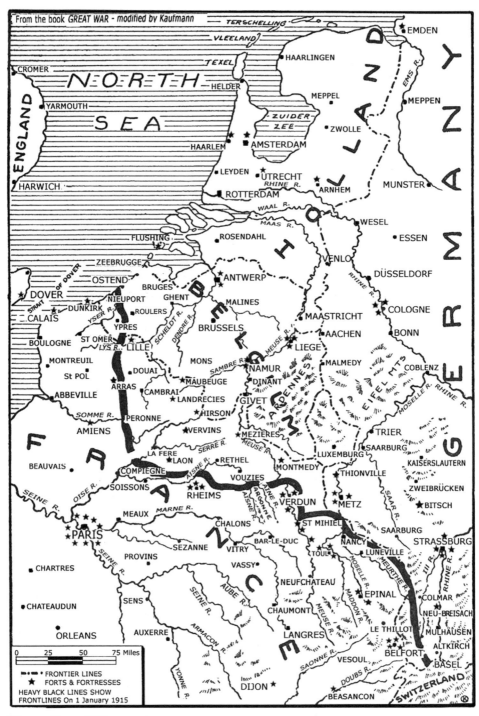

Western Front, 1915.

1902 150-mm Howtizter (s. F.h. 02)

98/09 105-mm Light Field Howitzer (l.F.H. 98/09)

Long 1913 150-mm Howitzer (lg.s.F.H. 13)

1916 105-mm Light Field Howitzer (I.F.H.16)

1913 150-mm Howitzer (s.F.H. 13)

GERMAN MEDIUM

FIELD ARTILLERY

1904 100-mm Gun (10 cm. K.04)

1914 100-mm Gun (10 cm K.14)

forces on the Western Front and blamed it on fruitless sideshows like the Dardanelles Campaign. In any case, it is doubtful that these diversions would have changed the outcome of his three failed offensives in 1915. Joffre and his generals finally began to realize that artillery must pave the way for the infantry and that infantry charges in mass formations with flags flying and bands playing were no longer practical. Elan and bayonets would no longer bring about victory.

'Artillery conquers, the Infantry occupies', asserted Pétain, but the problem for the French as well as the Germans was that they had not established a proper role for the artillery during the first months of the war. Trench warfare required an effective use of artillery, the new role of which was defined during 1915. It may have been less noticeable on the Eastern Front where trench lines did not dominate. After the Germans opened an offensive there, the artillery did not have to advance in order to breach non-existent Russian trench lines. However, the Germans did use their guns in the East to attack fortified positions or to open the assault in order to crush Russian defences. In the West, the continuous trench lines increased in depth in 1915 and the war took on the character of sieges where big guns were needed to break enemy positions. The Germans entered the war with howitzers and heavy mortars, the high trajectories of which allowed them to destroy enemy trenches. Their 77mm guns, like the French 75mm guns, were direct-fire weapons and they were ineffective against trenches or wire barriers. However, they proved more valuable when they were pushed up to the front in direct support of troops attacking strongpoints or in defence against infantry attacks. In 1915, the Germans developed more effective methods than the Allies did. The British, who had some success with the hurricane barrage at Neuve Chapelle, seemed convinced that a bombardment lasting days would be more productive. Although the extended bombardment proved to be rather ineffective, the Allies continued to employ it. After 1915, the creeping barrage followed by troops showed more promise, but timing, observation and effective communications were important to ensure success.

At the onset of the war, neither side would have imagined that trenches would become the dominant factor in the West. Before long, however, the trench lines stretched across France. They became increasingly sophisticated with the addition of troops and ammunition, shelters, communication trenches leading to the rear and multiple lines of trenches forming a defensive belt. They were reinforced with wood, sandbags and even concrete. Strongpoints, veritable miniature forts, appeared on the trench lines.[44] A 'no-man's-land' separated opposing lines. In 1915, the Germans began adding multiple strands of wire in intricate patterns to the original one or two strands. The French direct-fire weapons were unable to break up the wire barriers and wire cutters for the troops were in short supply for many months. Until 1916, only the Germans possessed enough trench mortars and heavy artillery to destroy the enemy's obstacles. Falkenhayn concluded that his troops had to 'acclimatize' themselves to trench warfare on the Western Front, which was not an impediment to sending new units and troops to the East.

In 1915, Joffre's 'nibbling' tactics, though costly in terms of French lives and generally futile, actually caused Falkenhayn great concern. Even though his losses were considerably fewer than Joffre's, his resources were stretched to breaking point. He constantly had to maintain a balance and keep his eye on other concerns. During the war's first winter, Falkenhayn wrote:

> almost every single shot had to be counted in the Western Army, and the failure of one single ammunition train, the breaking of a rail or any other stupid accident, threatened to render whole sections of the front defenceless. The requirements of the Eastern Army were always given the preference on account of its being composed of many units in which the process of consolidation was incomplete.[*]

Germany's Three-Front War

Shortly before Italy entered the war on 23 May 1915, Falkenhayn, concerned about the situation, had tried unsuccessfully to convince the Austrians to buy off

---

* General Erich von Falkenhayn, *General Headquarters 1914–1916* (repr. Nashville, TN: Battery Press, 2000), p. 44.

Italy with territorial concessions.[45] Meanwhile, neutral Rumania supplied food and other resources to the German war machine, but the Allies continued to pressure it into entering the war. When Falkenhayn eliminated Serbia at the end of 1915 with Bulgaria's help, he kept Rumania from entering the conflict for many months. The Bulgarian army was sufficient to keep the Allied forces bottled up around Salonika, Greece, for most of the war. As the Allies evacuated Gallipoli, the Germans opened the rail connection to Constantinople, which provided direct support to Turkey. That allowed Austria to redirect its troops from the Balkans to Italy.

Meanwhile, as the great Eastern offensive ended in the autumn of 1915, Russia began to lose its grip on its Polish salient as its troops evacuated the mid-nineteenth century fortress of Ivangorod on 4 August. The next day, the victorious German troops entered Warsaw. The Russian line of fortresses on the Northwest Front, which had slowed the German advances between Warsaw and Kovno during the first half of 1915, began to crack in July. On 5 August, however, the Russians repulsed the attack of the German *10th Army* at Kovno (Lithuanian Kaunas) on the Niemen River. On the Southwest Front, the Austrian *4th Army* defeated the Russians north of Lublin. On 10 August, German troops crossed the Vistula at Warsaw, took the suburb of Praga and laid siege to Fortress Novogeorgievsk, which surrendered on 20 August. The Russian forces had abandoned the Polish salient after 16 August and retreated to a line running from the fortress of Kovno to Osovyets (Polish Osowiec) to Brest-Litovsk. Mackensen's Austrian and German troops rapidly advanced toward the fortress of Brest-Litovsk and chased the retreating Russian forces across the Bug River on 17 August.[46] Meanwhile, the German *10th Army* finally took Kovno. One fortified position after another continued to fall: Brest-Litovsk on 25 August, Grodno on 2 September and Vilna on 19 September. The Central Powers' troops continued to advance until the end of September, completing the offensive that had begun in May and that pushed the front 482km (300 miles) eastward. The German and Austrian troops established a front line that ran from east of Riga in the north, through Pinsk in the centre and near Tarnopol in the south. Fortresses once isolated on the Eastern Front had failed to turn the tide for either side and they usually fell, which may have continued to influence Joffre's thinking on the Western Front.

While Joffre planned his grand offensives for 1915, he still had to relieve the fortress of Verdun that anchored both his right flank that ran to Belfort and his left flank that extended to the sea. The two main rail lines to the fortress had been cut and the only remaining rail link with the rest of France was a secondary one. Early in year, he tried to eliminate the St Mihiel Salient by ordering the 1st Army to attack in the Woëvre and the 3rd Army to push the Germans off the ridge west of Verdun from which their artillery interdicted the main railroad to Verdun that passed through the Argonne. Both operations served as a diversion from the Champagne Campaign. After the retreat from the Marne, the Germans pulled back from most of the Argonne. In early 1915, their renewed attacks were unsuccessful in regaining the ground they had lost in the Argonne. On 17 February, the French 3rd Army failed to dislodge them from their observation post at Vauquois, marking the beginning of a long stalemate in the Argonne. After late January, the French 1st Army attacked

Pétain, France's Rising Star

Henri Philippe Pétain, commander of the 4th Brigade of the 2nd Infantry Division of the 5th Army, had always been sceptical about the idea that elan would lead to victory and the *offensive à outrance* – the policy of going on the offensive everywhere at all times with whatever means. General Lanrezac, commander of the 5th Army, agreed with him. In mid–August 1914, Pétain's brigade was engaged in the defence of the Meuse and formed the rear guard during a retreat. His outstanding performance during those engagements did not go unnoticed. As Joffre sacked his ineffective generals one after the other, Pétain was promoted to *général de brigade*. On 29 August, General d'Espèrey, who replaced Lanrezac, launched a counter-attack near Guise following the doctrine of *offensive à outrance*. The first brigade went on the attack hoping that elan would carry the day. Pétain's brigade was the last. Having witnessed the slaughter of their comrades, his troops began to waver, but the general rode on his horse among them calming their fears. He deployed them in a loose formation and ordered the supporting artillery to put down a barrage before the attack. His brigade made good progress until the sun went down.[47] When the army began to retreat again, his brigade was once more in the rear guard. On 2 September, he was given command of the 6th Infantry Division, a broken formation at the time. He restored the unit transforming it into an effective force that performed with distinction at the Battle of Marne and later. The result was another promotion.

In October 1914, Pétain was awarded the Legion of Honour for his heroism and he received the command of the XXXIII Corps. He continued to promote a methodical approach to battle, instead of the *offensive à outrance* that Joffre employed through much of 1915. On 17 December 1914, the French 10th Army attacked in Artois and Pétain's corps entered the fray. The corps on Pétain's flanks employed the old methods and made little progress leaving his flanks exposed after his corps successfully advanced. Thus, his troops had to fall back. When Joffre attempted to take Vimy Ridge in May 1915, Pétain's corps led the way again. While the other two corps gained little ground, Pétain's broke through and advanced 4km taking the ridge thanks to his methodical attack. Since the two corps on his flank failed to advance, they left his troops exposed on both flanks forcing him to pull his divisions back from the ridge. It finally became apparent that Pétain's strategy was more effective than the one used by the army up to that point. On 21 June 1915, Joffre put Pétain in command of the 2nd Army.

As Pétain's reputation spread to the enemy camp, Joffre shifted him around as a decoy. However, Joffre continued to turn a deaf ear to Pétain's pleas to adopt more effective fighting tactics. While Joffre sent several of his generals to sit out the war at Limoges for alleged incompetence, Pétain's reputation as one of the few generals who could be victorious on the battlefield grew. In the autumn of 1915, Joffre moved Pétain's 2nd Army from the front in Artois to Champagne where, alongside the 4th Army, it would spearhead an impending offensive. Joffre hoped to achieve a massive breakthrough on a front of up to 40km wide, eschewing attacks on narrow fronts of only a few kilometres he had tried earlier in Champagne and Artois. The divisions of the 2nd Army breached the first line of German defences only to face a second even stronger line. The other armies were less successful. Pétain needed more time and resources to strike at the second line, but this was not to be. On 7 October, Joffre called off the offensive that had begun on 25 September thus ending major operations for 1915 on the Western Front.

In the summer of 1915, Pétain had already explained to Joffre that the war had become one of attrition and that the side with the last man standing would win. Joffre was not ready to accept this fact. He did not seem as concerned about the lives sacrificed as Pétain, who cared for his men and who could often be found near the front with his troops, unlike his superior. On the night of 24/25 February, Pétain was absent from army headquarters when his aide came looking for him. When the aide finally located him at a hotel in Paris where he was spending the night with his mistress, he informed him of orders to report to Joffre at Chantilly on the morning of 25 February. Joffre gave him command of the defence of Verdun, which turned out to be the most infamous battle of attrition of the war. Pétain, unlike other commanders, was unwilling to trade the lives of his men for those of enemy troops. He was convinced that this was not a war of men against men, but rather a war of men against materiel. He believed that artillery and other weapons should inflict the main damage. On the other side of the hill, German General Falkenhayn had already come to a similar conclusion during 1915. He carried it to the extreme when he planned his 1916 offensive in the West against Verdun since his objective was to whittle down the enemy army rather than to seize Verdun. Like Pétain, he preferred to inflict the damage with his artillery and other weapons.

several key points of the St Mihiel Salient. On 18 March, its objectives included the Les Éparges Butte, which gave a commanding view of the Woëvre. Although attacks in March and April were supported by new artillery and the French infantry managed to occupy part of the Les Éparges Butte, the operations failed. Joffre concluded that the artillery must demolish the first and second lines of trenches before the infantry could attack. Between December 1914 and the end of March 1915, the offensives in Artois and Champagne and the operations on the shoulders of the Verdun Salient were dismal failures. The French army lost about ¼ million men. For Joffre, who showed remarkably little compassion for the soldiers who paid the ultimate price, the bloody offensives represented merely his first big experiments in modern warfare.[48] Joffre justified the offensives of 1915 by saying they were needed to take the pressure off the Russians when their front appeared to be collapsing.[49] However, even though Joffre's efforts were mostly fruitless and costly, they were a nuisance for Falkenhayn who constantly had to maintain a balance of forces to ensure that he had enough troops to handle the situation.

In June, Joffre finally improved his command structure by creating three army groups. He had already created an informal Northern Army Group under General Ferdinand Foch and an Eastern Group under General Yvon Dubail. The Central Army Group was formed under General Noël Édouard de Castelnau. General Pétain took over the command of Castelnau's 2nd Army, which prepared for a new Champagne offensive that began on 25 September. On the first day, some French units advanced up to 4km and took thousands of prisoners. German counter-attacks pushed them back. The French lost 145,000 men and the Germans 95,000, with negligible changes. Also on 25 September, the BEF launched the Battle of Loos using poison gas, but gained very little terrain despite losing 50,000 men and inflicting 25,000 casualties on the Germans. At the same time, the French 10th Army attacked in Artois following a four-day bombardment that made little headway. The fighting paused in mid-October. The French lost an additional 48,000 soldiers and the Germans 50,000. Since the front lines barely budged, Falkenhayn's defence in the West proved successful while Joffre's approach did little to help the Russians. The 1915 campaigns came to a close with both Joffre and Falkenhayn initiating planning for 1916 to break the hopeless deadlock.

Chapter Two

Fortifications and Positional Warfare

'The symbol of the battle was a great fort, Douaumont, which the French had
  had the sense to abandon'
    Norman Stone, *World War One: A Short History* (New York: Basic Books, 2007)

In contradiction to the above conclusion:

'The battle over the last six months has been dominated by concrete and cannon'
                                    3rd Bureau of Pétain's Second Army, 1916

Forts and Fortresses

Even though the forts at Verdun played an important role during the battle, few
history books offer much information about them. Except for the forts of Douaumont
and Vaux, none of the other forts is described. The citadel at Verdun, however, is
mentioned even though it played a minimal role in the First World War. Actually
located in the city, it dates back to the seventeenth century. Its underground galleries,
extending 7km in total, were added between 1886 and 1893 and served as a depot for
weapons, powder magazines, other stores, kitchens and communications and could
shelter up to 2,000 soldiers in addition to civilians. In the twentieth century, the
walls of this old fort hardly provided any protection for the city. There were other
Vauban era fortifications at sites such as Lille, Montmédy and Longwy, but beyond
supporting a garrison and, in some cases, housing a few battery or combat positions,
they offered little in the way of modern defence.[1]

France and most of the other major powers had continued to improve their
fortifications until the beginning of the war. On the Western Front, the French and
Germans reinforced their fortresses with new or additional barbed wire obstacles
and interval positions only days before the war broke out. The Germans maintained
the fortresses of Metz–Thionville and Strasbourg–Mutzig where they expected to
receive the brunt of a French attack.[2] The French, despite being mostly concerned
about their main fortresses between Verdun and Belfort, also worked on the border
forts between Maubeuge and Longwy since they expected a German advance through
the Ardennes.

In 1903, the French army had allotted extra funds for ammunition, for work on
the fortresses in the east and northeast and for 105mm and 155mm guns.[3] In 1904,
when Joffre became the French army's chief engineer, the government underfunded
the work on the eastern frontier. This delayed the completion of the programme

by twenty years by which time the works would have become mostly obsolete. In 1905, Joffre failed again to obtain the required finances. In 1906, the new Minister of War finally allotted additional funds. In 1911, when Joffre became Chief of the General Staff, he discovered that the French army lagged behind the German forces in weapons and equipment and that the artillery was short of ammunition. If they were to equip the army adequately, Joffre and the War Minister would not be able to give priority to the fortifications, especially since the French war plans called for offensive action.

The Germans continued to work on their forts even though Schlieffen and his successors believed that they should build more railroads rather than forts. When the war broke out, forts took centre stage in the West more than in the East. In 1915, the Russian fortresses of Ivangorod (Polish Dęblin), Warsaw and Novogeorgievsk (Polish Modlin) secured the Russian Vistula River Line. The fortresses of Novogeorgievsk, Różan, Łomża, Osowiec, Grodno, Olita and Kovno held the Narew, Bobra and Niemen river lines by covering the major crossings. The Russian defence against German thrusts centred on these fortresses until late July 1915 when the Germans finally overcame them (see Chapter 1). Although some of these fortresses, like Novogeorgievsk, were of equal size as many of the fortresses in the West and included a similar number of forts, they were less impressive because they lacked armoured turrets.

At the onset of the war, the major powers assigned different roles to forts and fortresses in their plans. Many of the military leaders expected a brief war from which their own armies would emerge victorious shortly after mobilization. Most planned on offensive action supported by fortified sites, which were to serve as assembly and concentration points and shield the army during mobilization. The citizenry of the various countries was convinced that permanent fortifications would prevent invasions. The German military command, however, doubted that their intermittent line of forts in the East would stop the Russians. In the West, they hoped that the French would engage their fortified Metz–Thionville complex and advance into the Vosges allowing the German forces to thrust through Belgium and proceed unimpeded. They were prepared to take up entrenched positions deep inside this territory to halt a French advance.

Fortifications offered a sense of security to the minor powers, such as Belgium, Switzerland and the Netherlands, since their armies were too small to consider offensives against a great power. The Belgians were thought to have some of the strongest fortresses in Europe capable of holding would-be invaders, be it Germany or France, until another nation came to their rescue. Except for the water barriers, the Dutch fortifications were less impressive than the Belgian were. The Swiss forts combined with impressive mountain barriers, however, were formidable, but formed a national redoubt that offered little protection to the population centres. The Rumanians built some impressive fortifications near Bucharest, but their main line of defence faced the Russian Empire rather than the Central Powers. Other minor powers from Scandinavia to the Balkans relied mostly on geography and older fortifications.

Of the major powers, Germany possessed the newest and most impressive fortresses located in Alsace and Lorraine. According to the Schlieffen Plan, the fortresses of Metz and Diedenhofen (French Thionville) shielded the main route into Lorraine. The fortress of Strasbourg in Alsace, linked to Feste Kaiser Wilhelm II, was mostly a fall-back position for the field army, which was to use the terrain between Metz and the Vosges to delay a French advance and buy time for an unhindered German offensive through Belgium.

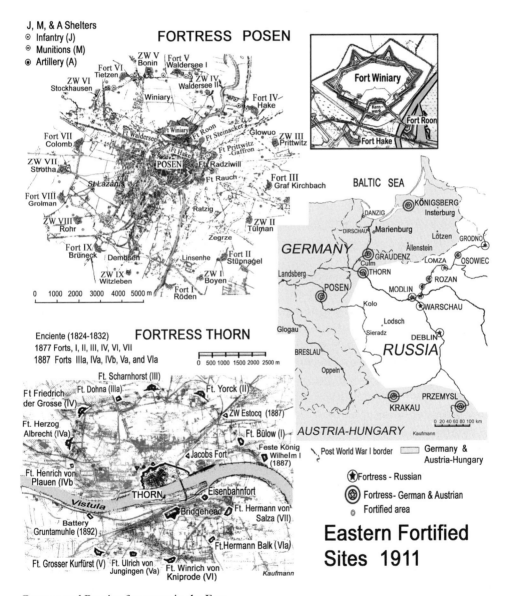

German and Russian fortresses in the East.

According to the French Plan XVII, the fortresses of Verdun, Toul, Épinal and Belfort were expected to cover the mobilization of the French army. Several forts linked the fortresses of Verdun and Toul and the fortresses of Épinal and Belfort. The Trouée de Charmes (Charmes Gap), which lay between these two fortress groups, included three river barriers (Vezouze, Meurthe and Moselle) that cut through the plains and rolling hills, the centrally located city of Lunéville and Fort Manonviller, a major *fort d'arrêt* – a 'stop' or blocking fort. According to the plan, the French armies were to advance into Alsace and Lorraine as soon as they assembled. However, Joffre, who expected a German thrust through southern Belgium and Luxembourg, modified the plan before the war.[4] After he obtained additional funds for the eastern forts, the army undertook work on older forts near Belgium in the northeast. Unfortunately, it was too little too late.

The Germans also had a string of fortresses on their Eastern Front: Posen (Polish Poznań), Thorn (Polish Toruń) and Graudenz (Polish Grudziądz). Fortress Königsberg served as an anchor on the German left flank with the heavily forested terrain and lakes of East Prussia between it and Graudenz. According to the Schlieffen Plan, the forces in the East would go on the defensive while the bulk of the German army took on the French in the West. The scheme did not work out because the Russians invaded East Prussia, which forced the German high command to transfer a couple of army corps from the Western Front to the East. As it turned out, the Germans repulsed and defeated the Russians before these reinforcements arrived. After his victory at Tannenberg, Hindenburg was forced to strip the East German fortresses of their garrisons to bolster his field forces and prop up the faltering Austrian Front.

Austria's plans were unclear. Although Italy was a member of the Central Powers, the Austrian high command did not trust it and continued to maintain and improve the forts on their sensitive mountainous border.[5] There were few significant permanent fortifications on the frontiers of Austria's Balkan provinces. There were two major fortress rings to defend the front with Russia in Galicia: Cracow and Przemyśl. Austria's plans did not dovetail with German strategy on the Eastern Front. Soon after the war broke out, the Austrian command foolishly opted for offensive action, which became a major rout and put a strain on the Germans in the East. The retreating Austrians lost most of Galicia and allowed a Russian army to isolate the fortress of Przemyśl.

The Russians also had a string of fortresses, most of which faced a possible German invasion from East Prussia and stood mainly between Warsaw and Grodno. The Russians planned to use them to cover their mobilization. These fortifications included old and new forts. In 1880, the Russian army prepared a plan for the construction of fortifications on the Narew and Bobra (Polish Biebrza) rivers that included defensive bridgeheads at Zegrze, Pułtusk, Różan, Ostrołęka and Łomża on the Narew River. Łomża's role required its conversion into a fortress. The fortress of Novogeorgievsk at the confluence of the Vistula and Narew and Fortress Osowiec on the Bobra secured the flanks of this covering line. The bridgehead at Zegrze consisted of a small fourteenth-century fort until 1898 when work began on two earthen positions reinforced with concrete positions on the escarpment above the northern bank of the Narew. The largest fort was an irregularly shaped hexagon with caponiers, observation posts and barracks. A second, but smaller fort, connected to it with a rampart for infantry and an artillery battery. Between 1906 and 1909, the entire position was modernized with new ramparts and additional positions. At Łomża, the Russians built five earthen forts between 1887 and 1889 on the left bank of the Narew and three forts on the right bank above the town. They updated the position after 1901 when they decided to turn Łomża into a fortress. The three forts on the right bank were renovated, provided a pentagonal trace, concrete barracks and a caponier in the gorge, troop shelters on the ramparts and counterscarp caponiers in the frontal ditch. A 1908 plan called for five new forts in an outer girdle on the right bank and the reconstruction of two forts on the left bank. When he took office in March 1909, General Vladimir Suchomlinov, Russian Minister of War from 1909–15, persuaded the Tsar to approve a decree eliminating the 'fortresses' in Poland, except for the largest, which included Warsaw, and those located between Novogeorgievsk and Osowiec. The 1909 directive ended work on the Łomża fortifications. In May 1910, plans were made to dismantle and remove the forts, but discussions delayed the process. It appears that the Russian army began restoring many of the fortifications between 1912 and 1913 with the intention of using them as shields during mobilization. Other locations such as Ostrołęka, where two forts defended the bridge over the Narew River, and Pułtusk, which consisted only of earthworks built before the war, were not as impressive. Work began on four forts at Różan on the Narew River in 1899. A fifth was never finished because of the 1909 directive. The Russian engineers opted for trapezoidal designs for two of the forts and rhomboidal for the other two, common shapes for modern fortifications. Construction began in 1902 and the last of the four forts was completed in 1910.

Kovno and Grodno on the Niemen River were built to block an eastward German advance. At Kovno there was a girdle of seven forts begun in 1882 and an eighth added later. A new girdle of twelve forts with supporting positions was under construction in 1912 and was due for completion in 1917. When work stopped in 1915, only one fort had actually been completed. The Russian engineers reinforced most of their forts with concrete in 1915. Grodno, located at the confluence of the Bobra and the Niemen rivers, had seven forts dating from 1887 and from 1900–12. A further fourteen forts and thirty-seven interval positions formed an outer ring around the city. To the southwest of the Bobra, stands the Osowiec fortress, and, surrounded by swamps, it secured the north flank of the line of bridgeheads on the Narew. This impressive position included two forts built between 1882 and 1890 that continually underwent modernization. A further two forts were added after 1900. The final phase of rebuilding began in 1912 with the construction of shrapnel resistant shelters. Additional works constructed between 1913 and 1914 successfully resisted German heavy artillery bombardment.

Novogeorgievsk , the largest of the Russian border fortresses, occupied a strategic location and was as important as Verdun was for the French. The fortress formed an impressive girdle at the confluence of the Vistula and Narew rivers. Originally fortified under Napoleon, construction of its first girdle of forts began in the 1880s. A second girdle was added on the north side of the rivers and a new front on the east side between the two rivers between 1912 and 1915.

Not as modern, but just as large, was Fortress Warsaw, which included a citadel built in the early 1830s and six surrounding forts completed in 1865. The fortress included several generations of nineteenth-century fortifications. After 1883, the Russians built an outer ring of fourteen forts (four on the eastern bank of the Vistula). In 1886, they developed an inner ring of five forts that were completed in 1892 and to which they later added interval positions. By 1900, an enceinte connected the inner ring and over twenty forts formed the inner and outer girdle on the left bank with a wall between the forts of the inner ring. Several forts formed the eastern part of the ring on the right bank. During the 1890s, the girdle of brick forts was modified when the brick was replaced with concrete or the concrete was used to cover brick sections. At this time, the French were carrying out similar renovations on their own forts as well. During a further modernization phase, some of the Russians forts ended up with two separate ramparts – one for infantry and the other for artillery – when a lower rampart was added and the length of the glacis was extended. However, despite their generally larger size, the Russian forts of Warsaw and other sites did not equal the fortifications of the West. They had no armoured gun turrets and usually lacked armoured components. The most modern addition to the Russians forts in Poland, beside electricity and communications, took the form of concrete shelters. Fortress Warsaw was included in the decommissioning order of 1909, but the years of indecision that followed prevented the liquidation of that fortress before the war.

The salient formed by Russian Poland faced the threat of a German invasion on the west and north sides and an additional threat from an Austrian incursion in the southwest where the Russians had fewer, smaller and mostly obsolete fortifications. The line of the Vistula formed the main barrier facing west with no major positions to the west of it near the German frontier. The old, bastioned fortress of Ivangorod, built in the second quarter of the nineteenth century, stood almost in the centre of the Vistula line with Warsaw to the north and little else in the way of fortifications to the south. It consisted of seven detached forts built between 1878 and 1882, making it the strongest position south of Warsaw. Further to the south and near the Austrian border, was Zamość, an old fortress that had acquired a circular casemated fort in the 1830s.[6] It had been decommissioned in 1866 and sections of its defences were later torn down. Well to the east of Zamość was the fortified town of Dubno with an ancient castle and two forts added in 1900s. Rovno (Polish Rowno) included seven earthen girdle forts from 1890, whereas Lutsk (Polish Łuck), on the Styr River, consisted of four earthen forts from 1890. Dubno, Rovno and Lutsk formed the Volhynian Triangle (a historical region in northwest Ukraine) and covered a possible Austrian invasion from the direction of Lemberg.

The Russian army designated the Bug River as a second line of defence, which covered the route from Brest-Litovsk to Minsk and Moscow. Brest-Litovsk, one of the newest Russian fortresses, was located on the western side of the large Pripet Marshes. The citadel, built on the central island between the 1830s and 1843, was known for its thick, red-brick walls. It was surrounded by three major fortifications, an earthen curtain with several brick casemates that stretched over 6.4km and a wet moat. The Russians added a girdle of ten artillery forts between 1878 and 1888 and modernized these earth-covered, brick forts surrounded with ditches between 1908 and 1911. The renovations consisted of pouring a layer of concrete up to 2m thick over the brick masonry. Between 1909 and 1915, the Russians added fourteen newer concrete forts and thirty interval positions. By 1914, only two of these fourteen forts had actually been completed.

In the late nineteenth century, the Russian army fortified several other sites, including Olita, which guarded a new railroad crossing. The main Russian defensive system included forts and fortresses that defended river crossings and stretched along the Narew and Niemen rivers facing East Prussia. It did not form a continuous line, unless the rivers are included as part of the defences.

The Russian rail system, much improved after the Russo-Japanese War, was more important than the road system, which often turned to mud in heavy rains. The Russians opted for broad gauge rails, which made it difficult for their armies to advance into enemy territory where they encountered the narrow standard gauge rail lines. It was easier for the Germans and the Austrians to use the Russian rail network because they could increase the length of the axles of the rolling stock and engines.[7]

Most Russian forts were two to three times larger than Austrian forts. Beginning in the 1890s, the Russians, like the other Europeans, started to use concrete in their forts, but they failed to add armoured components. In 1909, their army ceased work on their Polish fortresses, but maintained Novogeorgievsk and Osowiec. The modernization of the outer ring of Novogeorgievsk was not completed in time for the First World War. The Russian army quickly brought the decommissioned fortifications back into service at the onset of the conflict. The fortresses served as ammunition depots and artillery parks for almost all the Russian heavy artillery. This might have been a reasonable decision if the Russians had not found it difficult to distribute these resources in 1914 and 1915. In addition, when these sites fell into enemy hands, they contained vast amounts of weapons and munitions, which came as a boon to the Germans and the Austrians who suffered from shortages in 1914 and later.

There was a marked difference between the way the Russians used forts and fortresses and the French did. The French created a major fortified line that extended from Verdun to Belfort with only one significant gap of about 40km (25 miles), which, nevertheless, did include a few forts. The line consisted of two major segments of about 95km (60 miles) in length each. The entire line, including the gap, extended for about 230km (145 miles) and covered almost the whole front between France and Germany. The major fortresses of Russia, on the other hand, were 95km (60 miles) to over 240km (150 miles) apart and some controlled key points on major invasion routes. The only position that resembled a fortified line ran along the Narew, Bobra and Niemen rivers for about 360km (225 miles) and was thus almost 50 per cent longer than the main French line. In the Russian river line, the gap between the small fortresses was often 65km (40 miles) long or more, which was larger than the

Artillery and Turrets

What turned most modern forts into formidable positions was their protected artillery in armoured casemates and turret positions. The first requirement of an effective armoured gun turret is a breech-loading gun. In 1872, Charles de Bange, a French artillery colonel, designed the first successful breech system for cannons that prevented gases from escaping from the breech and injuring the crew. The 'De Bange System' 155mm L Mle 1877 was adopted by the army. The gun had to be pushed back into position after each firing, like most artillery of the day.

FRENCH ARTILLERY

75mm Mle 1897

155 mm Long de Bange Mle 1877

120 mm Long de Bange
Mle 1878

370 mm Filloux Mortar
1915

90 mm de Bange Mle 1877

Note: The two 155-mm guns and the 120-mm gun
above used the Cingoli system on their wheels

The most effective recoil system appeared on the French 75mm Mle 1897. The French 'Soixante-quinze' remained in position after firing while only the barrel recoiled on its carriage and returned to the firing position. The Nordenfeld breech mechanism allowed the gun to fire up to twenty-eight rounds a minute. In 1914, General Frédéric-Georges Herr cited an official document according to which the 75mm gun 'suffices for all the missions that can be intrusted to artillery in field warfare'. As an artillery officer, he decried the fact that long-range artillery was undervalued in France because it required direct observation, but then the best optical equipment available was limited to distances below 5,000m. The use of aircraft or balloons in reconnaissance and observation, he pointed out, was not even taken into consideration.[8]

In 1915, the French artillery service still relied mostly on direct-fire guns and was short of heavy artillery, which led to the removal of artillery from the forts in the autumn. Among these weapons, there were a number of old 155mm guns with no effective recoil system. The field army lacked modern indirect-fire weapons and the forts had a few obsolete mortars. Turret guns needed some type of recoil system because space limitations precluded kickback upon firing.

In the 1870s, Captain Henri Mougin developed the first approved turret for the French forts.[9] The Mougin Mle 1876 turret mounted two de Bange 155mm L (long barrel) Mle 1877 guns and had embrasures cut in its cupola. Descriptions of the turret vary between sources. According to an article of 20 January 1900 in *Scientific American* (Supplement, No. 1255), the sides of this wrought-iron turret were 60cm thick and its roof was 20cm thick. The cupola was made of five sections and the dome stood about 1.5m high. An armoured glacis consisting of several pieces formed a collar that surrounded the turret and was set in a layer of concrete, which also protected the subterranean masonry structure. It took eighteen men in teams of six to manoeuvre the turret manually until 1883 when a coal-fired steam engine took over this function. The army adopted the Mougin turret (built at St Chamond) in the 1880s. Mougin modified the design of the turret he presented at the Bucharest tests in 1886. The tests showed that repeated hits on the same section almost destroyed the armour. On the other hand, the French turret fired twice as fast as the German. There were twenty-five of these turrets in service including nine in forts of the main line facing the German border. In the 1900s, some of the turrets were removed and the masonry of their subterranean positions was replaced with concrete or reinforced concrete. German heavy artillery demolished a few forts with Mougin turrets at Maubeuge and Fort Manonviller in 1914.[10]

During the second half of the nineteenth century, turret armour kept pace with changes in fortifications. The Grüson works in Germany developed a secret method that gave them the edge in the industry for many years. In 1878, the French armour commission concluded that the steel in use shattered under excessive shock. The commission next considered either rolled iron or cast iron, which is not as malleable as wrought iron.[11] As wrought-iron plates increased in size, a process was developed to weld them together. The problem with the welding method, however, was that it had a tendency to split along the seams when it was hit. The commission decided to adopt both rolled iron and the less expensive hard cast iron. Hard cast iron is rigid, could break up the heaviest projectiles of the 1870s and lends itself to the creation of rounded surfaces. Rolled iron, on the other hand, is easier to shape and can reach required thicknesses.[12] In the early 1880s, carbon was added to steel to form a stronger metal. The addition of tungsten and chrome greatly increased the overall strength of steel.

The new high-explosive shells were made of steel, which gave them greater capabilities and volume. At St Chamond in 1884, tests showed that rolled iron armour was more resistant than hard cast iron to these steel shells. The Mougin turrets, made of hard cast iron, had already been installed when tests revealed that they were inadequate. The commission selected rolled iron for armour. The Mougin turret was rather flat at the top, but the Bucharest tests demonstrated that curved roofs were preferable for turrets. The commission also concluded that in the future it should strive to obtain eclipsing turrets, which meant that the guns could not extend beyond the embrasure. After tests at Chalons in 1887–8, the commission adopted two Mougin retracting turrets.

The commission also tested a couple of non-eclipsing turrets at Chalons. They rejected a St Chamond turret, very similar to the Mougin, but with gun embrasures closer to ground level and a laminated curved armoured dome instead of a cast-iron one. This experimental turret was installed at Fort St Michel (Toul). The Montluçon turret also had a curved dome but its gun embrasures for 155mm C (howitzers) were cut into its dome. This turret served as a detached armoured battery near Fort Lucey (Toul). The Bussière and Souriau turrets were among the first eclipsing turrets produced in France, but neither proved satisfactory. In addition, the price was up to four times higher than the non-eclipsing type. The Bussière eclipsing turret had a roof of rolled iron bolted to the turret sides. It mounted a pair of 155mm L guns and, like other turrets, included hydraulic brakes. Manoeuvring the turret required a steam engine. Its main weakness, concluded the commission, was its fragile operating system. The mixed metal armour of the turret's flat roof was .24m thick and consisted of two plates screwed together. The turret walls were .45m thick. The diameter of the turret was 5.25m. This turret was mounted next to Fort Souville (Verdun).

Colonel Souriau designed one of the most interesting turrets at the Schneider factory. His eclipsing turret mounted two 155mm L guns under a curved roof. His unique eclipsing system had the turret's vertical movement relying on a platform floating on water in a tank. However, the commission considered this system a liability due to the fact that water and metal would be in contact.

In 1892, Captain Galopin was assigned to study Mougin's new version of an oscillating turret which had gun embrasures pointed below the level of the glacis armour right after firing then tilted back up to the battery position. Galopin's own design was tested shortly afterward. His turret's eclipsing movement used counterweights and shifted from the battery (firing) to the concealed position in 2 seconds.[13] After the guns were loaded, the turret was raised and its weapons were aimed and fired in 4.5 seconds. The turret required a crew of six men in the turret and eleven in the block below the turret. The Galopin turret mounted two 155mm L cannons and the roof comprised 30cm of rolled iron lined with sheet metal. The sidewalls were made of 45cm-thick half-hard steel. The turret, 5.5m in diameter, included ventilators and a monte-charge for moving the ammunition. Fort Arches (Toul) received one of these turrets and three blocking forts (*forts d'arrêt*) of the Charmes Gap had five.

In 1903, the army engineer section redesigned the Galopin turret into a small single-gun turret with steel armour 30cm thick. The firing chamber weighed 70 tons (10 tons less than the two-gun turret). It housed a 155mm R (short barrel) gun with a range of 7,200m as opposed to the 155mm L that had a range of 7,500m. It had the same features as the larger turret, but the few modifications made it more affordable.[14] In a few years, it was adopted as the Galopin 155mm R Mle 1907 turret. By 1914, twelve of these turrets were emplaced.[15]

Bussière designed an eclipsing turret for two Nordenfeld 57mm guns in 1893. This may have been in response to a similarly armed Grüson turret and a mobile model that had grown in popularity. Although the French army purchased four of these turrets, it did not seem to be a good investment since it only mounted a small calibre gun. They were installed in three forts in the mid-1890s. The army modified two of the turrets in 1909 and replaced the 57mm guns with 75mm guns: one at the Ouvrage of Bouvron and the other at the Ouvrage of Est du Vieux Canton. The two turrets at Fort Manonviller were modified.

By the end of the nineteenth century, the 75mm guns became prevalent not only in field artillery but also in fort artillery, before the army converted the two 57mm gun turrets. Using the Galopin turrets as a basis for a new turret design, the French engineers developed a turret mounting two 75mm R (short barrel) guns. Although it was adopted in 1902, this new turret is usually identified as a Mle 1905. Some sources refer to it as Mle 1903. The turret roof armour was 35cm thick and the walls 25cm. It was installed in a combat block with the counterweights and balancer (in the lower level of the block) for eclipsing. Command and control occupied the intermediate level and the firing chamber in the turret was at the upper level. A manual ventilator in the turret removed escaping fumes from the guns. In 1912, ventilators were installed in some of the older turrets as well.[16] The steel roof armour was 30cm thick and the mantle 15cm.[17] Between 1903 and 1914, fifty-five of the seventy-three turrets of this type were emplaced on the main line and in other locations, including in coastal defences. The majority of these turrets went to the fortresses of Verdun (fourteen), Toul (eighteen) and Belfort (ten). Only four went to the forts at Épinal. Like a few of the old Mougin turrets, several of the Mle 1905 turrets remained in service until 1940 in the Maginot Line.

Before long it was decided that machine-gun turrets were needed to protect the fort. The Puteaux armaments work designed the first turret, the GF3 (Gatling Fusil) Mle 1895. It was lightly armoured with 12cm of rolled iron for the roof, and steel sides only 1.5cm thick.[18] There was one of these turrets at Fort Manonviller. When the more effective Hotckhiss Mle 1899 was perfected, the GF4 turret with a thicker roof and side armour was designed. Its side armour was thick enough to resist infantry weapons because the turret rose to the firing position after the enemy bombardment stopped in order to meet an infantry assault. The roof was thick enough to resist 155mm artillery rounds. The turret mounted two Hotchkiss 8mm machine guns, but the gunner did not fire them simultaneously. One man occupied the turret, firing the machine gun and directing movements. Another man stood nearby handing him ammunition clips for the machine guns. In 1914, eighty-seven of these turrets were installed, mostly in the forts of the main line.

The 155mm C (howitzer) Turret Mle 1908 was a late development. It was a non-retracting, single-weapon turret with a steel dome 30cm thick. Only two were installed in 1914, both at Fort Longchamp. There were plans to install two a short distance behind Fort Douaumont in 1914, but construction had to halt in August of that year.

In addition to the turrets, the army ordered a number of armoured observatories. These fixed turrets, called cloche, were constructed with steel about 25cm thick. They usually had three narrow observation crenels and were equipped with instruments to observe artillery fire. They often occupied positions near a gun turret.

single gap in the French line. The entire Russian frontier with Germany and Austria-Hungary was huge and it would have been impractical if not impossible to create a fortified line long enough to hold, especially in terms of nineteenth-century military thinking. The Russians, therefore, had to adopt a policy similar to the one followed by the Germans and the Austrians when it came to forts and fortresses rather than the French one. The Russian forts could do little more than guard key sites, serve as points from which to organize a general defence or function as bases for offensive operations. They were not able to present a solid fortified line that sealed an entire front. By nineteenth-century military standards, this was a reasonable mission, but it also required Russia to have an army capable of manoeuvring and engaging the enemy beyond the fortified sites. The only problem with this strategy was that by 1914 armies were larger than at any time before. The ability to manoeuvre, supply

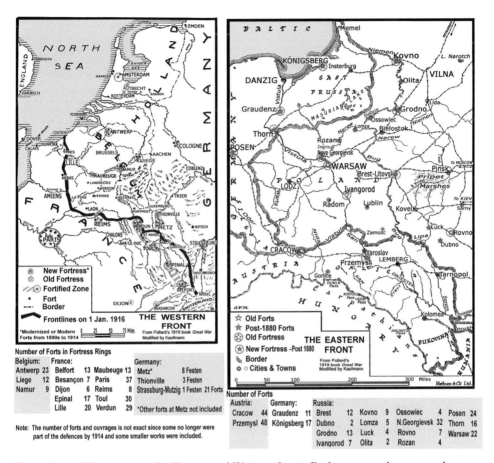

THE WESTERN FRONT

New Fortress*	⊛
Old Fortress	
Fortified Zone	
Fort	*
Border	
Frontlines on 1 Jan. 1916	

*Modernized or Modern Forts from 1890s to 1914

From Pollard's 1919 book *Great War* Modified by Kaufmann

Number of Forts in Fortress Rings

Belgium:		France:		Germany:	
Antwerp 23		Belfort 13	Maubeuge 13	Metz*	8 Festen
Liege 12		Besançon 7	Paris 37	Thionville	3 Festen
Namur 9		Dijon 6	Reims 8	Strassburg-Mutzig 1 Festen 21 Forts
		Epinal 17	Toul 30	
		Lille 20	Verdun 29	*Other forts at Metz not included

Note: The number of forts and ouvrages is not exact since some no longer were part of the defences by 1914 and some smaller works were included.

THE EASTERN FRONT

☆ Old Forts	
★ Post-1880 Forts	
⊗ Old Fortress	
⊛ New Fortress -Post 1880	
⊙ ○ Cities & Towns	
⊶ Border	

From Pollard's 1919 book *Great War* Modified by Kaufmann

Number of Forts

Austria:	Germany:	Russia:					
Cracow 44	Graudenz 11	Brest 12	Kovno 9	Ossowiec 4	Posen 24		
Przemysl 48	Königsberg 17	Dubno 2	Lomza 5	N.Georgievsk 32	Thorn 16		
		Grodno 13	Luck 4	Rovno 7	Warsaw 22		
		Ivangorod 7	Olita 2	Rozan 4			

Comparison of fortresses on the Eastern and Western fronts. Both maps are the same scale.

and even arm such large military forces required a highly industrialized nation with great resources. This meant that Germany and France were much better able than Russia to direct huge armed forces.

Of the major European powers, Russia had had the most recent experience in large-scale trench warfare. In 1904, during the Russo–Japanese War, Russian troops built defences approximately 80km (50 miles) long to hold Liaoyang. In 1905, they built about 160km (100 miles) of lines at Mukden. Despite these efforts, they ended up losing the battles that ensued. The line between Kovno and Novogeorgievsk, which covered over 320km (200 miles), was almost 100km longer than the French line between Belfort and Verdun and lacked major fortresses. The front between Novogeorgievsk along the Vistula extended for 160km (100 miles), but had only two fortresses. Along the Galician frontier, there was an additional 350km or more without fortresses. The river lines on these three fronts formed the main barrier for Russia. On the central front on the Polish plain, there were few barriers except for the wide Vistula and the Bug River further to the east. Even after the fiasco in the

Russo–Japanese War, the Russian leadership still failed to grasp the requirements of trench warfare and paid little attention to defensive operations, especially after the 1909 directive.

The German fortresses, among the most modern of the era, saw almost no action during the war, whereas the French, Belgian, Austrian, Italian and Russian fortifications were heavily involved in combat. Before the war, the Germans and

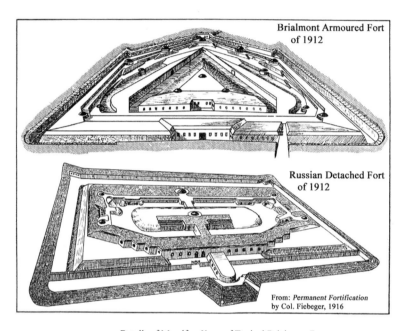

Details of Massif or Keep of Typical Brialmont Fort

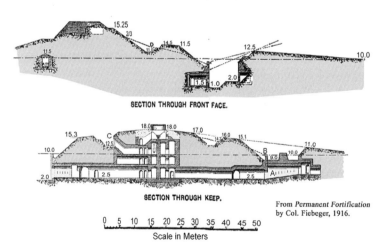

Examples of Russian and Belgian forts. The Belgian forts were much weaker than the French, and not made of reinforced concrete.

Austrians, mostly focused on eliminating enemy fortresses, strove to develop heavy artillery like howitzers of 305mm and 420mm. They also manufactured short-range mortars (*minenwerfer*) to tackle not only the enemy forts, but also the trenches they expected to encounter between forts. Before the war, the Germanic allies did not try to create a continuous defensive line on the Eastern and Western fronts. Germany's key fortified positions at Metz–Thionville and Strasbourg–Mutzig were designed to deny key strategic points to the enemy and relied on the Vosges and on other natural obstacles to channel a French advance. The Germans applied the same principles on their eastern border where a small number of fortresses relied on the wooded lake region of East Prussia to support a defensive action. The Austrians, on the other hand, built only a couple of fortresses on the Galician Front in the Carpathian Mountains to blunt an enemy advance if Galicia was lost. Along the Alpine front with Italy, the mountains formed the main obstacle and several forts effectively guarded the passes.

The Belgians had turned Liège, Namur and Antwerp into fortresses. They did not even try to create a continuous line. They intended to dig trenches to defend the intervals between the forts of each ring and wait for their allies to manoeuvre between them. Allowing a fortress to be isolated proved to be a bad idea during the First World War. Originally, Brialmont had built the Belgian forts of Liège and Namur with concrete that was not continuously poured, which weakened the structure. The Achilles heel of the Brialmont forts was that they had not been strengthened with reinforced concrete. Like the French and German forts, and unlike the Russian ones, they had armoured components, including gun turrets. Although their armour was intended to resist 210mm calibre guns, it failed to do so and it was no match for the 305mm and 420mm monsters that tore the forts apart. The catastrophe that befell the Belgian forts almost became a disaster for the French because Joffre and many of his fellow officers concluded their own forts must be equally vulnerable. Joffre took advantage of the situation to remove what artillery and ammunition he could from his forts in August 1915 to make up for the deficiencies in his field artillery. In 1916, the French discovered they had been mistaken about the worth of their forts.

The Fortress Line
The French had to protect their new border after the Franco-Prussian War of 1870–1. This task fell to General Raymond Adolphe Séré de Rivières who became Director of Engineer Services at the War Ministry in February 1874.[19] He developed plans for France's new defensive lines and the old fortress of Verdun fit into this new scheme. Work began on the first of six detached forts, which later formed the inner ring, within a year of the Prussian (German) evacuation of Verdun in September 1873.[20] These fortifications became known as the 'Forts de Panique'. At the same time during the 1870s, construction started on another ring of six detached forts, mostly on the right bank of the Meuse. In 1881, the outer ring was expanded with the construction of Fort Vaux and two other forts. Between 1883 and 1885, Fort Moulainville and five more fortifications were added. Fort Douaumont was one of the last masonry forts, begun in 1885.

The new line of fortifications was to consist of four fortress rings spanning the length of the new border region with Germany. Séré de Rivières established four fortresses, also known as entrenched camps (Camps Retranchés), each with a ring of forts around it.[21] The French army engineers worked on other fortresses as well. However, these fortifications were relegated to second or third class status by the end of the nineteenth century.[22] Séré de Rivières had to come up with new fort designs at a time when innovations in artillery came rapidly and rendered many fortifications obsolete almost as soon as they were built.

The period between September 1873 and the late 1880s was dedicated to the building of fortifications in France. Construction started simultaneously on the fortress rings of Toul, Épinal, Belfort and Verdun. In addition to these emerging fortress rings, the French built several forts on the Meuse Heights between Verdun

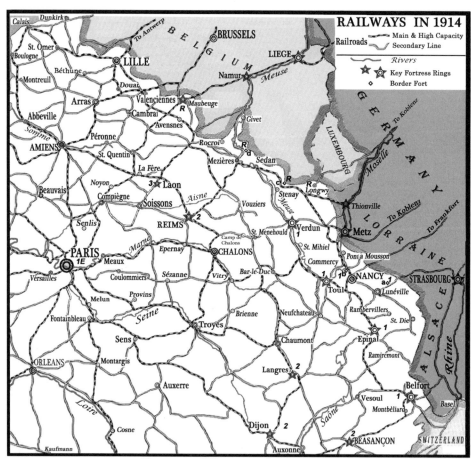

Border Forts
a. Ft. Manoviller
b. Ft. Frouard
c. Montmedy
d. Ft. Ayvelles
E Entrenched Camp
   of Paris

Classes of Forts and Fortresses
1 1st Class - Fully Operational & Updated. Garrisoned & fully stocked.
2 2nd Class - Maintained in existing condition. Limited garrision & stocks.
3. 3rd Class - Only maintained and in carekeeper status.
R Reclassified in 1914 to 1st class or 2nd Class.
Forts between main border fortress rings rated as 2nd Class

Fortified cites and main railways on Franco–German border.

and Toul, in the Charmes Gap between Toul and Épinal, the Moselle Heights between Épinal and Belfort, and the Belfort Gap. The French army established a fortified zone that extended from Verdun to Toul and from Épinal to Belfort and anchored each end of these sections with a fortress. The forts occupying positions in the Charmes Gap served as *forts d'arrêt* that dominated key points from which they were to hinder or actually 'stop', as their name implies, the enemy's advance. The individual forts along the Meuse and Moselle Heights, linking Toul to Verdun, and Épinal to Belfort, were not *forts d'arrêt*.[23] They were, in fact, part of a line linking each pair of fortresses. Leaving the Charmes Gap lightly defended was not a serious problem because a large section of this gap faced the Vosges Mountains, which formed a natural barrier. The Germans would have to advance from a direction leading towards Nancy where the *forts d'arrêt* would block the main routes. The French military thought that they

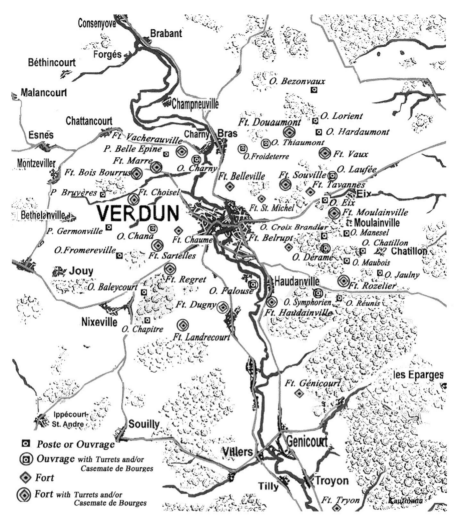

Map of Verdun Fortress area.

could easily rout a German force channelled through this gap. The first two French war plans were exclusively defensive and concentrated on holding the main positions and on counter-attacking against any point through which the enemy advanced.[24] The French command, like its German counterpart, planned to mobilize an army that could defend massive swathes of territory and would not allow the enemy to penetrate deep into their territory along the Franco-German border.

The year 1886 brought, according to the French, the 'Crisis of the Torpedo Shell'. A new type of shell, named for its cylindrical shape and filled with a high explosive known as melinite, was perfected. This high-explosive shell was made of steel instead of cast iron, had an overall weight that allowed it to carry almost eight times more explosive and achieved a greater range than other projectiles of the period. In that year the French tested the new shells by firing over 242 rounds from a 155mm

Mle 1877 cannon and a 220mm mortar Mle 1880 on Fort Malmaison (1878–83) at Laon. The result was extensive damage to the scarps, counterscarps, facades, armoured sections, artillery positions on the ramparts and the interior of the brick structures. The experiment demonstrated that the new high explosive had rendered masonry forts obsolete. The French needed to come up with a new solution quickly. Belgian General Brialmont thought he had already found one before he began to build his new forts in July 1888. He used concrete and designed his forts to resist artillery rounds of up to 210mm.

The crisis of the high-explosive shell ended the first phase of fortification construction that had begun in 1874. During a second phase that lasted through the remainder of the 1880s, entire sections of existing fortifications were reinforced with concrete. In France, priority was given to strengthening the masonry forts that had barely been completed and included Verdun and the other fortress rings rather than building new concrete positions. To achieve this the military engineers cleared the earthen cover from the roofs of important structures within the forts before pouring a layer of concrete about 2.5m thick. They finished the job by recovering the structures with earth. This new roof or carapace was up to 4m thick. They also covered exposed masonry walls with a concrete layer about 1.5m thick, and reinforced counterscarp walls with concrete at a few locations. After 1887, the new forts they designed were mostly made of concrete. Nothing was done to strengthen five of the twelve forts built during the 1870s at Verdun. However, of the ten that were built before 1886, all but two were reinforced with concrete. Similar arrangements took place in the other three major fortress rings. This second phase represents the first period of modernization.

The third and final construction phase began in 1892 and lasted until the war. As progress continued to be made in the development of artillery, the fortress engineers met the challenge by rebuilding parts of some of the fortifications with reinforced concrete. By the end of the decade, they added armoured positions of steel. In 1906, construction began on a generation of a few state-of-the-art forts. The French experimented with different types of concrete for their fortifications until they hit upon the right mixture of cement and aggregate for the greatest strength. They called it *béton spécial* (special concrete) and used it to reinforce fortifications during the second and third phases between 1888 and 1914.[25]

Once more, the area above the roofs were cleared, a cushion of sand was added and a layer of special concrete was poured to serve as a bursting layer after a shell penetrated the earthen layer above it. In some cases, the masonry roof had to be replaced with a concrete one. The caserne (barracks area that often included the large dormitories with bunks, kitchen, latrines, stores and other facilities) and magazines were covered with a layer of special concrete that often formed a shell over the structure. The facilities of the caserne were typically clustered together and usually occupied a large rectangular area of the fort. Often, the side of these casernes facing the rear ditch of the fort was exposed. The rear side of a ditch or moat (fossé) is known as the gorge. When the caserne had an exposed side facing the gorge, the latter often served as a courtyard. In some cases, the caserne opened onto a courtyard within the fort, while in others, a courtyard was located in the centre of the caserne. Forts built before 1887 often had large vaulted openings that allowed natural lighting. When the reinforcement was added, the exposed side of the caserne had to be covered with concrete leaving smaller entrance openings. Alternately, a new concrete wall was built in front of the original masonry wall, leaving a corridor between the two. Either way, natural lighting was greatly reduced. In some cases, part of the caserne was reinforced with a concrete shell and served as a wartime facility while the remainder of the masonry structure was used in peacetime. On the ramparts, masonry shelters (abris) of various types such as infantry or traverse abris were often given concrete protection.[26] Many of the entrances remained unprotected, except by an earthen cover, since they faced away from direct enemy fire.

During the final construction phase in the 1890s, additional renovations took place, but not in all the forts. The most significant was the introduction of reinforced concrete that owed its increased strength to the addition of metal bars. In general, the concrete was poured over rebars (steel bars or rods) linked together to form a grid. Reinforced concrete was used in the newest forts and only in additions to the older ones. A number of the older forts built before 1890 included caponiers – casemates extending into the fossé that included weapons positions to cover the length of the fossé to prevent the enemy from crossing. Masonry caponiers in the flanks or in the frontal sections of the fossé were exposed to direct enemy artillery fire, which could have ruinous effects, especially after the advent of the high-explosive shell in the 1880s. Thus, they were removed from many of the modernized forts. Gorge caponiers, however, often remained because they were not overly exposed. In many forts, caponiers were replaced with counterscarp casemates of reinforced concrete, or, in rare instances, only of concrete. Subterranean passages beneath the moat, usually of reinforced concrete, linked the coffres to the fort.

When the high-explosive shell appeared, it was deemed necessary to test its effects on forts. These experiments showed that the traditional fossé with high scarp walls was vulnerable. The solution was to demolish the scarp wall or greatly reduce its height, except in the gorge. Thus, in the new or renovated forts a gentle earth slope rose to the ramparts from the floor of the fossé or a low scarp wall. Since the ramparts had to be moved back in order to achieve the gentle slope, the size of the area enclosed by the ramparts was reduced. The counterscarp in the gorge remained vertical. This concept removed the rearward scarp walls from the direct line of enemy plunging artillery fire. A protective concrete slab was added over the top of a number of masonry counterscarp walls. The layer of earth was removed from the area behind the counterscarps (against the glacis) and was replaced with rocks to prevent artillery fire from penetrating the glacis. The fortification engineers recommended building concrete counterscarp walls in the new forts, but few were actually built. The older forts that formed the inner ring were seldom modernized. In 1906, Fort Chanot at Toul was converted from an ouvrage (see below) into a fort with concrete scarps and counterscarps. At the old fort of Tillot, also at Toul, two counterscarp walls were changed to concrete when its caponiers were replaced with counterscarp coffres during the first decade of the twentieth century. At Fort Uxegney at Épinal, two

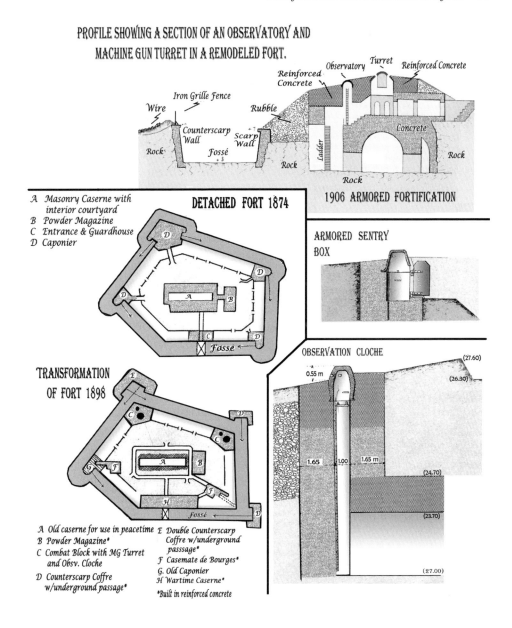

PROFILE SHOWING A SECTION OF AN OBSERVATORY AND MACHINE GUN TURRET IN A REMODELED FORT.

1906 ARMORED FORTIFICATION

DETACHED FORT 1874

A　Masonry Caserne with interior courtyard
B　Powder Magazine
C　Entrance & Guardhouse
D　Caponier

ARMORED SENTRY BOX

OBSERVATION CLOCHE

TRANSFORMATION OF FORT 1898

A　Old caserne for use in peacetime
B　Powder Magazine*
C　Combat Block with MG Turret and Obsv. Cloche
D　Counterscarp Coffre w/underground passage*
E　Double Counterscarp Coffre w/underground passsage*
F　Casemate de Bourges*
G.　Old Caponier
H　Wartime Caserne*
*Built in reinforced concrete

counterscarp walls were changed to concrete a few years before the war. At Belfort, the new Ouvrage of Meroux was built with concrete counterscarp walls.[27] Lieutenant Colonel Philippe Truttmann points out that early in the twentieth century the French army decided that replacing the scarp walls with a gentle slope was more economical, but it was not as effective as building concrete walls.* The war proved how ineffectual the earthen layer was, especially in the modernized ouvrages.[28]

---

* P. Truttmann, *La Barrière der Fer* (Luxembourg: Gerard Klopp, 2000).

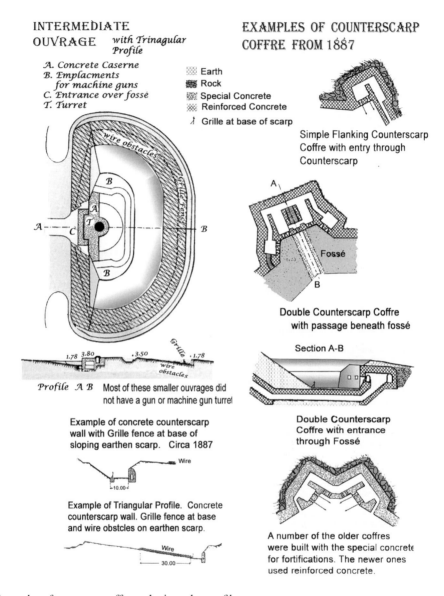

INTERMEDIATE
OUVRAGE   *with Trinagular Profile*

A. Concrete Caserne
B. Emplacments
   for machine guns
C. Entrance over fosse
T. Turret

Earth
Rock
Special Concrete
Reinforced Concrete
λ Grille at base of scarp

Profile A B   Most of these smaller ouvrages did
not have a gun or machine gun turret

Example of concrete counterscarp
wall with Grille fence at base of
sloping earthen scarp.   Circa 1887

Example of Triangular Profile. Concrete
counterscarp wall. Grille fence at base
and wire obstcles on earthen scarp.

EXAMPLES OF COUNTERSCARP
COFFRE FROM 1887

Simple Flanking Counterscarp
Coffre with entry through
Counterscarp

Double Counterscarp Coffre
with passage beneath fossé

Double Counterscarp
Coffre with entrance
through Fossé

A number of the older coffres
were built with the special concrete
for fortifications. The newer ones
used reinforced concrete.

Examples of ouvrages, coffre and triangular profile.

In the late 1880s, the army engineers introduced new and smaller positions called ouvrages (works) or redoubts between the forts for the infantry. They mostly filled gaps between forts in a ring and often served as advanced positions. Many were little more than shelters or field fortifications. In the early twentieth century, a number of these positions were modified. Known as modernized ouvrages, they were similar to new ouvrages built at that time. These improved ouvrages took on the appearance of a small fort with a fossé, a small caserne and often included armoured weapons positions. The older infantry ouvrages usually consisted only of a large abri (in this case for the troops) or a small caserne and a fighting position. In addition, mainly in the early 1900s, a number of concrete infantry abri were built to defend gaps between forts. A number of individual battery positions, some rather simple positions with an abri, others much like an ouvrage with a fossé, completed the inventory. The larger of these ouvrages, whether for infantry or artillery, presented a 'triangular profile'. In these ouvrages, the masonry counterscarp wall was 2.5m to 3m high and there was no scarp wall. With few exceptions, there were no coffres in the counterscarp

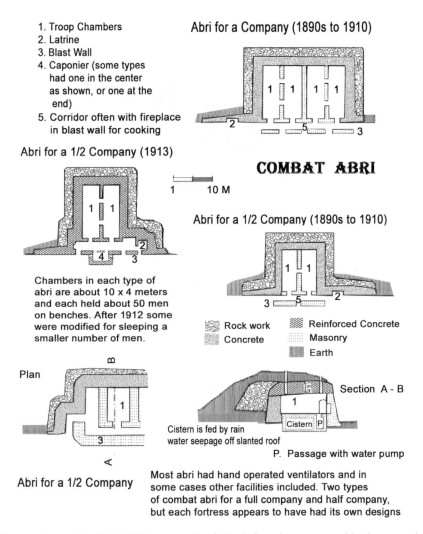

1. Troop Chambers
2. Latrine
3. Blast Wall
4. Caponier (some types had one in the center as shown, or one at the end)
5. Corridor often with fireplace in blast wall for cooking

Abri for a Company (1890s to 1910)

Abri for a 1/2 Company (1913)

COMBAT ABRI

1   10 M

Abri for a 1/2 Company (1890s to 1910)

Chambers in each type of abri are about 10 x 4 meters and each held about 50 men on benches. After 1912 some were modified for sleeping a smaller number of men.

Rock work
Concrete
Reinforced Concrete
Masonry
Earth

Plan

Section A - B

Cistern is fed by rain water seepage off slanted roof

P. Passage with water pump

Abri for a 1/2 Company

Most abri had hand operated ventilators and in some cases other facilities included. Two types of combat abri for a full company and half company, but each fortress appears to have had its own designs

The few combat abris built in 1913 were made of all reinforced concrete and latrines were inside. In some cases an escape tunnel was created in the cistern. They were company sized (for 200 men) with 4 large rooms and 3 outside latrines. Half-company size abris had only two large rooms and 2 outside latrines. Abris were spaced in intervals and behind forts and usually included infantry field works including concrete trenches.

Abri photos courtesy of Marcus Massing

Concrete
Roof Slab

Blast Wall

Latrines

Combat
Abri MF 1

Combat
Abri MF 2

Entrance to Ft. Tavennes   Munitions Bunker

Two French combat abris between the Meuse and Froideterre (MF).

to defend the fossé. The reason for this is that the outline of most of these ouvrages was oval, often bean-shaped so that most of the fossé sections were curved. In this arrangement, the fossé could only be defended from the ramparts. To make matters worse, repeated hits by artillery against the gentle slope between the base of the fossé and the ramparts tended to crumble the earthen slope causing sections to slide into floor of the fossé filling it so completely that the Germans were not even aware that they were crossing a moat. The French began to correct the problem in some of the last forts and ouvrages they built such as Fort Vacherauville (Verdun) and Fort Chanot (Toul) as they returned to vertical scarp walls. In the 1890s, barbed wire was introduced, mostly in fortifications without a scarp wall, but it was of little value if the earth of the sloped scarp filled the fossé after a bombardment. During the same period, the French also used a grille, a fence about 4m in height and surmounted with spiked bars set in concrete along the base of the fossé where the scarp wall would have been. The grille could also cover other vulnerable sections of the fortifications.

Several forts had a drawbridge entrance located between the counterscarp wall and the scarp in the gorge with the wartime entry beneath the ditch.

The forts' main purpose was to form strongpoints to deny access to the enemy. For this reason, they needed defensive weapons to repel an assault before it reached the fort and to throw back the enemy if they succeeded in penetrating into the fossé or beyond. Thus, the first forts built in the 1870s were provided with caponiers (casemates in the fossé) armed with machine guns and/or rapid-firing small cannon. Later, the caponiers were replaced with coffres equipped with similar weapons that covered the fossé from the counterscarp. The advantage of infantry positions on the ramparts was that they could cover the fossé and the glacis simultaneously. The forts required heavier armament that could not only defend the fort but also act as an offensive weapon against enemy troops trying to pass between gaps in the fortress ring or preparing to assault the fort. For this purpose, artillery of various sizes was emplaced on the fort. Mounting artillery in masonry casemates became inadequate during the period of the American Civil War when rifled artillery turned walls into rubble. As with the French built forts in the 1870s, the only satisfactory solution had been to replace the walled fort with an earth-covered masonry fort.[29] The artillery of these forts was mounted in open positions behind the ramparts with traverses separating the positions. If the enemy hit one gun position, the traverses protected the adjacent emplacements from the effects of an explosion. Masonry abris were built into the traverses to shelter artillery or troops. The army found this arrangement satisfactory until the high-explosive shell appeared on the scene in the 1880s. 'Torpedo shells' threatened not only the integrity of the earth-covered masonry of the forts, but also their artillery. In the 1870s, Captain Henri Mougin and other French fortification engineers worked on armoured casemate designs for the main-line forts.[30] The first specimens were expensive and usually housed only one gun of up to 155mm calibre. At Battery Éperon in the Charmes Gap two Mougin armoured casemates Mle 1878 for a 155mm gun were installed. Mle 1878 casemates for a 138mm gun were placed at Fort Parmont and Fort Château Lambert on the Moselle Heights.[31] The French army, however, was not fully satisfied with these armoured casemates. The best alternative appeared to be the armoured turret. Mougin was the first to develop one for the French fortifications in the 1870s. The army ordered several of these turrets for the land forts, but tests in the 1880s showed that they did not withstand the high-explosive shells. Thus, army engineers in Europe continued to search for another solution.

Armoured casemates, nonetheless, turned out to be valuable in coastal defences. A new type of artillery mechanism, the disappearing gun, was also a boon for coastal fortifications since it could be loaded before it was raised above the parapet to fire. The recoil brought the gun back into the loading position below the rampart. In some countries, they were adopted for land defences, especially in mountain positions.[32] In the 1890s, the search continued for a better and more effective armoured turret. Captain Alfred Galopin designed a turret for a pair of 155mm L (long barrel) guns and later, a similar retracting turret for a single gun 155mm R (short barrel), which was adopted by the army.[33] This turret began to appear in forts during the first decade

Siege Artillery

The belligerents required siege artillery to smash trench lines and to destroy forts. The French only used it against their own forts, which had been captured by the Germans. The Germans equipped their field artillery with howitzers, which gave them a tremendous advantage over the French in open as well as trench warfare, but they also produced siege artillery in preparation for breaking the Belgian and French fortress lines created in the 1880s and later. In the 1890s, the German army worked with the Krupp Company to develop the heavy 305mm Mörser which was designated a coastal weapon to disguise its actual purpose. The army had nine of these weapons by 1906. Afraid the Mörser would not be able to destroy the French forts, the Germans developed a newer weapon, which was ready by 1909, had a range of up to 12,000m and had greater penetrating power. Since the 305mm Beta-Gerät 09 howitzer was heavier than the 305mm Mörser, it was more difficult to move. There were eight of these mortars in four two-gun batteries and the two howitzers in one battery when the war began. These weapons required a number of train cars to move their components. The Krupp 420mm Gamma gun, developed after 1906, entered military service in 1911. This monster required more preparation and work to install than the older guns did. It was also more difficult to move than the 305mm weapons. These

130-mm Gun (13 cm.K.)

210-mm Howitzer - "Long Mortar" (lg.Mrs.)

150-mm Q.F. Naval Gun (S.15 cm. K. or 150 cm. S.K. L/40)

GERMAN HEAVY ARTILLERY

420 mm 360 mm 305 mm

1916   150-mm Gun (15 cm. K.16)

420-mm Gamma Howitzer

Several types of German Heavy Artillery.

fort busters were in service in two two-gun batteries by 1914 and a fifth howitzer went into reserve. Krupp produced five more of these weapons and a number of spare barrels during the war. An armoured cab added to the Gamma guns in 1916 protected the gun crews from French counter-battery fire, which was becoming increasingly effective. In 1911, Krupp designed a lighter wheeled version of the 420mm Gamma gun which was slightly more mobile and of a different design to the 1906 version. The gun had to be disassembled before it could be transported beyond a short distance. Only two were ready when the war began, but by the time of the Battle of Verdun, in 1916, six more had entered service.

When the war began, Germany had five batteries with two 305mm weapons, a one-gun battery with a single wheeled 305mm Beta and another battery with a wheeled 240mm L/12. The army also had two batteries with two 420mm Gammas each and a battery with two 420mm Big Berthas. In October 1914, a one-gun Gamma battery was added. When operations on the Eastern Front started in 1915, two additional two-gun Big Bertha batteries and a single-gun battery with a wheeled 280mm L/14 were ready. In 1916, a few more batteries with seven additional Big Berthas, three Gamma guns and four 305mm mortars were added. As the year and the Battle of Verdun drew to a close there was little need for fort busters.

The Austrians were the only other major power on the Continent with new heavy siege artillery. While the Germans worked on the 420mm weapons several years into the new century, the Austrians had their Skoda factories working on similar weapons. They developed the 305mm M.11 (1911) mortar. It was lighter than the older German 305mm mortar and had a greater range. The Austrians sent eight of these, with crews, to aid the Germans when the war began. The Skoda company designed 420mm howitzers for coastal defence in 1914. The army placed one of these 209.9-ton turret mounted weapons at a coastal fort protecting Pola and others followed. In 1916, the high command decided to move these 420mm howitzers from the coastal defences and make them mobile. This led to the designation of 420mm M.16. Including the two 420mm M.14s, Skoda produced a total of eight during the war. One of these survived the war, and took part in the bombardment of a Maginot Line fort in the Second World War when the French mistook it for a Big Bertha. The first two 380mm M.16 howitzers were ready in time for an offensive on the Italian Front in 1916. These guns had a longer range than most siege weapons and proved effective in blasting away at Italian mountain fortresses.

The Austrian siege guns were mostly motorized giving them more flexibility than their German counterparts, which relied heavily on railways. When the war broke out, the Austrians had twenty-four 305mm M.11 mortars, all motorized, in fifteen batteries. In 1915, they added five more two-gun batteries of M.11s. Between 1915 and 1917, the Austrians received seven additional 420mm howitzers and two 380mm howitzers, which they assigned to fortress artillery units with more 380mm howitzers under construction.

Table 3: Comparison of Heavy Artillery

Weapon German	Weight (Tons)/ Time to Emplace (Hours)	Range (m)	Weight of Round (kg)/ Rate of Fire (Per Hour)	Other Data
420mm M–Gerät* L/12	42.6/6	9,300	400 and 800/8 rounds	Big Bertha howitzer
420mm Gamma–Gerät L/16	150/24	14,000	800 and 1,160/8 rounds	howitzer
305mm Beta M–Gerät	47/8	20,500	345/8 rounds	howitzer
305mm Beta-Gerät L/8	30/12	8,200**	410/15 rounds	mortar
Austrian				
420mm M.16	112.7/?	12,700	1,000/8 rounds	Skoda howitzer
380mm M.16	81.7/7	15,000	750/12 rounds	Skoda howitzer
305mm M.11	20.8/?	9,600***	382/12 rounds	Skoda mortar****

* The Germans designated 'M' for a minewerfer or mine launcher to indicate the weapon fired a heavy round at a high trajectory. Gerät means equipment.
** 8,200m for armour piercing round and 8,800m for high-explosive round.
*** Light shell had a range of 11,300m.
**** Eight loaned to Germany.

Sources: Wolfgang Fleischer, *Deutsche Artillerie 1914–1918* (Germany: Motorbuch Verlag, 2013); Michal Prasil, *Skoda Heavy Guns: 24cm Cannon, 38cm Howitzer, 42cm Howitzer and Gasoline-electrical Trains* (Atglen, PA: Schiffer, 1997); Mark Romanych and Martin Rupp, *42cm 'Big Bertha' and German Siege Artillery of World War I* (Oxford: Osprey, 2014).

of the twentieth century. In 1901, the army also approved a retracting turret with two rapid-firing 75mm guns designed in 1897. This turret and the single 155mm gun turret became the main offensive weapons in most French forts. For protection, a machine-gun turret, designated GF4, also went into production early in the century. Since the forts also needed 'eyes' to direct the fire of the artillery turrets, positions were added on the forts for armoured domes (cloches) of three types (Type 1 Mle 1892, Type 2 Mle 1901 and Type 3 Mle 1912).[34] They held one observer who usually communicated with a command centre or turret block by means of acoustic voice tubes. Smaller observatories for lookouts, often set in a concrete block in the ramparts and protected by an armoured door, were added in 1902.

Another significant addition, the Casemate de Bourges – named after the test ground where it was developed, was adopted in 1899. The first was built for a pair of 95mm guns; others were redesigned to take two 75mm guns on a special mount. In addition to the gun chamber, the reinforced concrete structure included an observation position, a magazine for 500 rounds below the guns and a work/rest area for the 19-man crew. These casemates faced a flank of the fort so that, even though

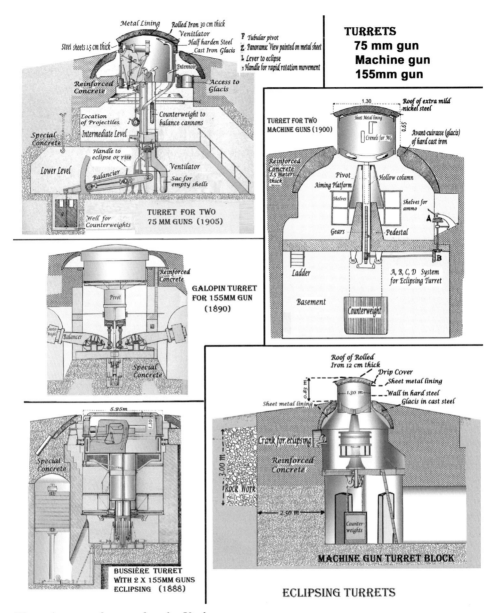

The main types of turrets found at Verdun.

their maximum wall thickness was only about .8m, their angled design kept them out of the direct line of fire of heavy enemy artillery. Their guns covered the gap between them and the next fortification with flanking fire.

Electrical power was added to many forts for lighting and operating the ventilation system and the turrets. Until the late nineteenth century, the fumes generated by the firing weapons were expelled through a small window-like vent above the gun

Ft. Moulainville

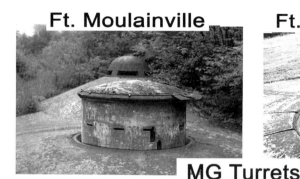

Ft. Villey Le Sec

MG Turrets

Ft. Villey Le Sec

Military railroad at entrance

Mougin Turret

Obsv. Cloche

Ft. Souville

Pamart Cloche

75mm Turret

Ft. Villey Le Sec

Destroyed 75mm Turret

Ft. Vaux

Examples of machine-gun turrets and Mougin turret for 155mm guns. (Photographs of Villey le Sac by Bernard Lowry and others by the author). Observation cloche. Pamart cloche for machine gun, also known as 'Elephant Head', were added to some forts in 1917. Turret at Fort Vaux destroyed by Germans during their retreat. (Photograph by Clayton Donnell)

embrasure.[35] Between 1904 and 1914, the French installed ventilation systems in a number of their forts. Hand-operated systems were put in at thirteen forts at Verdun: Haudainville, Froideterre, Moulainville, La Falouse, Dugny, Déramé, Landrecourt, Regret, Sartelles, Choisel, Borrus, Charme and Rozellier. An electrical ventilation system was installed at Vacherauville between 1912 and 1914, while work on a similar

Galopin 155 mm Gun Turret (Douaumont)

Machine Gun Turret (Froideterre)

GUN TURRETS

75 mm Gun Turret (Froideterre)

Bussière 155 mm Gun Turret (Souville annex)

(Second photograph from the top – control level of 155mm gun turret – by Frank Philippart; other photographs by the author)

system in 1914 only began at Douaumont and stopped when the war began. At Toul, twelve forts received manual ventilation systems (Bouvron, Bruley, Chanot, Domgermain, Écrouves, Est Vieux Canton, Francheville, Gondreville, Mordant, Tillot and Trondes). Between 1910 and 1914, ventilation systems were installed at Vieux Canton, Villey le Sec, Blénod and Lucey, including in the turrets. At Épinal electric ventilation systems went into forts Arches, Dogneville, Longchamp, Adelphes and Uxegney, while at Belfort they were installed at Bois d'Oye, Chèvremont, Côte

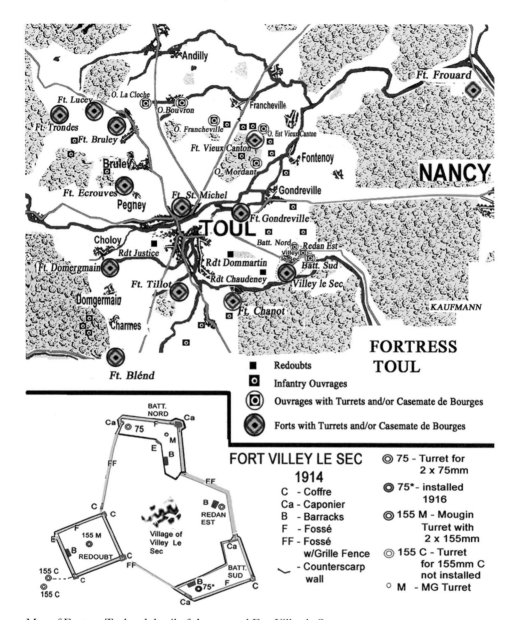

Map of Fortress Toul and detail of the unusual Fort Villey le Sec.

d'Essert, Fougerais and Salbert. Manual ventilation was set up at Fort Frouard in the Charmes Gap in 1910 and electrical systems at forts Manonviller and Pont Saint-Vincent. The forts of the Meuse Heights did not undergo any of these improvements,

Only a few forts were equipped with their own power generating system before the war because it was a new technology and required the building of a powerhouse (usine) on the premises that could house the dynamos, fuel storage, workroom, etc. At Fortress Verdun, the construction of a usine began at Fort Douaumont in 1914 whereas it had already been installed at the new fort of Vacherauville. It appears that higher priority was given to Toul and Épinal where five forts and ouvrages in each ring were provided with electric power between 1910 and 1914. Power generators were installed at the main forts of the Charmes Gap (Frouard, Pont Saint-Vincent and Manonviller) between 1910 and 1913 and in four positions at Belfort, which was more than at Verdun. The majority of French forts continued to rely upon candles and oil lamps for lighting. Some forts lacked an adequate water supply because it had not been possible to sink wells in them, so their water reservoirs had to be refilled by truck or pipeline.[36] Many forts included a filtering system for collecting rainwater. Unlike Brialmont's Belgian forts, the French forts were provided with latrines and kitchen facilities in secure and accessible positions. A heating system that used largely wood or coal for fuel served the kitchen ovens and warmed the barracks and other sections of the forts. The majority of the modern or modernized forts had sufficient storage and resources to resist for weeks if they were isolated.[37] By 1914, all the forts and ouvrages of Verdun were equipped with a telegraph post connected to the citadel of Verdun or to some of the nearby fortifications. In addition, many forts had optical signalling equipment. Once a fort was isolated, carrier pigeons sometimes proved to be the most effective form of communication. Most of the forts on the Meuse Heights had similar equipment. At Toul, the telegraph system connected to Fort St Michel, which served as the command post. They also linked with some adjacent fortifications. At Épinal and Belfort, the communications situation was similar. Only a few forts, located mostly in the Charmes Gap, had an underground telephone link.

A comparison of the four fortresses of the main line shows Verdun to be the strongest.

Table 4: French Fortresses of the Main Line

Fortress	*No. of Forts*	*No. of Gun Turrets*	*No. of MG Turrets*	*No. of Cas. de Bourges**	*No. of Guns***
Verdun	18 (+ 8 ouvrages) 15 infantry ouvrages	1 x 155mm (Bussière) 5 x 155mm R 14 x 75mm	29	23	411***
Toul	12 (+ 8 ouvrages) 19 infantry ouvrages 3 redoubts	2 x 155mm (Mougin) 2 x 155mm R 20 x 75mm	15	8	402
Épinal	17 (+ 7 ouvrages) 33 redoubts	3 x 155mm R 4 x 75mm	9	8	600
Belfort	9 (+ 5 ouvrages) 30 infantry ouvrages	2 x 155mm R 10 x 75mm	16	5	1,000

* Mounted two 75mm guns.

** Including in intervals.

*** Plus 258 in reserve at Arsenal of Jardin Fontaine.

The 155mm Bussière mounted two guns, as did the old Mougin turret and the 75mm gun turrets and the Casemate de Bourges. The Mougin turret did not retract. The 155mm R mounted a single gun. The MG turrets retracted.

Source: Marco Frijns, Luc Malchair, Jean–Jacques Moulins and Jean Puelinckx, *Index de la Fortification Française 1874–1914* (Welkenraedt: Auto-édition, 2008). Note that all sources do not agree with the number of guns or fortifications listed above.

If the number of 155mm gun turrets and Casemate de Bourges is a measure of strength, Verdun had the advantage, but Toul was better armed with 75mm gun turrets. Thus, it can be concluded that the Verdun–Toul fortified zone was the strongest when compared to that of Épinal–Belfort. Each of these four fortresses could hold a garrison of 50,000–70,000 men, including contingents for forts and

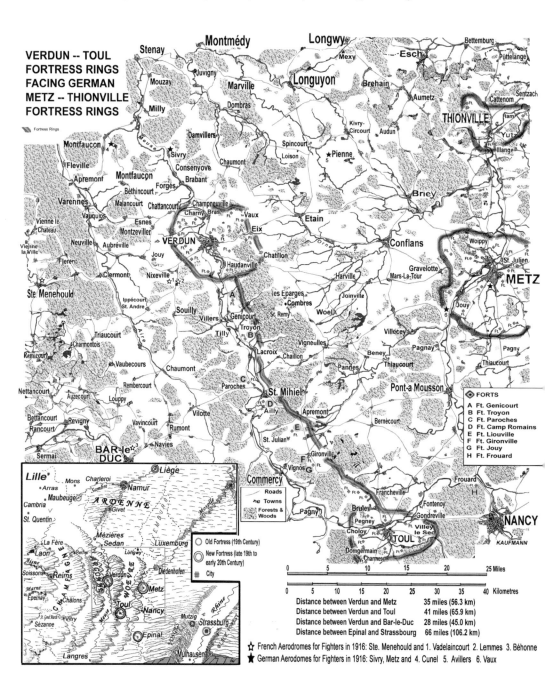

intervals. There were also numerous support facilities like casernes, warehouses for supplies and ammunition depots – usually a large magazine for each sector and smaller intermediate ones. Much of the artillery was located in an artillery park where it could be safely stored and maintained in peacetime.[38] In addition to the interval ouvrages, there were many abris for individual infantry and battery positions. The infantry combat abri varied in scale from half-company size to full-company size. Some of these fortresses included a military airfield and/or facilities for observation balloons and dirigibles. In addition to the regular national railroads that linked each fortress to the main line of supply, the army built 60cm-gauge military railroads in the fortress area that linked up with many of the fortifications.

A rough estimate of the number of artillery pieces of 75mm, 90mm, 95mm, 120mm and 155mm guns at the Verdun fortress emplaced outside the forts and ouvrages in 1914 is about 36 batteries of 90mm or 95mm (mostly 90mm), 25 batteries of 120mm and 15 batteries of 155mm guns. These batteries usually consisted of four, sometimes two guns. In the forts, there were five 120mm guns (about enough for one or two batteries) and forty 75mm guns from the Casemate de Bourges (and four 95mm guns). Thus, when Joffre stripped the fortress of its artillery, the forts of Verdun furnished enough weapons to form about twelve batteries of 75mm guns. Since the turret-mounted 75mm and 155mm guns did not have field mounts, removing the barrels to make up seven additional batteries of 155mm gun barrels and twenty-eight of 75s was not worth the effort. In addition, many of the weapons, especially the 90mm, 95mm and 120mm guns, were outdated. The army removed similar weapons from the fortresses of Toul, Épinal and Belfort.

Tactics of Trench Warfare

Trench warfare rendered traditional battlefield tactics obsolete in 1914. Since the time of Vauban, trenches were an important part of siege operations, but their use in the field was limited until 1864 in the American Civil War. Their use continued until 1914 when trenches formed long continuous lines across the front. Before the twentieth century, as armies took to the field, infantry and cavalry went into battle in company and battalion-size formations, which they maintained until they closed with the enemy and bayonets and swords came into play. Generally, the formations were similar to those on a parade ground with soldiers marching almost shoulder to shoulder, especially during an attack.[39] The British, who usually had smaller armies than their opponents in the eighteenth and nineteenth centuries, placed more emphasis on marksmanship, while the Germans stressed manoeuvre. In 1914, the main tactical unit was the battalion. The French, for example, deployed the companies of a battalion in columns or lines (sometimes referred to as a skirmish formation) for the attack, often with flags flying and bands playing in the rear. In some of the early French attacks against 'dug-in' German troops, the French Poilus, formed into almost parade-ground formation, advanced at a steady pace upon the enemy, bayonets fixed, to the tune of the national anthem or a military tune played by a military band.[40] Some of the officers, a sword or a pistol in hand, and a flag bearer marched along with them. French artillery, mostly 75mm guns, tried to hit the enemy

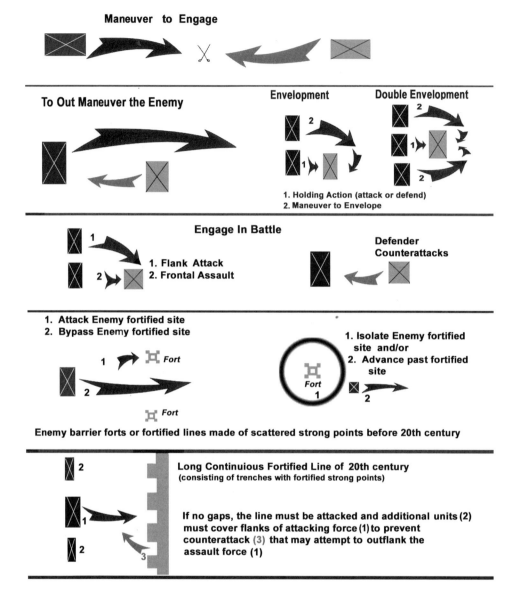

Maneuver to Engage

To Out Maneuver the Enemy

Envelopment

Double Envelopment

1. Holding Action (attack or defend)
2. Maneuver to Envelope

Engage In Battle

Defender Counterattacks

1. Flank Attack
2. Frontal Assault

1. Attack Enemy fortified site
2. Bypass Enemy fortified site

Fort

1. Isolate Enemy fortified site and/or
2. Advance past fortified site

Fort

Fort

Enemy barrier forts or fortified lines made of scattered strong points before 20th century

Long Continuious Fortified Line of 20th century
(consisting of trenches with fortified strong points)

If no gaps, the line must be attacked and additional units (2) must cover flanks of attacking force (1) to prevent counterattack (3) that may attempt to outflank the assault force (1)

positions with rapid fire before the troops advanced into the line of fire. These direct fire weapons did little damage to the entrenched enemy.

In October 1914, as the Poilus charged the German lines, they ran into few obstacles but came under a hail of German artillery fire. Shrapnel and high explosive rained down upon them tearing gaps in their formations, but adrenaline pumping, they raced towards the enemy lines as the thunder of the artillery drowned out their regimental music. Before the Poilus reached the German positions, the rat-tat-tat of the Maxim 08 machine guns joined the cacophony of sounds, with their enfilading fire mowing down the French formation more effectively than the other artillery combined. The few Poilus that survived swooped on their enemies in the trench and a savage hand-to-hand combat for the position ensued. If they succeeded in clearing the position, they would still have to face the enemy on both of their flanks and possibly more enfilading fire, but the traverses of the trenches might protect them. Additional troops would quickly reinforce them, but bringing up machine guns would require more time, especially over the cratered battleground. Friendly artillery support for a further advance was impossible unless the guns moved forward. However, before that could happen, the Germans would launch a counter-attack from a second trench a couple hundred metres to the rear. Their artillery was already within range of the lost forward trench. What's more, there were additional machine-gun positions between the first and the second lines.[41] The German rifleman's Mauser had a five-round magazine that he easily replaced, whereas this was not the case for the French Lebel's with a built-in eight-round magazine. Once his magazine was empty, the French rifleman had to fumble around loading the next eight rounds individually into his rifle while the enemy closed on him. The chances were good that the Poilu would be overrun. In 1915, all the belligerents followed similar procedures during their assaults in the West.

Once machine guns were produced in significant numbers, they changed the complexion of the battlefield where men in tightly packed formations were easily decimated.[42] When barbed wire appeared in front of the trenches late in 1914, the situation deteriorated further.[43] For an assault to succeed the enemy's machine guns had to be silenced and the wire entanglements had to be breached. To achieve this objective, each side had to deploy its infantry in loose attack formations and take advantage of the terrain. Colonel Pétain, who commanded a brigade in late August 1914, was ordered to take part in a counter-attack. While other brigades preceded his in mass and were shattered, his troops spread out into a looser formation. Thus, Pétain and several other generals launched the revolution in French assault tactics that would continue during 1915. The British still used the old method on the first day of the Somme in 1916, losing 90 per cent of their massive casualties to German machine guns.

Trench warfare bears a similarity to siege warfare, but with a significant difference. In a siege, a fortification such as a castle, fortress or city is surrounded. Either the besieged are starved into surrender or their defences are breached, ending the siege. Occasionally, the besieger is forced to lift the siege. In trench warfare when the trenches ran from one end of the front to the other, encirclement was impossible, unless the trench lines were part of a fortress ring. On the Western Front, the trench lines were anchored at one end by the English Channel and at the other by the Swiss border and encirclement was definitely unfeasible. However, both sides had plans to outflank the trench line by invading Switzerland if necessary. The British toyed with the idea of invading Germany from the North Sea coast. The Germans, on the other hand, had constructed some heavy artillery such as the 420mm Big Berthas and a limited number of trench mortars to smash the Belgian and French fortresses, not because they had envisaged a trench war. Since it was impossible to outflank trench lines on the tactical level without breaching them first, the attacks

Balloons: Hanging Around

When the war began, manned balloons were not a novelty. Balloons had been around for over a century and had served as observation posts during the American Civil War. The French employed them at the siege of Paris during the Franco-Prussian War as a means of escape and communication. The French and the British, as well as the Germans, had balloons, but they had not used them much before 1914. When these tethered balloons were aloft, they were visible for miles around. For this reason in the French army all but one balloon company were disbanded and their personnel became infantry replacements. The Germans proceeded in a similar way, but changed their minds after the Battle of the Marne.[44] French spherical balloons were almost useless on windy days. On the other hand, the German balloons – built by Parseval-Sigsfeldand and called '*Drachen*' (Dragon) – were sausage-shaped, had a single fin and handled like kites.[45] After they saw the Germans using an increasing number of these balloons for observation, the French considered doing the same.[46]

Eventually, Lieutenant Albert Caquot, considered one of the best military engineers in half a century in France, was put in charge of a balloon company equipped with Drachen type balloons. Since high winds made them ineffective, Caquot came up with his own design known as the Caquot dirigible. It could maintain its position in 60km/h winds thanks to its three fins. The Germans captured one and copied the design because it could attain greater heights and was more stable in windy conditions than the Drachens.

By 1915, both sides used these kite-like balloons for artillery observation. An observer dropped a weighted message with data for the artillery or used a telephone line connecting the balloon to the ground, which was obviously more effective. The weighted message could include a map on which the enemy positions were marked. Later, the army produced maps with coordinates so the observers could call in the information. The problem with the dropped messages was it could take the ground crew an average of 20 minutes to find them. After 1914, both German and French balloonists faced the ever-present danger of enemy aircraft. Keeping the balloons at a good distance behind the lines prevented enemy guns from targeting them. Some pilots became expert at balloon busting once machine guns were mounted on their aircraft. The pilots had to be at a safe distance before the hydrogen in the balloon exploded. The crew in the basket below still had time to use their parachutes.[47]

In an article published in the American *Field Artillery Journal*, Lieutenant Crivelli of the French Air Service explained that the consequence of improved heavy artillery was that 'Our own trenches were fired upon as often as those of the Germans, and everyone tried to put the blame on everyone else.'* Between

---

* Lieutenant Crivelli, 'Observation Balloons', *Field Artillery Journal* (January–March 1918), Vol. VIII, 342–8.

17 and 22 August 1915 – observed Crivelli – the weather had been excellent and some operations had been taking place at Verdun. Each squadron carried eight to fifteen observers. The balloon units deployed eight balloons for the divisional artillery, twelve for heavy artillery and two for the naval guns. Each balloon carried two to four observers. Whereas the aeroplane squadrons identified German batteries 521 times and performed ranging missions 690 times for the French artillery batteries, the balloons identified German batteries 1,064 times and adjusted the range for the artillery 1,078 times. Thus the balloons, which required fewer men and less equipment, outperformed the aircraft. However, this stellar performance was only possible when the weather was good and when the French had air superiority over the area. In poor weather, only the aircraft could perform missions for the artillery.[48] The presence of balloons often deterred artillery batteries from firing in 1916 and later.

In the summer of 1916 during the Battle of the Somme, the French targeted the German balloons. During the initial assault, they shot down nineteen, forcing the Germans to move them far behind the front. As a balloon observer during the Battle of the Somme, Crivelli himself was brought down 5 times on 5 successive days and his balloon was pierced with up to 300 bullet holes. In 1917, when incendiary bullets appeared, the balloons exploded and only a parachute escape was possible.

had to be frontal. On a strategic level, it was possible to attack the flanks of a salient in order to envelop the enemy forces there, but the tactical assaults at these points still had to be frontal. Thus, like in the siege of a fortification, the assailants had to find a weak point, such as a location manned with second-rate troops, a site too far from rapid support from reserves or have some other shortcoming. Combat patrols or raiding parties often went out at night to identify these weak points, to probe the enemy position or to bring back prisoners for interrogation. Air photography also helped to determine the location and condition of enemy positions and the depth of the defences.

After the soldiers dug the first trenches, they excavated a second line behind it and linked the two with narrow communication trenches. In many cases, they made a third trench. In the area between the front line and the rear trenches, they built other facilities such as first-aid stations, headquarters, shelters, etc. Troops in the second line could launch a counter-attack to drive the enemy from the first line if it fell. If the first line fell, an attack on the second line was still problematic because it took time to move forward the weapons supporting the assault. If no-man's-land was churned up with craters, movement was even more difficult.

In 1914, most attacks were launched with limited artillery support. As a result, the assaulting infantry was unable to take the enemy trenches or it was pushed out of them almost as soon as it captured them. In 1915, both sides realized that artillery had to plough the way for the infantry to advance and take enemy trenches. The Germans opted for the short hurricane bombardment, whereas the British and the French preferred prolonged barrages that could last several days. The belligerents further refined their assault techniques by developing the creeping barrage, which moved forward on a schedule and which was closely followed by the infantry. The German routine consisted of short bombardment, a short pause, followed by another round of firing, and repeating the procedure several times. During the storm of artillery shells, the defenders ducked into their shelters or crouched in their trenches. When the firing stopped, they returned to their posts, waiting for the infantry assault that was sure to follow. However, if nothing happened after two or three bombardments, they were prone to let down their guard and were slow to return to their posts thinking it was another false alarm. During one of those interludes, the infantry went on the attack.

During the offensives of 1915, Joffre and his subordinates first had to select their objectives. Next, they had to determine whether to assault on a narrow or broad front. Attacks on narrow fronts often allowed the penetration of the enemy's trench line, but yielded little gain and usually ended up in failure. Selecting a broad front and multiple sectors offered better prospects because it made it more difficult for the Germans to position their reserves and know when and where to send them until the battle had already developed. The broad front also allowed the possibility of neutralizing the enemy on the flanks of the main assault force. In 1915, the problem for the French and the British, though, was the lack of heavy artillery for breaking up wire obstacles and trenches.

During 1915 and later, the trench lines became more complex, especially on the German side. The French, on the other hand, wanted to avoid creating a feeling of permanency, which would hurt morale because it was their duty to drive the enemy from their homeland. A few kilometres behind the first defensive belt, which consisted of two or three lines of trenches, troops excavated a second and sometimes a third one, especially in vulnerable areas.[49] The Germans began building concrete shelters in their trench lines that could withstand most French artillery. They added strongpoints, sometimes made of concrete and even redoubts. These strongpoints often provided enfilading fire in front of the trench line. In late 1914, when barbed wire was provided in sufficient quantities, the soldiers strung out multiple strands in front of the first trench in no-man's-land. To alert the defenders of approaching enemy patrols, they added cans and other noise-making materials. On patrols and raids, both sides favoured hand grenades and rifle grenade launchers. Early in the war, the patrols included grenadiers protected by the other men in the group.[50] Assaults generally took place in daylight and were much more dangerous than patrol or raiding party duties were because machine-gun fire took a heavy toll and the attackers had no other shelter than shell craters. Wire entanglements slowed their advance if they were not breached. While the defenders were often able to keep their superiors apprised of the situation by telephone, the attackers had to depend on runners who had to scurry across no-man's-land to keep their own leaders informed.

Both sides looked for alternative methods to breach enemy defences. They developed the flamethrower to reduce strongpoints and terrorize the enemy. The belligerents considered poison gas as an effective way to clear the enemy trenches, but it turned out to be a disappointment, even with the development of phosgene and mustard gas. Most of these methods and techniques were mere improvements on medieval and ancient methods. Even a crude form of gas warfare dates back to ancient times; the Byzantine army developed a flamethrower using Greek Fire, which used susbstances that gave results similar to those achieved with modern napalm and could not be extinguished by water. An additional method used throughout history against fortifications was revived in trench warfare: mining. Instead of digging tunnels beneath castle walls, now the soldiers excavated them under no-man's-land to reach the enemy trench line. They filled the end of the tunnel with explosives and detonated right before a frontal assault. This procedure created a large crater and often left the surviving troops shell-shocked. Frequently the defenders detected the mining operations, but they could not necessarily abandon the targeted trench. Sometimes, the defenders dug a counter-mine and either broke into the enemy tunnel and fought with the attackers underground or they set off their own charges to destroy the enemy tunnel before it was completed.[51] Mining operations often resulted in some local successes but no massive breakthrough.

Thus, from 1914–17, trench warfare remained unproductive and both sides suffered heavy casualties as each tried to wear the other down to the point it could no longer hold the line as its reserves dried up. In 1915, the French and the British launched several offensives, but the Germans always managed to repel them as Falkenhayn juggled his troops between war fronts. In 1916, General Falkenhayn tried to take the initiative in the West in the hope of wearing down the Allies.

During the war, the Germans adopted a new tactical method to break up the stalemate on the Western Front – infiltration. Shock troops infiltrated enemy lines without tackling strongpoints, which were to be eliminated by the following waves of infantry. One problem, however, was that the follow-up troops often had to negotiate heavily cratered battlefields laden with their heavy weapons. The French and British had proposed similar methods on a smaller scale earlier in the war.[52]

The New Factor – Air War

The French military acquired aircraft in 1909 whereas General Helmuth von Moltke merely suggested that the aeroplane might have a military role. In 1910, Igo Etrich of Austria-Hungary designed a monoplane called the Taube (Dove), which became the first military aircraft for both Austria-Hungary and Germany before 1914 and was in use during the first months of the war. Italy had used it during the Italo-Turkish War in 1911. General Ferdinand Foch was not impressed with these small, fragile machines and commented that they were interesting toys and fine for sport, but offered no military value.

Count Ferdinand von Zeppelin built his first airship in July 1900 and by the end of the decade, the German military purchased several 'Zeppelins'. These dirigibles offered the potential for aerial reconnaissance and for bombardment of targets deep behind enemy lines. Tethered balloons had served in previous wars and offered a set of eyes above the battlefield for the artillery and the army commanders since they could communicate with the ground by various methods, but not radio until after 1914.

The French went to war with 162 aeroplanes and 6 dirigibles while the British had over 80 aeroplanes and 4 dirigibles and the Russians 190 aeroplanes. The German inventory included 232 aeroplanes – many Taube monoplanes – and 12 dirigibles (including 9 Zeppelins). Austria-Hungary had only about 70 aeroplanes and 3 dirigibles. Most aircraft operated from the headquarters of an army or army corps and there was no real strategic or tactical doctrine. When the war began aircraft had no armament, although they might carry a few small bombs or even fleches that the pilot or observer dropped over the side.

In the summer of 1914, the Germans built several aerodromes near the frontier such as at Metz. The French had 'aerostation' units assigned to Maubeuge, Verdun, Toul, Épinal, Belfort, Langres and Versailles with a depot unit a Chalons. In August, many of these French bases ended up too close to the front, but Maubeuge was the only one lost to the Germans.

The 'air war' began when *Zeppelin Z-VI* was sent on a bombing mission against one of the Liège forts in the first days of the war. Belgian riflemen riddled the dirigible with so many holes that it crash-landed in Germany. On 3 August, a German Taube monoplane flew a reconnaissance mission over Lunéville and dropped three small bombs and on 30 August, a Taube dropped bombs on Paris. On 21 August, two German dirigibles attacked French infantry marching into Alsace. Although they were at an altitude of about 800m, the French managed to bring both of them down. The Germans continued to use the Zeppelins on bombing missions in August, striking at several Channel ports and Lille. In August 1914, the British and French retaliated by bombing bases for dirigibles. On 12 March 1915, German dirigibles appeared over Paris after having attacked London in January 1915. Paris was not bombed again until January 1916 when another dirigible struck shortly before the scheduled Verdun Offensive. The Zeppelins continued long-range bombing missions in France and over Great Britain, but these ended during the Battle of Verdun.

Recognition was a problem for the troops, so German, French and British soldiers fired at almost anything that flew over them. The French damaged two of their own dirigibles, one in August 1914 near Lunéville, and the other on 24 September near Reims when the airship *Dupuy de Lôme* was retreating before a German advance. After these incidents, the French military forbade further dirigible flights until April 1915. On 16 August 1914, French troops shot down *Zeppelin L7* and on 23 August, German troops brought down their own *Zeppelin L8*. The French soon began to arm their dirigibles and the Germans followed suit. Accidental damage by friendly fire promoted the adoption of identification markings on all aircraft and airships. On 30 September, the Germans adopted the black Iron Cross as the insignia for their aircraft and airships. In late October, the British and the French marked their aircraft with a blue and red roundel. The main danger for the aviator came from ground fire, generally from rifles. However, machine guns and some light artillery were adapted to serve as anti-aircraft weapons before long. If the pilot was passing enemy aircraft, he could do nothing unless he carried a rifle or pistol. Even then, it was no easy feat to fly and fire a weapon at the same time unless it was a two-seater aircraft with an observer. On 25 September, several British BE-2 aircraft forced a German *Aviatik B* to land. On 5 October, a French Voisin III armed with a machine gun shot down an *Aviatik*. On 1 December, the Germans equipped the first aircraft with a radio for artillery spotting. In the meantime, the French test fired machine guns through a rotating propeller.

For most of 1914, aircraft and airships usually performed reconnaissance duty. On 22 August 1914 on the Eastern Front, *Zeppelin LZ5* spotted the advancing Russian 2nd Army in the Tannenberg region, which gave the Germans the edge in the upcoming battle. On 29 August, aircraft discovered another Russian force about to march. Only days later, in September, a French reconnaissance aircraft discovered that Kluck's army was turning away from Paris, which led to the Battle of the Marne.

Gabriel Voisin mounted Hotchkiss light machine guns on several Voisin aircraft, one of which scored the first victory on 5 October 1914. The gun of this pusher type aircraft was mounted on the observer's position in the front of the aircraft.[53] The French as well as the Germans also dropped artillery shells by hand from some aircraft on bombing missions. However, a German Taube or French Voisin had limited carrying capacity. In some cases, the pilots dropped darts and one even killed a German general with fleches. During the German aerial bombing campaign in 1914, Zeppelins bombed several rail stations on the Western Front. The French and British also launched a few bombing raids against the Zeppelin airship sheds in 1914, but accomplished little of significance.

Aerial bombing increased in 1915, but it had little effect. The arming of aircraft added a new dimension to the warfare as scout aircraft were turned into fighters that eventually became hunters of the sky. Formation flying evolved from the need to protect all types of aircraft. In 1915, most aircraft flew in groups and discovered that the 'V' formation was the most effective.

Joffre placed Major Joseph Barès, a veteran pilot of the Balkan Wars and ranking pilot, in charge of French aviation on 25 September 1914. His job was to organize the French aviation forces. One major step he took was to reopen flying schools and revive the aircraft industry, which had closed down in anticipation of a short war. That same month, he formed the first French bomber unit with eighteen Voisin LA5 pusher biplanes. The Morane-Saulnier monoplanes were chosen as pursuit aircraft and they formed the first fighter squadron of the war. The Caudron G III biplane was used for observation and artillery fire. The Maurice Farman VII also served for reconnaissance. Barès removed other types of planes with poorer performance. He soon doubled the number of French squadrons.

Trench Warfare in Modern History

Trenches, like forts, served as infantry and artillery positions for centuries before the First World War. In the seventeenth century, at the time of Sébastien Vauban, they formed siege lines to encircle forts or fortresses. Many of the trenching techniques, such as saps, persisted into the twentieth century.[54] The most significant changes in trench warfare emerged during the Crimean War and the American Civil War. In the latter conflict, the Confederates dug trenches to defend the front running from Richmond to Petersburg and built earthen forts at intervals to strengthen the trench line. The Union forces built a similar line of trenches opposite their enemy. Both sides added wood or gabion revetments, in use for centuries. Many of the American forts had bombproofs mainly for ammunition. There was no barbed wire, so the Americans used abattis, caltrops and other devices in front of the trenches to impede enemy advance. These same age-old obstacles were used in many a trench system during the First World War until barbed wire was delivered in sufficient quantities.

The next time trenches were used extensively was during the Russo-Turkish War of 1877–8. The Turks' use of trenches at the Battle of Plevna triggered a new trend not only in the employment of field fortifications but also in the development of permanent fortifications. Trench warfare dominated at the siege of Port Arthur during the Russo-Japanese War of 1904–5 when the Japanese took heavy losses storming the trenches. However, the Russians failed to make the best tactical use of their trenches because they neither selected the most advantageous locations for them nor took full advantage of their machine guns. Thus, some observers failed to appreciate the full potential of trench warfare in the next European conflict. The difference between early twentieth-century trenches and American Civil War trenches was that they were often deeper and provided overhead cover. In 1914 and later, armies were relatively well equipped with breech-loading rifles and artillery and they expended more ammunition in one day than armies in the previous century used in one month. They were also mostly equipped with high-velocity weapons that were less effective against trenches than the older, low-velocity artillery pieces with a high angle of fire.[55] However, breastworks, which had been used with or without a shallow trench, were not able to resist high-velocity weapons and no longer provided adequate protection. Many of the new rifles, such as the Martini, were able to penetrate even breastworks with earthen protection. To protect the troops, the trenches had to be deeper and have a low parapet for better concealment. The earthen parapet had to be widened to prevent bullets from penetrating it. However, it could not be too high or it became a target for high-velocity artillery. Overhead cover and underground bombproofs became necessary for the protection of the troops not only from an extended artillery bombardment, but also from bad weather.[56] They also helped maintain morale and the health of the troops.

In the 1877 war with the Russians, the Turkish soldiers, poorly equipped or supplied, demonstrated that the common soldier (as opposed to the well-trained professional) in field fortifications could easily hold off an enemy even if outnumbered three to one and short on artillery. Deep and narrow trenches with a low parapet protected the Turks from Russian field artillery, which consisted mainly of direct-fire cannons that were unable to hit the deep trenches. The overhead cover protected the defenders from shrapnel and other metal fragments from exploding shells. Although the redoubts, which served as strongpoints and protection for the Turkish artillery, stood largely above ground, their walls were thick enough to withstand most direct fire. According to Colonel Gustav J. Fiebeger, in daylight, the troops could not remain stationary without cover if they were within range of the breech-loading weapons.[57] The Russians ended up digging their own trenches before they launched assaults, and brought up heavy siege artillery to use against Turkish field fortifications. After over a month of siege and three failed attacks, the Russians kept some of the redoubts under heavy bombardment. This prevented the relieving Turkish battalions from occupying the position in daylight. The Russians concluded that night attacks had a better chance of succeeding than daytime assaults. The siege intensified in November. The Turks surrendered after a failed break-out attempt on 10 December 1877 even though they had managed to penetrate the Russians first line of encircling entrenchments at several points. Outnumbered by about three to one, the Turks had stalled the Russian invasion of Bulgaria for five months and demonstrated the value of trenches combined with rapid-fire rifles. Apparently, they also had a few Gatling guns, but the efficacy of the machine gun did not become apparent until the next century. The Battle of Plevna was a major event observed by military attachés and covered by the media. Unlike the Americans at Petersburg–Richmond, the Turks and the Russians largely used trenches to fortify a single point such as a town.

The Russo-Japanese War was the next milestone in military history. After the 1880s, barbed wire slowly became part of the war arsenal. It provided good protection to the forts built in the late nineteenth century. It was used extensively during the Spanish-American War of 1898. During the Russo-Japanese War, which was fought on a larger scale and in which field fortifications played a key role, it became even more prevalent. Smokeless powder, developed in the mid-1880s, also marked a major landmark in trench warfare because the troops were now able to fire without revealing their positions with a lingering trail of dark smoke. Maxim machine guns, which fired 400 to 600 rounds per minute, were an improvement over the rifles that could fire only 10 to 16 rounds a minute and became a weapon superbly fitted for trench warfare. Improvised hand grenades, which had been used for centuries, did not seem to garner attention until after the war. The Germans and the British began manufacturing them shortly before the First World War.

Although Russian field fortifications improved during the course of the war, observers claimed they were poorly constructed. Early in the war, the Russians placed artillery batteries on the crests of ridges and sited some of the trenches inadequately. In some cases, they used sand bags for revetments and barbed wire as an obstacle. Most of their redoubts, however, proved formidable. In the end, both the Japanese and the Russians learned that the attackers could take these positions only if they were willing to accept heavy casualties.

During the campaign in Manchuria, the Japanese also had to dig trenches to protect their troops, which confirmed Colonel Friebeger's claim that troops could not remain exposed. Comparisons of Russian and Japanese trenches showed that the Japanese construction and design offered much better protection. The Japanese-built trenches allowed the troops to get closer to the enemy by digging in after every small advance until it was time for the final surge. The Japanese army entered the war without machine guns, but soon realized their importance.

The need for heavy artillery became apparent during the war. The Japanese began using mortars with satisfactory outcomes. It seems, however, that only the Germans noticed the efficacy of these weapons since they were the only ones to manufacture them before the First World War. Although the military observers of most of the other great powers filed reports, their military leaders seem to have focused almost solely on offensive actions regardless of their high casualty rate.

The army engineers of the major European powers continued working on permanent fortifications until 1914. The fortress rings they created consisted of a group of forts around a town or city. If war broke out, they planned to build field fortifications between many of the individual forts to prevent the enemy from advancing through the gaps. The new German Festen at Metz consisted mostly of a series of scattered individual positions such as artillery blocks, infantry positions, casernes, etc. In some cases, the Germans also built concrete trenches within the individual systems to ensure the troops' protection. Before the First World War, they also created battery positions outside the Festen. The French did the same outside the forts of their fortress rings. The Belgians also realized that they needed field fortifications between the forts of their fortress rings, but they could not build them until war was imminent or had already begun.

The Balkan Wars of 1912–13 were too close to the First World War for most military leaders to absorb and implement what they had learned. During this conflict, it became apparent that trenches served not only for defence but also for offence when the defender dominated the battlefield with machine guns and indirect fire from concealed artillery. The Germans and the Austrians, who took heed of this lesson, continued to develop heavy howitzers and equipped their troops with entrenching tools to carry into battle. During their annual manoeuvres, units assigned to the defensive force practised digging in so entrenching was not new to their troops. German soldiers were also equipped with wire cutters for clearing the heavy barbed wire fences they expected to come across as they traversed farmland. The French were not so quick to grasp the necessity of developing these skills so their soldiers went into battle poorly equipped and poorly prepared, contrary to the claims made by German General Falkenhayn. Surprisingly, in his memoirs, Joffre claimed that he had pleaded for long-range field artillery and heavy howitzers before the war. He had not been able, however, to overrule the officers of the artillery department who were convinced that the 75mm gun was the ultimate artillery weapon.[58] In addition, the Germans realized that the machine gun was ideally suited for the infantry whereas the French continued to emphasize the use of rifles and bayonets. The permanent fortifications in the Balkans were mostly old and outdated so that defence devolved on trenches with redoubts. As a result, no one was able to assess the full value of the forts built or modernized in the first decade of the new century in Western Europe.

The Germans entered the war with a number of Taube monoplanes of limited value. They also had *Aviatik B.II*, the *LVG B.I* and *Albatros B.II* biplanes. Like the French, they established bomber units. However, reconnaissance or scouting aircraft were the mainstay of aviation in 1914, but they had their limitations. The aerial observers were able to impart detailed information to the ground forces after they landed, they could drop messages to men on the ground or they could use simple signals from the air. By the end of 1914, the German equipped the first aircraft with radios for artillery spotting. The French did not lag far behind; in 1915, they installed transmitters (no receivers) on Caudron G III aircraft to send Morse code messages. In 1915, the more powerful twin-engine Caudron G IV replaced the G III. The French attached a squadron of radio-equipped aircraft to each army corps to support its artillery. The Germans did not attach radio-equipped aircraft squadrons to their artillery until late 1915 when aircraft began to play a key role in artillery observation.

Fighting enemy planes in the air was a problem in 1914 because there was no effective way to mount machine guns. The Allies worked on a way to mount a machine gun so that it could be fired through the spinning propellers. The first method of placing a machine gun on an aeroplane was to put it on a swivel for operation by an observer located in the front in the case of a pusher engine aircraft or in the rear in the case of a tractor engine. One solution in 1915 was to mount the fixed machine guns on the nose of the craft and sheathing the propellers in steel to prevent them from being shot off. By 1916, the French mounted fixed, forward-firing machine guns on the top wing so they fired over the propeller. The problem with this method was the difficulty in changing magazines in flight. The French also tried to devise a more effective method, which would rely on the synchronization of the machine gun with the rotation of the propeller and required some type of interrupter gear. However, before they could perfect this method, Anthony Fokker, a Dutch aircraft designer, came up with a synchronization device in the spring of 1915, which allowed the Germans to beat the Allies to the draw. The first machine guns that fired through the propellers were mounted on Fokker *E.I* and *E.II* monoplanes. The Germans began to clear the sky of Allied aircraft during the 'Fokker Scourge' of 1915.

Meanwhile, in 1915, Roland Garros and Sergeant Jean Navarre gained instant popularity in France by downing five enemy aircraft each. The French press coined the term 'ace' for them. Shortly after that, Oswald Boelcke and Max Immelmann became Germany's first 'aces' flying the *Fokker E* model monoplanes. The 'Fokker Scourge' forced the Allies to shift their bombing efforts from day to night raids, which were less effective. Thus, the Allies lost the slight advantage they had held in the air on the Western Front since the beginning of the war. In 1916, the Allies finally managed to synchronize Vickers machine guns but they did not mount them on aeroplanes until the spring of 1916. Meanwhile, the French developed the Nieuport 11, known as the Bébé, which mounted a machine gun on top of the upper wing. This aircraft replaced the Morane-Saulnier Types L and N, which had a Hotchkiss machine gun that fired through the armour-sheathed propeller. These Nieuports proved superior to German *Eindeckers* (single wing) in early 1916. The Allies did not regain air superiority until many weeks after the Battle of Verdun began. Before the end of the battle, the Germans began to use new and more effective types of biplane fighters. Thus, during 1916, the biplane gradually replaced the monoplane in the air over the Western Front.

Both sides used aircraft to fly reconnaissance missions and photograph enemy positions as they slowly learned how to interpret aerial photographs. By 1916, these functions assumed greater importance over the Verdun battlefield, which forced the troops to begin camouflaging exposed positions. Balloons continued to be a primary source of observation for the artillery. Pétain even remarked that control of the air was critical during the battle. Before long, aerial observation became a dangerous duty for the observer since both sides converted some guns into a form of anti-balloon or anti-aircraft gun and it was not difficult to hit and set these hydrogen gasbags on fire. Some observers were issued a parachute to make a quick escape if the ground troops were unable to pull it to earth fast enough. Aircraft were able to penetrate enemy lines and send back reports as well as drive off enemy aircraft and attack observation balloons or airships. During 1916, the aeroplane added a new dimension to the battlefield as both sides strove to win air dominance over Verdun.

Chapter Three

Verdun Campaign, August 1914–February 1916

'General von Falkenhayn, the new Chief of the General Staff, who in the midst of the Marne disaster had grasped the reins with a firm hand, had for the moment only one thing to do, and that was to place the dislocated strategical position on a sounder basis.'

Crown Prince Wilhelm, *My War Experiences*
(London: Hurst and Blackett Ltd, 1922)

Creating a Salient

At the beginning of the war, the fortress of Verdun anchored one end of the French fortified line. In August and September 1914, the Germans tried to sweep around it while their main armies moved across Belgium and northern France. Crown Prince Wilhelm's *5th Army* formed the hinge of the German right wing that swung through Belgium and Luxembourg into northern France like an opening door. The Crown Prince's army was concentrated in the vicinity of Metz–Thionville where it observed French covering forces holding the Othain River Line and Étain on the direct approach to Verdun. On 17 August 1914, the *5th Army* was ordered to advance. It moved forward in concert with the *4th Army* on its right and passed through Luxembourg towards Longwy. The *VI Reserve, V* and *XIII corps* moved through Luxembourg. On 20 August, part of the *XIII Corps* was left behind to reduce the French fortress at Longwy. The *VI Reserve Corps*, on the left flank of the *XIII Corps*, passed through Esch and crossed into France on 20 August. On the *5th Army's* left flank, General von Mudra's corps at Metz pushed back the French outposts in the Woëvre on the direct route to Metz. Meanwhile, the German forces surrounded Longwy on 22 August and took the town on 25 August. On 23 August, Moltke sent the following order: 'The *5th Army* has freedom of movement. I want the enemy driven back from north to west past Verdun. Several French Corps are in action on the front of the *4th Army*. German right wing advancing swiftly in a southerly direction.'

On 24 August, the *VI Reserve* and *XVI corps* marched on Longuyon while the *V Reserve* and *XVI corps* reached the French outposts on the Othain River.[1] The Kaiser awarded his son the Iron Cross for his victory on the frontier. Mudra's corps and the *5th Army* tried to complete a double envelopment of French forces, but failed. The French forces on the Othain and north of Verdun escaped to the fortified zone. On 29 August, Moltke ordered the *5th Army* to advance to the Meuse. The previous day, the army had received orders to march on Chalons. The Crown Prince's army advanced north of the Verdun fortress. According to the Crown Prince, a 300mm Beta Mortar was sent to expedite the capture of Montmédy.

In September, after the *5th Army* crossed the Meuse west of Montmédy, it thrust southward and through the Argonne in order to trap the French 3rd Army, which had opposed it since the campaign had begun, and to isolate Verdun. The Crown Prince's army swept around the city and through the Argonne, anchoring the left wing of the German invasion force of four other armies intent on executing the Schlieffen Plan by invading Belgium and racing across northern France. Between

FORT CAMP DES ROMAINS

5 Traverse Abri on East side   4 Casemates for indirect fire weapon on East side
5 Traverse Abri on West side   4 Casemates for indirect fire weapons on West side
2 positions prepared for 155mm Mougin Casemates

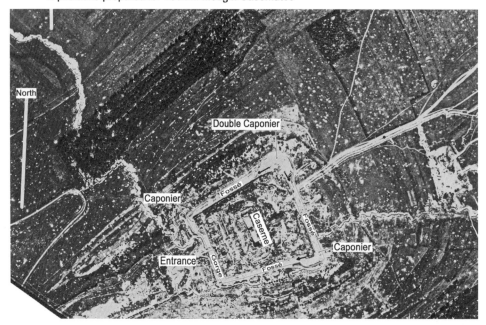

5 and 9 September, the campaign ended when the French forces defeated the invaders at the Battle of the Marne. During those first days of September, the German *XVIII Reserve Corps* advanced on Grand Pré and on its left, the *VI Corps* moved into the Argonne to take Varennes where it met up with the *XIII Corps* advancing south from Dun. To the left of *XIII Corps* was *VI Reserve Corps*, which crossed paths with *XVI Corps* near Montfaucon as they progressed without encountering much opposition. The *V Reserve Corps*, which held the front north of Verdun, redeployed southeast of Verdun in early September with the intention of isolating the fortress. General Mudra's *XVI Corps* stormed the key position of the butte at Montfaucon, a mere 10km to the northwest of Verdun, on 3 September and repelled French counter-attacks. The Crown Prince was ordered to send most of his divisions through the Argonne to complete the isolation of Verdun. After it advanced southwest of Metz across the Woëvre, the *V Corps* set out to capture the forts of Troyon and Camp des Romains and create a bridgehead at St Mihiel. The main force transiting through the Argonne was to drive towards St Mihiel on the Meuse and link up with *V Corps* to complete a double envelopment of the fortress. According to the Crown Prince, he was short of the special materiel and troops to achieve this objective. Therefore, at the height of the Battle of the Marne, his army launched the first campaign against Verdun.

Crown Prince Wilhelm explained:[*]

> We only had at our disposal for the attack against the Meuse forts the *10th Infantry Division*, with a battery of heavy field howitzers and an Austrian motor-mortar battery.... In order to secure a prompt execution of his task, we telegraphed to General von Strantz, informing him that the *5th Army's* front was facing east, towards the line Bar le Duc–Beauzée and to the north; we reckoned upon his attacking the enemy's rear immediately with his army corps.
>
> The fort of Troyon was silenced by heavy howitzer fire on the 8th September. It responded but feebly to our bombardment, and showed no further signs of life after 11 a.m. The 30 cm [305mm] Austrian mortar ... was expected to open fire at four in the afternoon, and it was hoped that the fort would be taken on the 8th September. Then the work of Les Peroches, on the left bank of the Meuse, was to be shelled by the heavy howitzers and taken under fire, and the mortars to be brought from Metz were to be directed against the fort of Génicourt to the north of Troyon. Our infantry lay about 100 m in front of the works of Troyon Fort. With the fall of Troyon and Les Paroches the gap still existing to the south in the circular front we were forming around Verdun was only reduced by seventeen km. But the most important thing of all was that the *3rd Army's* road to the French rear was now free. The Metz Main Reserve (the *3rd Reserve Division*) had remained in the Woëvre plain, between the Côtes Lorraines and the Moselle, to guard against any danger from Toul-Nancy. It had already strengthened its position in the area between Thiaucourt and Pont-à-Mousson, and had warded off a number of violent enemy attacks.

---

[*]   William, Crown Prince of Germany, *My War Experience* (London: Hurst and Blackett Ltd, 1922).

The *6th Army*, after much sanguinary fighting, was confining itself to the bombardment of the strong positons around Nancy. After their preliminary bombardment, they still hoped, with the expected steady advance of the *5th Army* beyond Bar-le-Duc to the south-east and towards the rearward communications of Nancy, to be able to break through the Trouée-de-Charmes between Nancy and Épinal. And thus forces which were badly needed elsewhere remained here involved in a hopeless struggle.

The Crown Prince doubted that this massive envelopment of the French fortified line Verdun–Toul was possible because of the critical situation developing on the Marne. Events vindicated his opinion. The *5th Army*, which acted as the German left wing, became involved in the Battle of the Marne. However, it made its last attempt to march through the Argonne on 8 and 9 September. The Crown Prince boasted that this advance was successful, but French General Herr, commanding the artillery brigade of VI Corps, claimed that his 75mm guns smashed a desperate German infantry assault. Whatever the case, the front of the *5th Army* in the Argonne area was pulling back on 11 September on orders from higher up.

Before the order to retreat, the *V Corps* and von Strantz's troops were unable to break the barrier of forts on either side of St Mihiel in time to cross the Meuse and expose Sarrail's 3rd Army from two directions. On 7 September, the Duke of Würtemberg's *4th Army* and the Crown Prince's army had been ordered to strike at the junction of the French 4th and 3rd armies respectively. The German *4th Army* advanced towards St Dizier while the *5th Army* marched on Bar-le-Duc. General Langle's 4th Army gave ground. Sarrail's 3rd Army, now reinforced, held the Crown Prince's army. The *XVIII Reserve Corps* had already reached Revigny on 9 September, while the *VI Corps* on its left had taken Ste Ménehould. Bar-le-Duc, on Verdun's lifeline, was threatened. During this march through the Argonne, the German *XIII Corps* had also moved through the forest while the *XVI Corps* on its left reached Souilly. This was as far as the Crown Prince's army's tentacles extended by 9 September. The German armies began to retreat on 10 September. Joffre ordered his armies to press forward and General Michel Coutanceau, Military Governor of Verdun, to attack towards the north and prevent enemy convoys from crossing the Meuse and his territorial divisions to attack eastward. When the German *V Corps* took St Mihiel on the Meuse it established a bridgehead, but it was too late to make any difference. When the Germans pulled back in the Argonne, Verdun formed a salient. One of its main rail connections was cut at St Mihiel and the other to the west soon was interdicted by German artillery located on the heights of the Argonne. The Germans occupied their own salient at St Mihiel from which they tried to penetrate the Côtes de Meuse.[2]

The battle for St Mihiel opened on 8 September with an artillery bombardment of Fort Troyon. To breach the river line, the Germans had to neutralize the forts. One objective in crossing the Marne in this area was to split the French 2nd Army from the 3rd Army. On 8 September, Joffre was so alarmed by the situation that he informed General Sarrail that he must maintain contact with de Langle's 4th Army on his left on the Argonne front and gave him permission to pull back from the fortress of Verdun, which could fend for itself, he believed. However, he was not authorizing Sarrail to retreat from the Meuse line south of Verdun.[3] On 9 September, only two French cavalry divisions – the 2nd near St Mihiel with a provisional brigade sent by Castelnau from Toul and the 7th near Troyon – stood to the east of the Meuse to cover the gap between the French 3rd and 2nd armies. As the French were still clinging to Nancy, the line of the Meuse would not fall without a major battle. By the time the Germans brought up their heavy artillery to deal with the forts between Verdun and Toul, it was too late for them to do anything besides establishing a salient at St Mihiel for future operations against Verdun.

Built in 1880, Fort Troyon had positions for twenty-two artillery pieces. Since it had undergone limited renovations, it still had to rely on its caponiers to defend its surrounding ditch and a large ravelin to cover the entrance when the war began. It occupied an advantageous position about 260m above the village from where its guns could cover the interval between itself and Fort Génicourt, Fort Paroches on its left and Fort Camp des Romains at St Mihiel on its right. In the 1890s, the army added concrete barracks. The garrison consisted of over 430 troops, including the gunners of the 2 120mm L Mle 1878 guns for indirect fire and the 12 antiquated 90mm guns – 4 on siege-gun mounts and the remaining on field-gun mounts. Machine guns as well as Hotchkiss 40mm revolver guns covered the fossé.

On 8 September late in the day, two days before Moltke's headquarters ordered a general withdrawal of the German army, the *10th Division* from Strantz's army detachment started bombarding Fort Troyon with 150mm guns, a detachment of 210mm Mörser and two Austrian 305mm Mörser. The next day, a German officer demanded the surrender of the fort, the commandant of which refused. The bombardment resumed, interrupted only by an infantry assault late in the morning, which was repelled after heavy losses among the attackers. The fort continued to resist the heavy bombardment and its 90mm guns fired upon the German troops busily digging trenches. By 10 September, only half of Troyon's 90mm guns were still serviceable, but the Germans had lost their chance to isolate Verdun. The bombardment continued. The artillery of the two neighbouring forts fired in support of Fort Troyon, which suffered additional damage during 11 and 12 September. The German bombardment ended when French reinforcements arrived. The fort took about 3,000 hits from artillery rounds of 105mm to 305mm calibre. It sustained some damage, but only four men died and another forty-one were wounded. During the week that followed, the garrison repaired the damage.

Meanwhile, the Crown Prince's army prepared for a new assault on the Côtes de Meuse (or Côtes Lorraines) to regain territory it had surrendered near Ste Ménehould. On 19 September, the Germans took Beaumont and marched on Fort Liouville and the two forts to the south at Gironville, which covered the eastern approaches to Commercy. Strantz's force was reinforced with the *Bavarian III Corps*, four Austrian 305mm Mörser and the *33rd Division* from the Metz reserve. The *V Corps* continued on its mission against Troyon, securing the crests of Combres and Éparges during its advance. Éparges became the scene of heavy fighting. The Bavarian corps moved against St Mihiel. The *XIV Corps* took up positions against the left flank near Fortress Toul. Additional siege artillery lumbered forward hindered by mud left after heavy rains. On 18 September, the French brought back several divisions they had removed from the area during the Battle of the Marne so the forts could defend the heights more adequately. Since the rains and late arrival of the Bavarian corps had prevented the Germans from getting all their units into position, the new offensive began on 20 September in piecemeal fashion. The German *10th Division* made the first move by bombarding Fort Troyon until 24 September.[4] According to the Crown Prince, his *V Corps* silenced the guns of Fort Troyon on 22 September. A 305mm round destroyed a magazine, killing eighteen soldiers taking shelter there. On 24 September, Troyon's commandant received permission from Verdun to evacuate the heavily damaged fort, which still remained under French control.[5]

After the Germans resumed the bombardment of Fort Troyon, they had to wait for their units to move into position before they could launch an attack on St Mihiel. On 22 September, the *5th Army* began operations against Fort Paroches and St Mihiel. The French 75th Reserve Division held the front near St Mihiel.[6] According to the Crown Prince, his artillery smashed the guns of Fort Paroches on the very first day. This fort, built in 1885 and typical of the interval fortifications between Verdun and Toul, still had caponiers to defend its fossé. Its armament consisted of six 120mm L cannons and two 90mm guns. On 22 September, its guns returned fire. Contrary to the Crown Prince's assertions, the bombardment of the next two days only destroyed one of the fort's 90mm guns. A heavier bombardment on 25 September smashed the other 90mm gun, but the remaining guns continued to fire until 26 September when a powder magazine took a hit. On 30 September, the garrison evacuated the premises, but stayed nearby in case the enemy infantry launched an assault.[7] The Germans suffered about 600 casualties in their failed siege of Fort Paroches.

Concurrently with the attacks on forts Troyon and Paroches, the *Bavarian III Corps* moved against Fort Camp des Romains and Fort Liouville with 210mm and Austrian 305mm Mörser.[8] Fort Camp des Romains, built in 1878, had undergone little modernization and still had caponiers to cover its fossé and two old Mougin casemates for a 155mm L gun from 1881. The fort's armament in 1914 consisted of six old 120mm L cannons, four 90mm guns on the ramparts and four old mortars. Its garrison of 530 men and a regiment of the 75th Reserve Division defended St Mihiel when the Germans approached on 22 September. The *6th Division* of the *Bavarian III Corps* stopped at the edge of St Mihiel in the afternoon of 24 September. The German artillery, directed by a tethered balloon, had begun to shell the fort on 23 September. The well-directed artillery forced the French gunners from the ramparts. On 24 September, the Bavarians occupied St Mihiel as the French regiment retreated across the Meuse. The assaulting battalion crossed the Meuse on one of the few footbridges left after General Sarrail had the bridges blown up on 8 September as enemy troops approached. The Germans established a small bridgehead at Chauvoncourt, but the guns of Fort Paroches made access difficult. Meanwhile, the fort sustained damage as the heavy bombardment continued. The

Germans cut the cable that linked Fort Camp des Romains with forts Paroches and Troyon. After a German attack late in the day failed, the bombardment resumed. Damage to the barracks rendered life intolerable for the garrison. On 25 September, an early morning shelling was followed by an assault from a Bavarian brigade. The attackers crossed the fossé, which was no longer defended, using ladders carried by the pioneers. The garrison, which had moved to the centre of the fort around the barracks, counter-attacked, but failed to dislodge the Germans. Before long, the fighting spread into the galleries and lasted for 3 hours until the French commander surrendered after 48 of his men were killed and 130 were wounded.[9]

On 25 September, the *6th Division* of the Bavarian Corps took on Fort Liouville, another old fort from 1880. Unlike the nearby forts, it had a Mougin turret for two 155mm guns added in 1881. Its Mougin turret had been reinforced, two of its caponiers had been replaced with counterscarp casemates and an observation cloche, a 75mm gun turret and a machine-gun turret had been added in 1909. The ramparts mounted seven 120mm L cannons, eight 90mm guns and machine guns in 1914. Over half of the over 700-man garrison consisted of artillerymen. On 22 September, the turrets and the 120mm cannons fired on German troops in the Varnéville sector. The next day, heavy German artillery targeted Fort Liouville. The gunners on the ramparts were vulnerable. That morning, a round penetrated the Mougin turret block between the turret and the frontal amour and sparked a flame that ignited the powder bags in the turret, injuring twelve men. It took hours to make the repairs. After several days, the fort sustained significant damage including to the artillery command post. On 25 September, the movement of the Mougin turret was blocked by pieces of broken concrete and the eclipsing mechanism of the 75mm gun turret was impaired by hits from large-calibre rounds. A shell struck the barrel of the right gun of the Mougin turret and later more debris blocked the movement of the turret. Problems multiplied for the fort on 26 September. A shell fractured the Mougin turret and one of the gun breeches of the 75mm gun turret was no longer serviceable. The next day the Mougin turret developed further mechanical problems, but there were no more spare parts left to repair it. The 75mm gun turret became increasingly difficult to operate due to previous damage and fresh hits from heavy artillery rounds. The mechanics repaired and returned the turrets to action on 28 September. The restored turret operated until 29 September when a 305mm round put it out of action for the remainder of the battle. The 305mm Mörser inflicted a great deal of damage on the fort. Finally, on 30 September, the fort commander moved his troops out, took up positions nearby and prepared to repel a ground attack. That day, another 305mm round pierced the frontal armour of the Mougin turret rendering it unserviceable. On 1 October, French troops came to relieve the fort and found the garrison sheltered in a nearby ravine. The German bombardment lasted until 16 October.[10] While the German *5th Army* assailed the Côtes de Meuse, the French counter-attacked its flank striking at the *XVI Corps* between the Meuse and Moselle. However, the Germans were left in possession of a salient at St Mihiel.

While *5th Army* tried to crack the Meuse Heights and secure a bridgehead near St Mihiel, the remainder of the German army launched a new offensive against the

Varennes area on the Argonne Front. The French had attacked on 20 September, but were repelled near Cuisy. The Crown Prince explained that on 22 September, the situation turned into a 'severe battle' when his detachments crossed the front line:[*]

> As early as 6:30 a.m. the enemy's front line trenches were surprised and passed. And yet how different was the fighting now from what it had been in the first phase of open warfare! The enemy had completely changed. At its battle Headquarters in Romagne-sous-Montfaucon the Army Headquarters realized from reports what difficulties our brave troops encountered in struggling forward against the French, who fought so magnificently and stubbornly for the smallest places.... The enemy artillery in the woods and near Varennes, Vauquois, Malancourt, Esnes and Cumières swept our roads of approach, as well as the valleys.... But had our troops also changed? The general impression derived from the various reports and observations ... compelled us to conclude that the aggressive spirit of the troops had been reduced in the first place owing to the enervating effects of the very bad weather ... and secondly by the dysentery which had just broken out, by the slippery state of the ground, and the impenetrable underwood of the forest. What must also have depressed their spirits was the fact that we were fighting for country which, for reasons quite incomprehensible to the troops, had been surrendered only a few days previously.

The Crown Prince's troops were more successful the next day, but the *5th Army* suffered from a shortage of ammunition for the artillery, resulting in his infantry taking heavy losses from lack of support. His troops, nonetheless, recaptured Varennes. In his memoirs he claimed that his offensive 'through Varennes and St. Mihiel had the lasting effect of keeping large French forces perpetually on the Verdun and Toul front'. On the other hand, he found that the 'enemy front from Toul to Verdun remained just as impregnable to our attacks as the upper valley of the Aire, south of the narrow defile of Varennes'.[**] From the heights in the vicinity of Varennes, German artillery interdicted the main railway line Ste Ménehould–Verdun. All attempts to drive the Germans from the heights failed. Fighting continued in the Argonne as the Crown Prince's army went on the defensive and began digging trenches.

According to the Crown Prince, during 1914, the Germans used aerial photography to fill in information missing from plans of the defences of Verdun in their possession. They began building standard gauge and military railways in the *5th Army* sector to bring heavy 420mm Mörser batteries, other siege artillery and sufficient ammunition to bombard Fortress Verdun. The pioneers of the *V Reserve Corps* erected a 25m–high tower on the heights of Crépion from which the Crown Prince watched his medium and heavy artillery respond to the 155mm gun of Fort Douaumont, which had been firing since September.[11] Crown Prince Wilhelm used the tower on 8 October 1915. Before long, the tower became a target for the French artillery.

---

*   William, *My War Experiences*, p. 104.
**   William, *My War Experiences*, p. 107.

The staff of the *5th Army* estimated that the ammunition necessary to sustain an attack of ten days, employing two-and-a-half army corps and their artillery, would require forty-eight-and-a-half trains. This would not include the requirement for the heavy siege batteries. Such an action would have been impractical in 1914 or 1915 when the Eastern Front took precedence. On 19 October 1914, the Crown Prince received orders to attack Verdun, but he was assigned a daily consignment of only nine-and-a-half ammunition trains and *Army Detachment Strantz* would receive four-and-a-half. Falkenhayn seemed to believe that Fortress Verdun would fall as easily as the Belgian fortresses and Maubeuge. Furthermore, he had little to spare because he was fully engaged in the 'Race to the Sea' in the north. The Crown Prince refused to undertake such an operation without enough ammunition to do the job. In addition, General Headquarters denied him the number of pioneers his staff requested.[12] The Kaiser agreed with his son after hearing about the problem. The operation was cancelled and some of the divisions of the *5th Army* were transferred to other armies. The shortage of ammunition kept the *5th Army* even from replying to French artillery fire for the remainder of the year. The struggle continued in the Argonne as the French lost a great number of men trying to penetrate the German position. At Christmas, a rare truce allowed both sides a brief respite.

In November 1914, in order to achieve more effective control and support, Falkenhayn gave the Crown Prince control over *Army Detachment Strantz*, Fortress Metz, *Army Detachment Falkenhausen* and *Army Detachment Gaede*.[13] This left him in control of the front from the Argonne to the Swiss border.[14]

The Argonne

The Argonne proved to be a barrier for both the French and Germans. In early September 1914, the German *5th Army* had moved rapidly through most of the region. The valley of the Aire could have provided it with a route for the encirclement of Verdun. On 10 September, however, all the German armies on the right wing were ordered to pull back. The Crown Prince and his chief-of-staff disagreed with the directive and appealed to the high command. After a final encounter with the French on that day, the *5th Army* began to retreat through the Argonne. At the end of the month, the *5th Army* advanced once again southwards through the Argonne trying to regain the ground it had lost in the withdrawal, but this time, the French did not yield quickly. The German troops recaptured Varennes, but they did not advance much further. The French tried to drive them from the key position of Vauquois (a butte 290m high) in one bloody engagement after the other. According to the Michelin guide to the battle published after the war, the Argonne is a hilly wooded area with no gentle slopes to prevent the infantry from easily establishing fighting positions. At the time, the 'impenetrable thickets' of this forested region could only be traversed by way of existing lanes and footpaths. The Argonne had plenty of water as numerous springs and streams ran through the clay soil that turned to mud once the rains fell. After a shower, the soldiers' trenches tended to fill with mud and most of the paths became impassable. From October 1914 onward, snipers infested the region and the crackle of rifle and machine-gun fire became almost incessant.

Once again, General Headquarters ordered the *5th Army* to go on the defensive and transferred some of its units for duty elsewhere. In the autumn of 1914, both sides dug trenches then saps leading to the opposing lines hoping to take the enemy by surprise as they quite literally emerged from the ground. They also adopted a more insidious method developed in ancient and medieval times: mining. It consisted of tunnelling until one reached a point under the enemy trench line, filling the end of the mine with explosives and detonating the charges. After the explosion, the attackers rushed to occupy and hold the crater they had created. Fighting at close quarters and dodging a hail of grenades was quite common.

Along the German front between Four-de-Paris and the Aire Valley, the French sappers were busy from January to March 1915 digging over 3,000m of tunnels and detonating fifty-two mine chambers. As time passed, the miners excavated larger mine chambers at the end of their tunnels and crammed them with ever larger amounts of explosives. The French II Corps had recaptured Four-de-Paris at the end of 1914. In January 1915, after an artillery bombardment, four French infantry regiments and the Garibaldi Legion attacked the Germans on the Bolante Plateau.[15] General Bruno von Mudra's corps handled most of the German defences in the region, and hung on tenaciously despite shortages of artillery ammunition. A 305mm Skoda battery was set up at Binarville and a second one at Apremont on each side of the Argonne. In late February 1915, during one of many bloody engagements in the Argonne, the French 9th and 10th Divisions of the V Corps attacked through the Aire Valley and tried to storm Vauquois from where the Germans directed artillery fire against the Ste Ménehould–Verdun railroad.[16] Supported by a heavy artillery bombardment, the 10th Division reached the summit and advanced across the butte where it halted in the village on the north end. However, Joffre refused to send much-needed reinforcements. Even though the fighting continued, the Germans maintained their artillery position overlooking the main rail line to Verdun. The V Corps sustained almost 27,000 casualties between mid-January and the end of March 1915 during this struggle. General Mudra received reinforcements from *5th Army* and kept the fighting going as mine warfare intensified. By May 1915, he had inflicted 8,000 additional casualties on the XXXII Corps of the 3rd Army, which held a position on the left flank of V Corps. The XXXII Corps was pushed back on a 7km front at the beginning of July.[17] The Crown Prince bragged that his four divisions had held off nine-and-a-half French divisions for most of the year. He was able to consolidate his positions during the remainder of the year. It made little difference which side had more troops in the Argonne because the terrain gave the edge to the defender. The French and the Germans continued their bloody struggle for control in the forest, but the front lines changed very little until 1918. The Germans never retook the southern section of the Argonne.

Verdun, September–December 1915

Although Verdun escaped complete isolation in September 1914, it formed a salient with only a secondary railroad connection to Bar-le-Duc for logistical support. During 1915, it became a relatively quiet front while the battle raged incessantly to the west in the Argonne. To the south of the salient, the French strove to wrest control of the Éparges Plateau from their foe and to eliminate the German salient of St Mihiel by striking at both sides of it.

In February 1915, a 420mm Mörser and a 380mm naval gun battery set up in a wood near Loison, to the southwest of Spincourt, fired upon Fort Douaumont. They were the largest weapons introduced to the Verdun Front in early 1915. The Crown Prince was impressed, even though the results were not spectacular. One round smashed through concrete protection of the 155mm gun turret, which remained in action nonetheless. The damage was minor. On 25 May, the Crown Prince climbed another observation tower in Consenvoye Woods, north of Verdun, to observe the cathedral of Verdun and French defensive positions while the 380mm naval guns fired on the military targets.

Joffre's big offensives of 1915 drained his resources and prevented him from eliminating the St Mihiel Salient or clear the Argonne even though he ordered smaller and more concentrated attacks against both. Army Group East was created in January 1915 with General Auguste Yvon Dubail at its head.[18] He ordered the first major assault against the Éparges–Combres Heights.[19] The Éparges Butte was 345m high and measured about 1,100m by 700m with a crest that extended east to west. At a point identified as 'X' on the northeast end of the crest, an observer had a clear view of the Woëvre. The French 12th Division (VI Corps) moved into

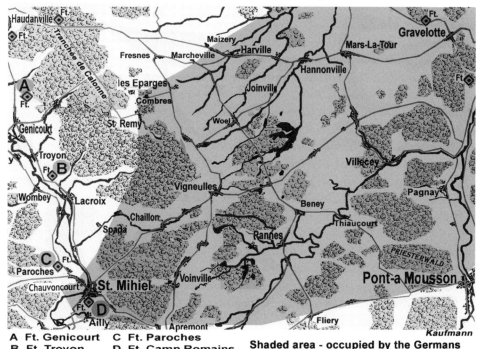

St. Mihiel Salient October 1914 to January 1916

A Ft. Genicourt   C Ft. Paroches
B Ft. Troyon   D Ft. Camp Romains   Shaded area - occupied by the Germans

position in November 1914. In January 1915, it seized the villages of Éparges and St Rémy. It left three battalions (one each from its 67th, 106th and 132nd Infantry regiments) in position around the village of Éparges below the heights. Meanwhile, the sappers dug mines into the butte. On 17 February, the French opened the assault by detonating four mines below the first German trench on the heights. The French soldiers reached the German first line only to find it abandoned. The next day, after the French had consolidated their position, the Germans responded with a counter-attack that drove them from their positions. The French counter-attacked. The fighting continued back and forth until 20 February when the French gave up after sustaining heavy losses and failing to take and hold the crest. On 18 March, the French 12th Division launched a renewed assault with an hour-long bombardment. Once again, they ejected the Germans from the first line, but not from the second. The Germans counter-attacked the next day and inflicted heavy losses on the French. On 27 March, additional French units including the 25th Chasseur Battalion joined the fray and despite a fierce battle, the Germans remained in control of the peak. During February and March, the French sustained 15,546 casualties (3,050 killed). The next encounter began on 5 April and lasted four days. This time, other divisions hit different parts of the St Mihiel Salient, which prevented the Germans from bringing additional reserves. After another heavily contested battle, the French 12th Division held the ground. General Herr, commander of VI Corps, declared it a victory, but French control of the area was incomplete since the Germans still clung to part of the heights at Point X.[20] Meanwhile, the Germans seized 4km of the French position along the Tranchée de Calonne, just west of Les Éparges.

In April 1915, as the intense struggle for Éparges continued, the French attacked as far east as Priesterwald, adjacent to Port Mousson on the Mosel in an effort to penetrate the St Mihiel Salient. The French launched another effort to clear the salient southeast of Étain against its northern end in the Woëvre. In early April, two newly formed French army corps participated in heavy fighting on the front between Maizery and Éparges–Combres. In April 1915, the French also thrust along the southwest part of the salient from Ailly-Apremont-Fliéry and both sides took heavy losses. At the end of April, the Germans, who held the salient with the *V* and *Bavarian III corps* and some reserve divisions, repulsed continued assaults on Fliéry at great expense. The French attacks of 1915 against the salient were generally costly for both sides and ended in failure. The continued pressure on the salient forced the Germans to transfer the newly formed *113th* and *121st divisions* from Sedan and St Avold as reinforcements. In July, the German *9th* and *13th Infantry divisions* repelled French attempts to retake the parts of the Tranchée de Calonne they had lost in April.[21] The rains, which had not let up since January, had turned the roads into quagmires and left the troops standing knee-deep in mud and water in the trenches. The French forced back the newly arrived German *121st Division*, which counter-attacked in the vicinity of the Priesterwald advancing up to 4km along a front of about 1.5km and taking many prisoners in early July. The fight at the Priesterwald lasted for weeks. The German defences of the St Mihiel Salient continued to be as solid as those in the Argonne were for the remainder of the war.

To the north, around Verdun, the German *5th Army* divisions saw limited action for much of 1915, while the French divisions hurled themselves against its left flank in the St Mihiel Salient and against its right flank in the Argonne. On 26 September 1915, the Crown Prince received command of an ad hoc army group that included his *5th Army* and the *3rd Army*. German intelligence identified the twenty-five French divisions opposite the three divisions of his *XVIII Reserve Corps* in the Argonne.[22] The French employed long-range artillery and aircraft to disrupt traffic behind his lines with great success. Falkenhayn sent the *5th Army* all available reserves on the Western Front, which included the *5th* and *56th divisions* and a few mixed *Landwehr* brigades. He also received the *X Corps* from the Eastern Front. The *VIII Corps* of the *3rd Army* was suffering heavily from constant French attacks. However, the attacking units sustained equally heavy losses. This combat was part of Joffre's second offensive in Champagne in 1915 and the prize was the Tahure Butte, which was eventually captured by Pétain's 2nd Army's XVI Corps. Crown Prince Wilhelm, with the German *3rd Army* under his command, had his first engagement with the French general whom he would face at Verdun in 1916. The fighting for the heights continued throughout the month. On 14 October, Joffre ordered a halt to the offensive, and four days earlier Falkenhayn had ordered the Crown Prince's two armies to go on the defensive.

In November 1915, the Crown Prince inspected the defences of the *3rd Army* and the Argonne. He reported the creation of a third trench line about 200m behind the first line near Binarville. His troops built the 'Crown Prince Fort', which he described as a model of field fortifications. It was a completely self-sustaining strongpoint surrounded by barbed wire entanglements 50m thick. A full-strength company that occupied the position had concrete shelters situated up to 5m underground to protect it from enemy shells. Sanitary conditions were good. The troops in the strongpoint had a field of fire to the front and flanks of up to 800m in clear weather. Several outposts provided additional security for the numerous occasions when fog covered the area. Like their comrades in the Argonne, the prince's soldiers prepared for the next winter along the front. As the year ended, the *5th Army* began to prepare for the next battle, the longest of the war.

Crown Prince Wilhelm did not fail to notice the changes warfare had undergone during 1915. The use of aircraft increased in the first year of the war. In the early morning of 3 June 1915, Stenay, where his headquarters were located, was bombed by about forty enemy aircraft flying in waves. They hit a barracks used as a hospital since no one had yet realized the need for marking such locations with a red cross. Other bombs landed in the market place killing some locals. The prince claimed that his own headquarters had been the target of 'bombs, grenades, and bundles of steel arrows'.[*] The French dropped 178 bombs in one of the first aerial attacks on an army headquarters. However, cellars offered adequate protection, wrote the prince, and the two-dozen or so casualties could be attributed to curiosity and foolhardiness.

---

[*] William, *My War Experiences*, p. 144.

There was not much he could do about the raid except order the 380mm naval guns near Loison to bombard a French headquarters in Verdun in retaliation.

It became obvious to the Crown Prince and every other officer on either side that there was a need for anti-aircraft weapons since friendly aircraft could only attack enemy planes if they were in the vicinity at the time of a raid.[23] The threat presented by aircraft was only beginning to be felt in 1915 near the front because most bombing raids had been directed at targets such as air bases, factories and cities. In 1915, aircraft engaged in long-distance reconnaissance as well as tactical missions. Scouting and observation aircraft became more effective in coordinating artillery fire, but they had not yet replaced the tethered balloons. In March 1915, the British introduced aerial photo mosaics to map enemy trenches. Air power played a significant role in the coming battle for Verdun.

Prelude to 1916

In December 1916, as winter set in after a year-and-a-half of bloody and largely indecisive warfare in the West, both sides began planning their strategies. Joffre tried to break the deadlock in 1915 by launching repeated offensives in Artois and Champagne with the support of the British army in the hope of destroying the German salient in northern France. During these failed operations and other battles between August 1914 and the end of December 1915, almost 16,000 French officers and 565,000 soldiers were killed and about 400,000 men, including over 6,000 officers, went missing in action. Many of the missing men may have deserted, become separated from their units, been taken prisoner or been blown to pieces leaving little to identify them. There were, in addition, 935,000 wounded, but this number may include soldiers with multiple injuries. This gave a total casualty list of 1,916,000 men.[24] In August 1914, The French army had mobilized approximately 3,500,000 men, 1,865,000 of which served in combat units.[25] The government called additional men to the colours during that first year-and-a-half. The numbers show that in order to maintain the 1914 troop levels, the French army had to induct as many men as they had mobilized in August 1914 because of the casualties incurred. Joffre had to rethink his strategy.[26]

Not known as a great strategist, the grandfatherly Joffre commanded, nonetheless, the affection of his troops. There was opposition to him among some of the French generals, and even the government was concerned about Joffre's strategy and tactics that had failed to remove the Germanic enemy from French territory and caused massive casualties. The burden of these results, however, was not totally his. He had wanted the government to acquire more heavy artillery before the war instead of relying on the French '75' for the needs of the field army. These rapid-firing guns, which had a flat trajectory, could only dominate a relatively level battlefield with no obstructions to block a direct line of sight or trenches to hide the enemy. The army had few indirect-fire weapons like howitzers, and little heavy artillery. In addition, they went to war, as did many nations, with only enough artillery ammunition for a few days of intense combat since the belligerents expected a short war. In August 1915, Joffre opted for a short-term fix. He ordered fortress commanders strip their

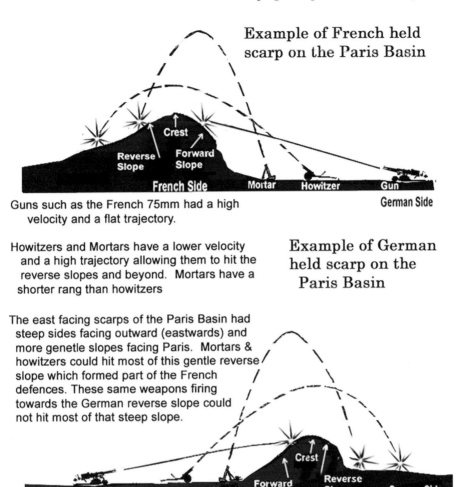

Example of French held scarp on the Paris Basin

Crest

Reverse Slope · Forward Slope

French Side · Mortar · Howitzer · Gun · German Side

Guns such as the French 75mm had a high velocity and a flat trajectory.

Howitzers and Mortars have a lower velocity and a high trajectory allowing them to hit the reverse slopes and beyond. Mortars have a shorter rang than howitzers

Example of German held scarp on the Paris Basin

The east facing scarps of the Paris Basin had steep sides facing outward (eastwards) and more genetle slopes facing Paris. Mortars & howitzers could hit most of this gentle reverse slope which formed part of the French defences. These same weapons firing towards the German reverse slope could not hit most of that steep slope.

Forward Slope · Crest · Reverse Slope

French Side · Gun · Howitzer · Mortar · German Side

Artillery trajectories and reverse slope defences.

forts of artillery and ammunition. This allowed for the creation of new batteries of heavy artillery, although these consisted of old 120mm and 155mm guns that lacked the modern braking system of the '75' and could fire only about one round a minute since their recoil resulted in the gun having to be realigned. The army also created a few new batteries of 75mm guns taken from the forts.[27] The value of these guns in Joffre's last failed offensive of 1915 in Champagne is debatable. The French leaders realized that elan alone would not win battles as the army learned new tactics, while paying a high price in casualties. General Pétain, one of Joffre's few successful generals, had shown that a methodical attack was best, but it would not produce the kind of breakthrough that would drive the enemy back quickly. Joffre and his British counterpart mapped out their strategy for 1916. It appeared to be more of the same. The plan was for a massive coordinated assault by the French and British armies along the Somme. If the Russians could recover from the disasters they had suffered on the Eastern Front in 1915, Joffre hoped they would launch a new offensive to maintain the pressure on their enemies.

The Germans had their own plans for France in 1916. General von Falkenhayn had to fight his own war against those that despised him for being a young upstart hoisted into the position of power in 1914 when he replaced von Moltke. He could not save the situation in 1914 as the Schlieffen Plan came apart. He did manage to secure the Western Front so that in 1915, when he gave in to the 'Easterners' and allowed the Eastern Front to take precedence, he was able to withstand all Allied assaults in the West and usually regain lost ground. Hindenburg, Ludendorff and Mackensen had achieved a number of successes in 1915, occupied Poland and driven the Russians back towards Riga and Brest-Litovsk. Still, as Falkenhayn had anticipated, the Russians, even after suffering crushing defeats, used the vastness of their empire to parry the German and Austrian assaults. Before winter set in, Falkenhayn had redirected the effort in the East to eliminating Serbia and opening a direct route to the Turkish Empire. Bulgaria's entry into the war helped defeat Serbia and keep Rumania neutral. Despite all this, the Russians had not surrendered, and the Austrians still had to deal with the Italians. The war would continue with Germany locked in a stalemate in the West, while the Western Allies continued to keep the war going and buoy up the Russians and Italians. There would be no German victory unless he could find a way to knock France and Great Britain out of the war. In December 1915, while Joffre worked on his plans for 1916, Falkenhayn did the same. Like Joffre in 1914 and 1915, Falkenhayn sought a knockout blow that would end the war.

Falkenhayn had a few options to examine:

1. Resume a new offensive in the East and continue to maintain a stalemate on the Western Front with minimum forces.
2. Shift additional German forces into Austria-Hungary and help their ally win a decisive victory against Italy.
3. Reinforce the Turks and eliminate the remaining Allies in the Balkans.
4. Launch a decisive action on the Western Front.

The leaves had fallen twice since August 1914 and the expected short war had become a never-ending bloodbath with no end in sight. All sides were suffering from some form of economic problems as the war dragged on. Food shortages for the Central Powers were far worse than for the Entente. The belligerents had to deal with a dearth of manpower as they called up more men. Women had to fill the gaps in manpower to maintain the economy. Medical services had not been prepared in 1914 for the massive amount of casualties they received. No one had prepared for this type of war and Falkenhayn was determined to end it.

Falkenhayn concluded that the first option of resuming an offensive in the East would not result in a decisive victory since the Russians would trade space for time drawing their opponent deeper into Russia. This would continue to widen the front and require more divisions and logistical support.[28] The Italian leadership proved itself incompetent, suffering massive losses in the battles of the Isonzo. Fighting in the mountainous terrain did not offer prospects for a quick victory, but even the collapse of Italy would not alter the situation on the Western or the Eastern fronts drastically enough to force the Allies to the peace table. Helping the Turks was simply a sideshow in which the Allies had already committed a number of troops with disappointing results in 1915. The forces of the Entente had failed at Gallipoli, and those in Salonika, sent to rescue the Serbs, offered no threat. The Turkish Minister of War, Enver Pasha, had led an invasion of the Caucasus region and suffered a major defeat at Sarikamish in January 1915. Forced to retreat, the Turkish forces sent to the Caucasus Front spent most of the year licking their wounds. A British threat from the south was checked when the Turks besieged a major British force in Mesopotamia at Kut at the beginning of December 1915. The only possible decisive action for the Turks was an assault on the Suez Canal. The British prepared the defences of the canal area in 1915 while allowing the Turks to occupy the Sinai. The difficult terrain and the distances would have limited any substantial German support beyond despatching advisors.[29] Victory in the Middle East or another effort on the Russian front offered no hope of bringing the Allies to their knees.

Falkenhayn concluded that only a decisive blow in the West could end the war. He also decided that he had to commit veteran troops to the Western Front since trench warfare required more experienced soldiers than the more fluid Eastern Front. The Germans usually established a belt of three lines of trenches. In 1915, the first line, which was most vulnerable to artillery bombardment, was manned sparingly. The troops were concentrated in the second and third lines from where they could counter-attack before the enemy soldiers could haul the artillery needed to support the assault on the next line of trenches through no-man's-land. Both sides ended up creating complex and extensive trench systems. The question that faced Falkenhayn was how to outperform the French in the attack. Falkenhayn had no illusions about breaking through to the 'green fields beyond' and return to a war of manoeuvre in the West.[30] He believed that his only option was to break the enemy's will to resist.

Falkenhayn summarized the situation in a letter to the Kaiser in December 1915:[*]

France has been weakened almost to the limits of endurance, both in a military and economic sense[31] – the latter by the permanent loss of the coalfields in the northeast of the country. The Russian armies have not been completely overthrown, but their offensive powers have been so shattered that she can never revive in anything like her old strength. The army of Serbia can be considered as destroyed. Italy has no doubt realized that she cannot reckon on the realization of her brigand's ambitions within measurable time and would therefore probably be only too glad to be able to liquidate her adventure in any way that would save her face.

… the chief among them cannot be passed over, for it is the enormous hold which England still has on her allies.

It is true that we have succeeded in shaking England severely – the best proof of that is her imminent adoption of universal military service. *But that is also a proof of the sacrifices England is prepared to make to attain her end – the permanent*

---

[*] Falkenhayn, *General Headquarters*, pp. 209–18.

elimination of what seems to her the most dangerous rival.... Germany can expect no mercy from this enemy, so long as he still retains the slightest hope of achieving his object. Any attempt at an understanding which Germany might make would only strengthen England's will to war as ... she would take it as a sign that Germany's resolution was weakening.

[*England*] *is obviously staking everything on a war of exhaustion.* We have not been able to shatter her belief that it will bring Germany to her knees and that belief gives the enemy the strength to fight on and keep on whipping their team together.

What we have to do is to dispel that illusion.

With that end in view, *it will not, in the long run, be enough for us merely to stand on the defensive.... Our enemies, thanks to their superiority in men and material, are increasing their resources much more than we are. If that process continues a moment must come when the balance of numbers itself will deprive Germany of all remaining hope. The power of our allies to hold out is restricted, while our own is not unlimited.* It is possible that next winter ... will bring food crises, and the social and political crises that always follow them, among the members of our alliance, if there has been no decision by then.... there is no time to lose ...

He continued, stating that Germany could not inflict a defeat upon the English on their home island since it was beyond the reach of the navy. Instead, the Germans must strike 'only against one of the continental theatres where England is fighting'. Thus:

We must rule out enterprises in the East.... Victories at Salonica, the Suez Canal, or in Mesopotamia can only help us in so far as they intensify the doubts about England's invulnerability.... Defeats in the East could do us palpable harm among our allies ...

In Flanders ... the state of the ground prevents any far-reaching operations until the middle of the Spring. South of that point [the Loretto Ridge] commanders consider that about 30 divisions would be required. Yet it is impossible for us to concentrate those forces on one part of our front. Even, as was planned, we collected a few more divisions from the German sectors in Macedonia and Galicia, in violation of our military conviction, as well as common prudence, the total reserve in France would still amount to little more than 25 or 25 divisions. When all these are concentrated for the one operation all other fronts will have been drained of reserves to the last man.

The document reveals Falkenhayn's logic for deciding on making 1916 the year of decision on the Western Front. This may be why he designated the operation name as 'Judgement'. The document also shows that he did not intend to use recognized methods to conduct this campaign:

As a rule the modern purely frontal battle means a slow start. Moreover, *the lessons to be deduced from the failure of our enemies' mass attacks are decisive against any imitation of their battle methods. Attempts at a mass breakthrough, even with an extreme accumulation of men and material, cannot be regarded as holding out prospects of success against a well armed enemy, whose moral is sound and who is not seriously inferior in numbers. The defender has usually succeeded in closing the gaps. This is easy enough for him if he decides to withdraw voluntarily, and it is hardly possible to stop him doing so. The salient thus made, enormously exposed to the effects of flanking fire, threaten [sic] to become a mere slaughter-house.* The technical difficulties of directing and supplying the masses bottled up in them are so great as to seem practically insurmountable.

In the document, he goes on to explain that an attempt to assault the British sector could only have the objective of driving the English from the Continent. Even if the German army succeeded, he felt that the British would not give up nor could he assemble enough troops to launch a follow-up assault on the French. The only way to hurt the British, in his opinion, was unrestricted U-boat warfare to bring famine to the island. On a positive note, he wrote, Italy's 'internal conditions will soon make her further active participation in the war impossible …', assuming Austrian successes continued. As for Russia, he claimed, all intelligence reports showed rapidly increasing domestic difficulties and internal problems might take the Russians out of the war. An offensive in the East would not be possible before April and he simply believed that would only put a strain on German resources and it might not bring an end to Russian resistance. Thus, he concluded, a decisive action in France was the solution:

The strain on France has almost reached the breaking-point…. If we succeeded in opening the eyes of her people to the fact that in a military sense they have nothing more to hope for, that breaking-point would be reached and England's best sword knocked out of her hand. To achieve that object the uncertain method of a mass break-through, in any case beyond our means, is unnecessary. We can probably do enough for our purposes with limited resources. *Within our reach behind the French sector of the Western front there are objectives for the retention of which the French General Staff would be compelled to throw in every man they have. If they do so the forces of France will bleed to death – as there can be no question of a voluntary withdrawal – whether we reach our goal or not. If they do not do so, and we reach our objectives, the moral effect on France will be enormous. For an operation, limited to a narrow front Germany will not be compelled to spend herself so completely that all other fronts are practically drained….* The objectives of which I am speaking now are Belfort and Verdun.[32]

Falkenhayn went on to explain that he chose Verdun because it was so close to the German railway system and a possible French assault from Verdun could also make the entire German front in the West untenable.

It is clear that Falkenhayn understood that he was no more likely to break the stalemate on the Western Front than the Allies had done in 1915. If Germany was to win the war, it had to be in the West and soon. He narrowed down possible objectives in the West to either Verdun or Belfort because British and French forces between Flanders and Champagne were too strong. Verdun had already been partially isolated during the 1914 campaign, which allowed the Germans to cut the rail line that passed through St Mihiel. In the Argonne, from the Vauquois area, German artillery interdicted the main rail line to Verdun from Paris. The question was whether the French would be willing to sacrifice their army to hold the city, which was reputed to be their strongest fortress. Falkenhayn did not know that Joffre initially had considered pulling back his forces from Verdun.[33]

Any attack in the West by the Anglo-French forces or the German army involved frontal assaults on a tactical level with a continuous trench system stretching from the North Sea to Switzerland. An offensive action involved either a broad front or a narrow front. With a broad front, the defender could not be certain where the actual main thrusts would take place and had to hold back his reserves and be careful not to commit them to counter-attacking against a divisionary thrust. The main problem was that before 1915 the French did not have enough heavy artillery for sufficient coverage of all sectors of a broad front making it easy to identify their point of attack. Pétain had already proclaimed, as did others, that 'Artillery kills' and that 'Artillery conquers, infantry occupies'. The French lacked sufficient artillery to achieve this on a broad front in 1915. The alternative was a narrow front where artillery could be concentrated, but that also revealed the location of the main assault to the enemy allowing him to send in his reserves. This might work well for the methodical attack, but that would not lead to a massive breakthrough. Once taking the enemy's first trench line, troops had to clear both flanks to prevent enemy enfilading fire into the line of advance. Meanwhile, advancing troops had to haul field artillery across no-man's-land, already obstructed by shell craters, wire obstacles and often muddy ground. The French and Germans had already learned that trying to strike the second trench line before artillery had moved forward and to eliminate the remaining resistance points with machine guns often resulted in failure since this was the time when the defender counter-attacked. Falkenhayn realized this, but he also intended to employ new methods, weapons and tactics developed during 1915 that would help overcome these problems, or at least he hoped so. He planned to attack on a narrow front, but have his artillery lay down fire on a broad front to prevent the French from guessing from where he would launch the assault.

Beginning in 1915, the Germans worked on developing poison gas and the flamethrower. After an unsuccessful attempt to use chlorine gas on the Eastern Front in early 1915, they employed gas canisters with limited success at Ypres in April of that year.[34] Both sides later utilized this deadly weapon and worked on developing counter-measures such as adequate gas masks. The German mask issued in the West from September 1915 until the end of the year included a face piece with a metal drum that held a filter. It was carried in a canvas bag that contained two additional screw-on replacement filters. The Germans called it a *Linienmaske* since it was made of a

GAS MASKS & MACHINE GUNS

1915

French Tambute Gas Mask

French Hotchkiss 8-mm Machine Gun

German Linensmaske

German Heavy MG 7.92-mm Maschinengewehr 08

CHAUCHAT
Mle 1915
8-mm

French Light MG

grey, rubberized cotton, although the official name was *Gummimaske* (rubber mask). The mask was effective against chlorine and tear gas. On 15 December 1915, the Germans tested the new phosgene gas, estimated to be almost ten times more deadly than chlorine, at Ypres by creating a gas cloud from cylinders. The British respirators designed only to deal with chlorine proved effective enough. The Germans only sent out patrols in an attempt to evaluate the results.[35] The Germans had used the new gas on a couple of other occasions in France before December. As a result, the French equipped most of their troops by February 1916 with the new Tambute masks.[36] The Germans lost the element of surprise with their early use of phosgene. Using both poison and tear gas as part of an assault forced the enemy to don their uncomfortable masks which limited their ability to see and engage the Germans.[37] Since the Allied masks resisted the German gas attacks, the only alternative was to increase the duration of gas clouds until the filters in the French masks needed replacing. In addition, the Allies had decided to add phosgene gas to their assortment while the German masks were still not yet effective against it. The French started using phosgene at Verdun early in the campaign and this resulted in the Germans having to improve their own masks. The use of gas canisters was still the main method of deployment of gas, but the French had already initiated tests with 75mm gas rounds and put them in use early in the battle. This also led to the Germans developing their own gas shells making it possible to put the gas right on target.

The flamethrower could eliminate enemy strongpoints and serve as a terror weapon. Developed in late 1914, the Germans first employed this weapon on 26 February 1915 against the French at Malancourt and then against the British near Ypres at the end of July. Neither effort had remarkable success. Major Bernhard Reddeman and Richard Fiedler developed a two–man portable version that had a range of less than 20m and sufficient fuel for less than a 2-minute blast.[38] The weapon's igniter turned the fuel into flame as it passed out of the nozzle. One man carried the fuel tank on his back and another held and aimed the hose that ignited and sprayed the liquid flame. A large stationary model had a range of about 40m and longer burn time. Their effect on the defenders was terrifying. Reddemenn commanded the first flamethrower unit. It included forty-eight pioneers with twelve small hand-pumped portable flamethrowers and two large stationary ones.[39] Before the flamethrower, the most effective way to take out an enemy strongpoint was with teams that included grenadiers carrying a sack of hand grenades and troops with rifle grenade launchers. Like the flamethrower team, they had to get close to the target. The flamethrower teams became targets of revenge because of the demoralizing effect of their weapon.

At Verdun in 1916, artillery finally took precedence over French infantry as the most important combat arm. The French used older weapons, many stripped from the forts, to compensate for the deficiency in heavy artillery pieces. Both sides had continued to develop new ways of employing artillery. In 1915, trench mortars and the big guns had rained death over the battlefields of Western Europe. The trenches offered the only protection and neutralized the effects of direct-fire weapons like the French '75'. However, they became death traps when they were pounded by howitzers and mortars, which were in plentiful supply in the German army early in the war. In 1915, only the Germans had a good mix of artillery but in the West, it mainly performed in a defensive role. The infantry commanders had learned to keep their first line lightly manned to reduce casualties during enemy bombardment. When that line fell, they could launch a counter-attack from the second line with the support of their own artillery.

Until 1916, only ammunition and weapon shortages had limited the scale of bombardments. The French lacked indirect-fire weapons during those years and could not effectively breach barbed wire barriers or neutralize enemy trenches. The British introduced the 'hurricane bombardment' to the Western Front at Neuve Chapelle in March 1915. This was a short and heavy bombardment designed to break up enemy defences. It allowed the British infantry to achieve surprise and advance rapidly before the Germans had time send in reserves. This method worked well, except in places where the shelling failed to break up barbed wire obstacles. When ammunition was available, the British and French preferred prolonged bombardments that lasted for many hours or days. This alerted the Germans to the coming assault and gave them time to prepare. In 1915, the French began producing heavier weapons and a greater number of indirect-fire guns like mortars since the '75' was almost useless in bombarding trenches.[40] In 1915, the French took one major step forward by founding schools for the instruction of artillery officers. In late November 1915, the French army also issued a new doctrine for the artillery that called for using counter-battery fire rather than concentrating on enemy infantry. Unfortunately, many artillery officers ignored this. Pétain always emphasized the use of artillery for properly supporting his troops. Paul Strong and Sanders Marble credit Pétain with the idea of using meteorological data, such as air pressure, to improve firing accuracy and of having gunners practise pre-registered fire as well as maintaining a close liaison between the infantry and artillery.[*] Since he considered it a form of siege warfare, Pétain planned his operations accordingly – methodically.[41] During the Champagne Offensive in September 1915, he moved his artillery as far forward as possible in order to give maximum support to his infantry during its advance to and past the first enemy trench. Once that goal was reached, he moved it forward to provide additional protection to the soldiers who moved against the next enemy position. In 1915, Nivelle went a step further as he came up with the creeping or rolling barrage. This prevented the enemy troops from leaving their shelters and taking up firing positions in their trenches after the barrage lifted but the infantry was still negotiating no-man's-land. With the creeping barrage, the infantry followed the line of exploding shells at a distance of about 80m or more as it moved forward. The barrage could lift after hitting the enemy trench line or could continue to advance striking possible strongpoints beyond the trench line. It could also block the approach of enemy reserves from the second trench line. This required close coordination between the infantry and artillery commanders since the time schedule had to be detailed and accurate. The box barrage gave flanking protection to the advancing troops when it laid down fire on three sides.[42] Signal rockets or flares helped control the artillery fire, but during the actual bombardment, they were often difficult to see.

During an Allied assault, the German long-range guns served in counter-battery fire, while the Allies generally tended to commit their guns to neutralizing the enemy infantry. Both sides continued to improve coordination for rolling barrages behind which friendly troops could advance. In one standard method, the barrage was often repeated several times to increase enemy casualties and produce false alarms. This caused the defenders to stay in their shelters longer, giving the assaulting infantry more time to reach the first line. By 1916, both sides acquired sufficient types of weapons – field artillery, trench mortars and heavy (siege) artillery – to give artillery a dominant role on the Verdun battlefield.

---

[*]   Paul Strong and Sanders Marble, *Artillery in the Great War* (Barnsley: Pen & Sword, 2011), p. 63.

Tactics had drastically changed since the beginning of the war. No longer did battalions assemble for mass regimental assaults. The infantry company and platoon had become the main manoeuvre elements for holding strongpoints and penetrating enemy lines. That did not prevent the use of massed regimental and battalion attacks. Captain André Laffargue produced a pamphlet for the French army entitled '*Étude sur l'attaque dans la période actuelle de la guerre*' in which he recommended the use of small units of specially trained assault troops whose efforts were coordinated with artillery support to breach an enemy defensive position.[43] He impressed Ferdinand Foch who reassigned him to the general staff where he was ignored. It is claimed that the Germans found a copy of Laffargue's pamphlet, which inspired then to create their own assault units and develop infiltration tactics.[44] Laffargue also accurately summed up most French offensives of the first fourteen months of the war:

> The characteristic of this attack is that it is not progressive but is an assault of a single rush; it must be accomplished in one day, as otherwise the enemy reforms, and the defense, with terrible engines of sudden destruction, will later recover its supremacy over the attack, which cannot quickly enough regain the mastery of this consuming fire. The whole series of frightful defences cannot be nibbled at successively; they must be swallowed whole at one stroke with one decision.[*]

He recognized that in these attacks that the troops employed in the assault were 'far from being assaulting troops'. Having taken part in these mass assaults for nine months, he claimed he had been 'part of the human canister', or, as others would say, 'cannon fodder'. He argued that assault troops needed well-established cohesion and special training. The men operating in the platoons and squads must work as a team. Extended duty in the trenches did produce stablility among small groups, but combat exercises and traditional training were needed behind the lines to achieve unit cohesion at battalion level. Serving too long in the trenches 'has a tendency to kill the offensive spirit of the troops'. He stated, 'A unit that has recently made a bloody effort is incapable of delivering a furious and unlimited assault.' He wrote that the troops should be given activities that kept them active both when out of the line and in the trenches. In the pamphlet, he describes his ideal method of attack, but makes no mention of 'infiltration' and only discusses bypassing certain strongpoints. Nor does he discuss the actual creation of special shock troops, although he alludes to the fact that not every soldier in the line can be considered qualified as an assault trooper. Before continuing the advance on the second enemy trench line, machine guns and light artillery are supposed to have followed the infantry into the first line.

In March 1915, the German High Command authorized the *VIII Corps* to create a detachment for testing experimental weapons and new tactics to overcome the deadlock on the Western Front. Major Calsow from *Pioneer Battalion 18* received command of

---

[*] André Laffargue, 'The Attack in Trench Warfare', *Infantry Journal* (Washington, DC: The US Infantry Association, 1916), p. 5.

this first unit of 'shock troops'. This test unit consisted of two pioneer companies and a detachment of twenty specially designed 37mm Krupp Sturmkannone. These guns had overhead shields and the troops could easily manhandle them. The unit, known as *Assault Section Calsow*, first went into action near the Loretto Ridge (northwest of Arras) where it took heavy losses partially because the awkward gun shields drew enemy fire. Next, the unit went to *Army Detachment Gaede* in the Vosges. The Sturmkannone proved impractical and a liability for those assigned to it. Captain Willy E. Rohr, from a Guards Rifle battalion, took over the unit and reorganized it in August. Modified captured Russian 76.2mm field guns replaced the Sturmkannone. The detachment's number of 'storm troopers' increased for operations in the Vosges the week of Christmas 1915 where it successfully took a key hill. Rohr's assault battalion was reassigned to the *5th Army* for the Verdun Offensive of 1916. In May 1916, the High Command ordered each army in the West to send six officers and NCOs to Rohr's battalion for training. It was not until October 1916 that orders arrived for all armies in the West to form a battalion of *Stosstruppen* (shock troops). Over a year earlier, many regiments had already formed their own storm-troop units ranging from platoon to company size. Thus, during 1916 more *Sturm* battalions formed with two to three shock-troop companies, a machine-gun company, a trench-mortar company and a flamethrower detachment. In 1916, these units received the first issue of new steel helmets and other equipment. They played an important role at Verdun.

The *Stosstruppen* carried a special assault pack instead of the normal infantry backpack, a canteen and a greatcoat. They also carried a bayonet and cartridge pouches, a haversack attached to their belt containing eating utensils, a canister with filters for a gas mask and an entrenching tool or wire cutters. Most of them were also armed with grenades, especially the famous M1915 stock grenade with fuses of 3, 5 or 7 seconds, or a percussion fuse that detonated on contact with a hard surface. By mid-1916, they were issued with a new 'egg grenade' that could be thrown up to 50m with a 5-second fuse. Many of these assault troops carried a bag of grenades and slung their rifle over their back during an assault. Some troops carried shovels to use when occupying an enemy position. Since they often advanced behind a creeping barrage, they often had their gas masks on or at the ready. The assault parties also received the Danish-manufactured Madsen 7.92mm light machine gun to provide fire support when they advanced.[45] Some assault units included flamethrower teams and a trench-mortar unit. They formed the advance force for an assault and had the weapons needed to breach the enemy trenches and isolate strongpoints.

Joffre's 1915 strategy of 'nibbling at the enemy' was over. He planned instead for a massive offensive against the face of the German salient in northern France, but Falkenhayn's Verdun Offensive would spoil his plans.

Why Verdun?

General von Falkenhayn had a choice of two fortress areas for the site of his great offensive. The question is why he would select a fortress zone over another section of the Western Front. He knew the French and British had concentrated their forces between Champagne and the coast. In addition, previous major Allied efforts on that front in 1915 had demonstrated that minimal German forces were sufficient to hold them in check. Even if the fortress zones had a smaller concentration of French troops, they could easily fend off a German assault long enough for reserves to reach them by rail. If he was aiming for a simple battle of attrition, he could have achieved it at many other points along the front if he launched an offensive as ineffective as those of Allies had been. It is possible that, like the French high command, he believed that the forts were mere shell traps and would fall easily. He may have also been aware that the French had largely stripped and abandoned their forts.

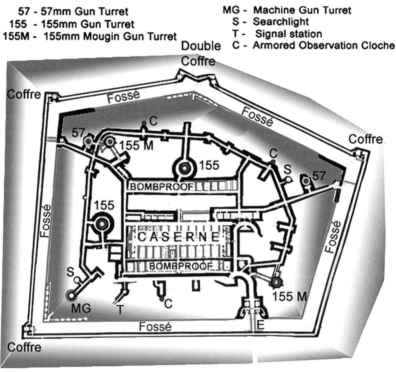

57 - 57mm Gun Turret
155 - 155mm Gun Turret
155M - 155mm Mougin Gun Turret

MG - Machine Gun Turret
S - Searchlight
T - Signal station
C - Armored Observation Cloche

FORT MANONVILLER

Note: **Iron grille fence**

German Demolitions

Fort Manonviller with photographs showing destruction caused by German demolitions after the capture of the fort. Also, detail of the iron grille fence of the same type used around other forts.

The record for forts on the Eastern as well as the Western fronts was not good. The Liège forts were the first to face the German juggernaut. Fortress Liège fell quickly because the intervals between its forts had inadequate defences. In addition, these concrete forts were not well built. Unlike most French and Germans forts, the forts built by Belgian General Brialmont had not been made of reinforced concrete.[46] Supposedly built to resist 210mm-calibre weapons, they were unable to withstand weapons of that calibre, much less the Austrian 305mm and German 420mm howitzers. Despite these and other problems, those forts did impose a small and unexpected delay on the German invasion plan. The Belgian forts of Namur and Antwerp suffered a similar fate. The French frontier forts a Maubeuge and other border locations also fell quickly, but in their case the reason was significant downgrading that had occurred well before the war. Fort Manonviller, a relatively modern but isolated fort of the Charmes Gap, also fell in 1914.

Even though it was considered 'modern', Fort Manonviller had been built a few years before Fort Douaumont. It had been updated with two Mougin Mle 1876 turrets (two guns each) shortly after its construction in the 1880s. Like other French forts, it underwent further modernization in the 1890s. In 1890, the army removed its two-dozen 120mm and 155mm guns and its old 220mm and 270mm mortars from the ramparts. In 1892, counterscarp casemates replaced its caponiers. In 1906, the fort received additional turrets that included two Galopin turrets Mle 1890 (each with two 155L guns), two turrets for rapid-fire 57mm guns, a GF3 machine-gun turret, two searchlight turrets and nine observation cloches. Thus, on the eve of the war, the fort had substantial firepower. On mobilization, its garrison numbered almost 800 men including 2 infantry companies and an artillery battery. On 11 August 1914, the fort's turret artillery supported a chasseur battalion in a nearby forest. On 21 August, units of the French 2nd Army were seen retreating after their failed offensive. German troops surrounded the fort by the morning of 24 August and the bombardment began the next day. The enemy artillery, which consisted of 210mm and 305mm Mörser, caused serious damage to the fort.[47] One of the Mougin turrets was jammed and could not retract. The big guns damaged parts of the kitchen facilities. In the afternoon, the Germans cut the underground telephone cable to Toul. On 26 August 1914, the German artillery inflicted additional damage knocking out a Galopin 155L turret. A 57mm gun turret was damaged and incapable of rotating. The Germans emplaced a 420mm Big Bertha that went into action the next day. The bombardment of 27 August brought more problems as toxic fumes from exploding shells spread through the fort. That evening, the fort surrendered. The Germans had bombarded the fort for 54 hours using over 5,800 heavy rounds from 150mm to 420mm and over 10,000 smaller calibre rounds. However, the fort's 155L Galopin turret and a 57mm gun turret were still serviceable. The concrete casemates and caserne had not suffered much damage although shells had severely damaged one counterscarp casemate. The garrison suffered only thirty-four casualties including four killed. Over 150 men were affected by toxic fumes from the explosives. Soon after they occupied the fort, the Germans went about destroying parts of it before they departed on 12 September. The French reoccupied the position on 13 September, but they could not readily distinguish the battle damage from the post-battle German demolitions, so the high command was not aware that the fort had continued to function before the surrender. Naturally, the Germans were aware of the fact that the fort had been still in relatively good condition when it had surrendered. Their demolitions prevented the French from realizing that their forts had resisted better than the Belgian forts.

The record for forts on the Eastern Front was dismal. The first fortress to face the test of battle was Przemyśl when the Austro-Hungarian forces reeled back from their premature 1914 offensive and the Russians surrounded the fortress. Hyped as the 'Verdun of the East' by some writers after the war, the fortress simply achieved little more than sacrificing a large number of Austrian troops. The fortress supposedly protected the Carpathian passes and occupied the main railway crossings of the San River, but in reality it defended very little of importance. At best, it anchored a defensive line that the Russians blew by, even after the garrison attacked the Russian flank on 21 September allowing the garrisons of Radom and Jarolsaw to escape. Over 100,000 troops held the fortress.[48] The defenders had dug about 50km (30 miles) of trenches to link all the forts and could hold out against several divisions of the 3rd Russian Army.[49] On 26 September, the Russians encircled the fortress and on 5 October began a bombardment, although they lacked heavy artillery. This culminated on 7 October with an assault against Fort I/1 Łysiczka. The Russians advanced the 500m and fought their way into the fort where Austrian forces trapped many and forced the survivors to surrender. Other attacks were focused on forts XIV Hurko, XV Borek, I/2–I/6 and IV Optyn and cost the Russians 10,000 casualties. On 8 October, the 3rd Army commander launched assaults against forts Xa Pruchnicka Droga, XIa Cegielnia, XI Dunkowiczki and XII Żurawica, but all these efforts failed on the glacis of these forts on the northern sector.[50] One source, of doubtful reliability, claimed the Russians suffered 40,000 casualties in all these failed attacks. Meanwhile, only two weeks after the first siege, an Austrian offensive began and that was one reason the Russian 3rd Army commander had launched those failed attacks. The day after the last of the assaults, 9 October, the Austrian relief force arrived from the Dukla Pass to break the siege. The Russians, unable to stop the advance, pulled back across the San River. The relieving forces were met with a jubilant celebration, but proceeded to use up some of the fortresses supplies. When Hindenburg called off his failed offensive in Russian Poland at the beginning of November 1914, the Austrian forces in Galicia moved back from the San River Line allowing Russians forces to return and again isolate Przemyśl by 8 November 1914. The fortress had received 128 trainloads to resupply its stocks before the Austrians retreated. Before the second siege began, Conrad chose to order the civilian population to evacuate the area, although he decided to maintain the garrison.

The Russian commander hesitated from launching attacks during the siege. The garrison sortied several times in November but failed to reach the relief forces. Conrad attempted more relief efforts in December, but the arrival of winter snows further complicated these attempts. On 15 December 30,000 troops inside the fortress attacked in a southwesterly direction hoping to break the Russian ring. The Austrian force penetrated no further than 25km and another relief force was

Russian attack on Fort Siedliska, Przemyśl.

a further 45km away in the Dukla Pass. On 19 December, the Russians pushed the Austrians back into Przemyśl and captured several positions. Three days of Austrian counter-attacks failed to retake the lost positions. The Russian 11th Army had taken over the siege operations from 3rd Army, but launched no further ground assaults and allowed their artillery to do the work. Conrad sent the Austrian *2nd* and *3rd armies* on another rescue mission in January 1915, but the last 2 weeks of the month resulted in 89,000 casualties or half its strength after the troops struggled through deep snow. The garrison attempted another break-out on 1 February, but again the Russians drove them back. Meanwhile, the Austrians attempted to fly in supplies with some of the primitive aircraft available at the time. They also used the aircraft to deliver mail.[51] Conrad's final attempt came at the end of February 1915 with *2nd Army*, *Südarmee* (a small German army sent to bolster the Austrian armies) and *3rd Army* with another 46,000 men lost. His bid to recapture the prestigious fortress had resulted in 800,000 casualties in 1915. One last attempt in March by the *2nd Army* resulted in another 51,000 casualties. Only the inability of the Russians to bring up siege artillery prolonged the resistance of the fortress. However, in March, their big guns arrived and were set in place. These included some Schneider 280mm guns purchased from the French and 152mm guns. A round from the Schneider struck at least one turret of a fort. On 10 March, the Russians captured several outposts and advanced positions on the northern part of the fortress that the garrison was unable to recapture. Conrad informed the Austrian commander, General Hermann Kusmanek von Burgneustädten, that he was on his own. So on 18 March, Kusmanek

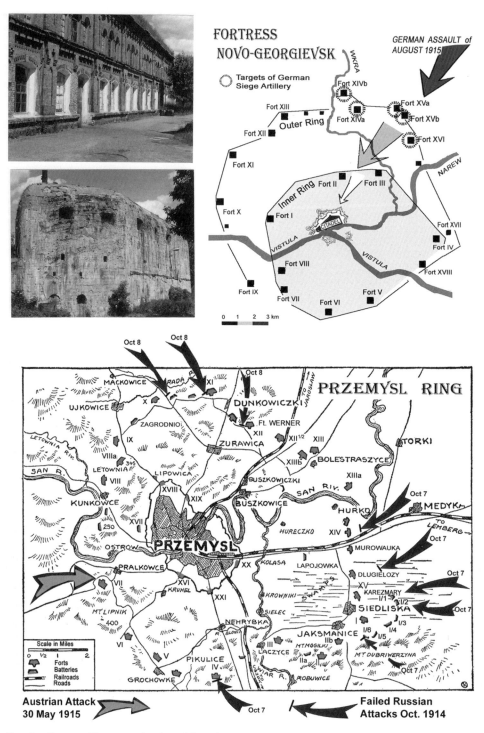

Russian Fortress Novogeorgievsk and Austrian Fortress Przemyśl. Photos of brick barracks and a concrete fortification of Fortress Novogeorgievsk.

launched a final break-out attack in the rain and snow using Hungarian troops. Instead of attacking in the obvious direction, their assault was directed eastward in an attempt to capture Russian supply dumps, but they failed to reach the Russian trench line. The Russians had built their own lines of circumvallation that successfully kept the garrison trapped. On 22 March, Kusmanek began the destruction of the fortress including blowing up bridges, stores and military installations as well as gun positions on the forts. None of the forts had sustained significant damage during the siege. The commanding general surrendered his remaining 117,000 men after 133 days (9 November 1914–22 March 1915).[52]

The Russians proceeded to repair the fortress for their own use and the Tsar even made a victory tour on 25 April. The Austro-German offensive at Gorlice-Tarnów in May broke the Russian front. Before the end of the month, the Russians in the fortress were under siege when Austrian 305mm mortars began bombarding the forts of the northern sector. On 17 May, the defenders forced back Austrian troops attacking Fort VII Prałkowce. On 30 May, the Austrians attacked again and captured Fort VII. A Russian counter-attack drove them out. A German force with a 420mm howitzer came to join the bombardment leading to the capture of forts on the left bank of the river. This was enough to convince the Russians to evacuate the fortress on 3 June, although it took until 5 June for the last forts to fall. The war was over for the fortress.

Przemyśl demonstrated that a twentieth-century fortress could withstand a siege of several months acting as a thorn in the enemy's side, but it also showed that when it was isolated the risk of surrender with immense losses was great. The fortresses' location was only strategic in the respect that it controlled several bridges over the San and blocked the main rail line to Cracow. The railway was of little use to the Russians, even if they controlled it because of the different gauge. Thus, the strategic value of the fortress was very limited. The Russians lacked the type of heavy artillery that could significantly damage the forts so when their big guns finally arrived they were not enough to prove the strength or weaknesses of the fortress. Thus, General Falkenhayn could not be certain how strong or weak this fortress was when it was subjected to the large-calibre weapons, but he did realize that the national pride of his Austrian allies was enough to make them fight tooth and nail for such a major fortress. Besides, the battle for the fortress had caused massive casualties. Thus, he could be almost certain that Verdun might evoke a similar reaction from the French.

The Russian fortresses, as previously mentioned in Chapter 2, were scattered along a line on the Russian northwestern front from Warsaw to Kovno, but had large gaps between them. They occupied a number of strategic points the Germans could easily bypass by cracking other parts of the defence line. With Warsaw abandoned on 5 August 1915, the fortress complex of Novogeorgievsk lost its strategic value. The Russians left its 90,000-man garrison to be encircled by 10 August.[53] The Germans brought in siege artillery that included four 420mm Big Berthas and a 305mm howitzer and in a preliminary bombardment shattered three forts before the battle. To these guns were added 10 305mm Skoda mortars and 2 420mm Skoda howitzers in 9 batteries with about 200 rounds per battery (approximately

1,800 rounds including 600 rounds of 420mm).[54] The attack opened on 13 August with a bombardment of forts XIV, XV and XVI for a few days. These forts, directly north and northeast of the citadel, were part of the outer girdle built between 1912 and 1915. They continued to resist. On the morning of the fourth day, German infantry began the assault on forts XV and XVI. The artillery continued to fire and a 420mm round hit an attacking company, but Fort XV fell that day. Despite this, the Russians continued to resist until forced to abandon their outer ring of forts. Soon three forts of the inner line (including fort II and III) fell followed by the citadel. The 24 battalions, mostly *Landwehr* troops, had the defenders trapped and by the morning of 20 August the fortress surrendered yielding a large number of prisoners and 700 artillery pieces.[55]

The Russian fortresses simply did not prove of much value when it came to assessing the strength of the forts and their ability to resist because the Germans avoided engaging them as part of any major battle. In the case of Kovno, the Germans arrived in front of it and began their bombardment in early August 1915 concentrating their efforts on the three oldest forts (almost all the forts were from the 1880s and the first seven were brick reinforced with earth). The fortress held 1,300 guns, but only about 240 were part of its defences and a second rate infantry division added to the defenders of the fort. The Germans brought up several batteries of siege artillery which included three 420mm Gamma howitzers, two 420mm Big Bertha howitzers, four 305mm mortars and a 280mm howitzer. Unlike, the action at Osowiec (described below) in February, aircraft and a tethered balloon provided observation for the artillery. On 15 August, the 420mm rounds shattered Fort I. On 17 August, German infantry overran four badly damaged forts. A week of bombardment left over 20,000 of the 90,000 Russian defenders as casualties and the fortress fell after only 11 days on 18 August.

A Russian fortress that successful resisted was Osowiec. This fortress occupied a site through which the Konigsberg–Łyck–Białystok railroad passed on a narrow strip of land surrounded by impassable marshes and crossing the Bobra River. The Russians built the citadel, Fort I, near the town and on the north side of the railway bridge Fort II between 1882 and 1892. Forts III and IV, built early in the 1900s, occupied a plateau southwest of Fort I. The defences took full advantage of the swampy terrain. The Germans placed the fortress under siege early in the war and assaulted it on 21 September 1914.[56] A frontal assault followed, but Russian artillery devastated the German attackers and counter-attacks on both flanks ended the assault. A second effort took place on 3 February 1915 with German artillery ranging from 105mm to 420mm firing a heavy barrage. In addition, four 305mm howitzers from the Western Front took part as the barrage reached a peak and ended on 16 February. The Russian high command did not believe the fortresses would last more than a couple of days, but that was wrong. Another bombardment began on 25 February and lasted until 5 March 1915. The German artillery already included two battalions of 210mm howitzers and one of 305mm mortars. A second battery of 305s was added and a 280mm howitzer along with a two–gun battery of 420mm Gammas. Marc Romanych and Martin Rupp state that the bombardment was ineffective since they fired blindly without any form of observation while Russian counter-battery fire hit both 305mm Skoda batteries. The town did suffer a large amount of damage, and the Russians claimed they silenced two of the 420mm Big Berthas, although that was not correct. The Germans withdrew their siege guns for operations elsewhere on the front.[57] They failed to reach the second line of defences when the attack ended. Hindenburg ordered the *8th Army* to launch another assault on 6 August. This time, since the siege artillery was gone, the guns fired chlorine gas shells. Once the Germans thought resistance was broken, over a dozen *Landwehr* battalions totalling 7,000 men from the *11th Landwehr Division* advanced on the fortress.[58] However, about sixty of the gassed Russians, coughing up blood and looking like the living dead, charged the Germans who had taken their first line sending them running. Their heroic counter-attack went down into history as 'The attack of the dead men'. A fortnight later, on 18 August, after the fall of the fortresses of Kovno and Novogeorgievsk, the victorious Russians forces at Osowiec found themselves in a precarious position due to the collapse of the flanks of the fortified line and they were ordered to withdraw to new positions. Before they left, the Russian engineers demolished much of the fortress.

The fortresses on the Eastern Front were not good examples of what such sites could achieve if properly built and defended when part of a larger defensive scheme. Thus, both the French and Germans could only use the Belgian forts and the French frontier forts to estimate the value of the 'modern' fort. During his time in charge of the army, Falkenhayn allowed the removal of half the 105mm gun turrets of Fortress Strasbourg and Feste Kaiser Wilhelm II at Mutzig in 1915, with the garrison reduced from 7,000 to about 2,000.[59] It is doubtful they had lost faith in their forts since the Metz–Thionville fortress complex remained strongly manned. On the other hand, Joffre stripped his forts of artillery in 1915 because the French army needed the weapons. He had possibly concluded that the French forts would not stand up to modern artillery. He had also seen that for most of the first twelve months of the war the Germans had made no serious attempt to break the French fortress line, instead concentrating most of their efforts in northern France.

Even if Falkenhayn had known the French were disarming their forts, he would have realized that with or without guns they still represented a serious obstacle if he directed an offensive to capture and/or pass through them. His choices for a decisive battle in 1916 did not include any location where he thought the French or the British were weak. As most historians have assumed, he did not seek a breakthrough that would return the element of manoeuvre to the campaign. He sought a battle in which his enemy would be defeated as decisively as at Waterloo or Königgrätz (Sadowa). His strategy was to select a spot where the enemy would not retreat to a new defensive position to continue the stalemate. His choices of Belfort and Verdun were easy to make. Belfort offered nothing more than a diversion to draw French forces as far away as possible since it occupied a gateway the French could not afford to lose. The main battlefront from Champagne to the North Sea, explained Falkenhayn, would not be decisive, as the actions of the past fourteen months had already demonstrated. The Charmes Gap lay between Verdun–Toul and

General Maurice Sarrail – Scapegoat?

Unlike most senior officers in the French army, Maurice Sarrail was a republican with socialist ideals. He maintained his position in the army while he had allies in the government. He was retired in 1917 when he lost support in the government. In 1907, he had been appointed as Director of the Infantry at the War Office. The next year, he was promoted from colonel to general. In 1908, he received command of the VIII Corps. In April 1914, he transferred to the VI Corps at Chalons, which became part of General Pierre Ruffey's 3rd Army in 1914.[60]

When the 3rd Army advanced in 1914, Sarrail's corps did not break during the assault of the German *5th Army*. During the first ten days of September 1914, Sarrail's V and VI Corps inflicted heavy losses on the German *5th Army* – estimated at 15,000 casualties. Shortly after that, Joffre began removing generals, Ruffey among them. Sarrail took command of the 3rd Army as Joffre thought he had the resolve to fight. In September 1914, his 3rd Army held the front on the Meuse between St Mihiel and Verdun and also had the responsibility for most of the Argonne sector to Verdun. Joffre ordered Sarrail to stop the divisions of the German *5th Army* that were sweeping through the Argonne and maintain a link with Langle's 4th Army on the western side of the Argonne. Joffre authorized him to break his link with Verdun if necessary to maintain a continuous front and prevent the Germans from breaching between the 4th and 3rd armies, which risked collapsing the French defences in Lorraine and eastern France. Sarrail chose to hold on to Verdun, and did not move fast enough as far as Joffre was concerned. It is generally assumed that his actions were not effective during that first week of September. When the Germans began to retreat after 10 September, he did nothing for 48 hours. Joffre telephoned Sarrail expressing his displeasure with his performance and said he wanted an investigation, which Sarrail skilfully avoided. Joffre accused some of Sarrail's regiments of being substandard and abandoning rifles and equipment, a problem caused by the division and regimental commanders.

According to some historians, with over 60,000 men, Fortress Verdun was a strong position that could have remained isolated for an extended period and that Sarrail should have allowed it to happen. It is true that Verdun was one of the strongest positions in Europe at the time, but no other fortress in the West had survived encirclement in 1914. At this time, the defenders' morale was fragile. Joffre had decided to concentrate all major reinforcements against the Germans at the Marne in an attempt to drive them out of northern France. The loss of Verdun might have weakened national morale because of its historical and strategic significance. The Germans could as easily have defended the terrain between Revigny and St Mihiel as they had done later at the St Mihiel Salient so the French would have had major difficulty in relieving Fortress Verdun.[61] Sarrail was accused of being slow in preparing for offensive operations in the Argonne (1914–15). This may well be the case; he had to hold the salient around

Verdun and supply it with only one small railway. French heavy artillery for these offensives involved old mortars and cannons. He may not have been an excellent tactician, but under the circumstances it is difficult to judge, especially since he had performed so well during the first weeks of the war as a corps commander.

The engagements in the Argonne during the first few months of 1915 resulted in heavy French casualties, and Joffre was slow to provide Sarrail with the necessary reinforcements. His V Corps might have cleared the butte at Vauquois if properly reinforced. Joffre wrote little about Sarrail's command of the 3rd Army in his memoirs, but he wanted him replaced and that was done by July 1915. In August 1915, Sarrail was sent to command the Army of the Orient, which was taking up positions in Salonika where it occupied a 'no win' position.

Joffre attempted to justify his actions in his memoirs:[*]

> I made no appointments and carried out no removals or changes except in the interests of the country. I have arrested the careers of those who were dear to me; I have promoted generals for whom I had no particular liking. I have made it clear that when I had to relieve General Sarrail of his command in July 1915, my decision was taken only after … an impartial expression of opinion from General Dubail….
>
> General Sarrail himself has never accused me of Caesarism, but merely of preparing the way for General Foch.

Dubail, the army group commander, did investigate for Joffre and reported inadequacies in Sarrail's tactics, and problems between the XXXII Corps commander and Sarrail. That was enough for Joffre. In addition, according to some claims, General Sarrail had accused Joffre of planning a coup. Historian Elizabeth Greenhalgh points out that Sarrail claimed that his removal was due to his left-wing views, but he also admitted that he had lost 80,000 men with little to show for it. On the other hand, he prevented Verdun from being isolated. It must be mentioned, however, that Joffre's leadership had resulted in almost a million French casualties, many of them from his nibbling and failed offensives, and that he failed to drive the Germans out of France in 1915.

A few months after Sarrail was sent to Salonika, Dubail, the commander of the Eastern Army Group, tried to warn Joffre of the impending threat to Verdun. He became the next target of Joffre's displeasure and he was removed. By 1917, Joffre himself was on his way out.

---

[*] Joffre, *Personal Memoirs of Joffre*, Vol. 2, p. 395.

Épinal–Belfort, but an offensive there would favour French defensive operations. Furthermore, striking at the fortresses of Toul and Épinal on either side of the gap would not force the French to overcommit themselves and to sacrifice everything for those towns. Thus, Verdun became the obvious objective for Falkenhayn's strategy. In 1915, it occupied a central point on the Western Front that acted like a hinge where the French defence line changed directions. In addition, the fortress of Verdun was a short distance from Metz and was the only location where France might mount a serious offensive within striking distance of German soil.[62] That appeared to be reason enough to keep Fortress Metz manned. The fall of Verdun would crack the French line. However, the French could easily pull back to a new position avoiding a decisive battle if they could accept the deterioration of national morale caused by the loss of Verdun. The illogical part of Falkenhayn's choice was that Verdun was considered the strongest position on the French front and his plan called for taking the French forts on the right bank to occupy the Meuse Heights and create a killing zone for his battle of attrition. Falkenhayn counted on the fact that the French army would not retreat from their greatest fortress, and the historic town it surrounded. However, he misjudged the French high command because Joffre had actually been ready to abandon Verdun when the offensive began and he was prevented from doing so by the French government.

Joffre Prepares for the Big Offensive

In 1914, the greatest threat to Fortress Verdun was the operations of the German *5th Army* in the Argonne and in Woëvre. Having virtually cleared the forested hills west of Verdun and crossed the Woëvre to attack St Mihiel, the German forces came as close as they ever would to isolating the fortress. Joffre closed the year with one last offensive in Champagne in the autumn while his 3rd Army continued the fight in the Argonne where a short period of calm prevailed in October before both armies resorted to mine warfare. During the next year, as the battle for Verdun raged, the Argonne between the Bolante Plateau and Vauquois became the scene of numerous mine detonations and artillery duels. Except for a growing casualty list, little altered on either front. In early 1916, the impending battle for Verdun brought change to the St Mihiel Salient when German troops swept across the northern part of the Woëvre towards the Meuse Heights. This move in effect widened the salient on its north side leaving it less exposed.

In December 1915, Joffre had to reflect carefully about the events that had unfolded in over a year of warfare. In the north, the Allies maintained control of a sliver of Belgium and the French Channel ports, but a huge German salient bulged into much of northern France enveloping Lille and putting Reims near the edge of the front. The Germans had taken control of the French mines in French Lorraine. Verdun, despite its forts stripped of artillery, stood like a rock in the storm, anchoring the French position and making it easier to maintain control of much of the eastern frontier to Belfort. The French army was increasing its inventory of heavy artillery, but it continued to rely heavily on older models. Late in the year, the French army adopted a new artillery doctrine and discontinued its reliance on elan-fuelled suicidal attacks. The troops were issued with the more modern horizon blue uniform and the Adrian helmet.[63] Airpower had proved its mettle during 1915 and the French air force finally acquired aircraft capable of taking on the 'Fokker Scourge'. Joffre had disposed of several subordinates who displeased him, including Sarrail, commander of the 3rd Army. Shortly before that, he had shifted the 3rd Army to the command of General Castelnau's Army Group Centre leaving Verdun under Dubail's Army Group East.

In the summer of 1915, Joffre invited representatives of each of the Allied armies to meet at his headquarters at Chantilly to coordinate future operations. In November, the Allies agreed to convene at Chantilly between 6 and 8 December in order to formulate a plan for concerted action in 1916. Joffre was pleased to gain unanimous agreement for the complete and immediate evacuation of Gallipoli, which he had always considered a drain on his resources. He believed, however, that creating an 'entrenched camp' in Salonika would leave an open option for future operations in the Balkans.

The Chantilly Conference opened on 5 December 1915. Joffre allowed his armies to rest shortly after his failed autumn offensive in Champagne to give them time to recover before launching a grand offensive in 1916. He also needed to await the delivery of new artillery and to build up ammunition stocks. The Russian army had suffered more than any major army, having been driven from the Polish territories. It certainly would not be ready to return to the offensive until a lengthy period of recovery. The Austrians had repelled the Italians, who had tried to knock them out of the war. Joffre did not expect the Italians to resume a major offensive on their Alpine frontier until winter was over. The Austro-German forces had crushed the Serbian army, the remnants of which had made their way via Corfu to Salonika where the Central Powers' new ally, Bulgaria, kept the Allied forces bottled up. The Turks had given the British Mesopotamian expedition a drubbing and at the other end of their empire, the Allies had evacuated their forces from Gallipoli. The Germans had opened a supply line directly to Turkey as the Berlin–Baghdad railroad was no longer blocked by Serbia. The British forces in Egypt had entrenched behind the Suez Canal awaiting a Turkish attack.

After the conquest of Serbia, German and Austrian forces were able to redeploy to other fronts, leaving the Bulgarians to hold the Allies in Salonika. Except for Bulgaria, every nation had taken heavy casualties by the end of 1915. The major powers had to conscript additional men to refill their ranks. If the end of 1914 had not exhausted most of the armies, the end of 1915 certainly sapped their strength. The Eastern and Western fronts stabilized on all sides during the winter.

Joffre was convinced that France was the key to victory or defeat. Falkenhayn, who was also making plans for 1916, was of the same mind. According to Joffre, 97 French infantry divisions and the equivalent of 37 territorial divisions had served in the war up to the end of 1915, 106 of these units on the Western Front.[64] He estimated that the Russians had 128 divisions, but lacked equipment, including rifles. His British ally, he claimed, had difficulties merely maintaining its seventy divisions, but would continue to grow in strength. He believed that the Germans would continue to direct their main efforts against Russia and that the Allies' main objective should be to destroy the German and Austrian armies. Falkenhayn, on the other hand had concluded that he must destroy the French army to achieve victory. Their methods for achieving similar goals, however, were dissimilar. Although the French realized in 1915 that the conflict had become a war of attrition, Joffre's objective was not to bleed the Germans dry.

The French as well as the Germans had stretched their human resources and realized that drafting new classes of males was not enough. They decided, therefore, to change their divisional structure. Joffre's infantry divisions began the war with two brigades, each of which had two or three regiments. This gave each division a minimum of four infantry regiments and some as many as five or even six. To save on manpower, the brigade headquarters were removed and each division maintained only three infantry regiments. In December 1915, these changes affected only two divisions. Between June and August 1916, nine more converted – five of them in the Verdun sector.[65] This modification did not actually weaken the French infantry division because emphasis switched to the artillery during 1916. In addition, the percentage of men assigned to the infantry decreased and the percentage of the soldiers assigned to the artillery increased. In addition, the distinction between active and reserve divisions disappeared in the French army during 1915.

The German infantry division began the war with twelve infantry battalions organized somewhat like the French into two infantry brigades, but each of these brigades consisted, with few exceptions, of only two infantry regiments.[66] The German reserve division often did not have the four machine-gun companies of the regular division and lacked sufficient artillery. One of the few notable exceptions was the 1st Guard Reserve Division. In August 1914, the German army went to war with 92 divisions, which included 51 infantry, 3 reserve, 4 *Landwehr* and 6 Ersatz divisions. More than two-dozen divisions were added at the end of 1914. In January 1915, the German army included 128 divisions, including 51 infantry and 54 reserve infantry. In March 1915, the Germans formed five new divisions numbered in the 50s, each of which consisted of one infantry brigade of three infantry regiments and one artillery brigade. An eleven additional infantry divisions were formed at the same time (numbered 101–23) and had a similar infantry brigade but only one artillery regiment. By the end of 1915, all German infantry regiments included one machine-gun company. At the beginning of 1916, the German army had 162 divisions that included 78 active infantry, 54 reserve and 20 *Landwehr*. By the end of 1916, the German army's strength had grown to 207 divisions including 115 active infantry, 55 reserve and 25 *Landwehr*. The army eventually converted all the infantry divisions to the single-brigade structure.[67]

Joffre appeared to have finally absorbed some lessons from his costly battles and even became more tolerant of the views of his subordinates. Years later, he wrote, 'No longer were men to be pitted against materiel, since France had suffered too many casualties this way.'[*] The most significant changes, besides the new artillery doctrine issued in November, were the guidelines formulated in the document entitled *Small Unit Combat Training*, issued to the infantry in January 1916.

---

[*] Elizabeth Greenhalgh, *The French Army and the First World War* (Cambridge: Cambridge University Press, 2014), p. 125.

After his letters failed to go beyond Joffre's staff, Colonel J.B. Estienne was finally able to contact the general at the end of 1915. He proposed the adoption of an armoured vehicle that mounted artillery, which was being developed by a couple of French manufacturers. In January 1916, Joffre witnessed the successful test of a modified Holt tractor and the government placed an order for 400 of these vehicles. The Allies required this type of weapon for delivering the close support the troops needed to reach the first enemy trench and go beyond. Estienne did not get enough of these vehicles to organize an armoured force until the end of 1916. Thus, Pétain, Nivelle and Estienne finally managed to convince Joffre to put the emphasis on artillery, and to pin his hopes of success on it.

In *The French Army and the First World War*, Greenhalgh, identifies other important changes that took place in the French army in 1915. When he was on the defensive, Joffre deployed his troops in three lines. About 20–30km behind the first line, he formed a second line where an army group deployed its reserves. Behind that, there was a third line where he positioned his general reserves, all located near railways. The doctrine for 1916 emphasized the slow methodical approach, abandoning the idea of achieving a quick breakthrough. Violent attacks and counter-attacks remained in effect, but now Joffre wanted his commanders to be in closer contact with the front. He demanded additional training with new weapons and tactics for the troops. To implement this policy, Joffre pulled the 2nd Army from the front and placed Pétain in charge of training reserve divisions late in the year.

As artillery assumed an increasing role on the battlefield, new technology was developed to either aid it or counter it. Each corps acquired technical sections for detecting enemy artillery by sound ranging and flash spotting. Sound ranging required at least one pair of microphones located a couple of kilometres apart and a stopwatch to determine the location of the gun based on the speed of the sound waves. The French often used five microphones for recording and charting the sound, but it was frequently difficult to determine which sound came from the enemy artillery piece. The Germans deemed the system ineffective, but they used a more primitive version of it. Flash spotting required teams of observers equipped with surveying instruments and placed at different locations to spot the flashes from enemy guns, measure angles and triangulate the gun's position. It was most effective at night. The system was not very successful until 1916 when the French used a high-powered instrument similar to a surveyor's theodolite. Neither system was of much use without detailed large-scale maps with grids for reference, which were prepared by the map service. Balloons, which had been effective in spotting enemy artillery, also needed the same type of maps to be more accurate. Observers in aircraft required maps as well, but in 1916, their aircraft were equipped with a wireless that allowed them to send information, but not receive messages.

At the Chantilly Conference, Joffre was confident that he could finally present a winning strategy based on all these changes and the military situation in Europe. Before the meeting, General Mikhail Alexeev, Russian Chief-of-Staff, gave him a general plan of action for the Balkans. It required the French, British and Italians to attack through Serbia and Albania, while the Russians advanced into Galicia and

Bukovina in the direction of Budapest where, it was believed, the front was less fortified. There was a possibility the plan might draw Rumania into the war. Joffre rejected the Russian plan because it required almost a million men from the UK, Italy and France. Initially the Allies agreed to Joffre's plan, but rejected it when it was brought up in December. Among the attendees at the conference were Field Marshal French (soon to be replaced by Haig), Gilinsky, chief of the Russian military mission, General Porro, Assistant Chief of the General Staff of the Italian army and General Wielmans, Chief-of-Staff of the Belgian army. They all agreed that to achieve a decisive result that they must coordinate offensives on all fronts. All must begin at the same time to keep the German and Austrian reserves tied down. However, they could not agree on a starting date since they had to consider weather conditions and other factors. The Russian representative warned them that his army could not be ready before June.[68] In the event of a major enemy offensive on one of the three major fronts, they agreed that each would attempt to provide assistance as soon as possible.

At Chantilly after the conference on 29 December, Joffre met with General Douglas Haig, who officially replaced Field Marshal John French on 19 December.[69] Haig agreed to relieve the French 10th Army in the Arras sector and to ready eighteen divisions for the big offensive. On 20 January 1916, Joffre visited Haig's headquarters at Montreuil to discuss further details of the planned offensive. On 14 February, they agreed to launch a contiguous and simultaneous attack on both banks of the Somme in late June. Haig refused to launch a costly preliminary engagement prior to the big offensive, opting for raids a few weeks before the operation. At the Chantilly Conference in December, they had agreed that if the Germans struck on the Russian front, they would begin their offensive in April. In 1916, General Foch worked out a final arrangement with Haig. Foch would employ 40 divisions in 3 armies with 1,200 guns for this offensive on a front of almost 50km between the Somme and Lassigny. They settled on 1 July for launching the offensive. Pétain's 2nd Army was in reserve for training behind the 6th Army, which held the front from the Somme to the Oise. To the north in the vicinity of Arras, British divisions gradually began replacing the French 10th Army, which would be free to shift to the south of the Somme. The corps assigned to open the offensive went into reserve for additional training or to rest. The Franco-British forces were to strike along the front of the German salient without repeating the previous attempts to envelop it from the flanks. Thanks to a continuous front, the Allies could shift reserves more quickly and concentrate their artillery instead of distributing it along widely separated points. The main problem was that the Germans had had ample time to build up their defences and install barbed wire entanglements in greater depth than ever before.

In February 1916, the Battle of Verdun was engaged. However hard Joffre tried to keep his plans for the big offensive alive, events did not work out as planned. By the end of the spring, he could only contribute eight divisions instead of forty to the offensive so that the 50km of front he had envisaged had to shrink, leaving the British to handle the bulk of the operation. The Battle of Verdun took precedence on the Western Front for all of 1916.

The Air War in 1916

The air war on the Western Front was anything but deadly before the summer of 1915. Aircraft remained a novelty until army commanders began using them for reconnaissance and artillery observation. The situation changed again when

FRENCH AIRCRAFT

Voison LA (recon, but some mounted 37mm gun)

Voison III (recon with one machine gun

Voison night bomber mounting 37mm gun

Caudron 4 (twin engine and machine guns)

Caudron G. 3 (recon)

Nieuport XI "Bebe"

Nieuport 16 with anti-balloon rockets

Examples of some of the more common aircraft. The Nieuport XI helped end the 'Fokker Scourge' in 1916.

weapons were mounted on aeroplanes. In 1915, the French assembled their first fighter or pursuit squadron (*escadrille de chasse*). They selected the Morane-Saulnier H or L single-seater monoplanes as fighters, and fitted the propellers with armour so the Hotchkiss machine gun could fire through it. The Germans copied the French aircraft and named it the Pfalz E-1. The Fokker series of Eindeckers (single-seat monoplane) also appeared in 1915. This aeroplane was more manoeuvrable and included a synchronized machine gun. In early 1916, the Germans used one or two fighters to escort their reconnaissance and bomber aircraft. From the fall of 1915 to early 1916, the German aircraft, usually flying individually, became the 'Fokker Scourge' in the sky. In early 1916, both sides started flying in increasingly formidable formations.

The French and the British used pusher type aircraft, as opposed to the tractor type with the engine in the front, because this provided a better platform for

Main types of German aircraft in the first years of the war.

forward firing machine guns before they developed synchronization. Next, came the Nieuport XI 'Bébé', a single-seater biplane more manoeuvrable than the existing monoplanes. On the top wing it mounted a machine gun that fired over the propeller. Of the 675 French aircraft that were operational in February 1916, there were 90 Nieuport XIs and 120 older, two-seater Nieuport Xs.[70] For the Verdun Offensive, the Germans had 168 aircraft, which included only 21 Eindeckers (Fokkers and Pfalz) available on the Western Front.

The French squadrons (*escadrilles*) consisted of up to ten aircraft. Each squadron was identified by a letter prefix before the unit number. The letter represented the type of aircraft, for example, C for Caudron, M for Morane-Saulnier, N for Nieuport, etc. The French formed the first escadrille de chasse (fighter squadron), N12, in September 1915. The French as well as the Germans selected their best pilots from bomber and reconnaissance/scout units to fly fighter aircraft. In 1915, the Germans used small flights of about six aircraft. They also built the *Flieger Abteilunger* (Flying Detachment) for reconnaissance and artillery liaison. Each German army corps had one.[71]

The best German pilots joined the *Kampfeinsitzer Kommand* (KEK) or single-seater fighter command, which consisted of two to four Fokker or Pfalz Eindeckers. When the battle for Verdun began, these KEK were sent to patrol the front and prevent French aircraft from penetrating German lines. However, the French scouts often slipped across before they could be intercepted. The few French pilots who got through on the first day spotted so many batteries that they were unable to judge how or where to direct their own artillery. The German ace Oswald Boelcke brought a change in tactics. Instead of sending the German fighters on patrol to intercept interlopers, he staked out observers at the front who notified his KEK by telephone when enemy aircraft approached. That way a pair of his aircraft could take off and head directly toward the enemy. His KEK operated from Sivry, about 11km from the front. Other fighter aerodromes were located at Cunel, on the west bank, and Avillers near Spincourt. From the first days of the battle, Pétain was concerned that his artillery would be blind without air support. On 28 February 1916, he ordered Charles Baron de Tricornot, Marquis de Rose to clear the sky. De Rose assigned *escadrilles* to the aerodromes at Lemmes, Vadelaincourt, Ste Ménehould and Béhonne from where they could effectively intercept German bomber missions and engage the enemy anywhere along the salient and behind the lines.

In March and April, the Germans lost control of the air to the French Nieuport XI and XVI pursuit aircraft. They had a similar problem facing the British DH-2 and SPADs on other parts of the Western Front. When the dominance of the Eindecker aircraft ended, the Germans had to find new models to regain control of the air, but it was already too late to change the situation at Verdun.

German bombing missions against the Sacred Way, rail yards and bridges were mostly fruitless. The most important contribution of aircraft during the battle was artillery spotting and aerial photography. Fighter aircraft became the best weapons against these activities.

Chapter Four

The Battle of Verdun, 1916

'Victory must be ours …'

From a letter by a young German soldier
who died only a few weeks after the war began

Happy New Year

Like two exhausted boxers, the Germans and the French armies rested to recuperate from their wounds and prepare for another round at the end of 1915. This time, both formulated actions for 1916 with every intention of delivering a knockout blow. The optimum time to begin a campaign is in the spring, after the thaw and the rains. Winter weather is the least desirable time for an offensive, especially when it involves trench warfare. General Joffre planned for concentric operations with his allies, which required him to wait until the summer for the Russians to be ready. However, he was prepared to go into action as early as April if the Russians were attacked. Since the Germans had remained on the defensive in the West throughout 1915, Joffre assumed that they would repeat this strategy in 1916. General Falkenhayn, however, had no intention of waiting for the spring since he believed that time was running out for Germany to achieve a decisive victory.

Joffre could not afford a repeat of 1915. The morale of the French troops improved, especially when generals like Pétain took steps to improve conditions on the front, gave them leave and provided them with postal services. Ordinary citizens, except those in the occupied lands, had not suffered too much. The Poilu's equipment and gear had improved. Despite the loss of valuable resources at Briey and Lille, French industry managed to increase production and the USA, which remained neutral, supplemented France's needs. Above all, the French fought on their soil against an invader and patriotism still ran strong. However, losses like those incurred in 1915 could spell disaster for the war effort. Joffre's plan for a great Somme offensive, if it were successful, offered the prospect of driving the Germans out of northern France, which would boost French spirits despite heavy casualties. It would also stretch Germany's resources to its limits, especially if the Russians had any success.

Time was running out for Falkenhayn. He could not afford a repeat of 1915 either. On the Eastern Front, his armies led by Hindenburg, Ludendorff and Mackensen battered the Russian army and occupied Russian Poland. As Falkenhayn had predicted, the Russians traded space for time and these losses would not force their surrender. He had successfully parried all British and French offensives on the Western Front, but that left the German front approximately where it had been at the end of 1914. Thus, he concluded, the war would not end if he concentrated

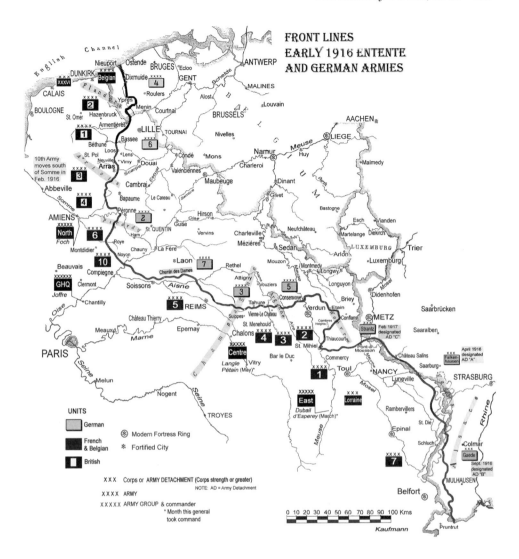

FRONT LINES
EARLY 1916 ENTENTE
AND GERMAN ARMIES

on the Eastern Front once more, where deeper advances into Russia ran the risk of repeating Napoleon's experiences of a century earlier. In addition, Germany was already suffering economically as much-needed imports decreased as a result of the British naval blockade. Neutral countries like Switzerland, Denmark and the Netherlands could not provide too much since they also relied on imports. Food shortages were felt in some parts of Germany where rationing of bread and other items was implemented. However, the problem was still negligible compared with the impending crisis of 1916. A U-boat campaign against Allied merchant ships in 1915 had limited success until the sinking of the British liner *Lusitania* in May provoked a reaction from the USA. The campaign to blockade Britain with twenty U-boats also had lacklustre success. When a U-boat sank the liner *Arabic* in August, the German government put an end to the submarine campaign against commerce.[1] In 1916, Falkenhayn wanted to renew the U-boat war against commerce and Grand Admiral Alfred von Tirpitz agreed, but the government leaders forbade it.

On Christmas Day 1915, Falkenhayn penned a letter to the Kaiser explaining his view.[2] France had been weakened militarily and economically to the limits of its endurance. Now – he wrote – the British were Germany's main enemy. 'John Bull' intended to bring Germany to her knees and would not negotiate or give up. Since the German navy could not transport an invasion force to the island, the army could strike at the British on the Continent by reaching the Channel and attacking them in northern France, while, at the same time, pushing the French back towards the Somme. However, Falkenhayn was not optimistic about this option. In his post-war account, he wrote that he would have been able to concentrate about twenty-five divisions for an offensive on the Western Front, which means that he would not have had enough men for a breakthrough attack. Reducing the strength of the units at the front, he noted, was not possible because they already averaged one man per metre of front.[3] He identified Verdun or Belfort as points where the Germans could expect a decisive victory because the French would feel obliged to stand and fight there for political and historical reasons. He made no mention of 'bleeding them to death'. His preference was Verdun because the front was only about 20km from the German railway system and because the site held great strategic significance. Taking Verdun, he claimed, would require a relatively small effort on the part of the Germans, and success would make the entire front untenable. Breaking the French would drive the British from the Continent, especially if the navy could launch a new campaign of unrestricted U-boat warfare to strangle the British economically. Even if the Americans were drawn into the war, he reasoned, they would not have the time to muster a military force adequate to intervene successfully before the Germans won the war.

If Joffre had been able to launch his Somme Offensive before Falkenhayn moved against Verdun, it is doubtful the Allies would have been any more successful than they had been in July. The Germans would have diverted several divisions, which they actually did when the offensive eventually materialized, to contain the threat. However, they may have prevented the Verdun Offensive and maintained a deadlock in the West throughout 1916. The offensive against Verdun offered a glimmer of hope for defeating France, whereas a purely defensive stance in the West would have prolonged the stalemate as shortages of food and materials increased in Germany. The likelihood of Joffre launching a major operation during the winter months was slim to none. Thus, Falkenhayn's decision to attack in February gave him the advantage of being the first to strike.

Joffre had changed Verdun's status from a 'Fortress' to a 'Fortified Region' in 1915. The decision to strip the forts of their armaments in August 1915 may not have been a mistake. The artillery that was actually removed from the forts consisted mostly of older pieces, many of which had occupied positions on exposed ramparts in the older forts, and 75mm guns mounted in casemates. The older pieces, like the 120mm guns, gave Joffre a temporary increase in heavy artillery. However, many of these cannons from the 1870s and 1880s lacked important features found in guns of the twentieth century, which limited their range, accuracy and rate of fire. Most of these weapons did not contribute greatly to the firepower of the forts, unlike the 75mm and 155mm turret guns that actually remained in position. If the forts had to be rearmed, it would not have been very difficult to reinstall 75mm casemate guns and other smaller defensive weapons.[4] Days after the battle began in February 1916, General Herr, the military governor of Verdun, made the gravest mistake regarding the forts when he had them prepared for demolition.

As far as Joffre and some of his subordinates were concerned, Verdun, which had been a relatively quiet front during most of 1915, required few preparations. In late 1915, Lieutenant Colonel Émile Driant raised the alarm by going over Joffre's head and alerting his friends in the government. As a result, Joffre sent Castelnau to check out the position. The inspection revealed that there were indeed deficiencies, which were only partially corrected. However, it was winter and Verdun was not a priority site. Driant and his chasseur battalions were stationed in a number of concrete bunkers in Caures Woods, north of Verdun. They occupied several positions, but did not dig a continuous trench line.[5] Driant complained of a shortage of barbed wire, the main anti-personnel obstacle in trench warfare. Other units defending the sector consisted of reserve divisions. French intelligence sources noticed an unusual German build-up in the area, but Joffre brushed off the possibility of a major attack.[6]

On the other side of the front, the Germans had been concentrating their forces in the area for weeks. Since the *V Reserve Corps* held the section of the front designated for the assault, its troops did most of the construction, which included bombproof munitions dumps in sheltered areas such as woods or ravines beyond the sight of prying eyes on the ground and in the air. To protect the assault troops in advanced positions, the pioneers built concrete underground shelters up to 10m below the surface called *stollen*. The construction of the *stollen* as well as new plank roads, light railways and other items needed on the front went on at night and in secrecy. Special care was taken to deceive air reconnaissance.[7]

The French intelligence service predicted an attack based on interrogations of deserters.[8] However, since they knew little about the *stollen* or the scale of the operation, they underestimated the enemy's strength. The Germans built enough shelters and new trenches to accommodate 6,000 assault troops in the first line. The *stollen* occupied positions within a couple hundred metres of the French front line. The largest held 1,000 men, but they had few facilities and no heat. These underground bunkers were prone to flooding, which made life for the troops waiting inside miserable. In February, foul weather delayed the assault for several days so the troops had to trudge back and forth at night and in the snow to spend some time in billets more liveable than the *stollen*.[9] The unsuspecting French defenders, in the meantime, awaited the end of winter in more comfortable quarters.

After December 1915, the Germans secretly moved munitions and other materials required for the operation to the front line. About 1,300 trains delivered over 2.5 million artillery rounds to feed the 1,300 to 1,500 artillery pieces of all sizes already emplaced in their concealed positions. Earlier in 1915, two 380mm naval coastal defence guns had taken up positions. Now, the Germans added 420mm Big Berthas and new 305mm howitzers. Everything was ready for the big offensive, except Mother Nature. It snowed and rained on 12 February 1916, the scheduled date for the attack. The Crown Prince ordered a 24-hour delay, but more than a week's postponement resulted from the inclement weather.

Other Considerations

The actual data is too flimsy and coloured by post-war interviews to be certain, but Falkenhayn appears to have envisaged a decisive battle for Verdun that would bleed the French army white. For Falkenhayn, the Verdun Salient presented a possible threat to Germany because of its proximity to the Metz–Thionville region. His claims, however, were greatly exaggerated. After the summer of

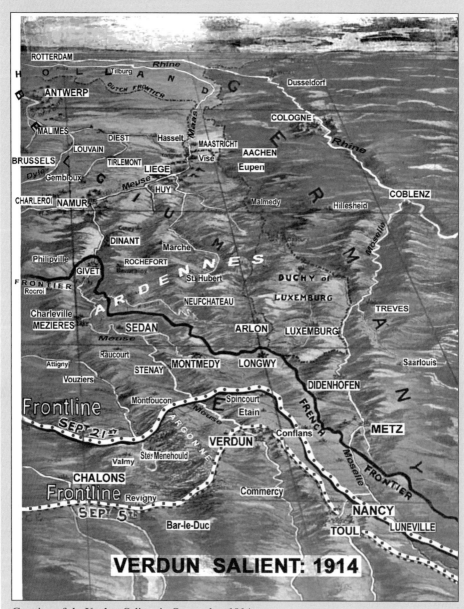

Creation of the Verdun Salient in September 1914.

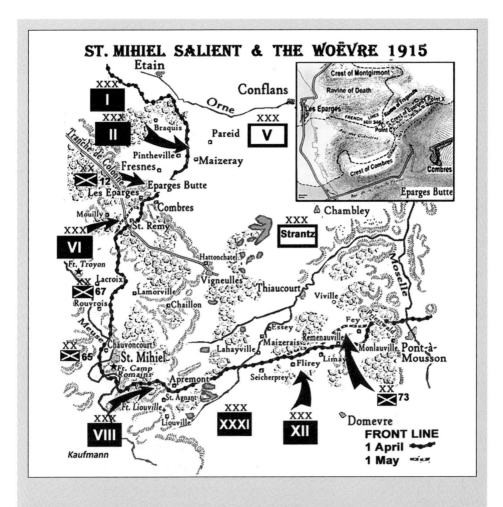

1915, one minor railway supplied Verdun and the salient was only about 35km (22 miles) wide. West of the salient, the Germans securely held part of the Argonne near Vauquois, and to the east was Éparges and the St Mihiel Salient that stood like a rock until September 1918. The Allies saw no reason or opportunity to concentrate a major offensive in this area until late in the war when they had sufficient forces to penetrate these main centres of German resistance. Therefore, there was no real danger to Germany from that quarter in 1916.

Falkenhayn was convinced that the French would fight for Verdun because its loss could collapse the entire front and for the French it was a matter of national pride due to its historic value. The Verdun Salient was at risk because it could still be isolated. In 1914, even Joffre had considered falling back to a more secure line if necessary and allowing Verdun to become isolated as the situation deteriorated. Its loss, he felt, would not crack the front unless the French army panicked during a withdrawal. The only factor that would motivate the French to fight was a feeling of national pride, as Falkenhayn had predicted. An offensive in the Champagne area or elsewhere – Falkenhayn calculated – might force the French to pull back, in which case he would not have sufficient reserves to exploit the situation. Thus, he concluded, he had to engage the French where they could not afford to retreat voluntarily and where he could inflict maximum casualties upon them. Although most historians say that he considered attacking either Verdun or Belfort, he made it clear in his memoirs that in Belfort he would not achieve his goals.

What remains a question was the objective of Falkenhayn's offensive. How far did he want to go, and was Verdun just one action or did he expect it to lead to others in the West? Historian Paul Jankowski explores the other possibilities as presented by the general's contemporaries:[*]

1. Count von Schulenburg, a staff officer in the *5th Army*, claimed after the war that Falkenhayn, who was a master strategist and planned his every move with care, had calculated that the French would have to weaken the fronts on the Aisne or Champagne. The British, in turn, would have to organize an offensive in Artois. German reserves would then attack the weakened French sector and counter-attack the newly recruited British forces, which would still be inexperienced at the time.
2. General Wilhelm Groener, in charge of the railways, claimed that Falkenhayn intended to take Verdun so he could launch another attack in either Artois or Champagne.
3. Colonel von Tappen, chief-of-operations at *Oberste Heeresleitung* (German Supreme Army Command), believed that Falkenhayn still considered operations against Belfort in December 1915 with about half a dozen divisions to draw the French forces away from another part of the front.[10] This would have allowed the Germans to strike at that weakened section of the front making an operation against Verdun or Belfort only a diversion. If von Tappen was correct, Belfort would have been a better choice.
4. The Kaiser, in exile after the war, recalled that Falkenhayn's explanation was that the French must attack and a British relief offensive was possible, to which a German counter-attack would be the response. This would bring a decision in the West that year. Verdun was to be the prelude. 'The hope persisted – added the Kaiser – to break up the English front.'[11] Falkenhayn clearly stated that his operations in the West in 1916 were to drive the British from the war, which corroborates the Kaiser's assertions.
5. One month before the offensive, Falkenhayn informed Hermann von Kuhl, chief-of-staff of Prince Rupprecht's *6th Army* in the Artois sector, to expect the British to retaliate by attacking on his front. Falkenhayn also warned Karl von Einem, commander of the *3rd Army*, soon after

---

[*] P. Jankowski, *Verdun: The Longest Battle of the Great War* (New York: Oxford University Press, 2013), pp. 35–6.

contacting Kuhl, to expect a French attack in his area. Both armies had orders not to initiate action, but to hold fast.

Thus, as Jankowski's research shows, despite his own post-war account, Falkenhayn initially intended to use Verdun as bait to draw in French and British forces. This would have allowed him to concentrate on directing a more decisive assault elsewhere on the Western Front. According to Jankowski, at a meeting on 11 February 1916, Falkenhayn ordered the chiefs-of-staff for all the armies, except Knobelsdorf of the *5th Army*, to meet at his own headquarters in Mézières.[12] Of the five men present, three claimed that Falkenhayn explained to them that the war could only be won in the West, but not with a single decisive battle. The Germans had to draw out the French and the British from behind their defensive lines, a move that would spell heavy losses for Allies. After this, the German attack could begin. Jankowski believes that this was why Falkenhayn carefully husbanded his reserves before and during the Battle of Verdun. Jankowski believes that even if Verdun was the initial target, Falkenhayn expected the reactions along the front to cause massive casualties for the enemy that would have the same effect. If that is indeed the case, the general was counting on the French employing the same methods they had used in 1915 and would draw them into more bloody battles. Therefore, whether Verdun was to be the scene of bloodletting meant to exhaust the enemy or a preliminary operation to ignite other parts of the front, Falkenhayn's 1916 strategy was to exhaust the Western Allies by inflicting irreparable losses on them.

In his Christmas Day memorandum to the Kaiser, Falkenhayn wrote that the Germans did not have enough forces to attack on the British front, but that 'an opportunity of doing so may arrive in a counter-attack'.[*] He claimed that the French, Russian and Italian armies were Great Britain's 'real weapons'. He went on to conclude that the British could be forced out of the war only if the French were eliminated since 'the strain on France has almost reached the breaking point …'. He ruled out a 'mass breakthrough', which 'in any case [is] beyond our means, [and] is unnecessary'. Behind the French sector of the Western front, 'there are objectives for the retention of which the French General Staff would be compelled to throw in every man they have …' and if they do, 'the forces of France will bleed to death – as there can be no question of a voluntary withdrawal – whether we reach our goal or not'. If the French allowed the German to take their objective, 'the moral effect on France will be enormous'. If this is actually the message he gave the Kaiser, we can assume that Falkenhayn, who also indicated time was short, intended to launch a massive campaign of attrition, be it solely against Verdun or several other points on the Western Front and that he did not believe he had enough forces for a war-ending breakthrough.

---

* Falkenhayn, *General Headquarters*.

Operation Gericht

There are multiple meanings for the word 'Gericht' and no one is sure which Falkenhayn intended. The most common translation is 'Judgement' and since Falkenhayn planned this to be the most decisive action of the war it could be the appropriate interpretation. One cannot be certain of the objectives for the Crown Prince's *5th Army*. The Christmas Day memorandum Falkenhayn prepared for the Kaiser does not specifically indicate his intention of 'bleeding the French army white'. It does emphasize the strategic importance of the city and its role as the cornerstone in the Allied line. Crown Prince Wilhelm and his chief-of-staff, von Knobelsdorf, thought that Verdun was their objective. They planned for operations on both banks of the Meuse, but Falkenhayn informed Knobelsdorf that he could not provide him with the necessary reserves or artillery to conduct an offensive on both banks. Thus, the main effort was focused on the right bank and no supporting operation on the left bank was to take place until later.[13] Falkenhayn pointed out that the winter and early spring weather had turned the Woëvre into a marsh and made the Argonne equally difficult to traverse. Thus, he explained, he could not approve of attacks through those sectors. It was better, he reasoned, to attack on a narrow front between the Meuse and the Woëvre.

From late December to February, on orders from Falkenhayn, each German army on the Western Front initiated small operations to keep the French guessing. In these encounters, neither side used poison gas and flamethrowers because of the weather. Crown Prince Wilhelm took two weeks' leave in early December. When he returned to Stenay, where he had initially prepared the operation with his staff, he discovered that his troops had been forced to abandon their flooded trenches. At about this point, Falkenhayn explained the situation to him and declared that the time was ripe for a major offensive in the West without, however, mentioning the date and the location for the impending operation. In January, the Crown Prince and his chief-of-staff were issued additional details regarding Falkenhayn's plans. Preparations were already in train. The Crown Prince recalled:

> I was filled with happy anticipations; yet I could not regard the future with a confidence altogether serene. I was disquieted by the constantly repeated expression used by [Falkenhayn] that the French Army must be 'bled white' at Verdun, and by a doubt as to whether the fortress could, after all, be taken by such means. I could only conclude that there lay before us a long and difficult struggle, which must place the utmost strain on the endurance of the troops; indeed, the limitation of the offensive to the right bank of the Meuse seemed to be motivated by a desire to engage as few troops as possible in the first stages, so as to ensure a continuous feeding of the front of attack over a long period of fighting.[*]

---

[*] William, *My War Experiences*, p. 166.

The Crown Prince's comments concur with those of other witnesses. However, his recollections may well have been coloured by other people's accounts after the war, especially when he mentions that Falkenhayn wanted to bleed the French white. He also claimed that he agreed with Falkenhayn that Verdun had to be taken quickly in order to avoid the continuous expenditure of forces and materiel inevitable in a lengthy battle. If it is true that Falkenhayn wanted a strong French reaction to his Verdun Offensive, it is debatable, however, whether he actually wanted the city to fall swiftly. He seemed more interested in taking the heights on the eastern bank where he could establish a killing zone. According to the plan, wrote the Crown Prince, 'Once the eastern bank is in our hands we can reduce the field works and permanent forts on the western side by flanking fire'.* A surprise attack with superior force covered by massive artillery would achieve this initial objective.

Crown Prince Wilhelm was given only one mission for 1916: the Verdun Campaign. To focus the Crown Prince's staff on the task, Falkenhayn detached the *3rd Army* from his command and replaced it with army detachments *Strantz*, *Falkenhausen* and *Gaed*. On 6 January, the Crown Prince and Knobelsdorf issued the 'Plan for the Artillery Attack' and on 27 January, they sent out orders to the commanders of the assaulting corps. They estimated that it would take five army corps to clear the east bank. Of these, three would attack from the north and a reinforced corps was to advance across the Woëvre northwest of Étain after the fall of the first French positions on the Meuse Heights. The *V Corps* was to coordinate an advance southeast of Étain with *Army Detachment Strantz*, but not during the initial attack. The artillery of the *VI Reserve Corps* with two divisions and *2nd Landwehr Division*, located west of the Meuse, would use flanking fire to neutralize French batteries. The *VII Reserve Corps* had secretly transferred from Valenciennes and joined the *5th Army* on 27 December 1915. It deployed behind the *V Reserve Corps*, which held sectors that formed the narrow assault front with its two reserve divisions. The assaulting corps would move past its divisions, which would remain in support. The *33rd Reserve* and *5th Landwehr* divisions occupied positions on the Woëvre Front from the vicinity of Fromezey southwards along the Orne.[14] In addition, the *VII Corps* was joined by the *XVIII*, *III* and *XV Corps*. According to Falkenhayn, these corps included nine trained and rested divisions. Each assault division was assigned to a front of less than 2½km. Later, three 'picked' divisions would move up to the front in preparation for an assault on the left bank when the opportunity arose. However, Falkenhayn would not allow any flanking attacks until he thought the time was right, insisting that there were not enough forces for a simultaneous attack on both banks.

The Germans managed to maintain secrecy on the *5th Army* front, despite deserters, and Falkenhayn directed each army to conduct aggressive operations on their fronts from January to February to keep the French guessing. *Army Detachment Gaed* in Alsace was to launch major divisionary operations in the Vosges region in an attempt to convince the French that an attack on Belfort was imminent. *Army*

---

* William, *My War Experiences*, p. 167.

Detachment Gaed had an early start on these operations since the French captured a couple of positions in the Vosges not far from Mulhouse between 28 and 30 December 1915 eliciting a response. *Gaed* troops counter-attacked and retook one position, but not the other. Both sides sustained heavy losses in an unsuccessful German attack on 8 January 1916. The *3rd* and *7th* armies launched trench raids on 4 January. The *3rd Army* penetrated the French line at several points near Butte de Massiges on 9 January. Although he was secretly preparing for the main assault and despite the cold weather, the Crown Prince allowed his *VI Corps* to launch a gas attack on 12 January in the Forges sector. Apparently, this action was meant to deflect French suspicions regarding the lack of activity on the *5th Army* front. On 23 January, the *6th Army* detonated twenty-five mines and launched a violent assault against the British in the Arras sector. The next day, the *4th Army* bombarded Nieuport on the coast. On 27 January, the *6th Army* attacked at Loos and Neuville while the *5th Army* kept its front active engaging in more mining operations against the French in the Argonne.[15] On 29 January, the *2nd Army* finally opened its own divisionary operations with an attack, including gas, near Lihons, south of the Somme. On 8 February, fighting in Artois heated up with over 700m of French trench line temporarily occupied. On 12 February, the *4th Army* and the *3rd Army* launched additional divisionary assaults in Flanders and Champagne respectively. The *3rd Army* made some gains, only to forfeit them to a French counter-attack on the following day. Meanwhile, *Army Detachment Gaede* captured several French positions in the Vosges. Falkenhayn wanted the *Gaede* operations to threaten the Belfort sector and to be on a larger scale than those of other armies. In February, the *4th Army* captured about 600m of enemy trenches along the Ypres Canal. The *7th Army* bombarded an area between Soissons and Reims on 14 February and launched a gas attack followed by an infantry assault north of Soissons on 16 February. The *4th Army* made three attempts to cross the Yser Canal on 20 February. Finally, on 21 February, the day the big offensive against Verdun was launched, the *6th Army* attacked near Béthune. As far as Falkenhayn was concerned, these diversionary attacks were successful as the French took heavy casualties and the Germans did not. In fact, his perception of the outcomes was rather rosy, since the Germans actually incurred significant losses, like the French. Nonetheless, when the Verdun Offensive began, Joffre was unable to ascertain if this was merely another minor action on the Western Front or something more serious. As a result, he did not send in his reserves in a timely fashion. In this respect, Falkenhayn had achieved one critical element he needed for the success of the operation: surprise. Thus, he had an advantage of a day or two before Joffre adequately reacted to the situation.

Despite some optimistic reports, the French positions at Verdun did not form a solid line of defence even after more than a year of relative quiet. A couple of French divisions pushed into the Woëvre and formed a line of mere outposts. Their position was much stronger in the Éparges sector. One of four sectors between Avocourt and Ornes in the northern part of the salient included Bois de Caures (Caures Woods) held by Colonel Driant's chasseurs. The 72nd and 51st divisions occupied other locations on the right bank and their situations were not much different. The 51st Division did not leave the southeast part of the salient to enter the line next to the 72nd Division until 11 February 1916.[16] The 67th and 29th divisions on the left bank held positions between Malancourt and the Meuse. The 14th and 132nd divisions held an outpost line in the Woëvre between the Orne River and the Meuse Heights. The 14th Division had only arrived on 12 February after a period of rest as of November 1915. Its troops trudged to their positions during the same period of bad weather that had delayed Operation Gericht. General Herr, military governor of Verdun, commanded the VII Corps (29th and 67th divisions), XXX Corps (14th, 51st and 72nd divisions), and a number of territorial battalions.[17] After he had pleaded for reinforcements for months, the 4th Division arrived in Lorraine on 13 January followed by the 37th Division on 12 February. The 48th Division transferred to his Verdun command on 16 February. The II Corps included the 132nd Division in the Woëvre and the 3rd Division, which had held the Éparges Front from December 1915.[18] The 67th, 72nd and 132nd divisions spent most, if not all, of their time in the Verdun Salient from the time mobilization in 1914 to 1916.[19] Joffre held the I Corps and the XX Corps in general reserve near Bar-le-Duc.

The two reserve divisions of the XXX Corps bore the brunt of the German assault and stood their ground for four days before their shattered remnants had to withdraw. Colonel Driant was more than justified in complaining about the weaknesses of the front since his worst fears were realized. Falkenhayn's offensive involved the largest concentration of artillery in the history of warfare up to that time. If he had been less methodical and not restricted the initial attack to a narrow front, the entire salient might have collapsed like a house of cards. However, that appears not to have been his goal.

The Generals

Among the generals who emerged as key players in the Battle of Verdun were Joffre, Pétain, Nivelle and Mangin for the French, and Falkenhayn and Crown Prince Wilhelm for the Germans. The two commanders-in-chief – Joffre and Falkenhayn – and the two generals most associated with guiding the course of the battle – Pétain and the Crown Prince – wrote books after the war, allowing historians a glimpse into their thinking. Naturally, since these men tried to vindicate their own actions, their accounts do not clearly explain what actually happened. However, between them, they caused one of the bloodiest confrontations in modern history, which failed to bring victory to either side in 1916.

Joseph Joffre led France into the war and took credit for the victory at the Marne in 1914. However, his early triumph was followed by one failed offensive after another until the end of 1915 as he ran up the number of casualties among his men without showing any significant gains. In 1914, when the French front was collapsing and the Germans struck at St Mihiel while another pincer advanced through the Argonne threatening a double envelopment of Verdun, Joffre seriously considered abandoning the fortress. Similar thoughts seemed to have run through his mind when the Germans launched their 1916 offensive. French political leaders changed between 1914 and 1915, but Joffre remained in command and exerted complete control over the front. He was not interested in sideshows and made it clear he was

Generals associated with the Battle of Verdun and Colonel Driant.

not pleased that the government had sent some of his divisions for operations in the Dardanelles in 1915. From 1914 on, he deemed incompetent any general who did not meet his standards or did not agree with him and assigned them to a meaningless position in Limoges. He usually stayed far from the battlefield and maintained a daily routine that made him appear quite aloof from his troops. Although his troops affectionately called him 'Papa', he showed little concern for their fate and wellbeing. Other generals tried to replace him, but they were not successful until his image was tarnished. After the failed offensives of 1915, he planned for a major Anglo–French offensive for mid-1916 in which the combined forces of both nations would drive the Germans from northern France. The only impediment to his great 1916 offensive was the Battle of Verdun.

During the winter of 1915/16, Joffre ordered defensive preparations to be made in locations where he expected the Germans to direct their offensive efforts. These sites included the area around Amiens where the Germans could drive a wedge between the British and the French, the Oise Valley around the city of Reims where they could take the direct route to Paris, the Argonne from where they could outflank and eliminate the Verdun Salient, the heights of the Vosges and the Porrentruy Gap along the Swiss border south of Belfort. 'Nor did the front around Verdun – wrote Joffre later – in view of the salient presented by its form, seem to me destined to become the theatre of the gigantic struggle …' that took place.* This was his justification, in light of a lack of material means, for not preparing Verdun and other positions. Furthermore, at a meeting on 29 December with President Poincaré and other officials, including General Gallieni and General Haig – Joffre claimed – everyone present concurred that the most threatened area was between Amiens and the Oise River.[20]

General Philippe Pétain, who had risen to prominence in 1915, was the only general who had achieved some success during Joffre's failed offensives. His tactics involved the methodical battle, which Joffre was reluctant to adopt in 1915. He often visited his troops on the front and valued their lives. No one could claim that he sat in headquarters moving troops around like pawns in a chess game. He had the skills needed to engage in offensive as well as defensive battle and win if he had the proper support from his superiors. When the Battle of Verdun opened, Joffre told Pétain to handle the situation by giving the 2nd Army responsibility for the defence of the fortress. Between 28 February and 2 May 1916, Pétain exercised control over the 2nd as well as the 3rd Army on the Verdun Front. The 3rd Army held the Argonne sector of the front. On 2 May 1915, Pétain was promoted to command Army Group Centre, replacing General de Langle.[21] Army Group Centre at Verdun included the 2nd and 3rd armies after 26 February and acquired the 4th and 5th armies in May.

General Robert Georges Nivelle took command of the 2nd Army on 1 May 1916, which gave him tactical control of the battle as Pétain assumed a more administrative position. However, Pétain still heavily influenced the conduct of the battle and continued to badger Joffre about rotating sufficient divisions to maintain the situation. Joffre became impatient with the demands of his army group commander, especially since they were taking troops from his planned Somme Offensive. However, he had little choice in the matter since France could not lose Verdun. Nivelle, who was confident that his own strategy and tactics would win the war, achieved some degree of success at Verdun. On 17 December 1916, his star rose even faster than Pétain's did when he was asked to replace Joffre as Commander-in-Chief. In 1917, finally allowed a free hand, he implemented his ideas with a disastrous offensive at Chemin des Dames which broke the morale of the French army. As a result, Pétain was asked to

---

* Joffre, *The Personal Memoirs of Joffre*, Vol. 2, p. 437.

replace him on 17 May 1917 and to restore order to the army. Nivelle was transferred to Africa.

One of Nivelle's subordinates at Verdun was General Charles Mangin, an extremely aggressive officer who rose from division commander at Verdun to commander of the 3rd Army in the last months of the battle. Known as 'The Butcher' for the heavy casualties caused by his methods, he was favoured by his superiors and the government as long as he was successful. Pétain disapproved of his disregard for the soldiers' lives, but Mangin was under Nivelle's command at Verdun. Mangin led the 6th Army in Nivelle's failed 1917 offensive, and like Nivelle, he was transferred out. He was brought back in time for the 2nd Battle of the Marne in 1918 where he redeemed his reputation.

General Frédéric-Georges Herr was put in command of the Région Fortifiée de Verdun (RFV) before the fateful battle. Joffre had created the Verdun Fortified Region in August 1915 when he had ordered the forts to be stripped of their removable artillery and their ammunition to form new batteries of heavy and field artillery.[22] The creation of the RFV meant that Verdun was no longer officially a fortress. As commander of VI Corps artillery brigade, Herr had smashed, with the help of aerial support, eleven batteries of the German army corps led by Bruno von Mudra on 10 September 1914. This action had taken place at the time Crown Prince Wilhelm's *5th Army* had tried to break through the French front in order to isolate the fortress of Verdun. The Germans had launched a mass bayonet attack on Herr's artillery north of Ste Ménehould, only to be driven back by his gunners.[23] At Verdun, General Herr was given limited resources and was unable to improve the defences significantly. The army used the fortress as a rest area for its troops since little action had taken place there after 1914. Joffre had transferred many of the infantry troops from the sector to the Champagne Front for the offensive of September 1915. This slowed Herr's efforts to build up the defences at Verdun with new trenches and barbed wire until the campaign ended and troops became available in late October. Herr warned General Dubail, commander of Army Group East, of heavy enemy activity in his sector.[24] General Herr and General de Langle, Army Group Centre commander, urgently requested reinforcements for the sector to improve and defend the positions. On the day of the proposed German assault, 12 February, which was cancelled due to bad weather, he alerted his subordinates of an imminent attack. When the battle began, Herr pulled back troops from the Woëvre to the more defensible positions on the Meuse Heights. Pétain arrived at Verdun on 25 February, a few days after the Germans launched their attack. He went to Herr's headquarters at Dugny to find the situation near collapse and to learn that Fort Douaumont had fallen to the Germans that very day. Herr had ordered the forts on the east bank and the bridges to be prepared for demolitions with disastrous results for Fort Vaux. Apparently, Herr, and General de Langle, thought that the east bank was lost and prepared to abandon it. When General Édouard de Castelnau, Joffre's second-in-command, was informed of the situation, he placed Pétain in charge of both banks of the Meuse.[25] Herr's plan to retreat to the left bank might have foiled General Falkenhayn's plan for a battle of attrition.

One more French officer, a colonel, influenced the course of the Battle of Verdun. He was Émile Driant, a commander of two battalions of *chasseurs à pied* defending

Caures Woods. He was a member of the Chamber of Deputies. As a reservist, he was called to active duty in 1914 at the age of 58. In 1915, he called the attention of other politicians to the inadequate state of the Verdun defences. Driant, who still served as a deputy, felt obligated to report the lack of men and materials – including barbed wire – necessary to improve the defences at Verdun. He also openly criticized Joffre's decision to disarm the forts of Verdun. However, little was done to correct the situation since the general opinion was that the forts would not be able to resist. Driant's criticisms caused the politicians to look at other weaknesses not only at Verdun, but also at Toul. The President of the Republic alerted the Minister of War, General Joseph–Simon Gallieni, who contacted Joffre on 16 December 1915.[26] Irate, Joffre replied in a letter of 18 December that on 22 October he had directed the respective army group commanders to improve all first and second positions on the entire front and to establish a system of fortified regions behind them. Some of the work, he claimed, had already been completed. 'I cannot permit men in military service – he groused – placed under my orders, to send to the Government … complaints or objection with regard to the execution of my orders'.[*] At the end of December, Joffre and Dubail, Army Group East commander, met with the president to report that the second line was completed and that they had begun work on a third line. Driant's complaints, which instigated these actions, may well have saved the situation at Verdun since Joffre had refused to believe that this area was threatened. Joffre sent his second-in-command, General Castelnau, to investigate. Since Castelnau reported few problems, Joffre was able to claim that he was informed that his instructions had been carried out as far as available resources permitted. Despite saying that the situation was satisfactory, he sent two divisions to General Herr. In order to improve coordination, on 1 February, he transferred the fortified region of Verdun to General de Langle's Army Group Centre. The work continued, but time was not on the side of the French.

Crown Prince Wilhelm, the eldest of the Kaiser's five sons, had a reputation with women that upset his father. In the military he rose to command a regiment, but when the war began, his father appointed him commander of the *5th Army* on 1 August.[**] Since he lacked command experience, the Kaiser told him, 'I have appointed you Commander of the Fifth Army. You're to have Lieutenant-General Schmidt von Knobelsdorf as chief of staff. Whatever he advises, you must do.'[27] Although he adhered to his father's instructions, the prince received credit for operations in the Ardennes in 1914 and shared some of the blame for the fiasco at Verdun.[28] However, the failure was not his because he followed orders from Falkenhayn, who did not always make his wishes clear. The Crown Prince and Knobelsdorf believed that they could have taken Verdun early in the battle and both were blamed by their troops for the insufficient resources that led to failure and huge casualties.

General Erich von Falkenhayn, commander of the army, was the youngest general serving as Chief-of-Staff Army (September 1914–August 1916) and as Minister of War (June 1913–January 1915) at the age of 53 in 1914. Before the war, he was

---

[*]   Joffre, *The Personal Memoirs of Joffre*, Vol. 2, p. 440.
[**] William, *My War Experiences*, p. 4.

promoted over many senior officers and he became a favourite of the Kaiser. Many other officers did not like him or the way he conducted himself. Among his detractors were generals Hindenburg and Ludendorff and Crown Prince Rupprecht of Bavaria, commander of the *6th Army*. Falkenhayn was probably solely responsible for the events that unfolded at Verdun. The evidence indicates that his subordinates did not fully understand his goals. His critics often accuse him of incompetency, especially since he believed that he could win a war by fighting a battle that would bleed the enemy to death. According to his critics, his offensive actions in the West in 1914 were failures, but they ignore the fact that he stabilized the front. In 1915, although he had preferred a Western to an Eastern strategy, he gave Hindenburg's front priority, which led to a massive defeat of the Russian army and he propped up Austria at the same time. Later that year, he engineered the conquest of Serbia. Even after Verdun, he was largely responsible for the conquest of Rumania.[29] Thus, despite his critics, he proved to be a largely successful general. Although his battle plan for Verdun seems senseless, if not absurd, there is no way of telling if it might have succeeded if it had been carried out the way he planned it. After all, there had never been a war of this scale in modern history and many experts had predicted that it would end quickly. Falkenhayn, unlike many other high-ranking officers, believed that in this 'modern' warfare with massive armies and huge fronts, Germany could not win by the traditional victory on the battlefield. He hoped that his plan for Verdun would whittle down the enemy forces to the point that they would surrender after this battle of attrition. Unfortunately, his new strategy proved to be as bloody and ineffective as those used by the other belligerents in 1915 had been.

Five Days in February

The battle opened with an artillery bombardment at approximately 8.00 am (German time) on 21 February 1916.[30] The opening shots came from the two huge 380mm Langer Max (Long Max) guns. These big 15in guns, originally intended for a battleship, had gone into service near Verdun in 1915. They fired a 2.2-ton round, had a range of over 22km and could strike almost anywhere in the salient, although it could take as long as 10 minutes between rounds. On that winter morning, they targeted the Verdun bridges and the railway station. The first round just missed one of the bridges, but crashed into the Bishop's Palace between the cathedral and the citadel. Another shell came down near the railway station. Then, the *trommelfeuer* (drum fire) of over 1,200 artillery pieces boomed across the countryside around Verdun. 'In the clear winter air – recalled Crown Prince Wilhelm – the thunder of the howitzers opened the chorus, which rapidly swelled to such a din as none of those who heard it had ever experienced hitherto.'* The German guns fired in sequence to achieve a continuous barrage for about 9 hours.[31] The slow-firing 420mm Big Berthas and Gamma guns joined in.[32] The artillery of the German army corps with fronts on the Verdun Salient laid down fire mainly on the French first line on the east and

---

* William, *My War Experiences*, p. 180.

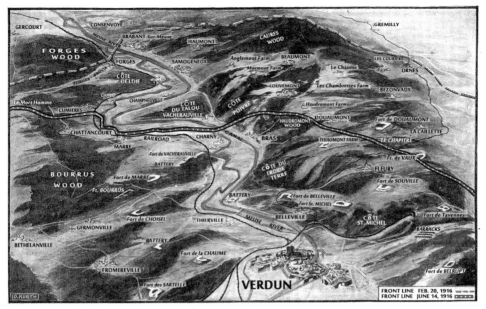

Bird's-eye View of the Battlefield of Verdun

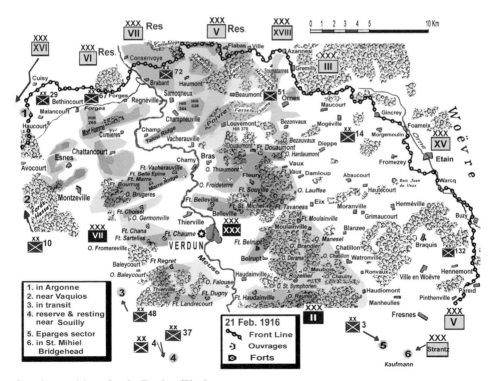

Opening positions for the Battle of Verdun.

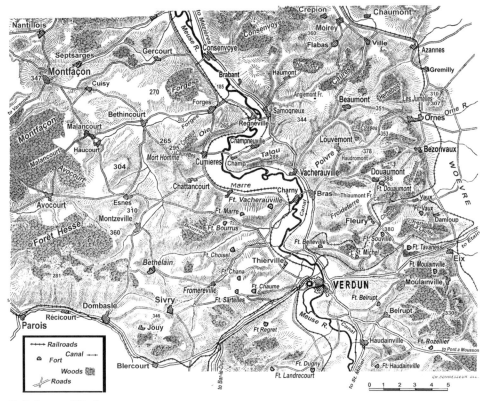

Relief map of Verdun.

west banks of the Meuse to keep the French guessing. It was becoming clear that the assault would not come from the Woëvre, but from the north against the Meuse Heights on the east bank and between the Meuse and the Argonne on the west bank. That was where Herr had concentrated four of his divisions. However, he was not to know that the left bank was not an immediate target for the Germans, who were about to concentrate on a narrow front. German artillery fire gave no clue until it started to concentrate on the areas intended for the ground assault and some batteries concentrated on counter-battery fire. As the day wore on, the barrages shredded the telephone lines between positions forcing Herr and his subordinates to rely on couriers to maintain contact with front-line units.

After Falkenhayn ordered them to prevent French aircraft from penetrating beyond the front line, the German aviation units flew patrols along the front, which took a toll on their engines. Some of the German reconnaissance units photographed the French positions while others flew artillery observation missions. On the first day, the German artillery received support from at least six tethered observation balloons, also known as kites.[33] The French balloonists were unable to locate the enemy batteries because they were targeted by German anti-balloon guns on the first day. German squadrons flew behind the lines to bomb railway stations in order

French Observation Balloon
at Verdun

French Biplanes protecting
an spherical observation balloon
against Taubens

Krupp Anti-Balloon Gun

Drawing of an observation balloon under attack and photograph of an anti-balloon gun (later referred to as an anti-aircraft gun).

to impede the transport of reinforcements into the salient. According to the French, the first wave of about ten German aircraft flew over Bar-le-Duc at about 10.00 am (French time). A second wave of five aircraft bombed Revigny at about 2.00 pm (French time). French pursuit aircraft reportedly shot down a couple of them as they fled. The best-known aerial operation of that day took place in the early evening over an airstrip near Revigny that had been lit up for returning French planes. Suddenly the spotlights fell on a yellow, fish-shaped object in the sky. It was a *Zeppelin L77* on a bombing mission. A battery of French 75mm autocannons (vehicle-mounted 75mm guns used as anti-aircraft weapons) opened fire at 9.00 pm (French time). Within 15 minutes, the dirigible took six hits, burst into flames and came crashing down to earth. There were no survivors.[34]

210 mm Howitzers open the batttle

Stormtroopers (post card)

In the late afternoon of 21 February, General Herr and his staff did not know where to expect the German strike on their front, but they must certainly have anticipated a big offensive since no one had yet witnessed a bombardment on this scale since the beginning of the war. Most of the divisions on the northern sector were not first rate and the soldiers had spent a cold winter sharing their trenches with rats. Fortunately, morale had been improving thanks to changes instituted to ease their daily lives. The constant artillery fire destroyed much of the first French position, but not to the extent hoped for by the Germans. At 5.00 pm (German time), the barrage shifted to the second French line and the German infantrymen emerged from their *stollen* expecting to reach and occupy the French positions easily. The battalions did not advance in normal assault formations, but adopted the newly developed storm-troop tactics. The advanced elements consisting of infantry and pioneer (combat engineer) companies were given the mission of moving quickly into the French positions and eliminating any strongpoints.[35] They advanced in small groups armed with grenades, light machine guns and small arms and they wore the new steel helmets. The pioneers carried flamethrowers and trench mortars to use against the strongpoints.[36] The weather was still cold and snow had still covered much of the ground before the bombardment. In many places, the snow was turning into slush. The assault troops had little cover between their own positions and the French first line because no-man's-land was wide, in some cases more than several hundred metres. Furthermore, the Germans had not dug sap trenches into it to provide advance jump-off positions for fear of alerting the French of an imminent attack.

Table 5: German Assault Units and Targeted French Formations with Objectives

French Corps Division Brigades			*German Assault Units*	*Objective*
VIII Res.	14th Res.	27th Res.	4 infantry companies: 1 regular, 1 guards, 1 reserve engineer company	Consenoye Woods –Haumont – 72nd Division's 351st Inf. Regt
VIII Res.	14th Res.	77th (attached from V Res. Corp)	6 infantry companies: 2 guards,1 reserve, 1 *landsturm* engineer company	
VIII Res.	13th Res.	28th Res.	4 jäger and 4 infantry companies: 2 regular, 1 guards, 1 reserve engineer company	Woods of Haumont – 72nd Division's 362nd Inf. Regt
XVIII	21st	42nd	20 infantry companies: 2 regular, 1 guards engineer company	Caures Woods – 72nd Division's 165th and 327th ** Inf. Regts and Driant's
XVIII	25th	49th	8 infantry companies:* 1 regular, 1 guard, 1 reserve engineer company	chasseur battalions
III	5th	10th	8 infantry companies:*** 1 guard engineer company	Ville Woods – 51st Division's 164th and 327th Inf. Regt
III	6th	12th	10 infantry companies: 1 regular, 1 guard, 1 reserve engineer company	Herbebois – 51st Division's 233 Inf. Regt

* From *115th Lieb Regt.*
** *327th* was from *51st Division.*
*** From a *Lieb Grenadier* regiment and a Fusilier battalion of a Grenadier regiment.

The follow-up infantry companies stayed behind until the assault troops broke into the first French line. Despite the massive bombardment, they were surprised to find surviving French troops stubbornly resisting at a number of points, especially in Caures Woods held by the chasseurs. Driant's two chasseur battalions, the target of

Typical German Supply Column

Shelter for Battery 426 in Bois de Ville

Entrance to German Stollen

German Shelter (Unterstand) for Artillery Commander

German Telephone Exchange

Main Road through Brabant after Bombardment

German attack, February 1916.

some 80,000 artillery rounds, had lost 60 per cent of their troops to the bombardment and many of their concrete shelters had been smashed. Yet the surviving chasseurs surprised the troops of the *21st Division* with their ferocity.[37]

East of Caures Woods, German troops advanced towards Ville and Bois-de-l'Herbebois where their artillery had destroyed some sections of the woods, but ran into stiff resistance from the French regiments of the 51st Division, particularly around Herbebois. While Driant's men held the *XVIII Corps* in check at Bois de Caures, the *VII Reserve Corps* made somewhat better progress at Bois de Haumont. Here the French troops of the 72nd Division occupied the high ground and a series of trenches with rows of wire obstacles blocked access and turned the heights into a formidable strongpoint. The German artillery had destroyed significant sections of the wire obstacles and, in some places, almost levelled the woods allowing their troops to take the position between 5.00 pm and 10.00 pm (German time). This gave the Germans a good jump-off position for 22 February as more of their troops and artillery poured into the Haumont area.

On 21 February, Driant's chasseurs prevented the Germans from advancing beyond Bois de Caures. As twilight set in early on that winter day, the Germans consolidated their positions. The soldiers on both sides spent the night shivering in freezing temperatures. German patrols went out to reconnoitre the remaining positions in the French first line and even the second line where it had collapsed. The next morning, the artillery received new firing data for another barrage. Much of the French 51st and 72nd divisions, which had reeled back in shock on the first day, prepared to launch desperate counter-attacks. The *VII Reserve Corps* continued to advance on the German right hoping to overrun the next French position quickly. However, the dazed and shocked survivors of the two French divisions who had weathered the shelling and assault had a brief reprieve that first night. The unrelenting bombardment had shredded many trees, levelled many of their trenches and smashed their shelters.[38] A repeat of a day like 21 February could have rendered the shell-shocked Poilus totally ineffective, yet they put up a strong resistance in some strongpoints and towns. The German storm units bypassed strongpoints that grenades or flamethrowers could not easily take out, leaving them to the mercy of the pioneers trudging behind with the trench mortars.

By the end of the first day of the German offensive, things looked grim for the French front-line divisions. General Herr faced a difficult situation with few resources to counter the enemy. The battalions of the 37th Division rushed into the northern sector to take part in counter-attacks the next day. The French artillery, especially 75mm guns, endured a bad day, but the batteries that survived the bombardment gave the advancing Germans an unpleasant surprise. After the war, General Joffre claimed that when 'the Germans hurled themselves against Verdun, the attack did not take us unawares …'.[*] If that was the case, the question remains why sufficient materials, such as barbed wire, and troops to finish the almost non-

---

[*] Joffre, *The Personal Memoirs of Joffre*, Vol. 2, p. 436.

existent second and third lines had not been sent in time. His explanation was that the first two positions in fortified regions were meant to channel an enemy advance and served as points of support for counter-offensives. In addition, he explained, before the German offensive, most critical sectors in need of strengthening were around Amiens where the British and French forces connected, in the Oise Valley which led directly to Paris, the area around Reims, the Argonne – a threat to the Verdun Salient – and the Vosges, which buttressed the French right wing. He had had to set priorities regarding where to build fortifications, and – he had no problem admitting – Verdun had not been first on his list.[39] In December, he had sent the VII Corps and the 15th Division to Bar-le-Duc for training, but not for reinforcing Verdun.[40] On 19 February, Joffre had gone to Bar-le-Duc to meet with Herr, Balfourier (XX Corps commander), Bazelaire (VII Corps commander) and Humbert (3rd Army commander). He was satisfied that Herr's command included twelve divisions and the VII Corps was detraining to reinforce Verdun. When the attack came on 21 February, Joffre decided he must maintain his reserve of twenty-six divisions echeloned along the Western Front. He admitted that at the end of 21 February he still did not think that Verdun was the main objective. Thus, Herr was left with little prospect of getting reinforcements the next day. It was not until the night of 24/25 February Joffre began to doubt his own judgement regarding the German offensive. However, he never thought to leave his headquarters to investigate the situation. He was satisfied with the notion that the surprise German attack had failed because it did not take Verdun. Despite his rosy views, the Germans successfully misled Joffre for several days. Their mistake was to attack only on the right bank of the river and to stop for the night after taking the first position.

General Falkenhayn and Crown Prince Wilhelm were satisfied with the progress of the first day, even though their gains were not impressive compared to their investment in the attack. On the first day, the Crown Prince drove to his battle headquarters at Vittarville, located about 10km from the front, while the bombardment was already underway. He arrived at the town at about 10.00 a.m. (German time) where General Knobelsdorf informed him that the French artillery response was weak and aimless, while their own guns were producing excellent results. Minutes later, French artillery shells fell in the town and near his headquarters. The Crown Prince and his staff promptly decamped to return to their old headquarters at Stenay, about 20km from the front, from where they operated for the remainder of the year.

During the night, the Germans moved their artillery forward and the second day of battle dawned with another violent bombardment. The troops of the *VII Reserve Corps* readied themselves in their newly occupied positions beyond the remnants of the French first line on the southwestern edge of Bois de Haumont. The *XVIII Corps* occupied positions in the French first line they had taken on the previous day. However, the remnants of the two French chasseur battalions still held much of Caures Woods and occupied several positions that covered the main road through the forest. Not far behind them, there were emplacements for 75mm and 90mm guns, some of which had been destroyed in the bombardment. At the entrance to the wood, the German artillery had brought down many branches leaving many of the remaining trees still standing. However, without spring foliage, the view of the ground was only slightly obstructed by the broken tree limbs. The *III Corps* held positions in Bois de Ville and Soumazannes. All its units had advanced the first day with light casualties, whose numbers increased in the evening of the first day when surviving French troops joined by nearby 75mm guns put up stubborn resistance.

On 22 February, the German artillery concentrated on the French second line and the towns of Brabant and Haumont, which were part of or behind the first line. At midday, the *VII Reserve Corps* launched its ground assault. The Germans encountered stiff resistance in the ruins of Haumont, but late in the day, the surviving French soldiers of the defending battalion, fewer than eighty men, finally surrendered. The *XVIII Corps* still had to clear Caures Woods. The chasseurs put up a heroic resistance that afternoon in the face of grenade and flamethrower assaults. By evening, the Germans secured with difficulty the woods they had been ordered to take at all costs. The *III Corps* advanced through Ville Woods. The troops from Rohr's detachment and the *6th Division* now faced the strongpoints in Bois de l'Herbebois on the northern and eastern edges where there was a double line of entrenchments and obstacles. Caures and Ville woods covered the west flank of the Herbebois Woods.

On 23 February, day three of the offensive, an infantry assault came on the heels of another morning bombardment. The *VII Reserve Corps* had moved artillery up to the edge of Haumont Woods to fire on the French positions running from the town of Brabant to the village of Haumont. Less snow had fallen then the previous day. The approaches to Brabant, located on the Meuse, were covered by several lines of barbed wire obstacles and trenches from the north. These defences extended eastward and combined with additional positions in the hills. That afternoon, the German troops fought their way into Brabant and secured the ridges to the east of the town as the French troops retreated. A few dozen French soldiers of a detachment of the 44th Territorial Regiment surrendered the town on 23 February.[41] General Étienne Bapst, 72nd Division commander, shifted his headquarters back and forth on 21 and 22 February, which caused command difficulties.[42] Bapst wanted to retreat, but General Adrien Chrétien, the corps commander, refused to give the order. By the time Chrétien had a change of heart, Brabant had fallen and other units of the division were in retreat. That night, the corps commander ordered a counter-attack to take back Brabant, but Bapst did not have enough troops. Troops of the 37th Division were sent in, but their attempts to counter-attack and help the troops of the 72nd Division failed.[43]

On the previous day (22 February), the *XVIII Corps* in the centre of the German drive had cleared most of Caures Woods. The last of the chasseurs' strongpoints fell and Colonel Driant was killed that night. The two neighbouring corps had to support the *XVIII Corps* in accomplishing its mission that day. On 23 February, the corps cleared the last of the resistance from Caures Woods despite a French counter-attack and moved to the south of the village of Beaumont. The *III Corps* on the left flank of the *XVIII Corps* fought its way into Herbebois Woods and took the French strongpoint in Wavrille Woods, incurring heavy casualties. It joined with the *XVIII Corps*, which was emerging from a small wood to outflank Beaumont. The German troops were unable to drive the defending French regiment of the 51st Division out of Beaumont that day. The French held off repeated German assaults and inflicted heavy losses before actually succumbing on 24 February. Some of the surviving Poilus fell back on positions at Louvemont. By the end of the day, three German corps had thrown the French back to their second position, which ran from Samogneux on the Meuse to Beaumont, through Fosses and Chaumes woods and to the town of Ornes. The Germans dominated Ornes from the twin hills of the same name, so the town was lost to all intents and purposes. This second line was far from complete when General Herr rushed in reinforcements. Thus, after three days of heavy bombardments followed by infantry attacks three relatively fresh German corps with six divisions and the largest concentration of artillery ever seen had advanced for 2–3km, had almost obliterated the French 72nd Division and roughed up the 51st Division. Although this was hardly impressive, it seriously alarmed the French. The next two days proved decisive for Falkenhayn's plan as well as for the French forces.

That evening, when he was informed that Samogneux had fallen, General Bapst ordered a counter-attack soon after midnight on 24 February. The remnants of one of his battalions still held the town, which had not actually surrendered. Meanwhile, Herr ordered his artillery on the west bank to fire on the position that was presumably lost, which devastated the poor defenders who surrendered the town to the Germans at 3.00 am (French time).[44] In the morning of 24 February, the Germans once again began the day with a heavy bombardment. The infantry emerged from its positions at about 2.00 pm (German time). The *13th Reserve Division* spearheaded the assault. French artillery from hills on the west bank mauled the *VII Reserve Corps* as it moved toward and past Samogneux.

The 37th Infantry Division, which was thrown into the battle piecemeal to stem the tide after the first day, was in poor condition by 24 February. Its two Zouave and two Algerian Tirailleur regiments of high-quality troops fared poorly in futile counter-attacks during the first days. On 24 February, General Léon de Bonneval, the division commander, received orders to defend the Côte de Talou and the Côte du Poivre (Pepper Hill). General Balfourier's XX Corps was on its way to the east bank, but only elements of the 153rd Division, its general and his staff arrived on 24 February. Elements of his 39th Division crossed the Meuse the next day. Thus, only the XX Corps had fresh units on the east bank to bolster the French third position that ran from Champneuville, through Louvemont and Bezonvaux, and south to Fort Douaumont and Fort Vaux. There was little left of Chrétien's XXX Corps. The 51st Division clung to Louvemont and the area around it while the 14th pulled back, but still held Bezonvaux and positions to the south toward Damloup. What was left of the 72nd Division assembled around Champneuville and the Talou Hill (or ridge), but had to be removed from the battle at the end of 25 February. On 24 February the Germans had penetrated the front running from Samogneux to Beaumont to Ornes, having already taken Samogneux early in the morning. The *VII Reserve Corps's* main achievement that day was the capture of Hill 344. Other corps moved through Bois de Fosses and Chaume Woods and the village of Ornes. During the night of 24/25 February, the French pulled back from Ornes to Bezonvaux, and, following Herr's orders, the French units on the north side of the line withdrew to an incomplete line that ran from Vacherauville to Côte du Poivre, Chambrettes Farm, La Vauche, Hardaumont and Vaux. This move apparently went undetected by the Germans.

The decisive day of the offensive was 25 February. Command changes on the French side altered the course of French strategy. In his memoirs, Joffre recounted that he did not learn of the German offensive until 10.00 am (French time) on 21 February. By the end of the day, he found out that the Germans were in the woods of Caures and Herbebois. Early the next morning, he was informed that Bois de Haumont and Caures Woods had fallen as well. The information about Caures Woods, however, had been erroneous. Reports that the French troops were performing admirably in heavy fighting buoyed his spirits. The news was no better on 23 February when, at mid-morning, he learned that the 72nd Division had abandoned Brabant and the Germans had taken most of Caures and Wavrille woods. The evening dispatches reported that his troops had a precarious hold on Ornes and Beaumont and that some positions were already lost. The ferocity of the German attack finally made him realize that he needed to commit fresh reserves. 'I Corps and XIII Corps – he wrote – had already been sent by motor transport to the region … and the commanders of groups of armies had been warned to be ready to furnish reinforcements up to the extreme limit of their resources'.[*] He had delayed in sending reinforcements because he had expected attacks on other fronts to follow this one. On the night of 23 February, Joffre sent Colonel Claudel, his assistant chief-of-staff, to investigate the situation at Verdun. On the afternoon of 24 February, Claudel telephoned to tell him that the attack had been slowed and that counter-attacks should be possible, apparently unaware of the condition of the divisions of XXX Corps. When the Germans renewed their assault with a ferocity equal to the previous days, Joffre could only say, 'the situation suddenly changed'. The Bois de Fosses, Louvemont and Hill 344 fell as French troops evacuated Ornes and German troops pushed into the Meuse Heights. General de Langle called Joffre at 7.30 pm to inform him that the situation was critical. Joffre authorized him to evacuate the Woëvre if he deemed it necessary, but told him that his forces must face northward and resist the German attack while maintaining positions between the Meuse and the Woëvre. According to historian Robert Doughty, de Langle had already anticipated Joffre's order.[**] On 24 February, Herr ordered his troops to prepare the bridges and forts for demolition. De Langle stopped all troop movements across the bridges to the east bank to keep them open for support troops evacuating the east bank. At 8.00 pm on 24 February, General de Langle ordered the outposts in the Woëvre to be evacuated the next day at 9.00 pm (French time). When he was informed of these measures, Joffre instructed Langle and Herr to rescind the orders concerning the abandonment of the east bank and

---

[*]   Joffre, *The Personal Memoirs of Joffre*, Vol. 2, p. 443.
[**] Doughty, *Pyrrhic Victory*.

the demolition of the forts. Herr obeyed his superior. Joffre also ordered the troops to hold the right bank of the Meuse and authorized de Langle to use the entire XX Corps to accomplish this mission. At this point, Joffre was becoming anxious because the situation was changing rapidly and he feared a collapse that would degenerate into a rout if the troops tried to make it to the left bank. The most important change on the east bank took place on 25 February when the XX Corps replaced the XXX Corps and took over the remaining divisions. This meant that General Maurice Balfourier and his staff would replace Chrétien whose XXX Corps was coming apart.

On February 24, Joffre concluded that one man needed to take command of the situation on the left bank. At 11 pm, he telephoned the 2nd Army headquarters to notify General Pétain that he was assigned that mission. That same night, Joffre had dispatched General Castelnau, his chief-of-staff, to Verdun and authorized him to implement any measures he felt necessary. Castelnau arrived at Avize, south of Reims, midway between Chantilly and Verdun, at 5.00 am on 25 February. An hour later, he issued the following order: 'The Meuse must be held on the right bank. There can be no question of any other course than of checking the enemy, cost what it may, on that bank.' Nothing would have pleased Falkenhayn more had he known about this order. The French were taking his bait. The Crown Prince and Knobelsdorf, on the other hand, would not have rejoiced to hear about this decision. President Raymond Poincaré and Prime Minister Aristide Briand made it clear to Joffre that he must

Timeline

The events of February 1916 are not only confusing but also controversial in some cases. The following information comes from Joffre and Pétain, but the accuracy of some of it may be questionable. Although Joffre always insisted that he had never wanted to abandon the right bank of the Meuse, there is a possibility that he may have made the decision to hold it only after a visit from the prime minister of France. None of the general officers described the weather in detail, besides mentioning that it had snowed before and after the battle began. They are equally unclear on the subject of the condition of the troops. According to Pétain, the troops of the XXX Corps 'exhibited astonishing, almost incredible, heroism' and that 'every centre of resistance, whether it were a wood, a village, a network of destroyed trenches, or a chaotic group of shell-holes, was used by our units and became the scene of gallant deeds …'.[*] Pétain did not mention who was at fault or the broken troops streaming back from the front. Accounts about actual conditions on the battlefield tend to be rather sterile. Pétain does not even mention that he had come down with pneumonia.

The basic facts can be summarized as follows:

---

[*] Pétain, *Verdun*, p. 63.

21 February: Bombardment began in the morning. Late afternoon, the German infantry advanced on possibly snow-covered ground expecting virtually no resistance. Despite the destruction of many trenches and shelters, they encountered stiff resistance in many places and from Driant's chasseurs in Bois de Caures. Many pockets of French resistance checked the German advance, but Haumont Woods fell.

22 February: Germans repeated the procedure of the previous day. The German infantry of the *VII Reserve Corps* took the towns of Haumont and Brabant. The *XVIII Corps* cleared most of Caures Woods. The *III Corps* advanced deep into Herbebois Woods. The French 72nd Division suffered heavy losses. The French 51st Division hung on to many of its positions. The 37th Division, consisting of North African troops, moved onto the east bank, but its regiments entered the battle piecemeal for the next three days to plug gaps. The weather, like the previous night, was wintry and bad. There is no consensus between various sources on whether Brabant was lost on 22 or 23 February. According to the Crown Prince, it fell on 23 February.

23 February: The *XVIII Corps* cleared the remainder of Caures Woods that day and the *III Corps* swept Herbebois Woods that evening. German troops advanced south engaging the French at Beaumont. Troops of the *VII Reserve Corps* marched on Samogneux. The French held their positions between Samogneux, Beaumont and Ornes until the evening. That night, General Herr ordered the XXX Corps to take up positions on a line between Vacherauville, Côte de Talou, Côte du Poivre, Louvemont and Bezonvaux.

24 February: Samogneux fell just before sunrise. The *VII Reserve Corps* took Hill 344. The *XVIII Corps* and *III Corps* moved through Fosses Woods. The *III Corps* swept through Chaume Woods, Carrière and Vavette and advanced upon Bezonaux, while the *V Reserve Corps* infantry moved on Ornes. The Germans broke through the entire position between Samogneux and Beaumont within a few hours. Herr ordered bridges and forts prepared for demolition. Herr and de Langle decided to evacuate the right bank. Late that night, Joffre sent Castelnau to investigate and to take charge.

25 February: French outposts pulled back to the heights from the Woëvre. German troops moved onto Poivre Hill (ridge) and Louvemont fell. The *III Corps* captured Fort Douaumont. The entire position on the east bank was near collapse. The French XX Corps took over the defence of the east bank. Pétain arrived at Verdun in the early evening, and Castelnau informed him he was to command the entire sector instead of the left bank only. Pétain designated the final defence line on the right bank and ordered the restoration of the forts to operational status.

'Considering the terrific force of the enemy's drive – stated Pétain – the fact that Verdun was still in our possession on February 25th constituted really a success.'*

---

* Pétain, *Verdun*, p. 83.

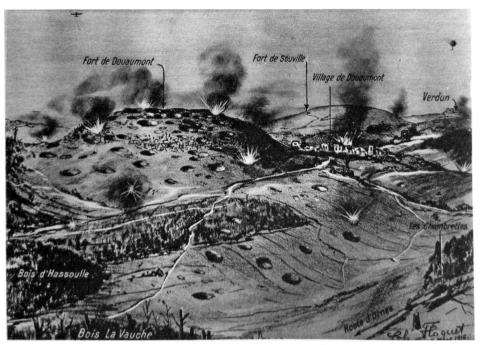

Drawing of the German attack on Fort Douaumont, February 1916.

hold Verdun. Joffre gave no indication that he disagreed, especially after a year of offensives that had ended in defeat.[45]

At about 8.00 am on the morning of 25 February, Pétain reported to Joffre for his instructions. He then drove to Verdun where he arrived in the evening after having travelled over sleet- and snow-covered roads in an open car. The next morning he was diagnosed with double pneumonia. Meanwhile, at 3.30 pm (French time), General Castelnau informed Joffre over the telephone that Herr was 'fatigued to the point of depression' from the events of the past few days, that he could no longer inspire his troops and that his staff was in no condition to support him. The best chance to save the situation, Castelnau opined, was to give Pétain command of both banks. When Pétain reached Souilly at about 7.00 pm, he met with Castelnau and de Langle. 'The reports were coming in slowly, – he complained – and seemed disturbing.'* He decided to drive on to Herr's headquarters at Dugny. On his way there, he came across long columns of troops blocking the roads, an endless line of supply convoys forging their way towards Verdun and a horde of fleeing civilian refugees. At Herr's headquarters, he found out that despite the XX Corps' valiant effort to maintain control of Douaumont village, Fort Douaumont had fallen earlier in the day to troops of the Prussian *III Corps*.[46]

---

* Henri Philippe Pétain and Margaret MacVeagh (trans.), *Verdun* (Toronto: Dial Press, 1930), p. 72.

That same night, at 11.00 pm (French time), General Castelnau informed Herr that he was now under Pétain's command. By this time, major reinforcements were reaching the front lines. The I Corps had detrained the previous day and the XIII Corps that very day. Additional artillery batteries taken from three new corps, according to Pétain, were also arriving. The next day, 26 February, some of these units reached the front. Late in the evening of 25 February, Pétain telephoned General Balfourier (XX Corps) on the east bank and General Bazelaire (VII Corps) on the west bank to inform them he was now in command. Their responses

BATTLE OF VERDUN   **FEBRUARY 1916**

A. 138.6 mm Mle 1910 Naval Gun

C.. 120mm C Mle 1890 Baquet howitzer

B. 164.7 mm Mle 1893 Naval Gun

Firing Trench in front of battery position south of Beaumont.

French Prisoners Feb 1916

Abandoned French Searchlight

A. In casemate and abandoned on in Bois-le-Fey and abandoned 22 Feb. 1916. A second gun captured at Vauche 24 Feb.

B. In casemate at Herbebois. One of 12 guns located at Verdun and Toul in 1914. Two were captured at Verdun in Feb. 1916

C. Damaged howitzer west of Beaumont.

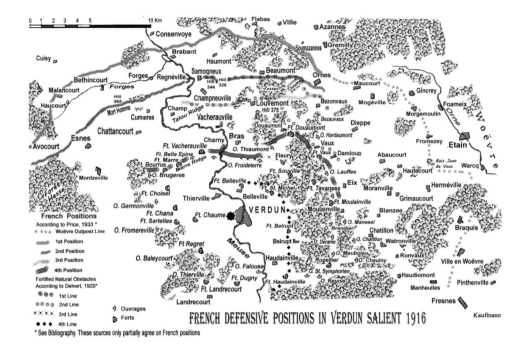

FRENCH DEFENSIVE POSITIONS IN VERDUN SALIENT 1916

bolstered his confidence in their performance. Shortly after that, just past midnight on 26 February, Pétain and his chief-of-staff reviewed the situation and prepared orders for every unit under his command during the next several hours. Despite his illness, Pétain worked tirelessly.

A New Command, 26 February–1 March 1916

General Pétain began his first day of command with double pneumonia. Refusing to rest and recover despite being 60 years old, he involved himself heavily in directing operations in less than healthy conditions. He was concerned about the loss of Fort Douaumont and Poivre Hill since this meant that the northern part of the front was on the verge of collapse with only two ouvrages and a poorly prepared defence line left between Douaumont and the Meuse. The shattered XXX Corps had to withdraw and rebuild. Generals Bapst (72nd Division), Bonneval (37th Division) and Chrétien (XXX Corps) served as Joffre's scapegoats.[47] Pétain's staff was on the way and his 2nd Army moved out of reserve to take over the Verdun Front. Joffre gave him tactical control of the 3rd Army on his left flank.

Pétain's final line of defence on the east bank and northern front ran from Thiaumont to Souville. The general wanted to keep the front between those forts as close to Fort Douaumont as possible. The eastern front ran through the forts of Vaux, Tavannes and Moulainville. On the west bank, the line stretched from Cumières to Le Mort Homme, Hill 30 and Avocourt. His Operations Order No. 1 specified that the mission of his army was 'to check at all costs the attacks of the enemy; to retake at once all lost ground' and for every man to do his best to hold the specified line. He designated the forts on

The Big Picture

The participants' recollections of the first critical days of the Battle of Verdun vary substantially. According to General Erich von Falkenhayn, the bombardment began on 21 February and it was followed by 'a successful infantry attack ... carried out with an irresistible impetus, and the enemy's first lines were simply overrun'. He concluded that 'the advanced fortifications, constructed in peace, [could not] stop the brave attackers, although these works were not much damaged by our artillery'.[*] Actually, the only French fort that fell was Douaumont, which – he claimed – was 'stormed' by the *24th Brandenburg Infantry Regiment* on 25 February. In the days that followed, Falkenhayn recalled, the Crown Prince's staff had to halt the advance because of violent counter-attacks mounted by hastily collected French troops, but his soldiers repelled these attacks everywhere and inflicted heavy casualties.[48]

Crown Prince Wilhelm, more closely involved in the battle, provided a more accurate description. By the evening of 24 February, his army 'held the whole of the enemy's main position!' and had not only shattered the defensive system of the French but had broken their morale. In his memoirs, he wrote that the French 'had nowhere been able to put up an effective resistance, and all his works, batteries and communications in his back areas as far as Verdun itself lay exposed to the effective and harassing fire of our artillery'. This was the time when his army had to prepare to smash the 'tottering edifice of his defence' before the French reserves arriving by lorry from Clermont could bolster the defences.[**] On 25 February, French artillery on the west bank brought the *77th Brigade* to a standstill in attacking the Talou Heights. The *XVIII Corps* in heavy fighting took Louvemont and the northeastern slopes of the Côte du Poivre. The *III Corps* passed through Chauffour Wood while one of its companies from the *24th Regiment* took Fort Douaumont. The *III Corps* drove the French from the ridge between Douaumont and Bezonvaux. The *V Reserve* and *XV Corps* pushed across the Woëvre. On the Meuse Heights, his troops fought off violent counter-attacks.

The *5th Army* headquarters ordered the heavy artillery of the attacking corps to move forward on the night of 25 February. However, the Crown Prince claimed that his only reserve was the *14th Reserve Division*, which had already been engaged during the first days of the attack. The promised reinforcements from Falkenhayn had not arrived. The Crown Prince complained that the *XXII Reserve Corps*, allotted to *Army Detachment Strantz*, had been left on the Woëvre and that Falkenhayn only dispatched the *Bavarian Ersatz Division* to *Strantz*, a unit not fit for offensive action. The French had been broken, he insisted, and he was 'within a stone's throw of victory' but had no reserves left to finish the job. His exhausted soldiers could not do it. In addition, instead of snowing, it rained turning the ground into a quagmire and filling even the smallest shell holes with water. Troop movement was hindered for days. Prince Wilhelm guessed that his chances of victory had slipped away on the night of 25 February when the French XX Corps reached the front.

---

[*]   Falkenhayn, *General Headquarters*, p. 233.
[**]   William, *My War Experience*.

this line as dominant positions because, after all, they occupied key points, some had turret guns and all had survived up to that point without significant damage. Pétain realized that most of these forts were better built than those that had fallen during the Battle of the Frontiers in 1914 and that they did not operate in isolation. On 26 February, he divided his front into sections. General Guillaumat's (I Corps) Group with 1st and 2nd divisions stood astride the Meuse and extended to the east. General Balfourier's (XX Corps) Group with the 14th, 39th, 51st and 153rd divisions held the Meuse Heights between Douaumont and Fort Vaux. General Bazelaire's (VII Corps) was west of the Meuse. The II and XIV Corps held the front on the east bank between Fort Moulainville and Éparges. Except for the remnants of the XXX Corps, there were no reserves. The XIII and XXI Corps were heading for Verdun and the XXXIII Corps was not far behind. Pétain asked Joffre to send more artillery instead of all these infantry divisions. The French had little room to manoeuvre on the east bank while the Germans held the dominant position of Fort Douaumont, the best observation point in the area. The French intended to fight to the death for Verdun from the east bank, and if necessary, from the west bank.

The events of 26–9 February are not clear, beside the facts that Pétain restored order and that the French were holding their ground. In a post-war account, historian Count Charles de Souza asserts that during those four days, the defenders strength increased as 'German assaulting waves dashed themselves in vain against the Talou heights, the Pepper (Poivre) Ridge, and the Vaux position.'[*] The Germans 'were ripped open with cannon, broken by the French bayonets, and driven back with fearful slaughter, time and again' until their battered units withdrew having lost 60,000 in a single week. As can be expected, his account exaggerates German losses. It places the French casualties at 20,000 when they were actually closer to 30,000. The Germans lost only a few thousand men less than the French did. Actually, at the end 25 February, the 37th Division had lost 30 per cent of its men (about 4–5,000 men) and the 72nd Division's casualties were 10,000 men leaving only 3,000 survivors. The 51st Division suffered 6,400 casualties. If these figures are correct, the numbers were a little over 20,000 for these 3 divisions alone.

On 26 February, the weather cleared again. The *VII Reserve Corps* sent patrols across the Talou Heights toward the quarries near Vacherauville. The *XVIII Corps* met strong resistance in the valleys and wooded area south of Louvemont. The *III Corps* fought off French counter-attacks against Fort Douaumont, but had no success in driving the French from the village. From the east, the *XV Corps* advanced across the Woëvre. The *V Reserve Corps* moved onto the Meuse Heights taking the small Ouvrage of Hardaumont to the east of Fort Douaumont and north of Fort Vaux. On the heights, recalled the Crown Prince, 'our attack had come to a standstill and the active defensive thenceforward adopted by General Pétain swayed the balance against us'.[**]

---

[*] Count Charles de Souza, 'The First Assault on Verdun', in Charles F. Horne (ed.), *Source Records of the Great War*, 7 vols (New York: National Alumni, 1923), Vol. 4.

[**] William, *My War Experience*, p. 184.

Falkenhayn's Strategy

No one can be certain of Falkenhayn's goals since even the Crown Prince and his other subordinates do not clearly agree on the subject. The Crown Prince thought that his objective was Verdun. Even with the forces available to him, if he had been allowed to attack simultaneously on both banks of the Meuse and all conditions had been the same, he probably would have taken the city in the first few days. If Falkenhayn had concentrated his forces on thrusts from the Argonne and the St Mihiel Salient, he might have isolated Verdun by envelopment, a tactic the Germans often used successfully. Instead, he went for a frontal attack and on

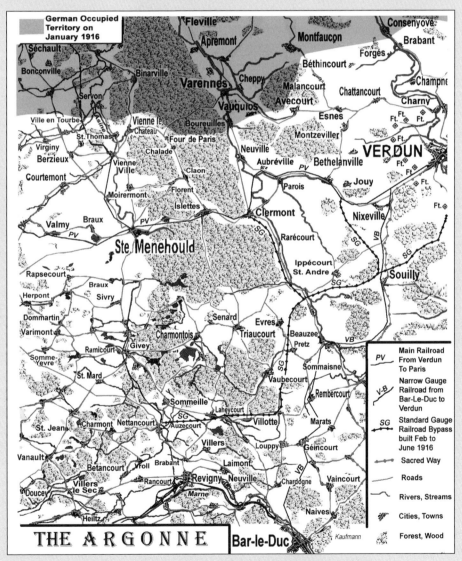

Map of the Argonne showing the railway and Sacred Way into Verdun, 1916.

a narrow front on the right bank against the Meuse Heights where the French defences should have been the strongest.

The first few days may give a clue to Falkenhayn's actual objectives. After the first two days, the German troops made significant advances. General Herr pulled his troops from the Woëvre and ordered the forts of Verdun prepared for demolition. He was ready to abandon the east and the Meuse Heights. What more could Falkenhayn want than control of the heights? If he had allowed a simultaneous frontal attack on the western bank and reached the line of forts there, Verdun would have been indefensible. Despite the French government's wishes, Joffre could have implemented his early plans and pulled his troops out of the salient into a new defensive position. The Germans could have claimed another small victory, but it would not have led to a triumphant end to the war on the Western Front. Falkenhayn wanted and anticipated French and British relief attacks, confident that his other armies would be able to check them. He wished for the French to fight for Verdun and hoped the battle would last long enough to cause unbearable losses. Only by securing most of the Meuse Heights from which his artillery could dominate the west bank and the city could he establish his killing grounds. The French, who still held key terrain on the west bank, could be drawn further into the battle even if they still controlled part of the Meuse Heights. The French would then have had to go on the attack in an attempt to push the Germans back and secure the old fortress perimeter. If the French committed enough divisions, the German *5th Army* could actually launch an offensive across the Meuse and apply more pressure or even attack from the Argonne and St Mihiel Salient if the French appeared to be reaching breaking point. For this to work, a battle of attrition had to be fought during the first month or so, if not longer and the French must lose at least two to three soldiers for every German soldier. If this was Falkenhayn's actual plan, it could only work if the French fell into his trap and stayed in the Verdun Salient.

It is conjectured that if the attack had gone as scheduled, despite the weather on 12 February, the Germans would have made more gains in the first days since the 51st Division had not moved into position. The 72nd Division, whose front was too large, may not have survived the first day and the Germans would have easily blown past the second French line. Assuming the weather did not hinder the attack, or even supposing it had been good that day, the Germans could have reached the line of forts so quickly that Herr would have evacuated the eastern bank, as he was about to do after 22 February. Verdun would have become indefensible and the French divisions in reserve would have had less time to move forward. This may have considerably shortened the Battle of Verdun, but it was most likely not the kind of victory Falkenhayn wanted. The only victory, in his mind, would have been a bloodbath for his enemy.

On the night of 27 February, the *VII Reserve Corps* tried to cross the Meuse near Samogneux, but could not get past wire entanglements in the riverbed. The Crown Prince and Knobelsdorf had hoped to secure this crossing for the *VI Reserve Corps* to attack the west bank. Falkenhayn released the *113th Division* at Metz to reinforce the offensive. *Army Detachment Strantz* tried to make some headway against the southern end of the heights on the east bank. The French position continued to grow stronger, but it did not expand.

Crown Prince Wilhelm lamented that no further surprises had been possible after 25 February. His troops were tired. By the end of April, he realized they could not crack the stubborn resistance, 'for every foot of ground' and that despite changing 'our methods of attack, a decisive success at Verdun could only be assured at the price of heavy sacrifces, out of all proportion to the desired gains'.[*] From that point on, he wrote, he did everything he could to end the futile attacks, against the wishes of his chief-of-staff who continued to order additional attacks. The public and the soldiers blamed the Crown Prince and called him 'The Butcher of Verdun'.

On 29 February, Castelnau returned to Chantilly and reported that Verdun was safe for the moment. Joffre recalled his reaction to the events:

> it seemed to me that the best way of arresting any succeeding efforts of the enemy would be by retaking the ground which he had conquered. Our ammunition was plentiful and our flanking positions on the left bank made it possible to bring the enemy under a convergent fire; this chance must, therefore, not be neglected, and when General Pétain took command, I indicated it to him as his earliest task.

He supposedly repeated this to Pétain during a visit at Souilly between 1 and 5 March and stressed that 'The most important of these operations should be the retaking of the fort at Douaumont.'[**]

---

[*]   William, *My War Experiences*, p. 199.
[**] Joffre, *The Personal Memoirs of Joffre*, Vol. 2, p. 448.

Chapter Five

On Ne Passe Pas

'Siege and defence will, in the future, be nothing but a number of artillery engagements, in which the opponents will severally hurl at each other thousands of tons of iron, and make their projectiles, by filling them with a large charge of explosives, have the effect of mines; thus ploughing up the whole battle-field and destroying all bulwarks. Fortresses which are well constructed … can now … serve as bulwarks and display powers of resistance with which they are now scarcely credited.'

> Colmar von der Goltz, *The Nation in Arms* (London: W.H. Allen and Co., 1887; English translation of Goltz's 1883 *Das Volk in Waffen*)

'"On ne passe pas" – "None Shall Pass"'

> General Robert Nivelle, spring 1916

March Madness

On 4 March 1916, an order from Crown Prince Wilhelm's headquarters exhorted the troops to make a supreme effort to take Verdun. General Falkenhayn decided to send the *5th Army* to seize Le Mort Homme Ridge and Cumières Wood on the left bank to protect the German rear and flank. However, snow followed by rainstorms delayed the operation, and deep in the trenches, the infantry on both sides hunkered down in misery, mud and slush. A massive bombardment began on the afternoon of 5 March in preparation for the assault on the west bank. From the beginning to the end of the battle, the defenders (French and German) took more losses than the attackers did since they were the prime target of the cannons. Attempts to improve defensive positions or captured ones became difficult under constant artillery fire and in bad weather. The soldiers often found it more practical to occupy and defend shell craters.

General Georges de Bazelaire's Group (VII Corps) held the western sector of the Verdun Front with four divisions on line and a fifth in reserve. The weight of the German assault fell upon the 67th Infantry Division. At the end of the first day of bombardment, the VII Corps reported, 'The whole area included in the resistance position and the zone of batteries behind it looks like a foaming trough.' The trenches on the reverse slope of Le Mort Homme and Côte de l'Oie were destroyed. On 6 March, the *5th Army* launched the ground assault on the west bank; a new attack on the east bank was to follow. The Crown Prince recorded a severe snowstorm on that day.

BATTLE of VERDUN   Feb. - July 1916

Be - Ft. Belleville   H - Ft. Haudainville   S - Ft. Souville
Bp - Ft. Belrupt   Ma - Ft. Marre   Ti - Ft. Thiaumont
B - Ft. Borurrus   M - Ft. Moulainville   T - Ft. Tavannes
Ch - Ft. Chaume   Re - Ft. Regret   Va - Ft. Vacherauville
C - Ft. Choisel   R - Ft. Rozellier   V - Ft. Vaux
D - Ft. Douaumont   SM - Ft. St. Michel
F - Ft. Froideterre   Sa - Ft. Sarfells

Forts

Front Line February 21, 1916
German Advance of July 1916

Days before the 5 March offensive, the *5th Division* had battled its way into Douaumont village. It finally wrested possession of this hot spot on 6 March. Due to heavy fighting, it was unable to move any further. When the right–bank offensive resumed on 7 March, the *113th Divis*ion had to take its place. Several other changes had occurred before the March offensive: a brigade of the *XV Corps* was detached to reinforce the *III Corps* and the *13th Reserve Division* (*VII Reserve Corps*) relieved the *25th Division* (*XVI Corps*). Falkenhayn dispatched the *121st Division* from his reserve to support the *V Reserve Corps*.

On 6 March, the *22nd Reserve Division*, attached to the *VI Reserve Corps*, opened the assault on the corps' left flank and took Regnéville.[1] Meanwhile, the *77th Brigade* of *VII Reserve Corps* crossed to the west bank to reinforce the attack. In the morning of 6 March, on the *VI Reserve Corps's* far right flank, German infantry surged late towards Malancourt driving back the French 29th Division. The corps' effort was concentrated across the Forges stream. The *feld grau* infantry encountered no major resistance until after it overran the lightly defended outpost line, took Forges village and marched up the slopes of Le Mort Homme and Côte de l'Oie. The next day, they overran Côte de l'Oie, but came face to face with French units. There ensued a ferocious battle with fixed bayonets for control of Corbeaux Woods on Côte de l'Oie. The French stopped the Germans from moving down the southern slopes and taking Cumières.[2] However, in the next few days, the Germans finally took Hill 265, part of Le Mort Homme, after heavy fighting on Côte de l'Oie. On 10 March, *22nd Reserve Division* continued its advance up the ridge and secured Corbeaux and Cumières woods. During this engagement, two French battalions were smashed. The surviving men were only enough to form a company sized unit. On the same day, the other divisions of the *VI Reserve Corps* were held up around Béthincourt and were unable to reach the northern slopes of Le Mort Homme (Hill 295) until 14 March.[3] On that date, the German artillery mercilessly bombarded the French infantry on Le Mort Homme crippling the defending unit and knocking out most of its machine guns. Both sides claimed they had taken light losses and inflicted heavy ones on their opponent. In actuality, both forces suffered heavily. The fight for Hill 295 became an almost endless succession of attacks and counter-attacks.

The German pressure against the XX Corps on the east bank compelled Pétain to reinforce it before it crumbled. He committed General Paul Maistre's XXI Corps to the east bank leaving only the XIII Corps to support the VII Corps, already under heavy assault, on the left bank. Pétain's main concern was that the Germans were sending as many as four divisions to reinforce the *VI Reserve Corps* on the west bank, which could trigger a crisis if they broke the French line from Malancourt to Cumières. The Germans had already taken Regnéville in the Meuse Valley creating a link with Samogneux on the other bank of the Meuse and opening a new route to the front. The French held the advantage since Pétain still had Joffre's full support and could count on getting reinforcements. The XXXIII Corps was heading to Bar-le-Duc by train and Maistre's corps was crossing to the east bank. The Crown Prince, on the other hand, could expect little from his commander-in-chief. As a result, his units had to fight to the point of exhaustion, which forced each corps to husband its own reserves to replace divisions at the front.

Hill 304, north of Esnes, dominated Le Mort Homme, which made it the next German objective. Just to the south of Esnes was Hill 310, which was also a significant feature in the area. Pétain thought that the Germans employed two corps with up to eight divisions supported by mortars and heavy artillery to assault the French lines from Hill 304 to Le Mort Homme in 'a frenzied duel [that] raged unceasingly' from 10–15 March. General Eugène Debeney, commander of the 25th Division and in charge of the defence, ordered no retreat.[4]

Across the Meuse, German troops had to contend with increasingly heavy bombardments as Pétain built up his artillery strength. Numerous French probing actions delayed the German assault scheduled for 7 March until 9 March. Pétain had made it clear to Joffre that his forces were not ready for a serious offensive and that he needed to build up his artillery. The French artillery proved effective in interdicting German supply lines to the point that the Crown Prince's forces on the east bank had to postpone their operations until ammunition was delivered to them. On 9 March, the *VII Reserve Corps* tried to clear the Poivre Ridge, but the French stubbornly resisted. The *77th Brigade* returned from the west bank to re-join *V Reserve Corps*. Further east, the *XVIII Reserve* and *III Corps* set off to clear the Vaux Valley and to take Fort Vaux. The *9th Reserve Division* approached Fort Vaux, but the *5th Army* failed to achieve its goals for that day. The Germans, recalled Pétain, 'hurled themselves with great violence against the fort of Vaux …' but after they reached its moat, his XXI Corps launched counter-attacks that drove them back. The Crown Prince attributed that day's failure to unbroken wire obstacles, French artillery barrages and flanking fire into the valleys from French positions. On 11 March, a 'violent artillery duel' took place along the entire front from *Army Detachment Strantz* in the St Mihiel Salient all the way to *XVIII Reserve Corps* at Douaumont. This action, combined with French flanking fire, slowed the advance of the *V Reserve* and *III Corps* across the Vaux Valley and prevented them from taking the fort. After the Germans sustained heavy losses the next day, the *19th Reserve Division* rushed by train from Upper Alsace to the *III Corps*.

The situation on the west bank was also eating up manpower, so the *58th Division* of *Army Detachment Falkenhausen* and the *113th Division* joined *X Reserve Corps*. Crown Prince Wilhelm's staff and Knobelsdorf continually had to juggle units by replacing divisions and corps temporarily and shifting divisions from one corps to another. For instance, the *19th Reserve Division* was sent to relieve the *6th Division* of the *III Corps*, but shortly afterwards it had to replace the *25th Division* of the *XVIII Corps*. This division next took part in the assault on the northern part of the front where it incurred heavy casualties. Both the *III Reserve Corps* and *V Reserve Corps* had to leave the front to rest and rebuild. Both German and French media sources concurred that these actions had been bloody, but one claimed that Fort Vaux had surrendered and the other denied it. This convinced the Crown Prince – or so he claimed – that he could only hope to inflict more casualties than he took since the possibility of taking Verdun had evaporated. He did not like the idea, since this was resorting to Falkenhayn's policy of bleeding the French army dry.

These relatively futile efforts continued throughout March. The only bright spot for the Germans occurred on 20 March on the left bank when the *11th Bavarian Division* launched an assault against the 29th Division holding the woods of Malancourt and Avocourt. The Bavarians overran the 29th Division, some elements of which fled while others stood their ground and became isolated. Nevertheless, the Bavarian's advance was slow. According to Pétain, the 29th Division was taken by surprise, but it 'quickly rallied and by 29 March fought their way back …'.* Supposedly, on 29 March, the division counter-attacked and began to close the gap it had left during its rout the week before. Whatever the case, the division lost Malancourt on 31 March and Haucourt on 5 April. On 8 April, it had to abandon Béthincourt before the town became isolated. According to the Crown Prince, the

---

* Pétain, *Verdun*, p. 112.

Bavarians took 3,500 prisoners, greatly depleting the division's strength especially if the wounded and killed are included.[5] During the month of April, the bad weather continued and the rain added to everyone's misery.

As the fighting wound down in April, the front of the *VI Reserve Corps* stretched from Avocourt Woods to north of Hill 304, to Hill 265 (northern part of Le Mort Hommes) and Côte de l'Oie. The next German objective was Hill 304 and the remainder of Le Mort Hommes. Once those positions fell, the next move was to advance all the way to the Marre Ridge from which the Germans could threaten the French defences of Verdun. To achieve this, Falkenhayn promised the Crown Prince the *XXII Reserve Corps* with the *43rd* and *44th Reserve divisions*. These divisions were of little use until they underwent intensive training in trench assault tactics. The *Western Attack Group* formed on 28 March under General Max von Gallwitz.[6] It consisted of *VI Reserve Corps* (*11th Bavarian Division, 192nd Brigade* and *11th Reserve Division*) on the right and *XXII Reserve Corps* (*12th, 22nd, 43rd* and *44th Reserve divisions*) on the left. The Crown Prince kept the *2nd Landwehr Division*, on the right of *VI Reserve Corps*, under direct control of the attack group.[7]

Meanwhile, Pétain carefully husbanded his forces and tried to wheedle more artillery from Joffre. He refused steadfastly to launch costly and fruitless attacks, despite demands from Joffre. However, he ordered his subordinates to hold the final positions at all costs, which produced costly counter-attacks. His policy was to keep the divisions at the front for only a short period and pull them out before they lost their effectiveness. Despite his policy of rotating divisions, he could not prevent them from taking heavy casualties during artillery bombardments or fierce infantry attacks and counter-attacks which occurred quite often during the months of hell at Verdun. His main goal was to let the artillery handle the main job of smashing the enemy so that the infantry would not have to make costly assaults. His methodical procedure for attacking did not produce dramatic victories, but it reduced French casualties.

Crown Prince Wilhelm realized chances for a major victory at Verdun had already slipped away and that, unless a dramatic change occurred, he would lose the battle. He blamed Falkenhayn for forcing him to continue engaging in a bloody and costly stalemate. The Crown Prince penned these sentiments after the war when he was trying to vindicate his actions, but it appears from his writings that, like Pétain, he had an emotional connection with his troops. On the other hand, empathy for the common soldier is clearly lacking in the post-war works of both Joffre and Falkenhayn. In reality, the Crown Prince was a mere figurehead, and his chief-of-staff, Knobelsdorf, handled the important decisions. Thus, it was Knobelsdorf who was the driving force behind the increasingly ruinous attacks. The Crown Prince tried to work with him and show that he did have a reasonable degree of competency as an army commander.

In mid–March, the Crown Prince and Knobelsdorf decided to take a different tack. Instead of continually shifting corps back and forth, as they had been doing, they ordered General Bruno von Mudra to leave his *XVI Corps* in the Argonne and to take command, with a provisional staff, of a newly formed *Eastern Attack Group*, consisting of the *V Reserve* and *X Reserve corps* on the east bank.[8] They hoped that

Mudra's skills would be the game changer. Probably as a result of his experience in the Argonne, he adopted, like Pétain, a more methodical approach. He felt a series of small local gains would be more productive. Knobelsdorf was sceptical of this method and preferred the all-out attack. Meanwhile, as the Germans reorganized, Pétain's artillery inflicted serious losses on the *V Reserve* and *XV corps* in the Woëvre.

On the east bank, the *XVIII Reserve Corps*, which had withdrawn to refit on 21 March, received new units to replace its infantry, while General Mudra planned another attempt at taking Fort Vaux. To prepare for the assault, he ordered the pioneers to push the saps and trench positions of the *V Reserve Corps* to within about 50m of the glacis of Fort Vaux. The troops also hauled up mountain howitzer batteries for close support. On 26 March, while the fighting was nearing a stalemate on the left bank, the *121st Division (V Reserve Corps)* took control of Vaux village. Mudra selected Caillette Wood and Fort Vaux as the objectives of a limited attack scheduled for 2 April. The *V Reserve Corps* was to take the Ouvrage of Thiaumont, the village of Fleury and the Ouvrage of Laufée on 6 April. Considering that Mudra had intended only small operations, these moves were still more than his troops could handle, especially when the French were growing stronger every day. As it happened, his planned offensive never materialized because the French struck first.

Courage, on Les Aura!

The French offensive opened on 2 April with a heavy bombardment of the front held by the *9th Reserve Division* and *121st Division*. The French infantry – recalled the Crown Prince – came on in four successive waves into the Vaux Valley, but ran into devastating fire from German cannons and machine guns. The German *58th Division* repelled an advance up one of the slopes of the valley wall. On 3 April, the French regiments attacking in Caillette Woods were pushed back as well. Mudra reorganized his forces during the next few days. The *X Reserve Corps* had reformed in March with the *19th Reserve Division* and *113th* and *58th divisions*.[9] However, the *58th*, except for its artillery, was relieved by the *21st Division* of the *XVIII Corps (21st* and *25th divisions)* on 9 April. Falkenhayn pulled the *113th Division* out of line on 12 April.[10] The *19th Reserve Division* remained at the front taking heavy losses in the days that followed.

The French attacks against Mudra's positions near forts Douaumont and Vaux early in April depleted several of Mudra's divisions, which had to be replaced so they could refit and recoup their losses. This assault and the German counter-attacks gave Pétain enough confidence to issue one of his rousing orders of the day on 10 April. 'April 9th was a glorious day for our armies – he declared – the furious attacks of the soldiers of the Crown Prince broke down everywhere.'[11] He closed this order with his favourite motto, '*Courage, on les aura!*' – 'Courage, we will get them!'

When his troops were ready, Mudra opted for single divisional operations. The first of these attacks on 11 April involved the *21st Division (XVIII Corps)*. The *21st* advanced on Caillette Woods, but French artillery stopped it in its tracks. Knobelsdorf, impatient with Mudra and highly critical of his small methodical attacks, sent him back to his old corps in the Argonne and replaced him with General Ewald von Lochnow of *III Corps* who opened an offensive on 17 April with the

VII Reserve Corps to gain control of Poivre Ridge.[12] The *XVIII Corps* captured a ridge and Thiaumont Farm, recalled the Crown Prince, and the *21st Division* fell back in the face of enemy counter-attacks. The *V Reserve Corps* was down to only four battalions on the front line and the *50th Division* had to reinforce it. The *1st Division* had to relieve the *121st Division* as casualties continued to mount. The *25th Division* faltered in its attempt to clear Caillette Woods on 20 April. The *III Corps* with its *5th* and *6th divisions* had to relieve the *XVIII Corps*. The *Eastern Attack Group* under Lochnow's leadership made few gains and showed that continued attacks would only increase German losses at Verdun. Crown Prince Wilhelm concluded that Operation Gericht was no more effective than Mudra's small-scale methodical attacks had been, and decided to end it. He refused to accept a strategy of attrition, despite the fact that Knobelsdorf 'with that steadfastness which was his finest characteristic adhered to his view that whatever happened we must hold fast to the idea of attacking and wearing down the enemy' (*My War Experiences*, pp. 194–5).

The actions on the left bank during April also contributed to the Crown Prince's pessimistic view of the situation. On 1 April on the west bank, the *VI Reserve Corps* made some gains near Béthincourt. However, the French hung on to Béthincourt and Haucourt until 5 April when they were pushed out of Haucourt by the German *192nd Regiment*. This presented a threat to the left flank of the French VII Corps and Hill 304, which, the Germans realized, was a key point for domination of Le Mort Homme. Fighting continued in the Forges Valley until the *11th Reserve* and *11th Bavarian divisions* began to make some progress on 7 April. The *12th Reserve Division* took Béthincourt on 9 April and the *22nd Reserve Division* pushed up the slopes of Le Mort Homme. His divisions, claimed the Crown Prince, 'melted away fast in stubborn fighting for trenches, which were usually badly damaged by constant rainstorms' and often crumbled in the saturated ground (*My War Experiences*, p. 201). Before long, the *192nd Brigade* and the *11th Bavarian Division*, followed by the *11th* and *12th Reserve divisions* were exhausted and needed to be relieved.[13] Renewing the assault on 22 April, the *VI Reserve Corps* fired a 3-hour barrage and sent in the *43rd Reserve Division* to plough through the muddy ground in front of their objective. Gallwitz assigned the newly arrived *4th Division* to the *XXIII Corps* to relieve the *12th Reserve Division*.[14] The objective was Hill 304. The Germans renewed their bombardment on 24 April. On the evening of 29 April, the French launched a strong assault on the front of the *XXII Reserve Corps* which stretched from Le Mort Homme to north of Les Caurettes. The fight for both Le Mort Homme and Hill 304 continued into May. The *4th Division* moved against Le Mort Homme between 4 and 8 May and captured some positions, but it retreated in the face of numerous French counter-attacks. It suffered heavy losses, but also took 1,500 weary French prisoners. On 15 and 18 May, the *38th Division* broke up several French attacks on Hill 304 that had repelled the *4th Division*. On 20 May, the *43rd* and *44th Reserve divisions* of the *XXII Reserve Corps* stormed the crest of Le Mort Homme taking 1,300 prisoners as the Crown Prince watched from a vantage point. 'Mort Homme – he recalled – flamed like a volcano and the air and earth alike trembled at the shock of thousands of bursting shells."* As he watched, the barrage lifted and his troops emerged from their trenches and charged the enemy. Before long, streams of French prisoners were being marched down the slopes. Knobelsdorf, who was observing the operation from the eastern side of the Meuse, thought the prisoners were retreating German troops and telephoned the Crown Prince to halt the attack. After the Crown Prince disabused him, the assault continued. On 24 May, the *22nd* and the *44th Reserve divisions* made concentric attacks and completed a line from Le Mort Homme to the south edge of Caurettes Woods and Cumières. Gallwitz ordered the corps to hold their ground and fortify the line. The *56th Division* came to reinforce the *XXII Reserve Corps*. The Germans' small victory in taking Hill 304 and Le Mort Homme at the end of May cost them 69,000 casualties.[15] However, on the west bank, between the new line and the Marre Ridge there were more hills and ridges followed by the forts of the northern part of Verdun's defences. This terrain favoured the French allowing them to inflict even greater losses on the Germans. The Germans never reached the Marre Ridge and they did not give up their attempts to retake and hold Le Mort Homme.

The Crown Prince realized the futility of continuing the campaign, but he had no choice in the matter. March, April and May were three of the bloodiest and most futile months of the battle. They characterize the senselessness of Falkenhayn's strategy more than any other period of the battle.

The rift between the Crown Prince and his chief-of-staff deepened before the end of April. On 21 April, General Knobelsdorf replaced Lieutenant Colonel von Heymann, a senior staff officer who had been able to mediate between him and the Crown Prince, with Colonel Count Schulenburg. Heymann was given command of a regiment. This change, however, did not help Knobelsdorf because it did not take long for Schulenburg to concur fully with His Highness about ending the offensive. Knobelsdorf and Falkenhayn agreed at a meeting that the campaign must go on. The Crown Prince had no recourse but to follow orders. The tremendous losses at that time forced Falkenhayn to send additional reinforcements to the Crown Prince's army.

Poor weather plagued both sides during the month of April. Heavy rains turned roads, trenches and shell craters into a muddy morass and some valleys and ravines into veritable swamps. The French remained in possession of their forts even though the Germans falsely bragged that they had taken Fort Vaux in March. When weather permitted, the soldiers tried to improve their positions; they also often used shell craters as foxholes. The French infantry regiments increased their firepower since the number of machine guns allotted to each of them went from six to twenty-four at the beginning of 1916. Now, the advancing Germans had to face numerous machine-gun positions that survived their artillery barrages. Since the battle had begun in February, the French had had learned to use their 75mm guns to deadly effect in support of their infantry. Pétain continued to receive additional artillery to replace his losses and slowly began to reach parity with his enemy. Although they were relieved

---

* William, *My War Experiences*, p. 203.

more frequently than their opponents, the French troops often marched to the front in high spirits only to return haggard, ragged and exhausted from their experiences. The nearly unceasing heavy artillery barrages left many a soldier shell-shocked and suffering from combat fatigue. More often than not, the French troops were relieved before the Germans could take advantage of their condition. The German troops often had to stay on line longer than the French did, and when they came off the front line to recover, they generally rested for a short period before being thrown back into the battle. In addition, the intolerable living conditions at the front took a heavy toll on their health and their morale.

Although the Germans continued to dominate the sky, their hold was slipping. They began the campaign in February with almost complete superiority, but beside spotting for the artillery, photographing French positions, and keeping their enemy from doing the same, they accomplished little else. The *5th Army* entered the campaign with four Zeppelins and several aircraft with limited bombing capability. The Germans engaged in some strategic bombing and targeted a few railroad stations with little effect. Their inadequate bomb loads could not cripple rail traffic from Bar-le-Duc to Verdun and any damage they inflicted was quickly repaired (see 'Pétain's Road to Victory' on p. 194ff.). The Germans did not attempt to bomb any of the numerous Marne bridges that supported the French forces on the right bank, but it is questionable whether their bombs could have caused any significant damage.[16] Both sides resorted to nightly bombing raids where pursuit aircraft were not a factor, but the French aircraft did not carry large bomb loads either.

The French, however, were making progress in using aviation for artillery coordination and mapping enemy positions, a field in which the Germans had held the advantage. In April, it was still common for a single Fokker monoplane fighter to escort several two-seater observation aircraft. During the year, the Germans grouped fighter aircraft into fighter squadrons. The German fighter aircraft, mainly the Fokker Eindecker, had been equipped with synchronized machine guns that fired through the propellers since mid-1915. Pétain encouraged and promoted the development of French aviation and the French army adopted the nimble Nieuport 11, which regained control of the air by the summer of 1916.

In April 1916, Pétain reorganized his forces. He replaced General Bazelaire's group (VII Corps) on the west bank with three formations: General Alby's XIII Corps, General Balfourier's XX Corps and General Berthelot's XXXII Corps. On the east bank, he formed two commands: General Descoins' XII Corps and General Nivelle's III Corps. He retained the VII and XXI Corps as a reserve claiming that their four divisions were in no condition to return to the front. Joffre grudgingly cooperated in maintaining Pétain's system of quick and frequent reliefs, so that no unit remained too long in action. Each division, Pétain explained, 'following a sort of rotary movement like that of a millwheel, after being called on to bear its burden of bloodshed and weariness on the Verdun front, returned to the rear …', or a quiet sector to recover.[*] In April, Joffre sent him the fresh IX Corps to keep the millwheel

---

[*] Pétain, *Verdun*, pp. 133–4.

turning.[17] Joffre recalled that when he gave Pétain this corps, he warned him that he would have to rely on his own resources after that. The divisions of the 2nd Army had taken a beating and, to Joffre's chagrin, Pétain insisted that it was not yet ready for the great counter-thrust Joffre insisted on at Verdun.

General Joffre and President Poincaré visited Verdun in early April. The government was worried about this battle because defeat could mean its own collapse. Foreign dignitaries such as Italian General Cardona also came to see Verdun. In March and April, Joffre made it clear to Pétain that retaking Fort Douaumont and launching a new offensive were top priorities. He was convinced that the 2nd Army commander was reluctant to go on the offensive and wanted to concentrate on defence. He complained that that Pétain requested additional reinforcements after every German attack. In part to satisfy Joffre, Pétain ordered Nivelle to prepare a methodical operation to take back Fort Douaumont in early March. Joffre wanted an operation on a grander scale than this, but when he visited Nivelle's III Corps on 10 April, he was pleased with what he saw. Still dissatisfied, Joffre decided nonetheless to find a way to remove Pétain from Verdun even though in public he called him the 'heart and soul of the action' that saved Verdun. Thus, he promoted Pétain to army group commander as of 1 May after retiring General de Langle from Army Group Centre. Informed by Castelnau of his impending promotion on 19 April, Pétain received the news with a decided lack of enthusiasm.[18] Joffre later explained that this move was meant to keep Pétain from constantly demanding new units, which had to be syphoned away from the build-up for the forthcoming offensive on the Somme. Joffre had wanted to assemble forty divisions for that big operation, but the Battle of Verdun had drawn off many of his resources so that by June he would only have twenty-four divisions at his disposal. Joffre feared that if he continued to agree to Pétain's requests there would be nothing left for the summer Somme Offensive. The new posting put Pétain in control of 2nd, 3rd, 4th and 5th armies.[19] His headquarters were at Bar-le-Duc. Nivelle assumed command of 2nd Army, which now was no longer under direct orders from Joffre at GHQ, but under direct control of Army Group Centre. Thus, Pétain had retained overall control of 2nd Army's operations, while Joffre felt free to wash his hands of the situation at Verdun and concentrate on his upcoming offensive. Joffre expected Pétain to rely on his army group's resources and make no further demands upon him. Pétain, on the other hand, encouraged Joffre to begin the Somme Offensive as early as possible to relieve the pressure on Verdun.

On 1 May, reported Pétain, the 2nd Army, now under the command of Charles Mangin, had 538,600 troops and 170,000 horses and mules, which included the men and animals supporting the combat units. The army had seven corps: Bazelaire's VII Corps, Curé's IX Corps, Berthelot's XXXII Corps, Descoins' XII Corps, Lebrun's III Corps, Baret's XIV Corps and Duchêne's II Corps.[20] Up to that date, forty divisions had passed through Verdun and Pétain had removed most of them from combat before they reached the point of exhaustion. Apparently, he left the 29th Division too long on line, because it broke under attack in March.

By the end of March, the French had to fill large gaps in the ranks as a result of casualties. To do this, the French government called the youth of the class of 1916 to the colours and recalled to arms the wounded who had recovered from injuries incurred in the first year of the war.[21] The majority of the French troops already serving had become seasoned veterans. According to Pétain, the Poilus were no longer motivated by enthusiasm but by the determination to defend their homeland from the invader, which made them more effective. However, in 1916 morale was deteriorating on the front as a consequence of the intense German bombardments that could shatter the will to resist in a short time. For months, the Germans had sufficient artillery engaged in the battle to maintain pressure. Later in the battle, the positions of the French and Germans were reversed and the German troops began to crack, especially those who had been engaged in the battle month after month. In May, Pétain estimated that the German *5th Army* consisted of eight corps and had a combat strength of about twenty divisions, but that only seven to eight divisions had been taken out of combat since 21 February. His intelligence service had identified twenty-six German divisions serving at Verdun since the battle began. He found that their method of deploying corps in sectors up the 20km or more behind the lines with depots for divisions and their sub-units allowed each corps to send up reinforcements quickly from within its area to keep operations going indefinitely, while pulling back front-line units to rest within the corps area.[22] It also made it more difficult to break a corps front and advance for a significant distance because of its depth. Yet the French divisions, which had continually taken a beating on defence or during counter-attacks between March and June, yielded very little ground to the Germans. Thus, by May and June the Germans were no closer to Verdun or to a significant victory than they had been at the end of February.

Reinforcing Failure

In May, after Gallwitz's *Western Attack Group* fought an almost month-long battle against repeated French counter-attacks it finally took and secured Hill 304 and Le Mort Homme. In the meantime, Lochnow's *Eastern Attack Group* went into action on the other side of the Meuse. The east bank assault opened at the end of April. The *19th Reserve Division* advanced with the *X Reserve Corps (5th* and *6th divisions* attached from *III Corps*) against the French line from Thiaumont Farm to Caillette Woods to Buttes Woods and northwest of the Vaux Valley. On 7 May, they took Thiaumont Farm, but *X Reserve Corps* ran into a heavy artillery barrage that inflicted severe casualties on the *5th Division*. The French counter-attacked and regained Thiaumont Farm. The *Guard Ersatz Division* relieved the *19th Reserve Division* from the intense fighting on 8 May. As the German thrust ground to a halt, army headquarters prepared for a new assault for 13 May, but this operation was delayed. Meanwhile, Pétain kept rotating his divisions and allowed the Germans to continue battering themselves against his positions along the final line of resistance on the east bank. Beyond the line of the Froideterre Ridge, Fort Vaux, Souville and Tavannes there was little to stop the Germans from reaching the Meuse besides a couple of old forts of limited military value.

At the beginning of May, General Nivelle and Lebrun worked out plans for the III Corps offensive to recapture Fort Douaumont. General Charles Mangin prepared his 5th Division (III Corps) and ordered the troops to train near the front. Mangin had the reputation of being more aggressive than the other French generals were and for pushing his troops. His actions at Verdun contributed to his nickname of 'The Butcher'. After the war, Winston Churchill wrote that Mangin was 'the fiercest warrior figure of France'.* Nivelle put Mangin in charge of the final planning and leading the operation. Mangin assessed the problems he would encounter after the Germans captured two ravines on either side of Fort Douaumont and the ridge to the west of the fort. Since the ravines would mask German troops moving to reinforce their front and endanger Mangin's operation, he requested four divisions to counter the threat. Joffre, however, refused to deplete the forces he was preparing for the Somme Offensive. Mangin received only one additional division, which was to serve as a reserve for the operation forcing Nivelle to reduce the number of objectives for the attack.[23] Colonel J.B. Estienne, who commanded the III Corps artillery during the operation, had 150 pieces of artillery and 10 heavy guns including 4 of the 370mm Filloux mortars.[24]

While Nivelle and Mangin worked on their plans, disaster struck their enemy at Fort Douaumont on 8 May. The Germans, who considered the fort a safe shelter, used its facilities to treat the wounded and quarter troops coming out of line to rest. The fort also served as a depot for munitions, flamethrowers and other equipment. Accounts vary as to the sequence of events, but most agree that some soldiers lit a fire to cook a meal near a store of flamethrowers or grenades. Sparks from the cooking fire set off a small explosion. The would-be cooks and the men around them, their faces blackened with smoke and soot, staggered out of the accident zone only to be mistaken for French African troops. Thinking that the French had breached the fort, their startled comrades lobbed grenades at them, one of which probably detonated a store of 155mm rounds for the turret gun. There followed a tremendous explosion that caused massive damage to the interior of the fort, killed 700 to 800 men and injured 1,800.[25] Elements of two regiments of the *5th Division* had occupied the fort at the time. After the medics and the pioneers sorted out the casualties and the damage, the fort continued to serve as a shelter/depot, but some troops were reluctant to stay in it. The turrets continued to serve as observation positions for the Germans.[26]

The Battle for Fort Douaumont

Fort Douaumont fell to the Germans on 25 February 1916. At the fort, the skeleton garrison was unable to implement fully General Herr's order to prepare the fort for demolition since the officer responsible never arrived on 25 February. Even had engineers completed the preparations, they would not have changed the situation because a small number of Germans took the fort by surprise on that day. The French infantry garrison left the fort after 22 February. The French battalions assigned to defend the area in front of the fort had also kept a good distance between them and the fort since it proved to be a shell trap as German medium and heavy artillery targeted

---

* William Martin, *Verdun 1916: They Shall Not Pass* (Oxford: Osprey, 2001), p. 69.

Fort Douaumont before the 1916 battle. On the right is a battery position which included an incomplete turret position that was converted into a machine-gun bunker.

it. In front and to the left of the fort, Zouave battalions of the 37th Division and the 95th Infantry Regiment held the line. On the right, there were regiments from the 14th Division and 51st Division, but this mixture of regiments from different brigades and divisions must have created problems in coordination.[27]

After September 1914, Fort Douaumont saw only occasional action. Its 155mm gun turret engaged the enemy in September and again in December. The Germans brought up a 420mm battery and their 380mm long-range naval guns to engage the fort in February 1915. The bombardment did not cause any substantial damage to the fort, but left its mark. Joffre's order to strip the forts of their artillery and ammunition came in the autumn of 1915. Fort Douaumont's only offensive weapon, the 155mm gun, remained with a supply of ammunition. The two 75mm guns also remained in their turret, but the other guns were removed. Adjutant Hippolyte Chenot, was in charge of the fort with fifty-six territorial troops and a few other soldiers that remained at the fort on 25 February.[28] They fired the 155mm turret gun at suspected German positions. The German bombardment, which caused little damage to the fort, forced much of the garrison to shelter deep inside to avoid the thunder of rounds striking the surface and the dust that that thickened the surrounding air. No one manned the observation posts or any position beside the single gun turret. When the German *5th* and *6th divisions* advanced in the area, it forced back the defending infantry. The fort was located in the sector assigned to the *5th Division*, but it was troops of the *24th Brandenburg Infantry Regiment* of the *6th Division* that actually moved on the fort due to a mix-up. Pioneer Sergeant Kunze and his squad-size unit worked their way up to the fort, found a gap in the obstacles created by an artillery round and climbed down into the moat.[29] Since his men refused to follow him, Kunze entered an unmanned coffre alone with nothing but a rifle in his hands, worked his way through the tunnels and captured the turret gun crew single-handedly. Meanwhile, Lieutenant Eugen Radtke and his platoon got into the undefended moat, crossed it and climbed up the scarp onto the fort. They proceeded to capture most of the remaining French troops. Captain Hans Joachim Haupt and Lieutenant Cordt von Brandis followed him. The fort fell without offering any resistance. Brandis became a national hero since his name was in the official report.[30] The French 37th Division pulled back on 25 February. On 26 February, the Germans repulsed a French counter-attack. The Germans, expecting a French attempt to take back the fort, readied the guns of the 75mm turret for action. In Germany, church bells rang celebrating the fall of the famous fort and the public became a little more confident of victory. Joffre, most likely as a result of pressure from the government, ordered Pétain to retake the fort. The French public eagerly read of the glowing but misleading reports of successful counter-attacks to take the fort published that month.

Finally, General Nivelle, after taking command of the 2nd Army, launched the first major attempt to retake Fort Douaumont late in May. The operation against the German *5th Division* was limited to Lebrun's III Corps spearheaded by Mangin's 5th Division. The French artillery bombardment began on 17 May and continued for five days. Even so, on 20 May, the French took heavy losses when the enemy artillery returned fire destroying trenches and other positions prepared in advance of the infantry assault.

Meanwhile, before the French assault on Fort Douaumont, General Knobelsdorf finally realized that the battle had become too costly to continue. He drove to Falkenhayn's headquarters at Mézières to ask him to abandon the offensive. The *5th Army* needed time to recover from these bloody operations which had brought them no closer to victory. However, Falkenhayn, not yet ready to call off Operation Gericht, promised Knobelsdorf fresh divisions from the *I Bavarian Corps* and told him to prepare to take the Ouvrage of Thiaumont and the Froideterre Ridge. Knobelsdorf agreed to fall in with these plans, but the Crown Prince was outraged and told Falkenhayn, 'I refuse to order the attack!' If ordered to attack, he said he would obey, 'but I will not do it on my own responsibility!'. Falkenhayn issued him written orders. At this point, even if the Germans took the east bank, they would still have to take the west bank where they had not even come near to breaking the fortress line. It was obvious that the French would continue to fight for Verdun. The attrition rate for the Germans turned out to be far worse than Falkenhayn's prediction of two Germans to every five Frenchmen.[31] Joffre was willing to fall into Falkenhayn's trap, but Pétain refused to waste his men on large, casualty producing offensives. On 16 May, Falkenhayn showed up at the *5th Army* headquarters to make his wishes clear. Thus, plans went forward for a new attack on the right bank on 22 May.

FORT DOUAUMONT

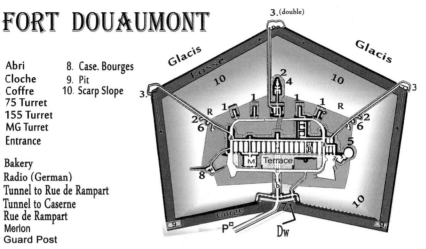

1. Abri
2. Cloche
3. Coffre
4. 75 Turret
5. 155 Turret
6. MG Turret
7. Entrance

8. Case. Bourges
9. Pit
10. Scarp Slope

B Bakery
R Radio (German)
a Tunnel to Rue de Rampart
b Tunnel to Caserne
c Rue de Rampart
M Merlon
P Guard Post

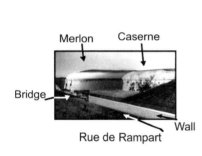

Merlon   Caserne

Bridge

Rue de Rampart   Wall

RL = Road in lower level
R = Road to Rue de Rampart

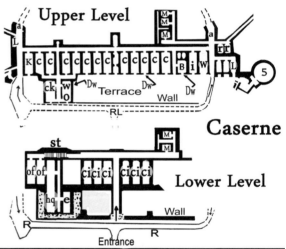

Upper Level

Caserne

Lower Level

In 1917 the French created tunnels to link the gun turrets and casemate to the caserne

The Germans did not use all the rooms for the purposes intended

c   Barracks
ci Cistern
ck Officers kitchens
e   Engineer materials
hq Headquarters
i   Infirmary
K   Kitchen
L   Latrines
M   Powder magazine
o   Officers quartrs
of Offices
r   Cartridges

s   Workshop
st Stairs
W   Weapon stores
w   Wash area

Dw Destroyed

Mangin pressed on with his plans as well. Pétain was sceptical because he thought that German artillery fire was superior to the French. The day before the assault, Colonel Estienne informed Mangin that his artillery had riddled Fort Douaumont. Mangin, like the Germans before him, was convinced that the artillery had obliterated the enemy positions and that his men could simply walk across the front and take possession of their objectives. The five-day bombardment heralded the assault on the fort giving the Germans time to prepare.

The French had finally wrested control of the air from their enemy and eliminated five of the six German tethered observation balloons hovering over the battlefield, blinding the enemy artillery.[32] French aircraft flew over the fort and photographed it to allow Mangin to assess the damage. The four 370mm mortars had landed several hits inflicting some damage, but none had actually penetrated the roof of the fort. The prolonged bombardment had reduced the two regiments of the *5th Division* (the *8th Liebgrenadiers* and the *52nd Infantry*) holding the line in front of the fort to a handful of men.[33] A large number of German troops had taken shelter in Fort Douaumont during the bombardment, but their situation became quite unbearable after some shells hit the exposed facade of the gorge. Dust, noise, flying fragments and noxious fumes and odours assailed the occupants. The heavy artillery damaged a gallery leading to the Casemate de Bourges causing it to collapse. The attack between the vicinity of Fort Douaumont and Fort Vaux was launched on 22 May, the same day as Falkenhayn's planned offensive. A brief German artillery barrage inflicted heavy casualties on the four French battalions before the assault. Just before noon (French time), despite losses, those battalions advanced under a rolling barrage laid down by 75mm guns.

Further down the line, the German *1st Division* (*X Reserve Corps*) repelled an attack coming from Fort Vaux, but the ferocity of the French assailants drove the *X Reserve Corps* back. The *5th Division* reeled back to the outskirts of Fort Douaumont. The *19th Reserve Division* and *6th Division* on either flank of the *5th Division* gave ground. The battalions of the French 9th and 10th brigades of Mangin's 5th Division were to converge on the fort.[34] They took losses from a German barrage but advanced under their own rolling barrage. German machine guns took a heavy toll as well. The French reached the fort and made it onto its superstructure where they set up positions on the glacis. Heavy fighting ensued. The Germans had installed machine guns in the empty Casemate de Bourges, but the French attackers took the casemate, the counterscarp coffre on the northwest corner of the fort and the double coffre. The Germans, however, had blocked the tunnels. The French soldiers set up defences inside the tunnel when they discovered that the Germans had blocked it with their own defensive position. The Germans used the northeastern machine-gun turret (the northwestern was badly damaged) to pin down the French troops on the superstructure. However, the French managed to reach the damaged machine-gun turret and access the passage to the barracks, only to find it blocked with debris. The French troops fruitlessly searched for ways to enter the fort. The Germans controlled the two gun turrets and the northeastern machine-gun turret, but the surface of the fort was crawling with French soldiers.[35] As the fighting for the superstructure of the fort intensified, both sides suffered significant casualties. The Germans used the 75mm gun turret to send light signals to headquarters at a higher elevation since the fort was virtually isolated and all means of communication were cut.[36] As the battle raged around and on top of Fort Douaumont from 23–4 May, Mangin pushed his troops to take the fort.[37] The Germans managed to sneak reinforcements into the fort during the night through the northeastern section that the French had failed to occupy. On 23 May, the French forced most of the German defenders back into the fort.[38] According to Pétain, two German companies stubbornly resisted while German batteries prevented French reserves from reaching the two battalions on the fort. The *5th Division* rallied on 23 May, and in a fierce counter–attack recovered its former positions and secured the village by nightfall. In the afternoon of 24 May, the remnants of the two French battalions clinging to the fort's superstructure were eliminated. Mangin's division had to be relieved that evening. The arrival of the *2nd Bavarian Division* allowed the *X Reserve Corp* to drive back the French troops. By the end of 24 May, the *Eastern Group* had regained control of its lost positions and cleared Thiaumont Woods with the help of the 19th *Reserve Division*. However, the troops holding Thiaumont Farm had to pull back. The *I Bavarian Corps* reached the battlefield at the critical point of the operation and moved between the *VII Reserve* and *X Reserve Corps* relieving the *19th Reserve Division* and taking command of the *5th Division*. The Germans took over 2,000 prisoners, but suffered heavy casualties. The German offensive planned for 22 May amounted to no more than an effort to push the French off Fort Douaumont and other positions.

On the Woëvre, the German troops of the *30th* and *39th divisions* and the *XV Corps* were subjected for months to constant bombardment that included gas shells in their relatively open positions, but they stubbornly held on under the watchful eyes of French observers on the heights. In the Argonne, on the *5th Army's* right flank, the *XVI Corps* continued the mine warfare and close combat in the forest and fought tooth and nail for possession of the craters left by mine explosions.

June Days – From Fort Vaux to Fleury

In June, Crown Prince Wilhelm and General Knobelsdorf had to settle for holding the line on the west bank between Hill 304 to Le Mort Hommes and Cumières while concentrating their main effort on the east bank. Their primary May objective, Fort Vaux, remained out of reach. Behind it lay forts Souville and Tavannes and two older forts of limited value.

Fort Vaux was a newer, modernized fort. In 1914, it had a single turret with two 75mm guns and a pair of Casemate de Bourges. Early in the war, the gun turret had fired on German troops on the Woëvre. When the Germans brought up the big guns to fire on Fort Douaumont in February 1915, Fort Vaux also became a target. A couple of rounds had penetrated the fort, causing a little damage. The fort, however, generally remained in good condition even though its garrison had been rattled by the dust and the din caused by repeated hits that made the situation appear far worse than the damage. Joffre's 1915 order led to the removal of the 75s from the casemate in 1915, leaving only the turret guns. On 24 February, when it appeared that the

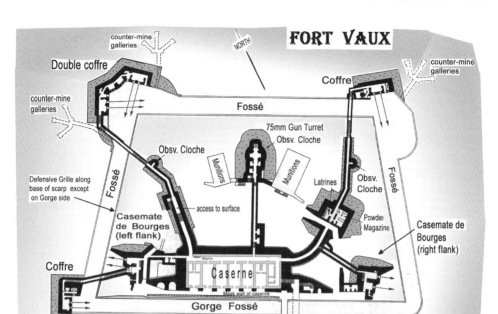

Fort Vaux, 1914.

Meuse Heights might fall, General Herr ordered the engineers to prepare the forts for demolition. When Pétain took charge late on 25 February, he countermanded these instructions. On the 26 February, the day after Fort Douaumont fell, the Germans turned their heavy 420mm artillery pieces on Fort Vaux. These guns damaged the counterscarp walls and one of the observation cloches, and literally tore another cloche out of its well. The big rounds also collapsed the double coffre in the northwest corner. The gun turret was blocked when the gallery roof caved in. Next, an explosion – caused by a 420mm round, according to some claims – detonated one of the demolition chambers damaging the turret. When he received the news, the commanding general of the sector ordered the fort destroyed. However, that same afternoon, another 420mm round destroyed the room containing the primers so that it became impossible to ignite the explosives. Shell craters pocked the fort surface and its glacis. On that day, the German *V Reserve Corps*, having received the order to take Fort Vaux, cleared the French from Hardaumont Ouvrage in preparation.[39] However, heavy French artillery fire repelled each German advance on Fort Vaux.

The next German attempt to take Fort Vaux was on 2 March, but it failed once again and the assailants took significant losses. An attack on 7 March met a similar fate in spite of a heavy preliminary shelling. Part of the problem for the Germans was that between the Hardaumont ouvrage, which they had captured, and Fort Vaux there was a ravine fringed on its west side by Caillette Woods from which the French enfiladed the soldiers advancing from the Hardaumont Heights into the gully. On the south side of the ravine, the Germans had to negotiate the steep slope of the hill overlooked by the fort and Fumin Woods. The French troops on the slopes of Vaux Hill and in Caillette Woods easily picked off the Germans moving across the ravine. Thus, repeated attempts to take Fort Vaux failed in April. Undeterred, the Germans tried again on 7 May and once again were unsuccessful.[40]

After March, the French began to clean up and repair Fort Vaux. After the army engineers examined the 75mm gun turret, they declared it beyond repair.[41] A detachment of the 44th Territorial Regiment with a less than stellar record manned the fort until a new garrison consisting of two infantry companies of the 142nd Infantry Regiment with machine-gun sections took over before June.[42] Since this was more men than the facilities of the fort could accommodate, one company took up a new position on the outside. However, the fort still lacked its own weapons. The fort attracted soldiers seeking shelter, which led to overcrowding and an increased depletion of supplies.

The new commander, Major Sylvain-Eugène Raynal, had been wounded three times before and declared unfit for service. When he was offered the opportunity to get back into the fray, he was eager to accept. On 24 May, he arrived at the fort a cane in hand and with a pronounced limp. Upon inspection, he realized that Fort Vaux was in poor shape indeed. Even though Pétain had ordered its rearmament, Fort Vaux had little to defend it beyond machine guns, a small number of trench mortars and a few small guns in the coffres. The Casemate de Bourges contained only machine guns. It had been impossible to return 75mm guns to the fort. The rest of the fort was in disrepair since nothing had been fixed since March. There was no well and the water pipes were broken so that the troops had to draw water from outside the fort. Sanitation was poor and a foul odour permeated the entire fort.

Raynal realized that repairs were urgently needed. He immediately set to work with the little manpower and few resources available. He discovered that the previous bombardments had created seven openings in the fort that could allow the enemy to gain an easy entry. They were located in the galleries connecting the two coffres on the front of the fossé to the western Casemate de Bourges and the entrances. Since the garrison was unable to seal these openings effectively, Raynal ordered the men build chicanes in the galleries.[43] After February 1915, the fort had no machine-gun turrets, only observation cloches and infantry weapons to defend the fort. The numerous heavy bombardments had partially filled the fossé.

In May, three army corps, the *I Bavarian*, *X Reserve* and *XV Corps* renewed the attack. This time, they were supported by eighteen howitzer batteries, including six heavy ones, transferred from the *Western Attack Group* to support operations east of the river. The batteries on the west bank strove to supress the French enfilading artillery on the Marre Ridge, which had impeded German infantry progress on the east bank since late February.

On the west bank, the *54th Division* (*XXIV Reserve Corps*) conducted mildly successful operations on 3 June. However, by 9 June it was pushed back to its starting position together with the *29th Division* (*XXIV Reserve Corps*). East of the *XXIV Reserve Corps*, three divisions of the *XXII Reserve Corps* had had to stave

FORT MOULAINVILLE

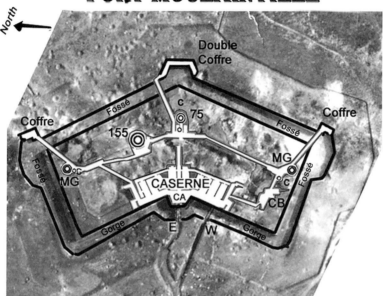

E - Entrance
W - Wartime Entrance
155 - 155 mm Gun Turret
75 - 75 mm Gun Turret
MG - Machine Gun Turret
C - Obsv. Cloche
CB - Case. de Bourges
CA - Caponier

off repeated French assaults aimed at Le Mort Homme since the end of May. The Germans lost about 250m of trenches on the southwest slope by dusk on 1 June. Knobelsdorf pulled back the *XXII Reserve Corps* (*43rd* and *44th Reserve divisions*). Its *56th Division* remained until mid-June when General von François, *VII Corps* (*13th* and *14th divisions*), took over the positions of the *XXII Reserve Corps*. French forces assailed Le Mort Homme once more on 14 and 16 June, but the German line held. The French artillery, however, prevented the Germans from improving their positions.

FORT MOULAINVILLE

View of right rear flank of Fort Moulainville.

On the east bank, the *5th Army* prepared for another major offensive involving the *I Bavarian* and *X Reserve corps*. The *VII Reserve Corps* (on the west bank) provided artillery support. The *XV Corps* formed the left wing. These forces concentrated on a 5km front of one of the mostly heavily defended sectors of Verdun. Knobelsdorf was convinced, or simply wanted to believe, that the defeat at Douaumont in May had greatly weakened the enemy. The Germans assembled 2,200 artillery pieces including the Big Berthas for another crushing barrage. The

420mm weapons contributed little because they concentrated their fire on Fort Moulainville during the offensive. Moulainville was the second largest fort on the right bank and somewhat similar to Fort Douaumont. It had become the Germans' main target after Fort Douaumont fell. It included a 75mm and a 155mm gun turret, which had remained in action since February causing difficulties for the Germans. Thus, during this latest attack, the 420mm weapons targeted Fort Moulainville instead of Fort Vaux or Fort Souville. However, their efficacy proved to be almost nil against Fort Moulainville.[44] During the campaign, they fired 339 rounds against the fort, scoring only 43 hits (just under 14 per cent), and they never came close to putting the fort out of action. This was not the first time the Germans had taken on Fort Moulainville. They had shelled it for a few days in March and April 1916. A 420mm round had struck the 155mm gun turret on 9 March, but the garrison had repaired it in two days. That turret fired over 5,800 rounds and its worn barrel had had to be replaced. The 75mm gun turret fired twice as many rounds and suffered minor damage during bombardments. The French had acquired more 155mm guns and their counter-battery fire targeted the 420mm howitzers and other heavy artillery in fixed positions with some effect.[45]

The French, who were still recovering from their failed May offensive, faced another massive onslaught. On 1 June, the *I Bavarian Corps* burst through the front southwest of Douaumont, the *7th Reserve Division* moved through Caillette Woods to the south of Fort Douaumont and the *1st Division* took the heights northwest of Fort Vaux and thrust into the Vaux Valley. The Crown Prince claimed that casualties were light as his troops took 2,000 prisoners. The French reacted with a heavy bombardment on 2 June that damaged a machine-gun turret and observation position at Fort Douaumont, which still afforded the only safe shelter for the German reserves in the area. The *50th Division* of the *XV Corps* took Damloup. On 2 June, three companies of its *158th Regiment* clawed their way onto the cratered superstructure of Fort Vaux. The French counter-attacked along the front of the *I Bavarian Corps* and *X Reserve Corps*, but were thrown back everywhere.[46] The East Prussians of the *1st Division* repeatedly tried to improve the German line to the northwest of Fort Vaux while French troops strove to eject the *7th Reserve Division* from Chapitre and Fumin woods.

Raynal had not been able to do much in one week to get Fort Vaux in shape. On 1 June, the German assailants succeeded in crossing the ravine, despite casualties, and forced the French back. Some of the retreating troops took shelter in the fort. The fort had a garrison of about 450 men including 150 men of a machine-gun company of the 53rd Infantry Regiment that had taken shelter there during the day. They joined the defence of the fort adding to its firepower. Other soldiers, who were not part of the garrison, overcrowded the fort and contributed nothing to the fighting. The fort endured heavy bombardment until 2 June when special German pioneers, trained to serve as storm troopers, joined in the siege of the fort. The French 101st and 142nd Infantry regiments of the 124th Division held positions around the fort. The German *158th* and *53rd Infantry regiments* advanced from their trenches to about 200m from the fort and engaged in heavy fighting not only with the French troops posted around the fort, but also with contingents emerging from the fort. The weapons in the coffres of the counterscarp stopped the German troops from crossing the moat. An attempt to destroy the machine gun defending the northeastern coffre failed, but the gun jammed eventually.[47] The fight next turned into a grenade duel until the thirty or so French soldiers in the coffre were overcome by fumes from a rubbish fire and surrendered after 2 hours of combat. Major Raynal, who had few means of communication at his disposal, sent a messenger pigeon to inform headquarters that the Germans had surrounded the fort.[48]

The Germans took over the coffre and began to explore the tunnel connecting it to the fort's caserne. As they explored the galleries, they came face to face with the defenders and an underground battle broke out. Meanwhile, other German soldiers tried to breach the double coffre without much success until the pioneers arrived with their flamethrowers. Since they had a short range, they lowered the weapon's nozzle from the top of the coffre, pushed it into an embrasure and injected a jet of flame. The machine guns in the coffre were instantly silenced. Before long, the Germans found an opening covered with sandbags, which they removed only to find the coffre empty. The defenders had evidently fled back to the fort through the tunnel. French counter-attacks from outside the fort failed while the fighting continued in the bowels of the structure. Using the remaining coffre and positions established in the gorge, the defenders kept the Germans from this quarter of the fort. By 3 June, the 124th Division was too weak to relieve the fort. When reinforcements arrived for the French early in the morning, they were pushed back and suffered heavy losses. The German regiments at the fort were relieved during the night of 3/4 June. The battle among the underground barricades continued. The Germans slowly worked their way through the eastern and western access galleries in the direction of the caserne. The attackers advanced with trepidation along the narrow, dark galleries as the defenders feverishly fired their machine guns and lobbed grenades from behind their barricades. The assailants brought up their flamethrowers to illuminate and burn the defenders. The French pulled back temporarily, and opened sandbagged positions in the gorge walls of the caserne to let in a rush of air to blow back the fumes and the flames when some rubbish caught fire. Before the Germans could get past the barricades, the Frenchmen came back at them weapons blazing. Still desperately holding on to the bulk of the fort, Raynal was informed that the water cisterns were empty. It seems that someone had miscalculated the amount of water they held. As the water and other supplies dwindled, Raynal devised a plan to move out hundreds of soldiers that were not part of the garrison at night. Only a few succeeded in escaping before the Germans realized what was afoot. The underground battle continued on 5 June. On 6 and 7 June, the *1st Division* repulsed numerous French attempts to reach the fort, the positions of which were obliterated. Raynal, his water gone, had no choice but to surrender on 7 June. Unaware that the fort had fallen, the French launched a final attack on 8 June, but sustained many casualties without anything to show for their efforts.[49]

Even though it was smaller and not as well armed as Fort Douaumont, Fort Vaux demonstrated the importance of forts in modern warfare. Its performance was

Destroyed Cloche

OUVRAGE OF THIAUMONT
1887-1916

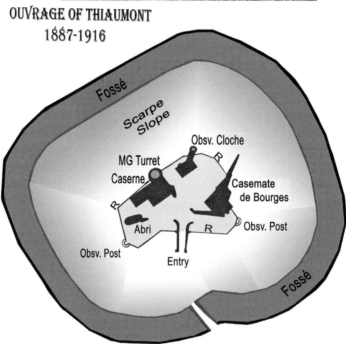

R= Infantry Rampart
Abri is masonry

remarkable especially since its main weapons – the 75mm turret guns and the missing guns of the Casemate de Bourges – did not take part in its defence. Pétain had been correct in February to order the restoration of the forts to full service and to provide each of them with up to two weeks' supplies so they could be self-supporting. The forts became the fulcrum of the French defensive positions. When the Germans secured the sector between forts Vaux and Douaumont, they could prepare a drive towards the Meuse. To do this, they had to eliminate the ouvrages of Thiaumont and Froideterre and the older forts of Souville and Tavannes. Since it had taken them months to take Fort Vaux, it was not likely that the remaining forts would fall quickly. Putting them under siege only promised to raise the number of casualties.

The Germans could also expect further losses in the effort to clear every ravine and wood between them and the line of ouvrages and forts.

After the fall of Fort Vaux, the German June offensive continued. On 8 June, the *1st* and *50th divisions* of *XV Corps* with the *I Bavarian Corps* on their right resumed their advance. The *X Corps* was scheduled to launch the attack at 4.00 pm (German time), but the French forestalled them by 10 minutes, only to be thrown back. The *2nd Bavarian Division*, supported by the new *Alpine Corps*, advanced to within 100m of the Thiaumont Farm taking 1,500 prisoners. On 12 June, the *Alpine Corps* replaced the *2nd Bavarian Division* and captured Thiaumont Farm.[50] As the Germans tried to consolidate their gains, they came under a vigorous French artillery barrage, which made it virtually impossible for them to carry out the task.

Before long, Falkenhayn sent orders to suspend the offensive because a Russian operation in Galicia was becoming problematical and the Austrians were once again on the verge of collapse. Shortly afterwards, however, the Crown Prince was told to renew the offensive and he was allotted the *4th* and *103rd divisions*. The *Eastern Attack Group* also received the *11th Bavarian Division* from *Army Detachment Strantz*. In addition, General Headquarters promised a large supply of Green Cross (phosgene) gas shells. Prince Wilhelm was not enthused; his heart was not in it, he said. He recalled these months at Verdun as the most painful of the war. He thought that the

HIGH WATER MARK OF THE GERMAN VERDUN OFFENSIVE

•••• **German Lines 23 June 1916**   0   1   2 Km

Ravines: 1. Bazil 2. La Dame 3. Chambitoux 4. Vignes 5. Fausse Cotes 6. Houyures 7. Fontaines 8. Caillette
9. Horgne 10. Fumin 11. Couleuvre 12. Helly 13. Hassoule 14. Poudrière

The last major German thrust. The Lion Monument represents the point of the maximum German advance.

French, who relieved their divisions frequently, did not suffer much more than his troops and, he lamented, 'now the balance seemed to me to be swaying the other way'.[*]

Once Fort Vaux surrendered, the plan was to capture Froideterre, the village of Fleury and Fort Souville. On 21 June, the German artillery fired phosgene gas at the French artillery batteries in an attempt to suffocate the crews. The *VII Reserve, XV* and the *Alpine corps* launched a preliminary assault, but they were checked by French artillery and machine-gun fire. This time, the French also targeted the rear areas to prevent the advancing troops from getting reinforcements and supplies. The Germans beat off French counter-attacks. A sustained bombardment heralded the main German attack. By 23 June, the poison gas finally seemed to take effect as French resistance faltered. The Bavarian troops took the Ouvrage of Thiaumont in a rapid assault. Other Bavarian troops and elements of the *Alpine Corps* assailed the village of Fleury. Further to the left, the newly arrived *103rd Division* and the *1st Division* advanced from Chapitre Woods, but they were halted by French machine guns that barred the way to Fort Souville. The *103rd Division* sustained heavy losses. Meanwhile, the *50th Division* cleared away French positions south of Fort Vaux. The French continued their futile counter-attacks. The Germans took 4,000 prisoners in these operations. On 24 June, the Crown Prince was informed that Falkenhayn intended to reduce expenditures of men and materials due to the general situation. Knobelsdorf insisted that the offensive should continue and Falkenhayn agreed despite a reduction in support for *5thArmy*. This offensive would be the last major effort on the part of the Germans to gain victory at Verdun.

During this offensive, as in the past, the German divisions fought until they reached the point of exhaustion before they moved to the rear for a short respite while other divisions took their places on the front. In some cases, Knobelsdorf had to replace an entire corps. On 1 July, Joffre launched his much-anticipated Somme Offensive. Falkenhayn's headquarters ordered the *5th Army* to assign two divisions to the High Command's reserves and to report on additional forces that could be made available. The Crown Prince drove to Falkenhayn's General Headquarters in Mézières to report that the *4th Division* and *21st Reserve Division* would be available for the reserves.

Late June to July – The Last Assault

At the beginning of June 1916, as disaster loomed on the Austrian Front in Russia, General Erich von Falkenhayn had to divert his attention from the Western Front. General Alexei Brusilov had launched a major Russian offensive in Galicia on 4 June. The Austrians had already caused difficulties for Falkenhayn when Generalfeldmarschall Conrad launched the Trentino Offensive against Italy in May 1916. Conrad wanted him to send German troops to support his campaign in Italy where his army had driven the Italians back, but suffered 150,000 casualties. In June,

---

[*] William, *My War Experiences*, p. 217.

Conrad had to divert forces to the east to reinforce his armies, which were collapsing in the face of Brusilov's offensive.[51] The Russian's four armies smashed the Austro-Hungarian front inflicting over 100,000 casualties in a couple of weeks, and took 200,000 prisoners before they outran their supply lines. The Germans, who were afraid that a defeat could trigger Rumania's entry into the war, had to prop up their ally. Brusilov renewed his offensive in late June, but had to slow his pace in July. A renewed Russian offensive failed in late July. The Germans had to take control of Austro-Hungarian forces on the Eastern Front. Falkenhayn's strategy based on his Verdun gamble was unravelling. On 1 July, while the Germans were still contending with the disaster in the East, the Western Allies opened their Somme Offensive.

Before the Russian front exploded and the Somme Offensive opened, the Germans had a piece of good news. Between 31 May and 1 June, the German High Seas Fleet had engaged the British Grand Fleet in the Battle of Jutland, the only major naval

The Somme Offensive

The great offensive began on 1 July 1916 on a 30km front stretching from Amiens to Péronne on both sides of the Somme River. It was heralded by an eight-day-long preparatory bombardment. Three armies, two British and one French, with a total of twenty-seven divisions engaged sixteen German divisions of the *2nd Army*. According to General Otto von Below, the *2nd Army* commander, German air reconnaissance had noticed the build-up since February. In May, Below complained that his army was weakened when many of the German artillery pieces were replaced with captured weapons.

The British bombardment, which began on 22 June, failed to destroy the barbed wire and the German first line. The French, however, did a better job on their part of the front. The first day, 1 July, was one of the darkest days in British military history as 58,000 men were lost in the assault, over 19,000 of which were killed. The Germans counter-attacked after the first day and regained their lost positions. It took over a week to capture the first German line. According to Below, the Allies not only outnumbered his troops but also had more aircraft and more equipment. He was forced to send in units piecemeal just to fill the breaches and prevent a collapse. The battle raged for almost five months. In September, the British launched the first tank assault of the war, but made only minor gains.

By the time the offensive ended in November, the British had lost 420,000 men, the French 200,000 and the Germans about 500,000. After this debacle, Hindenburg took over operations in the West and adopted a new strategy. Combined with Verdun, the German army was bled white, but the Allies still failed to break the stalemate. The Somme Offensive forced Falkenhayn to weaken his position on the Verdun Front. In September, Hindenburg ordered the creation of a new position, nicknamed the Hindenburg Line, to which he pulled back his forces at the end of the year. The Crown Prince anchored the German flank from the Verdun Front to the Aisne.

battle of the war. The British had caught the German fleet out of port, off the Danish coast, and attacked it. Whether or not it was a trap engineered by Admiral Reinhard Scheer made little difference.[52] The German warships inflicted heavy losses on their enemy before they made it back to the safety of their ports. However, even though the British suffered greater damage and losses than the Germans, the High Seas Fleet never accepted a similar challenge again. The British won a great strategic victory, but the Germans and their media relished the tactical victory. It was, however, only a feel-good triumph as the Allies' blockade caused greater shortages in Germany. In 1916, Grand Admiral Alfred von Tirpitz agreed with Falkenhayn that it was time to unleash unrestricted U-boat warfare, but the chancellor and government refused to allow it. Admiral Scheer had to order his submarines back to port in April 1916. Thus, the blockade could not be broken and the High Seas Fleet no longer presented a threat to shipping, a capability it never had since its warships were not designed for extended voyages.

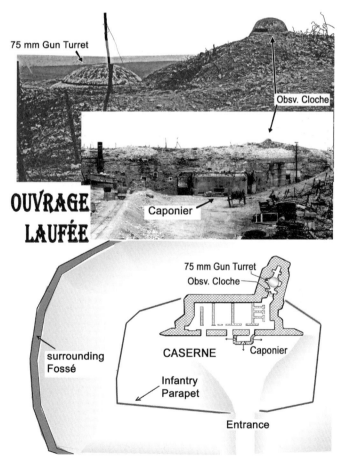

Ouvrage of Laufée. A caserne (bottom) with attached 75mm gun turret and observation block (top). The caponier on the caserne was added in 1916.

In July 1916, the entire front of the Crown Prince's army was engaged in the Battle of Verdun. At Vauquois, the French used 'new liquid fire trench mortar bombs ...,' he complained, 'with such powerful charges that even their own trenches were damaged,' adding 'that everywhere, on both banks of the Meuse, there broke out heavy bombing fights intended to hold our forces to their ground and distract our attention from the main action on the Somme'.* Falkenhayn needed the Crown Prince to tie down as many French divisions as possible to divert them from the Somme Offensive.

On 3 July, the German troops stormed the Damloup battery located on the edge of a steep slope just to the south of Fort Vaux. The fierce French counter-attacks that followed retook the battery and held it until 12 July, hindering preparations for the main German effort to clear the Meuse Heights.[53] The loss of the Damloup battery left the French with only the Ouvrage of Laufée in front of forts Tavannes and Souville. Laufée, which had been an infantry position earlier in the century, was enlarged by the addition of a large concrete structure that housed a caserne and a turret with two 75mm guns. The garrison of about one-hundred men covered the surrounding fossé with machine guns and rifles from the ramparts at the top of the earthen scarp. The gun turret had supported Fort Vaux early in June. After that, the turret gun was used to repel several attacks of the *50th Division* against Laufée itself.[54]

Bad weather delayed the artillery barrage. Falkenhayn became impatient and ordered the attack on Fort Souville to take place immediately so he could send some artillery from each corps on the east bank to the Somme Front. On 10 July, the German artillery on both banks of the Meuse laid down another massive bombardment that included more Green Cross shells than ever before. The main targets were on the east bank. The French gunners responded with their own poison gas shells. At 5.45 am (German time) on 11 July, the German infantry went on the attack focusing mostly on Fort Souville.

Fort Souville, a seven-sided fort, had begun the war with four 90mm guns and two mortars on its ramparts. It held a garrison of 250 men. Its main value was as an observation position, which made it a target of almost constant shelling in 1916. Between June and July, the 420mm guns scored two hits that collapsed the galleries leading to the powder stores. On 10 and 11 July, the fort was pummelled with artillery as well as gas shells. On 12 July, its machine guns mowed down German troops of the *103rd Division*. After this unsuccessful German assault, badly needed reinforcements reached the fort. The garrison lost 50 per cent of its men in that engagement. By the end of the year, an estimated 38,000 enemy rounds had hit the fort causing major damage and turning it into rubble. Amazingly, the Germans were unable to take it. The fort had no turret artillery, but an annex 385m to the west armed with an 1891 155mm Bussière gun turret was able to fire upon key points between the Ouvrage of Froideterre and Fort Moulainville. The turret had required repairs, which had been completed in October 1915, in time for the battle of Verdun. It was bombarded between 24 February and 16 March, but managed to return fire. After it shot about

---

* William, *My War Experiences*, p. 221.

600 rounds of low-quality ammunition, a shell finally burst in one of the gun barrels damaging the turret. The battery stayed out of action for the remainder of the battle, but served as an observatory.[55] The position consisted of a single turret mounted on a concrete block with only twenty men to serve it. The crew had to depend on field troops for close defence.

Like Fort Souville, Fort Tavannes had undergone little modernization. It had been pummelled with high explosive and gas shells between 25 February and the end of May. On 7 May, the day before the accident at German-occupied Fort Douaumont, its powder magazine blew up when a grenade detonated unintentionally. It was also targeted by the German artillery on 10 July. German troops charged it from the vicinity of Fort Vaux and Damloup, but stopped less than 1km away.[56] On 11 July, the *Alpine* and *X Reserve corps* attacked south of Fleury and advanced up to 400m. To the left of them, the French held up other German divisions in Chapitre Woods. The Germans' failure to take the objectives brought Falkenhayn post-haste down upon the Crown Prince. Expressing his extreme displeasure at the poor outcome of the operation despite the fact that he had lavishly provided the personnel, materials and Green Cross shells requested, he ordered the prince to go on the defensive.

In July, the French launched a major effort to retake the Ouvrage of Thiaumont, which had been lost on 23 June. This pushed Knobelsdorf to ask for permission to put the *5th Army* back on the offensive. Falkenhayn, unconvinced, ordered additional troops to the Somme that month. Meanwhile, as the French attacks against Thiaumont continued, the ouvrage changed hands several times and the mounting losses of the *4th Division* required the *14th Division* to move from the west bank to relieve it.

The Ouvrage of Thiaumont was a relatively small position that had been modernized early in the century. A caserne that included a machine-gun turret, a small block with an observation cloche and a Casemate de Bourges all in reinforced concrete and grouped closely together were added at that time. The French army removed the 75mm guns from the casemate in the autumn of 1915. During the first week of the German offensive in February, the shells broke up the surrounding parapets and damaged the barracks. In March, attempts to rearm the artillery casemate failed due to the constant bombardment. The machine-gun turret jammed and most of the wire obstacles and parts of the ramparts disappeared during the bombardment. The small garrison of about 70 men was withdrawn leaving the ouvrage to serve only as a shelter. On 20 June, the *I* and *III Bavarian corps* attacked towards Thiaumont and the Ouvrage of Froideterre. The Germans bombarded the position and took it on 23 June along with thirty prisoners. All French attacks between 24 and 29 June failed to regain the position. Until 4 July, both sides heavily contested the position, which changed hands several times. The Germans held its ruins between July and late October. In 6 days of combat, one French regiment lost over 1,200 men. When the Battle of Verdun ended, little was left of the position.

Before the Somme Offensive, Pétain said that 23 June was 'a specially critical day' since, he claimed, the Germans' bombardment had lasted two days and they had a marked superiority. He had warned Joffre that the Germans had a two to one

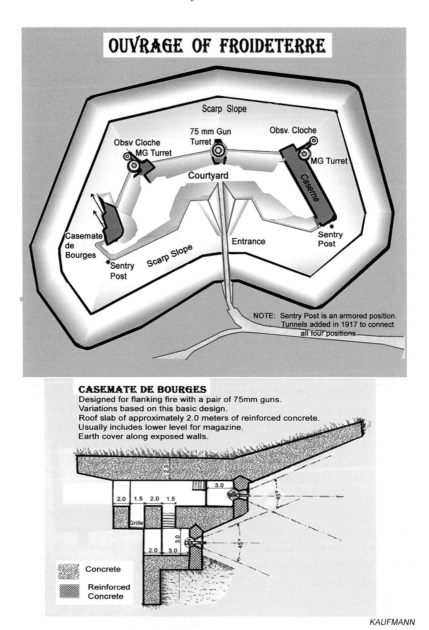

Top: Ouvrage of Froideterre. The combat blocks were not linked to the caserne until tunnels were excavated in 1917. Bottom: Basic design for Casemate de Bourges from 1899.

advantage in terms of artillery. The French II and VI Corps suffered heavily from the German bombardment, he pointed out, but they had managed to hold off the German assault several hours before they finally yielded control of Fleury and the village of Thiaumont. The German advance continued relentlessly along the crest of Froideterre. At this point, the French 2nd Army did not have enough fresh divisions to meet the demands of the situation, which could leave the right bank impossible to defend if the Germans achieved their objectives. Nivelle urgently requested reinforcements and warned his troops that the decisive moment of the battle was upon them. We 'must not let them pass!' he exhorted his soldiers. Pétain contacted Castelnau at General Headquarters that evening and warned him that the situation was critical and that he could not hold the enemy back with 'second class divisions'. Castelnau's response was to send four fresh divisions on 24 June; Nivelle's troops launched a counter-attack.

The Ouvrage of Froideterre stood beyond the Ouvrage of Thiaumont, near the end of the ridge. Its capitulation would give the Germans a dominating view over Verdun. This ouvrage, also modernized early in the century, was more widely dispersed than Thiaumont. Its positions, made of reinforced concrete, included a Casemate de Bourges, a block for a machine-gun turret and observation cloche, a block for a 75mm gun turret and a large caserne block with an emplacement for a machine-gun turret and an observation cloche. The two 75mm casemate guns had been removed in 1915. During the bombardment of February 1916, the observation position of the Casemate de Bourges was destroyed. In late March, the artillery casemate was rearmed. During the German offensive on 20 June, the ouvrage was shelled with heavy artillery including 305mm and 380mm weapons. The next day, 500 rounds rained down on the fort and included many Green Cross gas shells. The Germans continued to drop poison gas shells on the fort until the morning of the assault. The bombardment caused a great deal of damage, especially among the wire obstacles, and blocked the entrances, but the gun positions and the turret remained operational. On 23 June, after three days of bombardment, German infantry advanced on the ouvrage at about 7.00 am. The machine-gun turrets failed, blocked by debris, which allowed the Germans to reach the ramparts and enter the courtyard. The 75mm gun turret fired at point-blank range on the Germans in the courtyard sending them scurrying for cover. At 11.00 am, the machine-gun turrets were back in action. Before long, a chasseur battalion drove the Germans off the fort. The retreat from the ouvrage cost the Germans their best chance to control the ridge, albeit they did not give up. German artillery continued to pound the ouvrage. On 25 July, the glacis armour of the machine-gun turret on the caserne was pierced by a 305mm round. The turret became inoperable until it was repaired a year later. The infantry attack of 23 June was the last on the Ouvrage of Froideterre.

Before 23 June, the *25th Reserve Division* had made some progress near Froideterre. The *Guard Ersatz Division* had been stopped by heavy fire and the *21st Reserve Division* had taken an extremity of the Souville Ridge. Early in July, south of Vaux, the *50th Division* had captured Battery Damloup. Further efforts in July were futile in the face of French counter-attacks. The French penetrated the second line of the German *VII Reserve Corps* on the western part of the Poivre and the Germans could not drive them back. General Johann Hans von Zwehl, commanding *VII Reserve Corps* (and the commander of the *14th Reserve Division*), refused to counter-attack since months of combat had worn down his troops. On 3 August, the French retook Fleury and the ruins of Thiaumont only to lose the small ouvrage the next day. According to the

Pétain's Road to Victory

Before the battle in February 1916, Verdun had a logistical problem. The main rail line entered the city from the direction Chalons–Bar-le-Duc–St Mihiel but was cut by the St Mihiel bridgehead. German artillery, located in the Argonne near Vauquois, interdicted the other main line from Reims–Ste Ménehould–Clermont at Aubréville. This left only a small railway that ran between Bar-le-Duc and Verdun via Souilly. It lacked the required capacity to support French forces in the Verdun

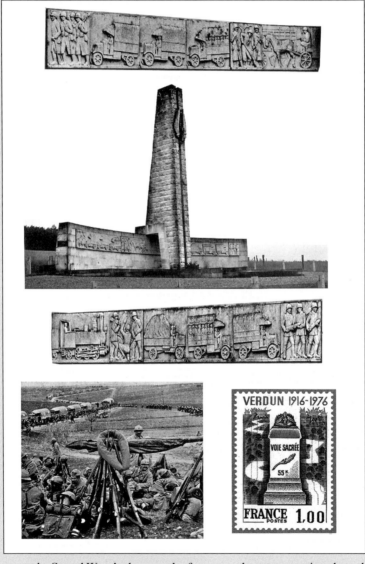

Monument on the Sacred Way. A photograph of troops and convoys moving along the Sacred Way.

Salient. A secondary road that ran more or less parallel to the railway was in poor condition. The narrow gauge railway, known as 'Meusien', carried a little over 80 per cent of the food supply for Pétain's army of over 436,000 men and 136,000 horses and mules between February and March. Its capacity of 1,800 tons a day rose to about 4,000 tons in March and 10,000 tons in June. A French infantry division, which had required 70 to 140 tons a day in 1914, needed 10 times that amount by 1918. That was the equivalent of 10 to 20 wagons in 1914. The small railway needed more rolling stock in February to increase its capacity from the 1,800 tons a day. During the following weeks, the army requisitioned the necessary equipment from throughout France and increased the railway's rolling stock to 75 locomotives and 800 railway wagons. The number of trains that made the daily run increased from twenty-two in February to thirty-five in April. The railroad was especially useful in evacuating the wounded on hospital trains, which often brought back 300 men at a time. Barracks and other large buildings were converted into hospitals at Bar-le-Duc and Revigny. Beginning in 1915, the 5th Engineer Regiment, specializing in railway work, improved the rail line leading to Verdun and doubled the number of tracks. On 23 February 1916, it also started building a new standard gauge line between Nettancourt and Dugny, finishing it by the end of June 1916. This improved the supply situation and the build-up for the big French offensive on the east bank. This new rail line was able to carry three times as much as the secondary road the army had heavily depended on and freed up many trucks for the Somme Offensive.

As soon as he took command, Pétain set out to improve the 75km road that became the lifeline of Verdun and which was eventually dubbed 'a Voie Sacrée' or the 'Sacred Way'.[58] This road began at Bar-le-Duc, ran through Naives, Rumont, Chaumont-sur-Aire, Souilly, Lemmes and ended at Verdun. It was widened in 1915 to accommodate two-way traffic. On 28 February, the thaw made it quite impassable. The road was divided into six sections controlled by an officer of the Motor Traffic Commission supported by military police. Pétain established many quarries near the road and assigned civilian labour and territorial troops the task of filling in the road as quickly as the vehicles wore it down. By the end of February, 8,800 men were involved in the building and maintenance of the Sacred Way and 3,900 motor vehicles moved back and forth across it. By 6 March, in little over a week, 23,000 tons of munitions, 2,500 tons of material and 190,000 men moved into Verdun on this route. The workers spread the stone, recalled Pétain, and 'the work of steam rollers to be done by the procession of motor-trucks'.* However, this was not the ideal solution because the partially crushed stones tore up the rubber tyres of the vehicles and the constant rattling put a stress on the engines, which required frequent maintenance.

In June 1916, over 12,000 vehicles plied the road as one passed every 14 seconds travelling at 5–20km/h. Drivers often drove for 18-hour shifts and

---

* Pétain, *Verdun*, p. 96.

remained with their trucks for ten or more consecutive days. Before long, about 9,000 trucks, cars, and ambulances operated on the road making it possible for troops and supplies to move in and out of the salient. Vehicles returning from Verdun to Bar-le-Duc often carried troops, mainly from units leaving the front lines. Fresh troops arrived by rail at Revigny, Bar-le-Duc and Baudonvillers (south of Bar-le-Duc) and boarded a convoy of trucks that headed down the Sacred Way to Verdun. Each day, the road handled an average of 13,000 troops, 6,400 tons of materials and 1,500 tons of ammunition. There is no doubt that the small railway and the Sacred Way not only provided logistical support, but also allowed Pétain to rotate divisions constantly in and out of the Verdun Salient. The road and railways were mostly beyond the range of most German artillery, and the German air force proved to be a minor threat. Thus, this lifeline was instrumental in preventing a German victory at Verdun.

Sources: Jean Boucheré's *Chemin de Fer Historique de la Voie Sacree* at http://translate.google.com/translate?hl=en&sl=fr&u=http://traintouristique-lasuzanne.fr/index.php/fr/l-histoire-du-meusien/la-guerre&prev=search

Ministère de la défense: http://www.defense.gouv.fr

Henri Philippe Pétain and Margaret MacVeagh (trans.), *Verdun* (Toronto: Dial Press, 1930).

Crown Prince, between 23 June and the end of August, the Ouvrage of Thiaumont was attacked thirty-four times and Fleury thirteen. Casualties mounted steadily on both sides.

The *Alpine Corps* illustrates how German units at Verdun operated for extended periods and its history highlights the problems associated with long service in the front lines. This corps lost slightly over 70 per cent of its infantry at Verdun between June and early August 1916. It transferred to the Argonne on 12 August to recoup its losses before it was sent to Rumania at the end of September.[57] The *Guards Ersatz Division* took part in operations at Verdun beginning in May. It drew back from the front at the end of August after having lost 50 per cent of its infantry. The *4th Division* reached the front in May and took heavy losses a few days later in the attack on Hill 304. In July, it incurred heavy further casualties in the fighting around Thiaumont. The *2nd Bavarian Division* showed up at Verdun in May. During operations near Douaumont in June, it lost 50 per cent of its contingent and had to be reconstituted. It returned to the front on 23 June and once again, it took such heavy losses that one regiment was left with only forty men. The division had to withdraw to the St Mihiel Salient to recover. The *7th Reserve Division*, which took part in the operations of early June and the attack in Chapitre Woods on 21 June, took over 50 per cent casualties. On 1 July, it was sent to the Argonne to reorganize. The *12th Reserve Division* was in the Verdun sector on the west bank when the battle began. It joined the fight in March. By mid-May, it had lost 70 per cent of its infantry and had to be sent into reserve. The *38th Division* reached the Verdun Front in mid-May 1916 and remained there until October. It had lost 52 per cent of its infantry when it transferred to the Somme. The *39th Division* fared even worse. It served with the *XV Corps* on the Woëvre from the beginning of the offensive. In March, it took heavy losses at Caillette Woods and became involved in fighting around Vaux in August ending the battle with 69 per cent infantry casualties. Although French and German units were decimated at Verdun, the Germans had the harder time of it. Their units stayed fully engaged for months with only enough respite to replenish their forces whereas most of the French divisions did their time, moved to another front and returned for a second or third round at Verdun.

Pay Back

July represented the high water mark for the Germans on the east bank of the Meuse. The French had already stymied their advance on the west bank in early June. The resolute French defence of Verdun in the spring should have made it obvious that Operation Gericht would be futile. The French had taken up the challenge to fight it out at Verdun, but they were not being bled white. The attrition rate did not reach the levels Falkenhayn had expected. In the summer, the Austrians were once again on the verge of collapse on the Eastern Front in the face of the Brusilov Offensive. On the Western Front, the Somme Offensive presented a major threat to the Germans. Both fronts began to sap the strength of the *5th Army*.

On 11 July 1916, Falkenhayn ordered the *5th Army* to end offensive operations, but he had a change of heart at the end of the month and he told the Crown Prince to launch another offensive on the east bank in August. The *5th Army* had already dispatched some divisions to the Somme on 18 July. The *X Reserve Corps* (*7th Reserve, 19th Reserve* and *9th Landwehr Divisions*) moved from the east bank to the Argonne.[59] The *XVI Corps* remained in the Argonne. The *Western Attack Group* still consisted of the *VI Reserve Corps* (*13th, 14th* and *20th Reserve divisions*). General Hermann von François replaced Max von Gallwitz as commander of the *Western Group*.[60] Höhn's *Group* (*4th* and *6th Bavarian divisions*) formed under General Maximilian von Höhn and *XVIII Reserve Corps* (*21st Reserve* and *Guard Ersatz divisions*) made up the remainder of the group.[61] The *Eastern Attack Group* consisted of the *XXIV Reserve Corps* (*38th, 54th* and *192nd divisions*) and *VII Corps* (*13th* and *14th divisions*). The *XV Corps* remained unchanged (*30th, 39th* and *50th divisions*).

The renewed German attack achieved very little. Höhn's Bavarians made minor gains near Froideterre, while the *Guard Ersatz Division* faltered in the face of machine-gun and artillery fire. The *21st Reserve Division* secured a small piece of Souville Ridge. The French counter-attacks ended this last German offensive with heavy casualties. On 3 August, General Nivelle's 2nd Army drove the Germans from the Ouvrage of Thiaumont and the ruins of Fleury, but the Germans retook the ruined ouvrage the next day. Fleury continued to change hands as well. In August, the French exerted heavy pressure on both the east and west banks smashing German positions with their artillery. As Höhn's Bavarian divisions neared exhaustion, the *14th Division* came from the west bank to replace the *4th Bavarian Division* on 6 August and the *33rd Division* from Mudra's *XVI Corps* in the Argonne relieved the

6th Bavarian Division on 8 August. The Crown Prince shifted additional divisions, including Mudra's remaining division – the *34th*, to the east bank to shore up the position. Mudra received the depleted *Alpine Corps* to replace his two divisions. The *1st Division* had already departed for the Eastern Front. The German front at Verdun had become a patchwork of formations.

Meanwhile, Nivelle's 2nd Army and Pétain's Army Group Centre finally wrested air superiority from the Germans and obtained new artillery and fresh troops. On 17 August, following a heavy bombardment, the French launched three attacks against the *Western Attack Group* that stubbornly clung to its positions. Meanwhile, French artillery laid down several heavy barrages on the east bank. French troops forced *Höhn's Group* and the *XVIII Reserve Corps* out of Fleury. The next day, additional units stormed the ruins of the Ouvrage of Thiaumont and cleared the Germans from the area south of Fort Vaux. On the east bank, the combatants were locked in heavy fighting. On 19 August, a French artillery barrage smashed a German counter-attack and the battle raged among the ruins of Fleury until 20 August. The *50th Division* had partially restored the front shattered on the 18 August. The *Guard Ersatz Division* was relieved by the *14th Bavarian Division*, which had to be relieved before long by the *84th Division*. As attacks and counter-attacks succeeded each other throughout the month of August, the German divisions were slowly decimated, but the lines around Verdun hardly budged.

General Knobelsdorf conferred with Falkenhayn about continuing the offensive operations against Verdun. This time, Falkenhayn did not share Knobelsdorf's enthusiasm for continuing the status quo because Germany's overall position appeared bleak at this point. Operation Gericht had failed to achieve his goals, the situation on the Somme was worsening and Rumania was about to enter the war. The Crown Prince, who was often dismissed as an amateur but had more aptitude than was attributed to him, sent a letter to Falkenhayn explaining the futility of continuing the attack. Knobelsdorf, on the other hand, insisted that he had to take the heights between Fleury and Fort Souville in order to secure the front east of the Meuse and prevent the French from dominating the lowlands to the east. General Lochow, who commanded the *Eastern Attack Group*, disagreed with Knobelsdorf and warned that an assault on Fort Souville would lead to endless combat and a repeat of the effort to take Fort Vaux. Falkenhayn's response came in a letter dated 21 August: 'The general situation renders it urgently necessary to keep the enemy in the Meuse area under the impression that the offensive on the German side has not been abandoned but will be systematically continued. It is left to the Army Group Command to decide how this can best be accomplished with the necessarily limited means at its disposal …'.

Falkenhayn's letter brought the conflict between the Crown Prince and Knobelsdorf to a head the week the French launched fierce attacks. Fed up, the Crown Prince asked his father, who was also disillusioned at the time, to transfer Knobelsdorf. On 27 August, Knobelsdorf was heading to the Eastern Front to command the *X Corps*. He was replaced with General Walther von Luttwitz from the Eastern Front and harmony was restored at headquarters. Meanwhile, Austro-German resistance finally stiffened against Brusilov's offensive in August. However, on the 27th, the

Rumanians finally joined the conflict, which threatened to tip the balance.[62] A few weeks later, the Russian momentum floundered, but not before changes were set in train in the West. Hindenburg replaced Falkenhayn, who was put in command of the *9th Army* in preparation for the invasion of Rumania. Hindenburg concluded that Germany's situation was unfavourable 'for lack of men we could not contemplate the idea of a relief attack either at Verdun or the Somme, however strong were my own inclinations for such a measure'.* He requested the Kaiser's permission to end the Verdun Offensive explaining that the 'battlefield was a regular hell and regarded as such by the troops'. In retrospect, he thought, it would have been better to abandon the gains the Germans had made and consolidate the situation at Verdun. 'The flower of our best fighting troops had been sacrificed …' at Verdun, he concluded.

The Germans bagged 65,000 French prisoners between February and the end of August at Verdun without managing to turn the tide. With the Hindenburg/Ludendorff team in command, they needed to find a way to replenish the fighting strength of the army. Hindenburg and Ludendorff met with the commanders of the *1st, 2nd, 4th* and *5th armies* on 8 September and informed them that, as a result of the battle on the Somme, *Landwehr* and *Landsturm* units would serve on the front to free first-line divisions for operations on the Somme Front. They also ordered each German division to release one regiment to form a new division. The *5th Army* provided the *4th, 19th Reserve* and *10th Ersatz divisions*. The front was readjusted so the headquarters of the *X Reserve Corps* moved to the southeast and the *XVI Corps* (now *Mudra Group*) took command of all troops on the Argonne Front (*21st Reserve, 9th Landwehr, 19th Reserve* and *16th Bavarian divisions* and *Alpine Corps*).[63] Mudra's sector extended from *3rd Army* to *Franke's Group* (*2nd Landwehr* and *4th divisions*) holding Hill 304.

The *Eastern Meuse Group* under Lochnow split into four commands: *VII Reserve Corps* (three divisions), *54th General Command* (three divisions), *XII Corps* (three divisions) and *XV Corps* (two divisions). In early October, *XV Corps* (*30th* and *39th divisions*) left *5th Army* and *XVIII Corps* returned from the Argonne to take over a sector of *Eastern Meuse Group* in the Woëvre. In mid-October, Viktor Kühne's *54th General Command* and one of its divisions came off line, but the Crown Prince received no replacement.[64] The *5th Army*'s reserve had one division on the left bank and two on the right bank and was no longer the formidable force it had been in early 1916. During this time, the French made no grand offensive in the area, but their artillery and aircraft asserted their presence as Pétain and Nivelle built up their forces. The German expenditure of artillery shells dropped to about 25 per cent of the June levels, but the French fired about seven times as many rounds as the Germans. Fewer than 70 of the Crown Prince's 140 original heavy artillery batteries remained.

During much of September and October, the German positions began to crumble under heavy French bombardments and almost daily rains made it difficult for the soldiers to repair and improve them. Nivelle continued rotating divisions at the

---

* Paul von Hindenburg, *The Great War* (London: Greenhill Books, 2006), p. 121.

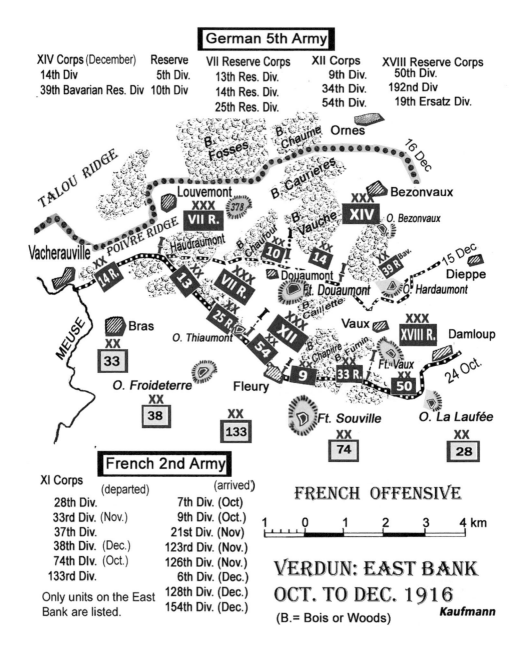

German 5th Army

XIV Corps (December)	Reserve	VII Reserve Corps	XII Corps	XVIII Reserve Corps
14th Div	5th Div.	13th Res. Div.	9th Div.	50th Div.
39th Bavarian Res. Div	10th Div	14th Res. Div.	34th Div.	192nd Div
		25th Res. Div.	54th Div.	19th Ersatz Div.

French 2nd Army

XI Corps (departed)	(arrived)
28th Div.	7th Div. (Oct)
33rd Div. (Nov.)	9th Div. (Oct.)
37th Div.	21st Div. (Nov)
38th Div. (Dec.)	123rd Div. (Nov.)
74th Div. (Oct.)	126th Div. (Nov.)
133rd Div.	6th Div. (Dec.)
	128th Div. (Dec.)
Only units on the East	154th Div. (Dec.)
Bank are listed.	

FRENCH OFFENSIVE

VERDUN: EAST BANK
OCT. TO DEC. 1916

(B.= Bois or Woods)   *Kaufmann*

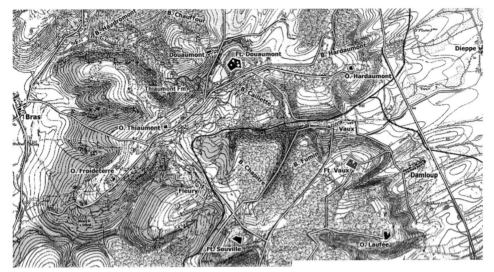

German topographic map with wooded areas added showing the main area of the battle over the forts for control of the Meuse Heights.

front. On the east bank, activity was maintained as fresh divisions came to occupy the area between Thiaumont and Chapitre woods. Among them was the 7th Division, which took its place on line in late August and assailed German positions in early September and on 20 September. The 73rd Division arrived at about the same time and took part in the fighting in Chapitre Woods during the first half of September. The 67th Division engaged in combat on the west bank in March, rotated out of Verdun and returned in September to serve on the east bank until it was replaced at the end of the month. The 73rd Division reached Verdun in late August, took part in the fighting in Chapitre Woods in early September and withdrew. The 38th Division (North African troops) was involved with the fighting around Avocourt Woods and Hill 304 for months in August. It moved to the east bank at the end of September to prepare for the impending offensive. The 55th Division, which had been involved in combat in the same area on the west bank until 20 June, did not move to the right bank until 21 September. The 130th Division participated in the June fighting to stop the German advance between the Ouvrage of Thiaumont and Chapitre Woods. Between 21 and 23 June, it fought for control of Fleury before moving to the Argonne for a couple of months. It returned to the east bank on 29 September to the same sectors and remained there until it was relieved on 23 October.[65]

Other divisions replaced most of the units on the east bank in expectation of the long-awaited offensive. General Arthur Guyot de Salins' 38th Division spearheaded the attack on Fort Douaumont on 23 October.[66] General Charles de Lardemelle's 74th Division retrained in August before moving into position with the objective of retaking Fort Vaux. General Fénelon Passaga's 133rd Division, stationed near Switzerland, arrived on 11 September with the objective of clearing Caillette Woods. The 37th Division, commanded by General Noël Garnier-Duplessix, had been at

FORT DOUAUMONT

Aerial Photo before 1916

After 1916 Battle

MG Turret

NW MG Turret Block

Abri VI converted to Obs. Bunker
1917

Obs.
Cloche

75mm
Turret

Cloche on
remains
of Abri VII

Fort Douaumont after the battle. The MG turret was replaced with a turret from another fort after the war. Abri VI was converted to an observation post, which was destroyed more than once after 1916. The cloche attached to Abri VII is all that remains of the structure.

Verdun in February and incurred heavy losses. In July, it took part in the attack on Fleury and went to rest at the end of the month. On 27 September, it returned to take part in the offensive. General Joseph Mangin's 55th Division, which was on the west bank near Hill 304 from June until 1 September moved to the east bank on 21 September. It remained there until to 2 November. The 63rd Division of General Joseph Andlauer, which had participated in the failed relief effort of Fort Vaux in June, was sent to the Vosges. It returned to the east bank in October. General Louis Arlabosse's 9th Division was at Vauquois until about October before it moved to the

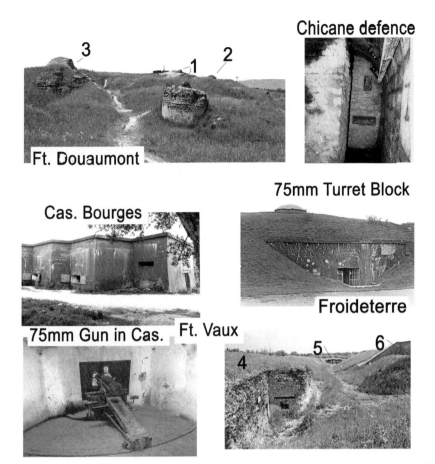

Sections of forts including defensive chicane built to protect entrances and tunnels. 1. Obs Cloche, 2. 75 Turret, 3. Converted to Bunker 1917, 4. Gorge Coffre, 5. Double Coffre, 6. Cas. Bourges.

east bank to support the attack on Fort Vaux. Thus, on 23 October, only a handful of German divisions faced an onslaught of seven relatively fresh divisions of the XI Corps.

The French finally launched their offensive on 24 October after a day of intense bombardment. The preliminary shelling began on 20 October after the weather cleared. The ordnance included gas shells, which kept the Germans tied down while the French guns systematically destroyed their positions. General Charles Mangin (XI Corps) was in charge of operations on the east bank. Pétain had obtained two of the huge 400mm railway howitzers firing a 900kg round up to 15,000m and 370mm mortars that lobbed a 489kg round about 5,000m.[67] On 23 October, the 400mm rounds inflicted the most serious damage Fort Douaumont suffered in the entire war. Fires broke out in the fort and the likelihood of another explosion like the one of 8 May became very real. The Germans had evacuated Fort Douaumont the next morning leaving behind thirty men and one officer who desperately tried to organize a defence.

Shortly before noon, three French divisions advanced on a 7km front shrouded in a thick fog behind rolling barrages. General Passaga's 133rd Division led the way and took control of the area between Fort Douaumont and north of the village of Vaux. Fog temporarily delayed Guyot de Salins' 38th Division in Caillette Woods, but its battalions took Douaumont village at 2.45 pm and the fort about an hour later, taking prisoner the remaining Germans. The German *25th Reserve Division* of the *VII Reserve Corps*, the *XII Corps 9th Division* and *54th Division*, which held the area between Thiaumont and Chapitre Woods, quickly capitulated. Only the reserves on the steep slopes north of Douaumont village held back the French while the *33rd Reserve Division* checked the French infantry. The French 74th Division on the right had to be replaced by the 9th Division after incurring heavy losses in its attempts to reach Fort Vaux. The *XVIII Corps 50th Division* held Vaux Hill for a few days. The *5th* and *10th divisions* rushed to the front to fill the gaps and in a few days relieved the shattered *9th Division* and *25th Reserve Division*. The 4 days of battle resulted in 47,000 casualties for the French.

The French renewed the attack on 25 October and on 2 November Fort Vaux fell, but a day after the garrison evacuated it. On 1 November, pioneers brought explosives and prepared the fort for demolition. The explosives blew the 75mm gun turret out of its well and propelled it into the fossé. French troops entered the abandoned fort on 2 November. Despite all the damage, the fort could be repaired, except for the gun turret block, like Fort Douaumont.[68]

A new offensive launched by the French in December ended by mid-month. The French troops drove the Germans back over Côte du Poivre and took Louvemont, Bezonvaux and Damloup to the south. The threat to Verdun was over. The French set about restoring and improving their forts and added new positions and underground galleries during 1917. The number of French and German casualties can only be estimated. The French incurred 300,000–500,000 casualties including about 150,000 dead. Germans casualties ranged between 280,000 and 430,000. These numbers were smaller than for the French, but did not reach the ratios Falkenhayn had optimistically expected to achieve. At this point, the Germans retained about 5km of conquered territory of limited military value.

Chapter Six

Conclusion

'The Mill of the Meuse'

A phrase sometimes attributed
to General von Falkenhayn

The Battle of Verdun embodies most of the ideas we have formed about the First World War. Except for the tank, all the weapons associated with the war played a significant role on this battlefield. The artillery churned up the entire battleground and pockmarked it with deep craters that persist to this very day. Both sides used a variety of deadly gases extensively. They were not only released from canisters at the front, but also pumped into artillery shells and fired into enemy trenches and on enemy batteries with large-calibre guns. Airpower increased in importance providing aerial photos for intelligence and directing artillery fire. Before long, control of the air became more critical and both sides formed fighter or pursuit units to clear the skies of the enemy. The Germans began to use storm-troop tactics on a large scale and adopted flamethrowers. Other innovations in the military arsenal included more powerful artillery, mainly for the French, steel helmets, etc. Both sides used some of their biggest guns at Verdun: the German 420mm weapons and the French 400mm railway guns. Trench warfare reached its zenith as much of the battle revolved around control of the forts of the Verdun ring. Like most of the battles on the Western Front, Verdun turned into a massive stalemate during over a half a year of fighting. On 23 June 1916, when the German advance reached its zenith, the Kaiser's troops had taken little more than 10km since February. In June, their progress had dwindled to about 2km, most of which was lost within a matter of weeks. Falkenhayn had hoped that the battle would force the enemy into capitulation. For the French, on the other hand, the Battle of Verdun was a matter of national pride and morale rather than strategic importance. The main leaders of the battle –Joffre, Pétain and Falkenhayn – were eventually removed from key commands, although Pétain, the hero of Verdun, made a quick comeback. Others such as Nivelle and Mangin rose to higher command, but lost their ascendance because they emphasized the offensive. Hindenburg and Ludendorff, who replaced Falkenhayn, only played a role in winding down the battle. Crown Prince Wilhelm, who performed well under the restrictions imposed upon him, was to receive more than his fair share of the blame, but remained in command. The battle brought down many commanders, but it also saw many others rise to higher positions. Sadly, more than ½ million men died or lay wounded as a result of a conflict that accomplished nothing but a stalemate.

The ossuary was built after the war. Skeletal remains found since then that cannot be identified are placed in various rooms on the lower level. The unidentified remains of about 130,000 soldiers are interred here. The cemetery has 15,000 graves. Middle: victory monument. Bottom: monument to member of parliament and army sergeant André Maginot on the battlefield. The defeat of the Germans at Verdun, with the help of Maginot, inspired a new philosophy regarding the role of forts which culminated in the construction of the Maginot Line.

The battle concluded in December 1916. The decisive victory General Falkenhayn had hoped to achieve did not happen. Instead of 'bleeding the French army white', he almost crippled the German army. After General Hindenburg replaced him, Falkenhayn took over the command of an army in the Rumanian Campaign where he redeemed his reputation. Crown Prince Wilhelm took command of an army group, but he could never shake off the blame and regret for the needless expenditure of life during the battle that earned him the undeserved sobriquet of 'The Butcher of Verdun'. 'The mill on the Meuse – he wrote – ground to powder the hearts as well as the bodies of the troops.'* Falkenhayn, whose strategic and tactical plan had prevented the Germans from taking Verdun early in the campaign, never spared a thought for the men who lost their lives or their health fighting in the trenches. His only concern appeared to be continuing the battle even when it became apparent that the only obtainable objective was increasing the number of casualties.

By rescuing Verdun, General Pétain saved the day for France and he was hailed as the saviour of France. It is undeniable that the fortifications played a major role in the defence of Verdun and Pétain must be given credit for their restoration thereby creating an unbreachable barrier. Even though the Germans hammered the refurbished fortress line and even took Fort Douaumont, they gained no easy victories against the remaining forts. It took bloody and exhausting combat to take control of Fort Vaux, despite the fact that its main defences had already been destroyed. Fighting raged around the Ouvrage of Thiaumont for months and its ruins changed hands many times. The Ouvrage of Froideterre continued to resist even though German troops crossed over its ramparts. The defenders threw them back and put a stop to their chances of taking the position from where they could dominate Verdun. The Ouvrage of Laufée and Fort Moulainville checked additional German attempts to penetrate beyond Fort Vaux. The badly damaged forts of Souville and Tavannes proved to be effective even though they were not as well armed as the others. It must be noted that all the forts and ouvrages occupied key points and were better designed and built to resist German heavy artillery than trenches and scattered bunkers were. To a great extent, Pétain owed his victory to his idea of rearming and returning these forts to their defensive function and making them his last and main line of defence on the east bank.

General Nivelle took command of the 2nd Army, and his subordinate General Charles 'The Butcher' Mangin went on the offensive with almost the same enthusiasm as in early 1914. In May, their attempt to retake Fort Douaumont failed even though their troops reached the superstructure of the fort. Mangin's 5th Division lost over 5,300 men in its worst 2 days of the war. Despite the growth of the French heavy artillery, the French infantry was beaten back and suffered heavy losses that spring. After the Somme Offensive was launched, the Germans went over to the defensive at Verdun. In October, Nivelle and Mangin again tried to retake the lost forts. In a memorandum of October 1916, General von Zwehl observed:

---

* William, *My War Experiences*, p. 223.

The value of Fort Douaumont, leaving aside the great political importance of its possession by us, lies in the possibility of our artillery dominating the terrain in front of it, thanks to the excellent observation posts in its armoured turrets.

We can only prevent a surprise of our first line by its means. Moreover, to a certain extent, the fort gives our reserves good shelter two kilometres from our first line.

This time, Pétain obtained two of France's largest railway howitzers. These 400mm weapons inflicted enough damage on Fort Douaumont to force the Germans to evacuate it before the French infantry attack. The big guns succeeded in part because their rounds landed on the rear sections of the fort, its weakest point. Taking the two forts was almost an anti–climax. This time, the French surprised and overwhelmed the defenders after short intense bombardments followed by swift infantry advances. The French suffered significant losses nonetheless.

General Pétain was sidelined when General Joffre was replaced by Robert Nivelle. However, Nivelle's Champagne Offensive (2nd Battle of the Aisne) of 1917 did not bring the promised decisive victory in two days. Instead, the French suffered over 180,000 casualties in less than a month of combat between April and May. The resulting French Mutiny brought Pétain back into the limelight. By this time, Verdun was no longer a major concern.

Surprisingly, Field Marshal Paul von Hindenburg provides in his own memoir, *The Great War*, the best summary of the battle and its importance to Germany. The Verdun Offensive was undertaken at the cost of putting the Eastern Front on the defensive. Hindenburg and his colleagues had remained silent on the subject in February because of their own doubts. Despite that, he wrote, 'the idea of capturing Verdun was a good one'. Taking the fortress would 'remove the salient at our most sensitive point' and open new strategic possibilities.

In my opinion the importance of this fortress justified an attempt to take it. We had it in our power to break off the attack at any time if it appeared impossible to carry it through, or the sacrifices it exacted seemed to be too high. Moreover, had not the boldest and most improbable actions in attacks on fortresses succeeded brilliantly time after time in this war?

After the end of February the word 'Verdun' was no longer uttered secretly, but loudly and joyfully. The name 'Douaumont', like a beacon of German heroism, lit up the far distances of the East… .

As time went on Verdun was spoken of in yet another tone. Doubts gradually began to prevail… . Why should we persevere with an offensive which exacted such frightful sacrifices and … with no prospects of success?

Once the Kaiser appointed him as Falkenhayn's replacement, Hindenburg had the opportunity to end the slaughter:

On purely military grounds it would have been far better for us to have improved our situation at Verdun by the voluntary evacuation of the ground we had captured. In August, 1916 I could not adopt that course. To a large extent the flower of our best fighting troops had been sacrificed in the enterprise. The public at home still anticipated a glorious issue to the offensive. It would be only too easy to produce the impression that all these sacrifices had been incurred in vain.

At the end of October the French opened a largely-conceived and boldly-executed counter-attack and overran our lines. We lost Douaumont, and had no longer the strength to recover the field of honour of German heroism.[*]

On 25 December 1916, General Hindenburg issued a secret order titled 'Experience of the Recent Fighting at Verdun'. Some of the more salient points of this order addressed the construction and manning of defences that became part of the 'Hindenburg Line' in 1917 when he made a strategic withdrawal in northern France. What he wrote is not exactly new, since Falkenhayn had already employed some of these methods. Hindenburg explained that 'Single lines of trenches do not suffice' and 'A fortified zone must be constructed, organized in depth ...'. He decided that the rearward portion of the zone would have to consist of a system of strongpoints, machine-gun nests and other postions that merged towards the front to create a close meshed network of trenches. He forbade the use of deeply excavated dugouts in the front-line trench saying that they were mantraps.[1] The dugouts were to be placed towards the rear and in the intermediate zone and should be made of concrete and masked from enemy observation. Large underground accommodations would serve only the reserves and placed far to the rear. He also ordered his subordinates not to build the large *stollen* near the front where they could become mantraps. Wide obstacles near the front trench and in no-man's-land, he decided, could be destroyed in a vigorous attack. It was better to place the greatest number of obstacles within the fortified zone all the way to the rear where they would be integrated into the strongpoints. The idea was to entrap enemy forces that managed to break through and to protect the troops still holding out in the front line. 'At Verdun – he wrote – where there were too many dug-outs in the front line trench, a proportion of the infantry did not get out of them quickly enough. A close-meshed network of trenches was lacking, as were also obstacles running perpendicular to the front.' He did not overlook the fact that the morale of the German troops defending the area was low. However, he felt that the troops in the rear did not show enough initiative to counter-attack and rescue their comrades trapped in the forward positions. He claimed that many German soldiers had surrendered without offering much resistance due to low morale. He told his commanders to increase training, drilling and education to revive the flagging spirit of the infantry. Furthermore, their living conditions had to be improved. Hindenburg also criticized the use of artillery at Verdun claiming that

---

[*] Hindenburg, *The Great War*, p. 121.

in many cases it operated mechanically instead of seeking out targets. The lessons of Verdun formed his blueprint for future operations in the West.

Over commitment to Verdun placed both German and French in a 'no retreat' situation to maintain morale. According to Hindenburg, the French army under Robert Nivelle threw away its advantage by returning to bombardments of long duration in 1917. The shelling eliminated the element of surprise and allowed the Germans to maintain their positions and inflict heavy casualties on the attackers.

The Battle of Verdun also marked the renaissance of fortifications after the debacle of 1914 when, in the Battle of the Frontiers, the Belgian and French forts had fallen and seemed to be unsuited to modern warfare. The Russian fortifications had not fared much better. Thus, by 1916 the Allies had largely written off forts as obsolete behemoths. Pétain, however, thought that the forts were of 'great assistance to our troops during the battle, and contributed largely to our success'. In addition, 'the forts, in spite of their imperfections, demonstrated that they were indisputably superior to every other system of defence'.* It is clear from an announcement he made at German headquarters in November 1916 that even General Erich von Ludendorff agreed:

> The forts of Douaumont and of Vaux played an important part in the battle of Verdun so long as they remained as French forts in the hands of the defenders. In order to weaken the Verdun position they had to be rendered inoffensive; deprived of their fighting means and largely destroyed, they possessed only a limited value for the assaulting party from a tactical point of view immediately the attack upon Verdun had been interrupted.**

Only the new Fort Vacherauville and Ouvrage of Falouse had been built of reinforced concrete, whereas the older fortification on the right bank had not. Despite that fact, these obsolescent fortifications were able to take a tremendous battering and keep on functioning. Thus, the French decided to improve and modify their forts in 1917 creating new subterranean links, repairing and adding positions. This work included the construction of a tunnel from the caserne to the 75mm gun turret block at Fort Douaumont and the replacement of the sandbagged barracks face of Fort Vaux with defensive machine-gun casemates. Work began on a deep tunnel system for Fort Vaux, and a tunnel system from the caserne of Froideterre to the combat blocks of Froideterre. In some forts, such as Fort Souville, tunnels extended to outside positions. The Battle of Verdun changed the negative image of forts that had prevailed after the fall of Liège and the Battle of the Frontiers. The successful defence of Verdun led to the birth of the Maginot Line in France and a new wave of 'Fortress Mania' in other nations after the war.[2]

---

*   Pétain, *Verdun*, p. 219.
** Erich von Ludendorff, 'The Verdun Counter-Attack', in Horne (ed.), *Source Records of the Great War*, Vol. 4, p. 376.

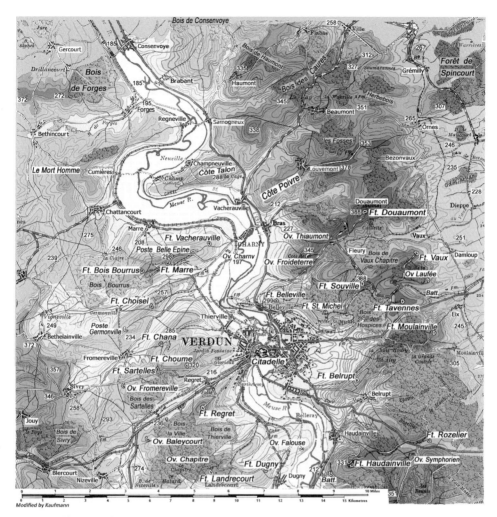

Topographic map of Verdun.

Many famous personalities took part in the Battle of Verdun, including post-war politicians and generals such as Edouard Daladier, Charles de Gaulle, André Maginot and Heinz Guderian. In addition, some of the most famous French and German 'aces' flew over Verdun. Even the Escadrille Americaine, which, for political reasons, changed its name to the Escadrille Lafayette, served at Verdun. This battle truly characterized the First World War all the way to its indecisive conclusion which allowed the war to drag on.

Table 6: Fortification and Year Completed (Years of Modernization)

1st SECTOR	TM	Obsv	75T	Obsv	155T	Cas B	OPr
Froideterre 1888 (1902–5)	2 (1905)	2 (1905)	1 (1905)			1 (1905)	
Thiaumont 1893 (1902–5)	1 (1905)	1 (1905)	[1]			1 (1905)	2 (1905)
Douaumont 1891 (1887–9, 1901–13)	2 (1902) [1]	2 (1902)	1 (1913) [2]	1 (1913)	1 (1908) [1]	1 (1907)	
Vaux 1884 (1888–95, 1904–6, 1910–12)		2 (1906)	1 (1906)	1 (1906)		2 (1906)	
Le Laufée 1888 (1904–6, 1913–14)	[1]		1 (1905)	1 (1905)			2 (1905)
Tavannes 1879 (1889–90)							
Belleville 1879							
St-Michel 1877							
Souville (PC) 1879 (1888–9, 1890–1)					1* (1891)		
2nd SECTOR							
Moulainville 1885 (1889–91, 1905–9)	2 (1909)	2 (1909)	1 (1909)	1 (1909)	1 (1908)	1 (1907?)	
Déramé 1888 (1902–6)	1 (1906)	1 (1906)	[1]			2 (1905)	1
Rozellier 1879 (1890–91, 1902–13)	3 (1904)	2 (1904)	[1]	1 (1908)	1 (1908) [1]	2 (1909)	
St-Symphorien 1889 (1900, 1902)						1 (1904)	1
Haudainville 1879 (1900–2)	2 (1902)	2 (1902)				2** (1902)	2
Belrupt (PC) 1877							
3rd SECTOR	*Citadel (PC)*						
La Falouse 1908 (1907–14)	1 (1912)	1 (1912)	1 (1912)	1 (1912)			
Dugny 1877 (1901–2, 1902–8)	2 (1908)	2 (1908)	1 (1908)	1 (1908)		1 (1905)	2 (1908)
Landrecourt 1886 (1891, 1904–6)	2 (1906)	1 (1904)	1 (1905)	1 (1904)		1 (1907)	2
POSITION REGRET							
Sartelles 1883 (1894–7, 1904–6)	2 (1905)	1 (1905)	[1]		[2]*		2 (1905)
Chana 1885 (1906–9)			1 (1909)	1 (1909)			4
Le Chaume 1877 (1884)							
Regret 1877 (1902, 1909)	2 (1909)	2 (1909)	2 (1909) [1]	2 (1909)		1 (1909)	2
POSITION CHOISEL							
Vacherauville 1915	1 (1915)	1 (1915)	1 (1912)	3 (1912)	2 (1915)		3
Bourrus 1886 (1891–4, 1904–7, 1913–14)	3 (1906)	2 (1906)	[1]		[1]*	2 (1907)	4 (1907)
Belle Epine 1886	[2]		[1]	[1]			

1st SECTOR	TM	Obsv	75T	Obsv	155T	Cas B	OPr
Marre 1878 (1888–9, 1906–8)	[2]		1 (1908)	1 (1908)		[2]**	
Charny 1888 (1902–4)	1 (1904)	1 (1904)				1 (1904)	1
Choisel 1883 (1894–7, 1905–14)	2 (1909)	2 (1909)	1 (1908)	1 (1908)		2 (1906)	3 (1912)

FORTS LINKING WITH FORTRESS TOUL

Geincourt 1880 (1890, 1900–10)							
Troyon 1880 (1890, 1900–11)	1 (1909)	2 (1909)	1 (1908)	1 (1909)		1*** (1911)	
Paroches 1885 (1890, 1900–10)							
Camp des Romains 1878 (1890, 1913–14)						[1]***	3 (1914)
Liouville 1880 (1890, 1907–8)	1 (1909)		1 (1908)	1 (1908)		1*** (1911)	
Gironville 1875 (1890, 1900–10)							
Jouy 1885 (1890, 1900–10)							

TM = Turret for Mitrilleuse
Obs = Observation Cloche for TM
75T = Turret for 75mm guns
Obsv = Observation Cloche for 75T
155T = Galopin turret, except where noted
Cas B. = Casemate de Bourges
OPr = Armoured lookout post in concrete in ramparts
PC = Command Post for sector
(1900) = year installed
[1] = number of this type of position approved but not completed
* A Buissière 155mm gun turret installed in a position outside the fort with an obsv. Cloche and a Pamart casemate at Souville. Two Galopin 155mm gun turrets planned for similar position outside Sartalles, Bois de Bourrus and Marre.
** Armed with older 95mm guns instead of 75mm guns.
*** Mougin turret.
Several of the interval positions are not included above. The forts without an armoured artillery (turrets) listed above still had artillery mounted on ramparts or in some cases casemates.
Source: Le Guy's *Verdun, Les Forts de la Victorie*, and Cédric and Julie Vaubourg's Internet site 'La fortification Séré de Rivières' at *http://www.fortifsere.fr*.
NOTE: Dates and some details vary from the above and other sources.

Appendix

Weapons of Trench Warfare

Trench warfare varied from front to front. On the Western Front, a continuous system of trench lines extended from one end to the other. On the Eastern Front, continuous trench-line systems did not exist because of the length of the front. In the Balkans and in northern Italy, mountainous terrain imposed a discontinuous trench system.

Although the rifle was the main infantry weapon at the beginning of the war, only the British made marksmanship key to training and combat as they had done throughout the nineteenth century. The French, on the other hand, preferred to 'fix bayonets', attack the enemy in mass formations and overwhelm its positions.[1] According to French military doctrine, the charge combined with elan would carry the day. In reality, however, the number of deaths by bayonet was rather small. The French infantryman carried a Lebel Mle 1886/96 firing an 8mm round. This rifle was slow to reload since its eight rounds had to be loaded one at a time and its accuracy was poor. In 1915, the 8mm Manlicher-Berthier with a box magazine of three, and eventually five and six, rounds began to replace the Lebel. The German soldier used the Mauser Mle 1898 (Gewehr 98), which was an accurate weapon and had a five-round magazine for 7.92mm bullets. The British used the Lee–Enfield III (1907) firing a .303in bullet with a magazine for ten rounds. All three rifles took a bayonet. However, the French bayonet was longest. In trench warfare, the rifle, equipped with telescopic sights, became deadly in the hands of snipers who, often camouflaged, took up positions, preferably in shell holes in no-man's-land, where they patiently waited for a target to present itself. As a result, the men in the trenches had to keep their heads down and eventually started making loopholes in trench ramparts. Most rifles had a range of up to 2,500m, but lost accuracy beyond 550m.

When the war began, the number of machine guns per battalion of the opposing armies was small, but they soon became the dominant weapons in trench warfare. These weapons were the main killing machine for defending the trenches. The French used a Model 1914 air-cooled Hotchkiss machine gun that weighed 110lb including the tripod. It fired an 8mm (.315in) round in thirty-round strips. Even though continuous firing could overheat its barrel since it was air-cooled, it was a reliable weapon. The British went to war with the belt-fed Maxim machine gun firing 7.7mm (.303in) rounds that was later replaced with an improved Vickers model, which weighed 42lb, but had a tripod that weighed 48lb. The Germans used a 1908 model (MG 08) water-cooled Maxim machine gun, almost identical to the British version except that it used a 7.92mm (.312in round). The gun weighed 55lb, and about 150lb with the tripod. Machine guns positioned in the trench lines or in individual strongpoints could cover the battlefront and mow down exposed troops crossing no–man's–land.

Early in the war, the belligerents developed a lighter machine gun that the troops could carry into battle. Except for the German model, these weapons were air–cooled and fired each army's standard rifle rounds. The British machine gun was an air–cooled Lewis, which went into service in 1915.[2] It weighed only 27lb and mounted a forty-seven-round ammunition pan. Later that year, the French developed the Chauchat Mle 1915. It used a twenty-round magazine and weighed only 21lb. This cheaply made, difficult to use and unreliable weapon that often jammed turned out to be the least satisfactory of the main types of light machine guns in use. The German trimmed down the MG 08 into the lighter MG 08/15 which weighed about 47lb (just under 40lb without the water). This weapon, however, did not appear on the battlefield until 1917.

The above-mentioned rifles and machine guns remained in service through the next world war for the most part. This was true of many weapons either in the original or modified form. Various types of grenades and the flamethrowers also increased the infantryman's arsenal during this period.

Only the Germans went to war with a ready supply of grenades.[3] None of the Entente members went to war with a stock of hand grenades and it took them until the spring of 1915 to acquire some and these were rather ineffectual. It took the French until 1916 to develop an effective grenade somewhat similar to the British Mills bomb (grenade). The percussion grenade, which exploded on contact, turned out to be the least favourite because of its tendency to explode accidentally. On the other hand, the grenade with a spring-loaded mechanism that ignited after its pin was removed gained popularity. The British and the French experimented with various types of grenade until mid-1915 when the British designed the No. 5 Mills bomb, which weighed 1.5lb. The Germans perfected the stick grenade with a bomb attached to a wooden handle. It had a fuse that burned for 3–5 seconds – the time was stamped on the handle. While the Allies' grenades were mostly based on fragmentation, the German types, including an egg-shaped model of 1917, relied on blast. The *Stielhandgranate* or stick bomb nicknamed 'potato masher', which came into service in 1915, became the most popular in the German army.

Before long, several devices were perfected to increase the range of the grenade. Among them were a small catapult that gave a range of up to 145m and a trebuchet that gave 225m. Their use was discontinued between 1916 and 1918. The rifle grenade was adopted in 1914; the British model achieved a range of 180m. The Germans also used rifle grenades until 1916. The French rifle grenade, unlike the others, used a live round instead of a blank to ignite the grenade's fuse.

The flamethrower also facilitated the elimination of enemy positions during the assault, assuming the soldiers carrying it could get close enough to the target (see Chapter 4 for more details). The Germans first employed this weapon in combat in the woods of Malancourt on 26 February 1915.[4] It was, however, rather ineffective against the French position. At the end of July, the Germans used flamethrowers against the British in the Second Battle of Ypres. Their portable model weighed about

80lb and its flame had a range of less than 20m and lasted for less than 2 minutes. By 1916, each company of the German *Guard Reserve Pioneer Regiment* had thirty-four portable flamethrowers. The regiment was assigned to general headquarters, but its units were attached to various armies. After the Second Battle of Ypres, the British developed their own flamethrower with almost twice the range of the German, but they seldom used it. The French perfected a portable flamethrower with a range of about 100m with a single burst or up to 25m with eight short bursts, but they did not use it until 1917.

The most lethal infantry weapon with a greater range than the grenade or flamethrower was the trench mortar. It served as artillery for the troops in the trenches, but, more importantly, could break up wire and other obstacles. The Germans originally developed it for use against fortresses. It became known as a 'trench mortar' because it was mostly a short-range weapon used in front-line trenches, often to drop bombs into enemy trenches. Once again, the inspiration for the development of this weapon came to the Germans from their study of the Russo-Japanese War. The Germans called it *Minenwerfer* (bomb or mine thrower). When the war began, they had about 150 of these weapons to use against French and Belgian forts. The Rheinmetall Company produced the 170mm (6.69in) *Minenwerfer* from 1913 after approval from the army. Production increased during the war. This over 1,000lb weapon fired a 110lb shell at a rate of twenty rounds a minute at ranges of up to 1,500m, but it was only accurate under 300m. The Germans had about forty of the heavier 250mm *Minenwerfer*, which they had adopted in 1910. This weapon had rifling to increase accuracy and fired a 210lb shell with an effective range of about 540m and a maximum range of 970m. It weighed about 1,700lb and it was reputed to fire up to one round every 3 minutes. Its production increased soon after the beginning of the war. A third German trench mortar was the 75.8mm (2.99in) *Minenwerfer*, which weighed about 200lb and was mounted on a two-wheeled carriage that could be manhandled into position. It fired a 10lb bomb and had an effective range of about 300m and a maximum range of about 1,100m. It went into production in the summer of 1914.

The French and the British had no mortars of this type when the war began. In late September 1914, when they had to find methods of lobbing bombs into enemy trenches, they developed the makeshift grenade launchers previously mentioned. In 1915, the French produced the Batignolles heavy mortars and even resorted to pulling out museum pieces from the previous century.[5] The Batignolles mortar, designated Mortier de 240mm (9.45in), weighed over 1,900lb and fired a 180lb projectile at ranges between 600m and 2,070m.[6] Its six-man crew could fire one round every 6 minutes. It first went into action in September 1915 during the Second Champagne Offensive. In early 1915, the French developed a 58mm (2.3in) mortar, which became the standard trench mortar and was nicknamed *Crapouillot* ('Little Toad'). The weapon weighed 165lb, its carriage 498lb. It fired shells ranging from 40lb to 77lb with a maximum range of 1,450m and required a crew of five.

At the end of 1915, the British fashioned a simple mortar from a 4in pipe that fired a bomb up to 1,300m without any accuracy. In 1916, Wilfred Stokes designed mortars of different calibres that reached the front in the same year. The most common calibres were 3in (76.2mm), 4in (101mm) and 6in (152mm). Unlike the German weapons, the Stokes mortars were smoothbore, but the parts (barrel, bipod and baseplate) were light enough for the crew to carry them into battle. The 108lb 3in mortar needed only a two-man crew and fired a 10lb round at a range of up to 750m and a maximum rate of over twenty rounds a minute.

The trench mortars were gradually improved during the war. Without these weapons, it was much more difficult to breach enemy trench lines. Placed close to the front and controlled by the attacking infantry, mortars could take out targets the artillery missed. Their ability to break up wire obstacles was a bonus for the Allies.

The weapon that sowed absolute terror in the trenches and could rip massive openings in the enemy front was poison gas. Both sides had tested irritants like tear gas without major effects. At the Second Battle of Ypres the Germans, in violation of the terms of the Hague Convention, introduced poison gas, accusing the Allies of having used it first. The only delivery methods at the time were gas cylinders and letting the poison fumes drift across the battlefield. At Ypres, French colonial troops panicked when they were hit with a green wave of chlorine gas. Since neither the French nor the German army had an adequate gas mask at this point, they had to resort to expedients. It was many months before artillery rounds were able to deliver the gas. The Germans had to be careful because the dominant western winds could blow the deadly fumes back upon their own trenches, which did happen. The British were the first to retaliate by using gas during the Battle of Loos on 25 September 1915. They launched smoke bombs with their Stokes mortars before they opened the gas cylinders because they thought that the German masks were good for only 30 minutes and they wanted to confuse the enemy. This operation was initially successful and resulted in the capture of Loos. However, shifting winds caused casualties among the British who then discovered that their gas protection equipment was ineffectual. Both sides used chlorine gas until December when, on the 19th, the Germans released phosgene against the British near Ypres. Chlorine gas had a strong odour similar to bleach and formed a yellow-greenish cloud. It attacked the lungs, but troops standing above the trenches were less affected than those seeking cover in the trenches. Phosgene was more difficult to detect because it was colourless and had the musty odour of freshly cut hay or grass. It was also more deadly than chlorine, but could take more than 24 hours (up to 48 hours in some cases) before the exposed troops came down with the incapacitating symptoms. It caused an estimated 85 per cent of all deaths from gas during the war, but did not bring about any breakthroughs on the battlefront. Mustard gas proved to be the mostly deadly, but it did not come into use until July 1917. It had a yellow-brownish colour and smelled of garlic and instead of damaging the lungs it went through the skin.

Gradually, however, artillery weapons began to dominate in trench warfare. The infantry attack had to be preceded by a coordinated artillery bombardment. The French army relied too heavily on the 75mm cannon, which had little value in trench fighting because, like most direct-fire cannons, it was ineffective against wire obstacles. The Germans, on the other hand, entered the war with an assortment of heavy artillery and batteries of howitzers, which, like the heavy German Mörsers, had the ability to drop heavy artillery rounds on the enemy trenches and break up wire obstacles. It took the French time to produce howitzers and heavy artillery in sufficient numbers. Thus, they were at a distinct disadvantage in 1914 and much of 1915, when they launched several major offensives.

Other innovative weapons and equipment that became part of the arsenal of trench warfare included the tethered observation balloon and aircraft. Both served for observation and reconnaissance of enemy positions. An observer in the balloon could provide valuable information for artillery targeting, although the observer himself was very vulnerable. The aircraft could use an aerial camera by flying over enemy lines and taking photographs that helped map out and target the enemy's positions. Aircraft also strafed and bombed enemy positions. The Germans had even produced a ground-attack aircraft by 1917 and both sides had to develop anti-aircraft guns to protect both the front-line troops and targets behind the lines.

Glossary

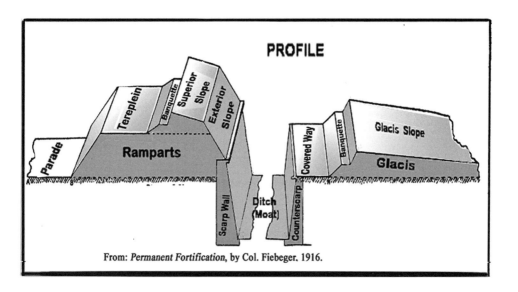

PROFILE

From: *Permanent Fortification*, by Col. Fiebeger. 1916.

Abbatis   An obstacle traditionally formed from branches and bushes, but can include uprooted trees and other materials.

Abri (Fr.)   A shelter for troops or ammunition and when built for fortifications usually made of concrete.

Aerial torpedo guns   Trench mortars that fired large finned bombs.

Anti-balloon guns   Artillery pieces, often up to 75mm in calibre given a mounting, sometimes on a truck, that allowed a high angle of fire. They were intended for shooting down observation balloons, but soon became 'anti-aircraft guns' as the aeroplane became a weapon of war.

Avant-cuirasse **(Fr.)**   In reference to turrets on forts, this comprises the armoured plates that surround a turret position to prevent artillery rounds from penetration and reaching the turret well. The term translates into forward armour, but is also known as a glacis (or circular armoured glacis) for a turret. In English, it is often referred to as a 'turret collar' and in German '*vorpanzer*'.

Bunker   A vague and generic term that can describe almost any type of fortification from a small blockhouse to concrete submarine pens. The French generally describe small bunkers as blockhouses, casemates or abri of various types.

Caponier   A projection from a fort's rampart into the moat or fossé with weapons positions for covering the side of the moat.

Caserne   A barracks or garrison area that includes the barracks and often other facilities such as the kitchens, latrines, cisterns, etc.

Chasseurs à pied **(Fr.)**   A term from 'hunters' referring to light French infantry, in this case foot soldiers as opposed to light cavalry. In the twentieth century these were elite light French infantry and some were identified as Chasscurs Alpin or elite mountain troops.

Chicane   An obstacle that prevents direct passage. Sometimes referred to as a 'zigzag' in English. It often consists of two sections with one on the left side of a passage or road, and the other on the right side but a small distance apart. Each of these two or more sections cover at last half the passage, but not the full width. Thus, one must pass around the side of one and then turn in the space between the two sections and go on to pass around the other section. They may include embrasures.

Cloche **(Fr.)**   Refers to a non–rotating dome shaped armored position generally used for observation. The term comes from the bell shape.

Coffre **(Fr.)**   A counterscarp casemate with firing positions to cover the fossé.

Concertina wire   Barbed wire formed in coils that the troops pulled out to form an obstacle. This wire, once extended to form the obstacle, was secured by stakes.

Counterscarp   The outside wall of a moat or fossé, usually a vertical masonry wall.

Elan   An enthusiastic spirit instilled in the troops used to motivate them to win.

Feldkanone (Ger.)   Field cannon. It is also abbreviated FK and followed by the last two digits which represent the year of that model, for example, FK 96 is 1896 and FK 16 is 1916.

Feld grau **(Ger.)**   Field grey colour of German uniforms which was a grey-green colour.

Fort d'arrêt   Literally a 'stop fort' or in English a 'barrier fort' that is generally isolated and blocks passage at a key point.

Fossé (Fr.)   Generally refers to a ditch or moat surrounding a fortification, but can also be a ditch.

Foxhole   Possibly a British term that appeared in the First World War referring to what formerly may have been known as a 'rifle pit' for one to three men. It is usually a rather simple entrenchment and not linked to a trench or anything else.

Glacis   A sloping area, usually descending from the counterscarp that provides clear fields of fire from the ramparts. Also refers to the armour sections surrounding a turret which in French is called the *avant-cuirasse* or forward armour.

Gorge   The rear section of a surrounding fossé where the entrance to the fort is found. It is often wider than other parts of the moat and one or both sides of it may include facilities of the fort's caserne.

Grand Quartier Général (GQG) **(Fr.)**   French General Headquarters.

Heer **(Ger.)**   German army.

Landsturm **(Ger.)**   German home guard made up of men aged 17–20 and 39–45.

Landwehr **(Ger.)**   German territorial army made up of men aged 27–38 after serving their time in the regular army and reserve.

Left and right banks of a river   These are oriented towards the mouth of the river. From a section of a river assume the direction of the river's mouth (where it ends) as 12 on the face of a clock and the source (where it begins) as 6. The side of the river that is where 3 would be on the clock is the right bank and the side where 9 would be is the left bank. This can be done using directions such as north and south since not all rivers end with their mouth in the north. In the case of the Meuse, the right bank is also the east bank and the left bank the west bank, whereas with a river like the Rhone (flows south to its mouth) the right bank is the west bank and so on. Depending on the way a river bends and changes it can have sections with east and west banks and other sections with north and south banks and so on.

Minenwerfer (**Ger.**)   'Mine thrower'. It was a short-range mortar, a trench mortar.

Mitrailleuse (**French**)   French term for a machine gun. The first of these in the mid-nineteenth century were multi-barrel weapons similar to the American Gatling gun.

Monte-charge (**Fr.**)   An elevator or lift. These were mainly intended for moving ammunition and could be large enough for men and cases in a gallery leading to a combat block or small enough for carrying rounds of ammunition in the control level of a turret block up to the guns in the turret.

Mörser (**Ger.**)   Term for an indirect-fire weapon, for example, a mortar or howitzer. Usually if over 100mm calibre it is a howitzer and a mortar if less.

Oberste Heeresleitung (**OHL**) (**Ger.**)   German Supreme Army Command.

Ouvrage (**Fr.**)   A work. Before and up to the First World War, these were generally smaller intermediate works or fortifications, located in gaps between forts. In the 1930s the large forts of the Maginot Line were also known as ouvrages.

Pillbox   A British term used to describe some of the first small bunkers of the First World War because of their shape. It soon became a generic term for almost any type of bunker with a weapon.

Pioneer   German and French combat engineers. Also, German engineer troops involved in construction and destruction of fortifications. Many armies used the same term.

Sappers   British and French military engineers who were known as Pioneers. The term comes from trench excavator, usually while under enemy fire. By the end of the eighteenth century in the French army it soon referred to troops that carried axes to clear the way through enemy obstacles.

Scarp   Inner wall of a moat or fossé. In some forts, a masonry scarp wall was replaced by or built with a gently sloping earthen scarp.

Schützgraben (**Ger.**)   Firing trench.

Stollen (**Ger.**)   Underground troop shelter with exit(s) to the surface. These could include the use of corrugated iron encased in concrete, timber and other building materials.

Traverse   A position, usually earthen, on the ramparts between gun positions. Often large traverses included a shelter for ammunition or troops.

Turret   In modern fortifications this generally refers to a rotating and sometimes retracting cupola. The French refer to fixed cupolas as cloches. The term turret can also mean a small tower in older fortifications.

Verbindungsgraben (**Ger.**)   Communications trench.

Notes

Preface

1. Archival documents might help in this case, but the only copies of the Schlieffen Plan were supposedly destroyed in the bombings of 1945. It is a curious fact that no historian or archivist typed a copy of such an important document.

Chapter 1

1. Between 1905 and 1914, German military intelligence had failed to notice that the Russian rail network had vastly improved after the end of the Russo-Japanese War as a result of financial investments made by Russia's allies.
2. The actual existence of this plan, which demanded almost 90 per cent of the German forces in the West to be concentrated for the flanking movement through Belgium, has become a subject of debate since it was only mentioned by name and its supposed details were not presented until after the war. In addition, the plan called for a much larger force than the German army could mobilize and for a number of non-existent units. Many historians blame Moltke the Younger for weakening the right wing to assure protection of his left along the frontier with France. Moltke may not have been wrong since it is doubtful that he could logistically maintain such a large force advancing through Belgium. Such a large number of divisions pushing through Belgium would have had to live off the land to some extent because supply priority went to ammunition to maintain the offensive. In addition, the rail link between Aachen into Belgium via Liège formed a bottleneck with the only other major German rail line about 100km to the south, along the Moselle and then through Luxembourg and southern Belgium.
3. The sequence of events was as follows: 28 July, Austria declares war on Serbia; 29 July, Russian mobilization begins; 31 July, Germany gives France 18 hours to declare neutrality; 1 August, Germany begins general mobilization and declares war on Russia as France mobilizes; 2 August, Germany demands passage through Belgium; 3 August, Germany declares war on France, Belgium rejects ultimatum; 4 August, Belgium invaded and Great Britain declares war on Germany; and 5 August, Austria declares war on Russia.
4. General von Falkenhayn, Minister of War, replaced Moltke the Younger in September 1914 after the Battle of the Marne. Although many other Prussian officers like Hindenburg did not like this young upstart, he had the Kaiser's support and trust. He held both positions until early 1915 when the Chancellor replaced him with General Heinrich Adolf Wild von Hohenborn as Minister of War.
5. When the Germans began their assault, they removed the Netherlands from their plan because it could serve as a window for neutral trade with Germany. This turned out to be a wise choice in the long run.
6. The rail and road capacity of northern Belgium, even without the delay imposed by the Belgians by blocking those logistical life lines, was not sufficient to bring victory since the German army was not large enough to execute the bold plan of either outflanking the French west of Verdun or taking Paris.
7. Until the end of the previous century French plans had been largely defensive. A new school of thought based on Charles Ardant du Picq (1819–70) and Louis Grandmaison (1816–1915)

called for *offensive à outrance* (offence or attack to excess) relying on *élan* rather than weapons and tactics to overcome the enemy. Joffre adopted this doctrine.

8. The taxis that carried troops to the Battle of the Marne mark the first time that motor vehicles were credited with helping win a battle even though they carried only a few thousand troops. During the Battle of Verdun, motor vehicles played a much more important role in keeping the French army supplied.

9. During this period, Darwinian Theory led the Germans and others to believe in their own cultural and ethnic superiority.

10. It took much of 1915 before Joffre realized a knockout victory was not possible and *élan* and *offensive à outrance* would not work.

11. In early August, the French 1st and 2nd Armies invaded Lorraine only to be beaten back by the German rearguards. Elements of the 1st Army advanced into Alsace and took Mulhouse, but a German counter-attack on 9 August drove them out of the city. These French units were reformed into the Army of Alsace on 10 August and sent back to the front. However, this army was defeated and dissolved late in the month when its remnants became the new 7th Army.

12. According to Norman Stone, *World War One: A Short History* (New York: Basic Books, 2007), the Belgians sabotaged only about $\frac{1}{6}$ of their rail system in early September. In addition, supply relied mainly on horse transport. Priority was given to ammunition. Tens of thousands of horses died from eating green corn (living off the land) and from the summer heat. The German army had a small number of trucks totalling about 4,000, but only about 1,300 of these were still operational after the end of the first month (pp. 43–4).

13. Many historians accused Moltke of reducing the right wing that advanced through Belgium to strengthen the left. However, this decision did not alleviate the logistics problem Schlieffen had failed to anticipate.

14. The Aisne forms a 64km (40-mile) east–west trench with steep walls that drop to a flat floor about 150m below containing the meandering, narrow and deep river. The Chemin des Dames (Ladies' Path) refers to the road and ridge on which it runs and which was held by the Germans. Limestone quarries left extensive galleries, which were used by the Germans. The first French assaults between Compiègne and Soissons, hindered by the flooded Aisne and heavy rains, failed. The British had a similar experience east of Soissons. By 14 September, the Allies were only able to cross to the north bank with the Germans situated above them. The German 2nd Army held on to the Suippe River, a tributary of the Aisne. The first stalemate began here with the Battle of the Aisne, 12–18 September. The Germans retook their lost positions overlooking the river (Douglas Wilson Johnson, *Topography and Strategy in the War* (New York: Henry Holt & Co., 1917), pp. 39–40).

15. Fort Manonviller, located in an isolated position blocking the Charmes Gap and one of the most heavily armed French forts, came under heavy bombardment, including 305mm and 420mm weapons, for over two days before surrendering on 27 August. The commander gave up since he did not appreciate the ability of the fort to continue to resist and did not believe French forces would rescue him. The Germans destroyed the fort days later when they had to retreat.

16. Hew Strachan points out in *The First World War* (New York: Penguin, 2003), p. 136, that Ludendorff through self-aggrandizement created his reputation as the conqueror of Liège by seizing the undefended citadel and then claiming Liège would fall in the first 48 hours. He was wrong, since the forts of the Liège ring took another ten days before the last one fell.

17. The battle, which actually took place at Allenstein (Polish Olsztyn) rather than Tannenberg, lasted from 26–30 August 1914. After crushing Samsonov's Russian 2nd Army, the Hindenburg/Ludendorff team turned against Rennenkampf's Russian 1st Army, handing it a defeat in the 1st Battle of the Masurian Lakes between 7 and 14 September. In each of these battles the Russians lost over 125,000 (nearly 300,000 according to some sources). Samsonov committed suicide, while Rennenkampf retained his command until he was relieved later in

1914 for another failure. Some historians combine the battles of Tannenberg and the Masurian Lakes into one.

18. The Gniła Lipa and Złota Lipa rivers are tributaries of the Dniester.

19. General Ivanov, a non-stellar veteran of the Russo–Japanese War, was very cautious and deliberate. These qualities prevented him from achieving an even greater victory in August/ September 1914. He was relieved for incompetence after the German Gorlice-Tarnów Offensive of 1915. His replacement, Alexi Brusilov, had commanded the 8th Army during Ivanov's offensive with great success.

20. Hindenburg took a couple of corps from *8th Army* and troops from large fortress garrisons and the *Landwehr* to create the *9th Army* in the latter half of September.

21. Hindenburg became Commander-in-Chief of Eastern Front on 1 November 1914 and he was promoted to Field Marshal on 27 November.

22. As in Galicia, the September and October rains turned roads and fields to mire.

23. The Russians did not have time to bring up their heavy siege artillery during the two-week siege.

24. General Mackensen commanded a corps in the *8th Army* during the Battle of Tannenberg. During Hindenburg's advance to the Vistula, his corps tried to break through the defences of Warsaw. Like Hindenburg, he was overconfident and looked down upon the Slavs as inferior people. In addition, like Hindenburg, it was only a matter of months before he received promotion to Field Marshal for his operations against Russia.

25. The Battle of Łódź raged until 6 December when the Germans finally took the city and temporarily stabilized the Eastern Front.

26. Casualty figures on the Eastern Front for both sides vary widely, more so than those of the Western Front. In fact, many sources disagree upon dates because the Russians still used the Julian calendar.

27. In December 1914 the Russian troops received their first shipments of barbed wire.

28. Many of the young men, who had recently come from universities and served in units with few experienced officers, charged the enemy in the old fashioned way, like the French. The press called it the 'Massacre of Innocents'.

29. Some historians place the beginning of 1st Champagne in February 1915 because there was no major action before that month.

30. Alsace had fewer mineral resources.

31. Potiorek was in charge of Archduke Franz Ferdinand's security at Sarajevo in 1914. After his humiliating defeat in Serbia, the government forced him into retirement on 23 December 1914.

32. The Aubers Ridge, over 6km long and 14m high at its highest point, dominated, nonetheless, its surroundings much like the Vimy Ridge, which was more impressive at about 7km long and 60m, above the Douai Plains.

33. Both sides worked on developing poison gas. In early 1915, gas cylinders were the only practical delivery method since the use of artillery shells in gas attacks had yet to be perfected. Unfortunately for the Germans, the prevailing winds were westerly, which could blow the gas right back at them if they were not careful. Neither side had yet provided their troops with gas masks, although research was underway.

34. The German divisions were part of the German *Sud Armee*, formed to help the Austrians.

35. The 'hurricane bombardment' tactic has often been credited to Colonel George Bruchmüller, artillery commander of the *86th Division*. He perfected it to take the achieving enemy by surprise and neutralize him. It consisted of several hours of intense bombardment. The British employed a similar method at Neuve Chapelle in 1915. In the first years of the war, the Allies generally devoted 30 per cent of their artillery to destroying the enemy wire. Since the hurricane bombardment failed to achieve this objective for the Allies, who lacked indirect-fire weapons in 1914, their barrages often lasted up to a week or more, alerting the enemy to the impending attack.

36. The Germans used poison gas against the retreating Russians on 31 May. They experimented with tear gas shells against the Russians at Bolimov, west of Warsaw, at the end of January 1915 (before 2nd Ypres), but the liquid did not vaporize because of the cold weather.
37. In 1941, the German army ran into the same problem when it invaded Russian (Soviet) territory.
38. The Austrians established well-built defences with communications and zigzag trenches. This was the only battle where the Austrian losses exceeded the Italian ones. Cadorna was convinced that infantry could attack uphill and defeat a well dug-in opponent (or enemy) with appropriate artillery support and elan. He firmly believed in frontal attacks and claimed that the campaign in France supported his views. Overall, his strategy proved as preposterous as Conrad's, his opponent, since neither man factored in weather, terrain and the enemy's capabilities.
39. This expansion often resulted in a large amount of defective ammunition.
40. The 77mm Feldkanone 96 fired up to twelve rounds a minute at a maximum range of 7,800m. The new gun ready in 1916, the 77mm Feldkanone 16, fired fifteen to twenty rounds a minute at ranges up to 10,700m. The French 75mm Mle 1897 had a range of up to 9,500m and could fire fifteen to eighteen rounds a minute with greater accuracy than the German 77mm FK 96.
41. The French replaced the flamboyant army uniform with a light-blue (known as horizon blue) one at the end of 1914. The government had considered the change before the war began.
42. The US military adopted a modified form of the German design late in the twentieth century.
43. In 1915, French Captain André Laffargue's pamphlet entitled 'The Attack in Trench Warfare' recommended a similar attack procedure. The French high command, however, rejected his proposal and the Allies were slow to adopt such methods. The Germans refined these methods at Riga in 1917 and then in the West in 1918.
44. Small forts or strongpoints were not an uncommon feature of the trench lines, and were common in the US Civil War.
45. The London Pact of April 1915 offered the Italians Austrian-controlled Trentino and the South Tyrol, the Istria Peninsula, sections of the Dalmatian coast and other territories and concessions.
46. The Russians built the Kovno Fortress complex between 1882 and 1903. It consisted of nine forts and eight battery positions. The fortifications were modernized with reinforced concrete. The Germans brought up a 420mm Gamma howitzer and reduced the forts one by one in 11 days, inflicting 20,000 casualties among the 90,000–man garrison. The Osowiec Fortress, built in 1882, consisted of four brick forts and several water defences that received reinforced concrete late in the century. The Germans bombarded it in September 1914 and in February– March 1915. In August four 420mm Big Berthas moved into position. On 6 August 1915, the Germans opened a new bombardment and assault, this time leading off with chlorine gas. As three regiments prepared to assault the fortress 60 dazed and bloodied Russians, still choking from the chlorine gas attack that had killed over 2,000 of their comrades, emerged from the rubble like the living dead, ready to fight back. According to legend, the 'Dead Men's Attack' so spooked the Germans that they broke off the assault. Finally, as the Germans moved to encircle the fortress, the front started breaking up and the Russians evacuated the site on 18 August.
47. In his book, *Pétain: Verdun to Vichy* (Dulles, VA: Potomac Books, 2008), Robert B. Bruce provides additional details on Pétain's rise from colonel to general early in the war in addition to this description.
48. Unlike in pre-twentieth century wars, the commanding general seldom commanded from the front since battlefields now extended over many kilometres. Sites from which a commander could observe the entire operation of all units involved and direct the action were rare. Modern communications made it possible for commanders to maintain contact with units that were out of sight. Thus, most generals only arrived on the battlefield to inspire their troops or for a first-hand view of the conditions.

49. Planning for the Artois offensive began before the German offensive in Russia. The French 10th Army took one of the key objectives, Vimy Ridge, but lost it soon afterwards.

Chapter 2

1. Some of these older fortifications were partially modernized. According to Clayton Donnell, author of *Breaking the Fortress Line 1914* (Barnsley: Pen & Sword, 2013), the old citadel of Montmédy was modified by Séré de Rivières in the early 1880s when new casemates, magazines in one of the bastions, and underground barracks were built. Traverses were added before 1890. Plans were prepared for Galopin Mle 1890 turrets for 155mm guns, but they were not carried out. In 1914, the old fortress held a garrison of 2,300 men and included 4 120mm guns on the ramparts. Longwy also had a Vauban era fortress with fifty guns on its ramparts, twelve of which were 120mm Mle 1878 cannons. Lille, like Verdun, had an old citadel and it was surrounded by a ring of six forts from the 1870s and thirteen ouvrages from the early 1890s. Maubeuge also had a ring of seven detached forts from the 1870s and seven intermediate works built between 1886 and the late 1890s (details from Rudi Rolf's *Dictionary on Modern Fortification* (Middelburg: PRAK Publishing, 2004)).

2. The Vosges formed a barrier along the border between the Rhine Valley and the Alsatian border with France. They offered only two significant invasion routes: through the Belfort Gap down the Rhine Valley and through the Saverne Gap towards Strasbourg. The Metz–Thionville fortified region blocked the main transportation route into the more open terrain of Lorraine.

3. In March 1913, the Schneider works produced a 105mm howitzer. Joffre had limited success in obtaining medium and heavy guns, and indirect-fire weapons for the army. A few long-range 105mm guns were ordered in 1913. Thus, France went to war without a field howitzer and its troops paid dearly for the lack of such a weapon. In August 1914, each French army corps had 120 75mm guns. In contrast, a German army corps had 108 77mm guns, 36 105mm howitzers and 15 150mm howitzers. The French army had 104 Mle 1904 Rimailho 155mm guns and 96 Bacquet Mle 1890 120mm guns. The Bacquet gun had a recoil system. This gun and the Bacquet 155 C Mle 1890 cannon were considered the first French heavy field artillery. They were replaced by the 105mm Mle in 1913. There were 20 batteries (about 100 guns) equipped with the long De Bange 120mm Mle 1878 gun on a Cingoli mounting. The Cingoli system consisted of a plated track over the carriage wheels which increased gun mobility. The German army had 360 100mm guns, 360 130mm guns and 128 howitzers of 210mm. The French siege artillery consisted of old 120mm guns modified to be tractor drawn and short 155mm guns on a mobile platform. These weapons lacked the modern recoil system of the French '75' so they had to be realigned every time they fired. The French also had long 155mm, short 155mm guns and 220mm howitzers. The army ordered eighteen 280mmm howitzers in late 1913 (delivery began after November 1915). The French did not develop weapons similar to the German *Minenwerfers*, the design of which was influenced by the Russo-Japanese War. (Sources: Joseph Joffre, Colonel T. Bentley Mott (trans.) and Colonel S.J. Lowe (trans.), *The Personal Memoirs of Joffre*, 2 vols (New York: Harper & Brothers Publishers, 1932), Vol. 2, p. 589 and Guy François, Pierre Touzin and Francois Vaulliller, *Les Canons de la Victoire 1914–1918*, 3 vols (Paris: Historie & Collections, 2006–10), Vol. 1).

4. Joffre expected the main German advance to go through the Ardennes instead of Liège, whereas in the 1930s, Pétain among others concluded that region was 'impassable' to a modern army.

5. Italy did not enter the war with the Triple Alliance; instead, it joined the Entente in the spring of 1915.

6. Known as the Rotunda, this fort was used by German security police in the Second World War and became a site for executing prisoners.

7. It was not possible for the Russians to shorten the axles on their railway vehicles.

8. General Herr's evaluation was published in the American *Field Artillery Journal* in 1927. He mentioned that the Germans developed a 77mm gun, which, in his estimation, was not as

good as the French gun. The German actual response to the French gun, he claimed, was curved or indirect fire provided by the 105mm howitzer Model 1898, which was modified in 1909. This was a quick-fire weapon equipped with shields to protect the crew and had the mobility of field guns. According to the German artillery regulations of 1912, 'the light howitzer accomplishes the same missions as the field gun. It has a much greater efficacy than the gun against defiladed artillery, objectives protected by overhead cover, against localities, and against troops placed in heavy woods.' According to Herr, the French 75mm gun was not effective in counter-battery fire whereas German doctrine emphasized counter-battery fire.

9. In Belgium, Brialmont had already installed a turret on a fort at Antwerp in the 1860s and mounted six more in two forts in the same ring in 1870.

10. Mougin turrets were found at forts Liouville (turret damaged and destroyed during bombardment of September 1914), Pagny, Frouard, Manonviller (both turrets were out of action when the fort surrendered in 1914), Pont Saint-Vincent, Lucey, Villey Le Sac, Longchamp, Parmont and Girmagny.

11. The French term for rolled iron is 'laminated iron'.

12. The rolling compressed the metal sheets (iron or steel). A full hard roll resulted in the greatest reduction in thickness (about 50 per cent), whereas a half-hard roll did not decrease the thickness appreciably.

13. These Mle 1890 turrets are not to be confused with a second one-gun turret designed to reduce the cost.

14. Compared to the 1890s Galopin turret mounting two 155mm guns, this 1907 model cost 60 per cent less (500,000 Francs compared to 850,000 Francs). It cost more than three times as much as a 75mm twin gun turret of 1902 (800,000 Francs to 140,000 Francs). Thus, for the price of one single 155mm gun turret the army could purchase three twin 75mm gun turrets (1 x 155mm gun or 6 x 75mm guns). The prices cited come from various sources and represent the price at the time of installation.

15. At Verdun, one each was installed at forts Douaumont, Moulainville and Rozellier and two at Fort Vacherauville. At Toul, Fort Lucey received two, the forts at Épinal three and the forts of Belfort two.

16. On his Internet site (http://www.fortiffsere.fr/), Cédric Vaubourg claims that this was due to the fact that an exercise at Toul revealed that poisonous gases were released in the turrets during firing.

17. There is some confusion regarding the type of metal used in the turrets. Plans and descriptions published in a 1909 French manual on fortifications for army engineers indicate that the roof armour was made of rolled iron, but according to other sources, a form of nickel steel was used instead. In 1890, the *Bulletin of the American Iron & Steel Association* stated that the nickel-steel plates made by the Creusot works were tested at Annapolis and performed better than other metals when a 6in projectile penetrated them creating a hole, but no cracks. Nickel steel alloy contains about 3.5 per cent to 5 per cent nickel. At the time, however, sources of nickel were limited and its price was high. By 1900 it was replacing compound armour.

18. Some sources state the roof was constructed from 320cm-thick mild nickel steel and had 125cm-thick sides.

19. He was promoted to the rank of general in 1872 and in June, he held a position on the Defence Committee that studied the problems of security on the eastern border during the war.

20. Although the Franco-Prussian War ended in 1871, the Germans did not remove their troops from the last occupied sections of France until September 1873 when all reparations had been paid in accordance with the Treaty of Frankfurt of February 1871.

21. Séré de Rivières had responsibility for the defence of other locations in addition to those along the Franco-German frontier. Some of these other fortified sites closely related to the Eastern Front including Reims and the fortified locations on the Belgian frontier.

22. This does not include coastal fortresses or those on the Alpine Frontier with Italy since they remained important.

23. Forts like those between Maubeuge and Verdun, and Fort Manonviller are *forts d'arrêt* since they are isolated and there are no nearby forts to support them.

24. War Plan I was formulated in 1880, but at that time, Séré de Rivières had been forced to retire after government officials decided that he had gone well over budget on his fortifications.

25. Of the three types tested, *béton spécial* used the least aggregate to achieve the greatest strength. Plain cement (no aggregate added) was much weaker than cement mixed with aggregate (concrete).

26. A traverse abri was built into a traverse. The traverse was usually an earthen position built between gun positions on the ramparts to protect the gunners from explosions on the adjacent positions.

27. More information, including plans of all the forts and ouvrages, can be found on Cédric and Julie Vaubourg's Internet site l'association Séré de Rivières at http://www.fortiffsere.fr/.

28. See Philippe Truttmann's *La Barrière der Fer* (Luxembourg: Gerard Klopp, 2000). for more details on these modifications.

29. Casemates were not entirely eliminated. Fort Liouville, built on the Meuse Heights in the 1870s, had two gun casemates (two guns each) and two special casemates for mortars that faced to the rear. During the same period, Fort Giromagny at Belfort was provided with several indirect-fire casemates located below the level of the ramparts. There were other forts – mostly mountain forts like Fort Écrouves at Toul and Fort Camp des Romains on the Meuse Heights – where the casemates were still effective and remained in use after the 1870s. In the early 1900s, most casemates in these main-line forts, especially those for mortars, were disarmed.

30. In the mid-1870s, Captain Henri L.P. Mougin served on the Armour Commission, created by the Defence Committee, and was able to develop and test his ideas on armoured casemates and turrets.

31. Each fort had one of the one-gun casemates. See Marco Frijns, Luc Malchair, Jean-Jacques Moulins and Jean Puelinckx, *Index de la Fortification Française 1874–1914* (Welkenraedt: Autoédition, 2008) or the Internet site http://www.fortiff.be/iff/index.

32. In the early 1900s, disappearing guns, which had no overhead protection, became vulnerable to armed aircraft. Some countries, nonetheless, maintained them until the Second World War, especially for coastal defences.

33. In the early 1890s, Galopin was a captain in army engineers specializing in military railroads until he was assigned to the commission on armour. He was promoted to commandant (major) in the early 1890s. Unlike other army engineers, he did not retire and join an armaments company, but remained in the army. He attained the rank of general during the First World War.

34. There is some confusion regarding the model year for each of these three types. This selection comes from Frijns et al., *Index de la Fortification Française 1874–1914*.

35. This method was used on some early Renaissance era forts.

36. Metal and concrete reservoirs replaced masonry cisterns, which could not withstand the effects of the vibrations set off during heavy bombardments.

37. The Germans developed a new type of fortification known as the Feste in the 1890s. The first of this type was Feste Kaiser Wilhelm II near Strasbourg. By the early 1900s, the Germans completed two rings of Festen around Metz and Thionville to block a French invasion. Each Feste consisted of well-dispersed positions that often included one or more batteries of turret artillery, casernes, power plants and infantry positions. Many were still under construction early in the war. The French inherited them after the war. They did not see combat until the Second World War and proved extremely formidable in 1944.

38. At Verdun, the artillery park was located at Jardin Fontaine near the Citadel.

39. In the Franco-Prussian War the Germans found it better to disperse their troops in the attack to reduce casualties, but the Prussian Guard infantry still had success with massed formations. As a result, between wars most generals wanted to avoid mass attack formations, but early in the war the older method prevailed until heavy casualties brought change.

40. The term 'Poilu', meaning the 'hairy one', had been associated with the French infantryman since the Napoleonic era, the same way the term 'Tommies' has referred to British troops since the eighteenth century.
41. The Germans began the war with more machine guns in their battalions than the French did. The French had tried to replace artillery with the *mitrailleuse* in the 1860s and they kept these weapons secret. However, they developed no tactical role for them. As a result, they had a negative experience with machine guns in the 1870 war.
42. During the American Civil War, trench warfare was fought according to similar principles followed in other parts of the world in the nineteenth century. It did not trigger a major change in battlefield tactics since the assaulting troops continued to advance in dense battle formations. The main weapons were still the rifle and the cannon, which, unlike the machine gun, were not as devastating to infantry.
43. In some cases, only plain wire was available, but by 1915 barbed wire was widely used, especially for low entanglements and higher fences. Concertina wire appeared later. The troops usually emplaced the wire at night and used various stealthy methods so as not to alert the enemy. Before barbed wire became readily available, the troops fashioned crude caltrops, which they placed in front of their trench lines along with broken glass and anything else that might impede the enemy including abbatis.
44. Various sources disagree about the Germans. According to a reliable source, they had eight balloon companies when the war began whereas a less reliable source claims they had only nine balloons on the Western Front in February 1914. Both may be correct, although the Germans probably did not begin using them for artillery observation until 1915.
45. Due to its unusual shape, the British also called it the 'Testicule'.
46. According to some historians, the Germans had successfully used balloons and aircraft in 1914 and 1915 for artillery observation.
47. Parachutes were attached to the balloonists' baskets. Aeroplane pilots normally did not have parachutes. Some did not consider it honourable. In 1916, during the Battle of Verdun, the French equipped Nieuport XI aircraft with Le Prieur rockets to be used against airships. When the rockets tore a hole into the balloon, the escaping hydrogen was ignited by the flame from the projectile.
48. Based on the numbers of aircraft and type of weapons listed, it appears that the article was referring to August 1916 and not 1915. During that period in 1915, there was little action around Verdun.
49. A second and third belt of trenches served as a backup in case the first belt was lost, but they were often only partially complete.
50. Later in the war most infantrymen could handle grenades and grenadiers or bombardiers were not needed for that role.
51. The French and Germans began work on counter-mines in some of their forts before there was a threat.
52. General Oskar Hutier successfully used these tactics in September 1917 at Riga on the Eastern Front. In 1916, the shock troops in the first wave brought their own heavy weapons and tackled the strongpoints.
53. Single-engine pusher aircraft had the engine on the rear of the fuselage while tractor aircraft had it on the front.
54. Saps were trenches that extended forward from the trench line and allowed soldiers to begin the construction of a new trench line closer to the enemy. They could also be used as positions from which to launch an assault. The troops often dug them while under enemy fire. The sappers also used various types of protections such as gabions (usually an earth-filled cylinder made of brush and wired or roped together) or some type of screen they pushed in front of them as they dug.
55. Few armies had an adequate supply of modern mortars and howitzers. The German army was the exception, but it had to borrow some heavy artillery from Austria.

56. In *The Rocky Road to the Great War* (Washington, DC: Potomac Books, 2013), Nicholas Murray notes that overhead protection was provided mainly for ammunition before the First World War. He also details the developments in trench warfare during the nineteenth century and up to 1912.

57. Colonel Gustav J. Fiebeger was a military expert at the turn of the century and an instructor at the US military academy from 1896 until 1922.

58. Change came slowly in the French army. Thus, while the artillerists put all their faith in the 75mm gun, they absolutely refused to support the development of howitzers and other indirect-fire weapons. Before the war, when the Parliament tried to replace the soldiers' blue and red uniform with a more serviceable one, it encountered stiff opposition.

Chapter 3

1. The *5th Army* included the *V Corps* and *V Reserve Corps*.

2. Côtes de Meuse (Meuse Heights) is a hilly and wooded plateau that begins north of Verdun and runs to Commercy. Most historians refer to the forts located between Fortress Verdun and Fortress Toul as the forts of the Côtes de Meuse, even though the fortifications at Verdun are on the same heights. Few French troops defended this area since General Sarrail diverted several divisions to the Battle of the Marne in the Argonne sector.

3. Joffre lacked confidence in Sarrail and was concerned that the 3rd Army had a front on the Meuse to the east and another to its northwest where the Germans might emerge from the Argonne. He considered the latter front of greater importance. If the 3rd Army became separated from the 4th on its left, it ran the risk of getting completely cut off along with Verdun and the 1st Army. Joffre had already begun transferring corps and divisions from the forces in the East. In September, the remaining divisions of the 2nd Army along the Meuse were assigned to the 1st and 3rd armies. The 2nd Army headquarters took command of several units sent to the north.

4. The *9th Division* was on its right, in the vicinity of St Rémy, and took part of the heights.

5. The French removed the remaining artillery, but held the fort for the rest of the war.

6. The French did not consider their reserve divisions adequate to participate in major operations, especially in offensives. This unit, which came from the Avignon region, was first sent to the Alpine Front and next, on 22 August, to Étain where it engaged the Germans. It was driven back from the Woëvre towards Verdun. Between 7 and 9 September, it took part in the battles of Revigny and Souilly. It remained in the vicinity of St Mihiel until it was disbanded in November 1914.

7. Fort Paroches did not fall to the Germans. It was used as a position from which to observe the Germans at Fort Camp des Romains and at St Mihiel for the remainder of the war.

8. The *Bavarian III Corps* attacked Fort Paroches, St Mihiel (Fort Camp des Romains) and Fort Liouville.

9. The Germans turned Fort Camp des Romains into an observatory and added a new entrance.

10. Fort Liouville served as an observation post after the battle. In 1916, the badly damaged Mougin turret was turned into a concrete observation post. The 75mm gun turret was repaired in 1916 or 1917 and the machine-gun turret removed to be installed in the Verdun citadel. Much of the data on these forts comes from Cédric and Julie Vaubourg's Internet site http://www.fortiffsere.fr/. Most written sources are in disagreement on the details, but the research on this Internet site appears to be the most accurate.

11. The heights of Crépion are located over 10km north of Verdun.

12. The German army mobilized ten pioneer regiments for siege operations in August 1914.

13. *Army Detachment Strantz* was formed by the commander of *V Corps*, Hermann Christian Wilhelm von Strantz, on 18 September to act as an autonomous part of *5th Army*. *Army Detachment Falkenhausen* and *Gaede* formed at about the same time as *Army Detachment Strantz* from units of *6th* and *7th* armies when General Headquarters moved those armies from Lorraine and Alsace to the right wing.

14. According to Crown Prince Wilhelm, three army groups were formed in November 1914, but he seems to have confused the year with 1916.

15. Italian volunteers formed the 4th Régiment de Marche/1st Regiment Foreign Legion. Giuseppe Garibaldi II, grandson of the Italian patriot, and his four brothers created this unit of over 2,000 men at the start of the war. Garibaldi II was put in command in November. The first engagement was in the Argonne the day after Christmas in 1914. One of the brothers was killed in a successful assault near the Bolante Woods. Another died in the next engagement at Four-de-Paris on 5 January. In March 1915, the Legion was dissolved and the troops, minus 300 dead, returned to Italy to fight the Austrians.

16. This was one of four major French assaults against Vauquois between the end of October 1914 and 1 March 1915.

17. According to Elizabeth Greenhalgh, author of *The French Army and the First World War* (Cambridge: Cambridge University Press, 2014), the Germans drove the XXXII Corps from these 7km of trenches and inflicted over 10,000 casualties in four days. Joffre ordered an immediate counter-attack and sent sufficient heavy artillery and two additional divisions. He blamed General Sarrail, the commander of the 3rd Army, for failing to prepare his two corps in the Argonne speedily enough. The Germans launched another attack delaying the French counter-attack, which followed eventually. In less than a month the 3rd Army lost over 33,000 men.

18. In 1915, General Dubail took command of the new Army Group East and General Pierre Roques replaced him as commander of the 1st Army. Much of the 2nd Army shifted to the northern front leaving several divisions under the command of the 1st Army, which became the army on 3rd Army's right flank. In June 1915, General Pétain replaced Édouard de Castelnau at the 2nd Army.

19. The French called it the Battle of Éparges and the Germans, the Battle of Combres. The butte is located between both villages. The fighting took place around the Éparges Crest as opposed to the Combres Crest.

20. Abel Ferry, a deputy in parliament and an infantry officer who wrote a report on losses for 1914 and 1915, claimed that the three-month operation against Éparges cost 20,000 to 25,000 French lives. Point X did not fall until 1918, by which time about 300 mines had been detonated.

21. Tranchée de Calonne was actually an almost straight road that cut through the rough wooded terrain. The Germans incorporated its ditches into their defences.

22. The Crown Prince claims probably overestimate the actual size of the French force.

23. The Germans already had anti-aircraft weapons that were designated as anti-balloon cannon since that was their original purpose.

24. This does not include almost 30,000 casualties in other theatres of war outside France.

25. These statistics come from Greenhalgh's *The French Army*. During the entire war the army had mobilized 8.4 million soldiers or about 2 million each year. Of this total 1.4 million died or were missing and 4.22 million wounded. Over 900,000 of the war's total dead or missing were on the casualty list by the end of December 1915.

26. Greenhalgh puts the French army at 93 infantry, 11 territorial and 10 cavalry divisions in January 1916 with no distinction remaining between active and reserve with the call of veterans recovered from their wounds and older classes.

27. The French had lost a number of 75mm guns from barrels destroyed by faulty ammunition. The poor quality ammunition resulted from the rush to produce more shells.

28. The Eastern Front was like a funnel with the west end being the narrowest part. The further east the Germans advanced, the wider the front became while at the same time the roads and railways became further apart. For the Russians moving west it was the opposite.

29. The Germans had already reorganized the Turkish army before the war with Liman von Sanders, and others would follow, including Falkenhayn in 1917 who joined Sanders to guide it.

30. One of the possible origins of the phrase 'To the green fields beyond' comes from an unofficial motto of the British Royal Tank Regiment formed in 1917. It was 'From mud, through blood, to the green fields beyond', describing the goal of breaking through the devastated area created from the bombardment of the trench lines and into open country.

31. Italicized sections are by authors.

32. The complete text (English version) of this document can be found in Falkenhayn's *General Headquarters 1914–1916* (rpr. Nashville, TN: Battery Press, 2000).

33. If anything, Joffre was pragmatic and not one to try anything new and not proven. He believed he must take the offensive not only to win, but also to take pressure off Russia. Verdun was threatened on both flanks and if the Germans threatened to isolate the salient, Joffre was prepared to pull back to a more defensible position. He had no plans in December 1915 for his own offensive towards the Metz–Thionville Stellung.

34. This initially took the Allies by surprise and was the only German offensive on the Western Front that year, supposedly to cover the transfer of troops to the East.

35. Some may question this method of testing a new weapon and giving the enemy time to prepare for it. This was just what the British did by committing a small number of tanks in 1916. The Germans found that phosgene gas alone would not be enough to break the Allied lines.

36. Supposedly designed by a French sergeant of the same name.

37. The Germans first used phosgene in October 1915 when it was mixed with chlorine. They created a gas cloud be releasing it from 14,000 cylinders near Reims. The French did not detect the presence of phosgene and assumed their casualties came from improper use of gas masks.

38. Reddemann was a *Landwehr* officer before the war, and in April 1916 commanded a Reserve Guard Engineer Regiment with three four-company battalions each. Each of these companies had thirty to forty portable flamethrowers and about a dozen heavy models. Fiedler, a civilian engineer, patented the first flamethrower in 1901 and received funds from the army to continue working on it. In 1905 the army engineers authorized him to conduct further tests using an army Pioneer (Engineer) company. Reddemann had been working on his own version at the time using a converted steam pumper from the city's fire brigade at a fort of Fortress Posen in 1907. The two men joined forces in 1908. (Source: *The Soldier's Burden* at http://www.kaiserscross.com/40029/76401.html.)

39. By March 1915, additional flamethrower companies formed and they included portable flamethrowers.

40. The 155mm GPF cannon, one of the most important artillery pieces used by the French and Americans, was not available before 1917. Several other modified or new types of large calibre artillery did not become available to the French until mid-1916 or after.

41. A proper siege is conducted in stages, i.e. methodically.

42. Except for the first British 'hurricane barrage' and Nivelle's creeping barrages, there is not much agreement among various historians about types of barrages and when they came into use. The Germans used a procedure called 'drum fire' which was supposed to be a constant barrage with guns firing in succession.

43. An English version of the pamphlet was published in the *Infantry Journal* (Washington, DC: The US Infantry Association, 1916) and translated as 'The Attack in Trench Warfare'.

44. It seems unlikely his pamphlet inspired the Germans.

45. Late in the war they were among the first troops to receive the new Bergmann MP18 9mm sub-machine guns.

46. His forts were completed in concrete before the French and others started adding reinforced concrete to their forts. The Belgian government apparently felt it unnecessary or too expensive to modify their forts.

47. Both these weapons identified as Mörser or mortars were howitzers.

48. Some sources estimate 127,000 troops, which was over 70,000 men more than the garrison. There were also about 18,000 civilians. In *The First World War: Germany and Austria-Hungary 1914–1918* (New York: Arnold, 1997), Herwig gives a similar number of 127,800 troops and 18,000 civilians for the second siege indicating the civilians had not left.

49. Actually about half a dozen divisions, most of the 3rd Army, remained to deal with the fortress.

50. Most of the data on the defence of the fortress and numbers comes from Tomasz Idzikowski and his book *Forty Twierdzy Przemyśl* (Przemyśl: Regionalny Osrodek Kultury, Edukacji I Nauki w Przemyślu, 2001). He specializes on the history of this fortress and has the most reliable information, so all details of both sieges are based on his work.

51. This may well have been the first attempt to supply a major encircled force by air, although nothing substantial could be delivered. It may also be the first air mail service.

52. Most of the dates and statistics come from Herwig's *The First World War*. Most sources disagree on the details.

53. In *The Eastern Front 1914–1917* (New York: Penguin, 1998), pp. 30–1, Norman Stone describes the Novogeorgievsk fortress as one in which the ring of outer forts was not at a sufficient distance to protect the citadel from new artillery. In addition the new ring of forts, although built of concrete and then changed to brick, were left unfinished. The high command expected the fortress to hold out for six months, but it did not receive quality troops and the weather did not offer an advantage such as mud that helped the Austrians at Przemyśl. He also stated that a single shell blew up one of the forts.

54. Details from Mark Romanych and Martin Rupp, *42CM 'Big Bertha' and German Siege Artillery of World War I* (Oxford: Osprey, 2014).

55. Some sources claim up to 1,600 guns captured. Allied propaganda, as shown in the *Illustrated London News* of 11 September 1915, presented the surrender at Novogeorgievsk as a kind of victory in that the 'brave' rearguard held the fortress as its garrison withdrew. The garrison did not escape and despite the destruction of the forts by the heavy siege guns, much of the garrison appears to have resisted tenaciously. The article also mentions the 'Polish Quadrilateral' consisting of the fortresses of Novogeorgievsk, Warsaw, Kovno and Brest-Litovsk. Other sources also refer to this 'Quadrilateral', but it is a bit of an exaggeration since Kovno and Brest-Litovsk are too far away to be considered part of such a position that had little in between. Other sources list the Quadrilateral as including Ivangorod instead of Kovno, but the distances are still great.

56. A Polish source claims captured batteries of Russian 203mm Mle 1877 were used, but that seems doubtful.

57. See Romanych and Rupp, *42CM 'Big Bertha'*. The siege artillery moved south to join Mackensen's *11th Army* in the attack on Przemyśl in May 1915.

58. The division was formed with two brigades of two regiments each in Germany during February 1915 and moved to the Russian front along with the *1st*, *10th* and *15th Landwehr* divisions (the latter from the Western Front).

59. This reduction in troops was not related to the strength or value of the fortresses. Even on the Eastern Front Hindenburg in 1914 had already drawn off troops, mostly not first-line troops, from fortress duty to supplement his army at the front. Falkenhayn in 1915 had to shift troops between fronts, so taking them from garrisons of fortresses not directly threatened by the enemy made sense.

60. According to a popular author, Sarrail was ineffective in carrying out operations in the Argonne-Verdun regions since he came from Carcassonne in southwest France and apparently was not acquainted with the rest of the country. However, his VIII Corps was at Bourges and his VI at Chalons so he was not utterly unfamiliar with eastern France. Before the war, senior officers had prepared for years for a war in eastern France and not along the border with Spain.

61. According to Holger Herwig, author of *The Marne: 1914* (New York: Random House, 2009), Sarrail boasted of being the 'Saviour of Verdun' because of his actions in September 1914.

62. In this case, the French considered this as 'stolen' territory from 1871, not German soil.
63. Louis Auguste Adrian, a retired officer, re-joined the army in 1915. After realizing that over half the wounds were to the head, he designed the steel helmet named after him. His was lighter and cheaper to produce than the British and German helmets, but less effective against shrapnel or bullets. In 1915, he was involved in developing camouflage techniques and served in the quartermaster section of the army where he designed other items for the troops.
64. During the war the French army had active and reserve infantry divisions numbered 1–78 available in August 1914. Infantry divisions 120–34, 151–4 and 156–8 formed mostly in 1915 (two began as ad hoc formations in September 1914 and the 134th was created in the summer of 1916). Infantry divisions 161–8 formed in 1916, followed by 169 and 170 in 1917. The territorial infantry divisions numbered 81–92, 96–8 and 100–5. The colonial infantry divisions included numbers 1–3 when the war began, 10, 15–17 formed in 1915 and 11 formed in 1917. One Moroccan division formed in 1914 and another in 1918. Cavalry divisions 1–10 were available in August 1914. (Source: Michael Cox and Graham Watson, *Pour la France: A Guide to the Formations and Units of the Land Forces of France 1914–18* (Solihull: Helion & Company, 2012).)
65. Between November 1916 and December 1917 most of the infantry and cavalry divisions had been converted.
66. The German reserve divisions numbered 43–54 and included two reserve infantry brigades and one field artillery regiment plus cavalry and pioneers. The next group or reserve divisions numbered 75–82 and the *8th Bavarian* had a single infantry brigade with three regiments and an artillery brigade of two regiments.
67. In 1917, Hindenburg reduced the infantry battalions from 919 to 650 men. (Source: Hermann Cron, *Imperial German Army 1914–18* (repr. Solihull: Helion & Co., 2006).)
68. On 18 March 1916, the Russian 2nd Army attacked the Germans at Lake Naroch losing a third of its men in an attempt to put pressure on the Germans during the Verdun offensive.
69. The situation for the British army changed at the end of December 1915 with the introduction of compulsory service.
70. The Nieuport X was modified and the observer/gunner in the front seat was eliminated making it a single-seater, but larger than the Nieuport XI and less manoeuvrable.
71. The standard unit was the *Feldflieger Abteilung* (Flying Field Company or Detachment) of four aircraft for reconnaissance and artillery spotting (usually two-seater aircraft). The strategic bombing groups of the army high command were the *Kampfgeschwader der Obersten der Heeresleitung* (*Kagohl*) that were organized into five to seven *Kampf Staffels* (*Kastas*) or combat squadrons with six aircraft each. Selected from these groups, the best pilots joined the *Kampfeinsitzer Kommand* (KEK) or single-seater fighter command, which consisted of two to four Fokker or Pfalz Eindeckers. These were mono-wing aircraft. The Pfalz, a copy of an inferior model, was used to supplement the fewer Fokker models available.

Chapter 4

1. The Americans and others protested about the German violation of the Hague Convention. The procedures for sinking unarmed ships required a submarine to surface and then send a warning. Striking without warning was viewed as barbaric, and the Germans wanted to keep America neutral.
2. This Christmas memorandum is much like the Schlieffen Plan in that no copies exist. Supposedly, an Allied bombing in 1945 destroyed the archive that held both of these documents. Oddly, it seems that no historian had researched and recorded the information on them, although it seems unlikely the Weimar government would have classified them as secret after the war. Falkenhayn quoted the contents in his book and this takes up more than a page in length. There may never have been a memorandum and he may have made the claim to clear his reputation.

3. Falkenhayn further explained in his book that his allies could not help since the Turks had too few troops, the Bulgarians would not send troops out of the Balkans and the Austro-Hungarian troops did not have sufficient training for operations on the Western Front.

4. The situation made it impossible to rearm Fort Vaux and Ouvrage Thiaumont with their 75mm casemate guns.

5. According to Alistair Horne, author of *The Price of Glory: Verdun 1916* (New York: Penguin, 1978), Driant set up a line of outposts on the outskirts of Caures Woods. Behind those outposts, he positioned independent strongpoints, each with a platoon. Behind that, in the woods, was a support line and to its rear, the 'R Line' consisting of structures he called concrete redoubts, one of which served as his command post.

6. Horne noted (in the *Price of Glory*, p. 62) that the Germans had broken up a spy ring before the offensive, which hindered French Intelligence (Deuxième Bureau de l'État-major general or 2nd Bureau of the General Staff, the British counterpart of which was MI5 – Military Intelligence, Section 5).

7. According to Horne (in the *Price of Glory*, p. 63), on 17 January, the weather was so bad it was unsuited for aerial photography. However, until 17 February, no officer from the reconnaissance squadrons was attached to General Herr's headquarters at Verdun to analyse the few available photos. The French aircraft that penetrated the German air screen missed the huge artillery concentrations northeast of Verdun and only spotted a few dozen gun emplacements.

8. On 15 February, three deserters of *172nd Infantry Regiment* warned of the coming offensive. Their unit was part of the *39th Division* formed in Alsace. In fact, several Alsatian deserters warned of the impending German offensive.

9. During the campaign, German Pioneers continued to build *stollen* including some in October 1916 near the front in advance of Fort Vaux and other locations. These structures were used as shelters for assaulting infantry, pioneers and ammunition. Often built into the slopes of a ravine, they had two entrances and several metres of earthen cover.

10. *Oberste Heeresleitung* (OHL), or Supreme Army Command, included the Supreme Warlord (the Kaiser), his Great Headquarters located at Spa for most of the war and the General Staff of the Field Army. The General Staff was the main element of OHL. The Chief of the General Staff of the Field Army (Moltke, Falkenhayn and eventually Hindenburg) headed the General Staff. Ludendorff, Hindenburg's assistant on the General Staff, took the title of First Quartermaster General.

11. This is taken from Paul Jankowski, *Verdun: The Longest Battle of the Great War* (New York: Oxford University Press, 2013), p. 36. The comments of the Kaiser, Tappen, Schulenburg and Groener come from documents in the Bundesarchiv Militärarchiv dating from the 1930s. Post-war accounts are often biased or intended to justify someone's actions, but they must be considered and evaluated.

12. The Crown Prince wrote that Knobelsdorf had met with Falkenhayn in Berlin, apparently before the meeting in France that he did not attend. Knobelsdorf submitted a plan for flanking operations by *Army Detachment Strantz* from St Mihiel and Mudra's corps in the Ardennes, but Falkenhayn rejected it, forbidding any strategic envelopment to be part of the *5th Army* plan. It would appear he did not want to force the French to withdraw and avoid a major battle.

13. According to the Crown Prince, he and his chief-of-staff argued with Falkenhayn to no avail. Falkenhayn told them he needed the reserves to deal with an expected British relief offensive. They felt that was impossible at the time because the British were in the process of reorganizing their army. Although the Crown Prince claimed these discussions took place before Christmas, other sources are adamant that they did not occur until after Christmas.

14. It is not clear to which corps these divisions belonged.

15. Tunnelling and detonating mines in the Argonne, like in the Éparges sector, was almost a continuous affair.

16. The 72nd Division had been assigned to the Verdun area as a fortress division since the war, just as the 57th Division at Belfort, the 71st Division at Épinal and the 73rd Division at Toul.

All four were reserve divisions. Driant's two chasseur battalions (reserve units) were attached to the 143rd Brigade of the 72nd Division.

17. Some sources list a 106th Territorial Division consisting of the 212th and 213th Territorial brigades commanded by General Pierron. One of these sources is Nafzinger, who took it from German documents. Michael Cox and Graham Watson, in *Pour la France: A Guide to the Formations and Units of the Land Forces of France 1914–18* (Solihull: Helion & Company, 2012), found no such unit in the official French history. The brigades may have been in the vicinity, but employed as a labour force, which was not uncommon with territorial units. There is no indication of any of the brigade's regiments taking part in a combat role besides caretaker detachments placed in some forts like Douaumont.

18. The II Corps, commanded by General Denis Duchêne, occupied the south part of the salient. His divisions moved into combat on 22 February between Eix and Éparges. On 21 February, its 4th Division was in reserve. The VII Corps, commanded by General Georges de Bazelaire, included the 37th Division, which was resting at Souilly when the offensive began. Earlier, the 14th Division joined the XXX Corps and took up positions on the northeast corner of the salient. The VII Corps withdrew on 26 March 1916 and returned on 10 April remaining on the line until 5 July. The XXX Corps held the northern section of the Fortified Region of Verdun (RFV) on 21 January 1916 under the command of General Adrien Chrétien.

19. The 132nd Division, originally formed as the Division de Marche de Verdun, received its number in July 1915. Division de Marche was a provisional division initially created with units available. It was not a previously established division.

20. See below for Émile Driant's role in bringing about this meeting.

21. General Fernand de Langle de Cary had only assumed command of the army group on 12 December 1915 and replaced General Noël Édouard de Castelnau who had moved up the GHQ.

22. Only the casemate guns and those remaining on the ramparts of the older forts could be considered to be removable. Most were older weapons, except for the 75mm guns. The turret guns remained because they did not have mobile mounts.

23. Holger Herwig describes this action in *The Marne: 1914* (New York: Random House, 2009). However, in *My War Experiences*, the Crown Prince makes no mention of implying instead that his forces had conducted an orderly withdrawal with few casualties.

24. Army Group Centre, formed in late June 1915, took over the Verdun sector late in the year.

25. Castelnau was Joffre's chief-of-staff and helped develop Plan XVII. In June 1915, he received command of the newly formed Army Group Centre and in December 1915, he was replaced by General de Langle as he returned to serve as Joffre's chief-of-staff. When Joffre was replaced by Nivelle, Castelnau retired, but he was recalled in 1918 to command Army Group East.

26. Gallieni had been in charge of the defences of Paris in August 1914 and was one of the men credited with the victory on the Marne in September. He was appointed Minister of War in October 1915. In a conflict with Joffre over control, Gallieni resigned in March 1916 and died a few months later.

27. Knobelsdorf was relieved in August 1916. The Crown Prince did have some good ideas, but Falkenhayn ignored him. Since the Crown Prince was not in favour with his father, Falkenhayn could do that with impunity.

28. In November 1914, the prince told the press, 'Undoubtedly this is the most stupid, senseless and unnecessary war of modern times' and it was not Germany's fault.

29. Falkenhayn was sent to the Middle East after that, but with a Turkish army of inferior quality he was at a disadvantage and he failed to stop the British from taking Jerusalem in 1918.

30. German time was an hour ahead of French time. The French recorded the time as 7.15 am French time.

31. A short intense bombardment was called a hurricane bombardment. Although many historians have used the term to describe the bombardment of Verdun, it seems inappropriate in this context. Hurricane bombardment is defined as a bombardment of short duration. Falkenhayn's bombardment, intended to take the French by surprise, lasted about 8 hours.

32. In February of the previous year, a Big Bertha had bombarded forts Douaumont and Vaux inflicting some damaged. The French claimed their 210mm weapons destroyed or damaged the 420mm Mörser mount.

33. Each of the three attacking German corps had the equivalent of two (the *III Corps* had three) balloon squadrons with about six 'kites' each. They also included an aviation detachment for directing artillery fire. Photo reconnaissance units also helped the Germans map out the French positions before the attack began.

34. The details of these air operations come from the newspaper *Le petit parisien*, dated 24 February 1916. The details may not be accurate, but they are based on eyewitness reports. In *Price of Glory*, Alistair Horne indicates that this happened on 20 February instead of 21 February. Some newspapers do not give a date. It was claimed that the Zeppelin was loaded with bombs and was hit by incendiary shells. The *British Journal of Nursing* of 18 March 1916 included the account of a nurse stationed at Revigny who recalled a morning attack by about fifteen Taubes that were driven off by French guns. Apparently, they returned at 3.00 pm. At about 8.30 the surgeons reported that 'star shells' were seen in the sky causing them all to go outside to see a Zeppelin burst into flames. The exact date was not given. Some sources indicate that a second Zeppelin was hit and that there may have been three of the four assigned to *5th Army* on the same mission.

35. Most of these small units, often called *Sturmtruppen* (storm troops), did not come from *Sturm Battalion Rohr*, which was not given that title until April and was only known as *Assault (or Sturm) Detachment*. However, the most common order of battle used today shows it listed as a battalion. The same order of battle shows it attached to the *6th Division* of *III Corps*. Apparently, Rohr's men only formed the storm units for the *III Corps*. The detachment had trained other troops from December 1915 and they probably formed the storm units of the other corps. According to Bruce Gudmundsson in *Stormtroop Tactics*, in many cases the infantry battalion commanders did not know how to employ these specialized troops effectively.

36. Rohr's *Sturm* battalion was attached to the *6th Division* of *III Corps*. It was the only actual *Sturm* battalion at the time, but other divisions employed troops in a similar role for the initial wave of the offensive. It performed so well that it set up a training programme for other units that year. Major Herman Reddemann's *3rd Guard Pioneer Battalion* had six companies of flamethrowers (twenty large and eighteen portable units). Each of the flamethrower platoons had four to eight of these weapons and they were assigned to individual detachments of troops that served as storm troopers. The battalion's Guard Pioneer companies were attached to each of the corps.

37. Only about 120 of Driant's 1,300 men survived the first 2 days of battle and then managed to break out towards Beaumont. A relief attack by a French infantry regiment failed on the second day.

38. Comments have been made about the undergrowth being swept away, but there may not have been much of it during the winter months and the snow may have covered what did exist. Photos show German troops, late in February, camped in some of these woods that were targets of the first two days of the offensive and it does not appear that they were all turned into 'matchsticks' by the bombardment.

39. In his 18 December 1915 letter to the Minister of War, Joffre did not give the same explanation for his actions, but tried to placate him by saying that in October he had instructed his army commanders to prepare the two lines of defence on the entire front and to include passive obstacles, i.e. barbed wire, abattis, etc. This was the letter in which he complained about his subordinates – i.e. Lieutenant Colonel Driant – not going through proper military channels to make complaints to the government.

40. The deployment of the VII Corps seems to have created some confusion. It was identified with its two divisions, the 37th and 48th in the Bar-le-Duc resting area in February 1916. At the same time, it was listed as including the 29th and 67th divisions stationed between Avocourt and the Meuse. The 29th Division was apparently detached from the XV Corps

when it left the Argonne in late 1915. The 67th Division detached from the XV Corps in 1915 after serving on the southeastern part of the salient and moved to the north side of the salient on the left bank in February 1916. On 12 February, the VII Corps inherited the defence of the area between the Meuse and Avocourt and took over these two divisions, while its other two divisions were still near Bar-le-Duc. The 37th and 48th divisions were assigned to XX Corps on the right bank on 25 February 1916. The XXX Corps was withdrawn from the right bank on that day. The 15th Division was part of VIII Corps, which held a front on the St Mihiel Salient from 1915–16.

41. The 44th Territorial Regiment is only listed on the Nafzinger order of battle and other sources. It appears as a single battalion.

42. According to Alistair Horne (*Price of Glory*, p. 103), he had been ordered by Chrétien to move his headquarters forward to Vacherauville on 21 February. He did, but found the facilities inadequate and was allowed to return to Bras. Arriving there the next day, he found his old headquarters already put to another use. This did not help his command ability, but neither did the loss of almost all telephone communications on 21 February which forced even Chrétien to rely on runners.

43. The 37th Division formed in Algeria and consisted of native and colonial regiments formed in that region. It was a first-class division.

44. See Alistair Horne, *Price of Glory*, for more information. Not all sources agree with some of his details, but his work is the best in English and even his critics seem to repeat much of his information.

45. In *Pyrrhic Victory: French Strategy and Operations in the Great War* (Cambridge, MA: Belknap Press, 2005), p. 271, Robert Doughty mentions that Briand reached Joffre's headquarters on the night of 24 February, and fearing the fall of the government, made it clear to the general that Verdun must be held. While he was waiting to see Joffre, the marshal's staff lectured the prime minister on the advantages of letting Verdun fall and taking up a more defensible position along the river. As Joffre was walking through the door, he heard Briand's angry outburst. He hastily reassured Briand that he would not give up the east bank. According to Doughty, Joffre never told Poincaré that he considered abandoning Verdun.

46. Although it has been questioned whether Joffre was initially ready to give up the east bank, it makes little difference. He gave no indication that he would have approved such a move, nor does he mention the demands made on him by the government to hold Verdun. In *Pyrrhic Victory*, p. 270, Doughty explains that de Langle told Herr to hold at all costs on 22 February and that on 24 February de Langle informed Joffre he had ordered the troops in the Woëvre to withdraw since he was afraid that the two territorial brigades would panic. Joffre approved the move. Doughty also points out that after giving Pétain command Joffre warned him that if he had to withdraw to the west bank, he must prevent the enemy from crossing the Meuse. Thus, Doughty concludes, Joffre never ordered Castelnau or Pétain to hold the right bank at all costs.

47. These three generals were the first 'Limoges' at Verdun, but that was preferable to court martial. Castelnau wanted to court martial Bonneval. Herr remained under Pétain for a while before he followed the other three generals into exile.

48. Considering the importance of the first week of the battle, these comments in a few paragraphs are all the general had to say in his book *General Headquarters 1914–1916* (repr. Nashville, TN: Battery Press, 2000) and in an article, Count Charles de Souza, 'The First Assault on Verdun', in Charles F. Horne (ed.), *Source Records of the Great War*, 7 vols (New York: National Alumni, 1923), Vol. 4.

Chapter 5

1. The *11th Bavarian Division* was also attached to the corps and took up positions next to the *2nd Landwehr Division* on the right wing. Both the *11th Bavarian* and *22nd Reserve divisions* were part of the *X Reserve Corps* according to the Crown Prince, although each operated on a different flank of the *VI Reserve Corps*.

2. Corbeaux Wood was located on the southern side of the Côte de l'Oie. Adjacent to it on the southern slope was Cumières Wood, seldom marked on most maps.

3. Although most sources identify Mort Homme as a hill, it is actually a ridge or butte consisting of Hill 265 and Hill 295. In French, it is referred to as a 'butte' which can be translated in several ways, but in English it also translates as butte.

4. The 25th Division entered the battle on 7 March 1916.

5. According to Paul Jankowski, author of *Verdun: The Longest Battle of the Great War* (New York: Oxford University Press, 2013), reports showed that morale was low in the 29th Division and troops began deserting or surrendering in droves. Alistair Horne, in *The Price of Glory: Verdun 1916* (New York: Penguin, 1978), states that an entire brigade of the division became surrounded and surrendered. It was unlikely the brigade and all the regimental commanders were captured with most of the troops because the remaining two regiments, also having taken losses, rallied to fill the breach as Pétain claimed. Michael Cox and Graham Watson, authors of *Pour la France: A Guide to the Formations and Units of the Land Forces of France 1914–18* (Solihull: Helion & Company, 2012), note that days before the German attack, two regiments from the shattered 72nd Division replaced two of the division's regiments.

6. Max von Gallwitz was brought from the Balkan front to take command on 29 March. He was an artillery officer, who had commanded an army on the Russian front and captured a couple of major fortifications in 1915. Later, he had led the *11th Army* in the Serbian Campaign.

7. Days after the *11th Bavarian Division* routed the 29th Division, the *11th Reserve Division* took enemy positions near Malancourt and cleared the entire village by 31 March.

8. This group was created days before the *Western Attack Group*.

9. The *19th Reserve Division* had been part of the original *X Reserve Corps* in 1915 until the corps was broken up. The division transferred to Verdun in mid–March 1916 and rejoined the corps. The *58th Division*, which formed in March 1915, joined it at the same time to reform the *X Reserve Corps*. That division fought on the Western Front before it was sent to Russia during the summer and returned in October. The *113th Division*, also created in March 1915 near Sedan, served in the Woëvre area during the year and rested near Conflans in February 1916. In late February, the division was sent to the Verdun area.

10. The *113th Division* had already lost about 2,000 men in attacks near Douaumont on 8 and 9 March and by April it was badly in need of rest and replacements. It was sent to the quiet sector of the *7th Army*. The *58th Division* was not in much better condition than the *113th Division* when it moved to Rethel to rest until it was involved in the Battle of the Somme.

11. Strangely, in his memoirs, with Margaret MacVeagh (trans.), *Verdun* (Toronto: Dial Press, 1930), Pétain makes no mention of this French offensive in early April. This was what the Crown Prince identified it as, but it may have comprised only counter-attacks. Pétain does not correct the Crown Prince's account, although he often refers to it in his own writing. It is not really clear what happened on the east bank for much of April other than it involved heavy casualties for both sides.

12. Von Lochnow had commanded the Brandenburg *III Corps* since the war began. This unit first served on the Western Front under *1st Army* and then in October 1915 von Lochnow took it east to join the Serbian Campaign. He then brought the corps back to France as part of *5th Army*. This corps captured Fort Douaumont and took over 6,000 prisoners during February.

13. The *192nd Brigade*, formed in June 1915, reorganized as the *192nd Division* in June 1916. As a brigade it consisted of the *192nd*, *193rd* and *25th Bavarian regiments* in 1915 and 1916.

14. The *11th* and *12th Reserve divisions* were relieved and sent to rest near Thionville. The *11th Reserve Division* was relieved by the *54th Division*.

15. Supposedly, the heavy bombardments reduced Hill 310 by 7m to 12m (depending on the source) in height.

16. The Germans actually targeted some bridges with their heavy long-range guns such as the 380mm, but their aim was not accurate enough to knock out the bridges.

17. Joffre claimed this was his only fresh corps.
18. According to Joffre's memoirs, Joseph Joffre, Colonel T. Bentley Mott (trans.) and Colonel S.J. Lowe (trans.), *The Personal Memoirs of Joffre*, 2 vols (New York: Harper & Brothers Publishers, 1932), when he sent Castelnau to Souilly in April to ask Pétain when he wanted to assume command, he learned of the general's displeasure at losing command of 2nd Army. On 3 May, Joffre met with him at Bar-le-Duc and they both went to visit the command posts of 2nd Army. During this trip, Pétain appeared to be very pessimistic so Joffre told him to write about his views and plans. On 7 May, Pétain submitted a long letter stating that the 'German system of making their attacks with a small amount of infantry and a large number of guns, we were slowly but surely becoming used up, and … if the Allies did not soon intervene we would finish by being beaten'. He felt at Verdun in 1916 that France had fulfilled its duty to its allies and that they should make no further demands. He was not advocating France's withdrawal from the war, but wanted the British to take on a greater share of the burden. If Joffre correctly recorded the content of this letter, it might give a clue into Pétain's thinking in 1940.
19. At this point, the 2nd Army no longer came directly under Joffre in the chain of command, but went through Pétain, so this did not actually remove the general from the operations at Verdun. It is curious that if Joffre wanted Pétain removed from operations at Verdun, he placed 2nd Army back under Army Group Centre's command.
20. Léonce Lebrun replaced Nivelle at III Corps, when the latter became commander of the 2nd Army. Lebrun remained in command of the III Corps until the end of the war.
21. Pétain noted that the Germans had to mobilize their class of 1916 before the French did.
22. According to Pétain, the Germans used up *III* and *XVIII corps* so quickly in the spring that both corps had to be temporarily withdrawn and rebuilt.
23. See Christina Holstein's *Fort Douaumont, Verdun* (Barnsley: Pen & Sword, 2002) for additional details. In *Verdun*, Pétain claimed that the division that served as a reserve included a single brigade of infantry.
24. In July 1916, Joffre reassigned Colonel Estienne to General Headquarters to work on organizing armoured units. According to Alistair Horne (*Price of Glory*), the commander of Fort Moulainville warned him that the 370mm weapons would be inadequate against Fort Douaumont since the German 420mm howitzers had done little damage to his own fort.
25. With many bodies torn asunder and some buried in the rubble, there was no way to get an accurate count, but the number was higher than estimates. Many believe there were more than the official 679 identified bodies. Holstein mentioned there was a problem with disposal of the bodies so some were interned in shelters on the Rue de Rampart, but many lie within the fort.
26. The Germans used the 75mm gun turret for sending light signals through the gun tubes.
27. Those regiments thrown together to hold the right wing came from several divisions: 44th Regiment of 14th Division, 208th Regiment of 51st Division, 95th Regiment of 16th Division, 414th Regiment of 153rd Division.
28. Adjutant is a rank sometimes compared to that of warrant officer or senior NCO, but it is not an exact match to American or English ranks. An American warrant officer is considered an officer, but this French rank is like an American master sergeant. A warrant officer in the British army is the highest NCO ranking, so the British consider it in a similar way. Thus, American writers refer to it as a sergeant and the British as a warrant officer.
29. Despite all the accounts written of the fall of the fort, none include the name Kunze.
30. According to Alistair Horne (*Price of Glory*), Brandis manned one of the machine-gun turrets firing into Douaumont during the fighting for that village the next day.
31. The casualty ratio varied during the battle, but probably never amounted to more than three Frenchmen for every two Germans lost which was not enough to cripple the French army without having the same effect on the German army.
32. Some sources report six of eight balloons.

33. *Liebgrenadier* has no English equivalent. Some authors equate it to a life guard or body guard grenadier unit, but this is not correct.
34. The 10th Brigade on the right with 75th and 274th Infantry regiments advanced against the rear and eastern flank of the fort where a German machine-gun position, stood on an incomplete observation position for an unfinished exterior 75mm turret site, held them up. The 9th Brigade with 36th and 129th Infantry regiments faced the left flank of the fort.
35. The ammunition for the 155mm gun was removed after the accident of 8 May. It is not clear why the Germans only aimed signal lights through the 75mm gun barrels instead of firing the guns. It is possible that they had no other means of communication since the bombardment had destroyed the small radio stations on the superstructure and it was more important for them to maintain contact than to fire the guns.
36. According to Christina Holstein (personal communication with the authors), the Germans used the fort's 75mm gun turret in early March and possibly in June and the turret's magazine had a good supply of ammunition. There was a gun crew available at all times.
37. While Mangin began his offensive against Fort Douaumont on the east bank, the Germans renewed their efforts to push the French out of the Mort Homme–Cumières line on the west bank. Thus, the Crown Prince and Nivelle both had to divide their attention between two major actions on opposite banks of the Meuse.
38. Details of the fighting and damage to the fort come from British historian Christina Holstein's *Fort Douaumont*, probably the best English title containing details on this fort during the campaign. She describes the German efforts to clean up the fort after this battle when the German commander received orders to fortify it. The fort was no longer to be merely a shelter for German troops. The Germans removed the debris, decomposing bodies and even the French 155mm rounds to prevent another accident like the one of 8 May. The German pioneers improved the other defences, made repairs to damaged facilities and turrets, and created new positions. They even installed an engine for electric power, but that took months.
39. Hardaumont Ouvrage was a small position consisting of an abri that could accommodate a company sized unit. It also had two machine guns.
40. Most of the details about the German operations against the fort and the damage it incurred come from Christina Holstein's *Fort Vaux* (Barnsley: Pen & Sword, 2011), which like her book *Fort Douaumont* is one of the best descriptions in the English language.
41. Holstein wrote that the Germans also inspected the turret after the fort surrendered and found they could put it in working order.
42. The 44th Territorial Regiment had troops garrisoning Fort Douaumont when it fell and the town of Brabant.
43. Christina Holstein (*Fort Vaux*) mentions that Raynal had these replaced with loop-holed barricades of sandbags that completely blocked the tunnel unlike the chicane-type example seen in the forts today.
44. Alistair Horne, in *Price of Glory*, notes that the 420mm barrels wore out causing both types of 420mm weapons to lose accuracy and efficacy. It is possible, but historian Marc Romanych informed the authors that these weapons had spare barrels so this should not have been a problem.
45. In *42CM 'Big Bertha' and German Siege Artillery of World War I* (Oxford: Osprey, 2014), Marc Romanych and Martin Rupp explain that the 420mm howitzers suffered from premature detonations in the barrels due to faulty ammunition. On 22 February, such an accident destroyed both weapons of KMK Battery 7 at Verdun. Other such accidents eliminated one of these weapons in KMK Battery 5 and Battery 6 and one Gamma howitzer in KMK Battery 2, Battery 8 and Battery 9. During the spring of 1916, the batteries had to be reorganized. In July, some batteries went to other fronts and by September, only six batteries totalling seven guns remained at Verdun, but they included more 305mm Beta Mortars, which had been used against intermediate fortifications. KMK refers to *Kurze Marinekanone*, or

short-barrelled naval cannons, since Krupp built these weapons for the coastal artillery. It is likely that Alistair Horne (*Price of Glory*) received faulty information regarding the causes that took these guns out of action. Popular belief attributed the accidents to counter-battery fire before data became readily available in the 1960s.

46. The German attack front had the *I Bavarian Corps* on the right, *X Reserve Corps* in the middle and *XV Corps* on the left.

47. The French converted this coffre into an entrance because of damage to the gorge entrances.

48. The fort also used signal lights to communicate with Fort Souville, but did not receive replies to its messages.

49. See Christina Holstein (*Fort Vaux*) for details on Raynal's plans.

50. The *Alpine Corps* included a division of the same name (*Alpinekorps*).

51. The Italians had a similar number of casualties.

52. Admiral Scheer replaced Admiral Hugo von Pohl in command of the fleet in January 1916. Pohl, suffering from cancer, died the next month.

53. The battery mounted four 90mm guns in 1914 and was totally destroyed by the time the French recaptured it in October 1916.

54. In August 1916, several rounds hit the turret, including one of 305mm. Although it penetrated the turret's glacis armour, it caused no damage. Not long after this, a heavy round damaged the turret preventing its full rotation. It could not be repaired until after the battle, in 1917.

55. In 1917, the turret was repaired and the steam engine that operated it was replaced with an electric engine. An observation cloche and a Pamart cloche for machine guns were added, but the threat from the Germans had receded. In addition, an underground gallery was added to link it to the fort in 1917.

56. An estimated 30,000 rounds hit the fort. Some improvements took place in 1917.

57. This refers to the two brigades that made up the division size unit known as the *Alpinekorps* in 1916.

58. In *Price of Glory*, Alistair Horne notes that the French army had only 170 vehicles in 1914. He also mentioned that 700 trucks could carry 1,250 tons daily, but that the 2nd Army at Verdun required 2,000 tons a day and an additional 100 tons for each new division. The French Ministry of Defence gives the same figures, but states that the number applies to the period before the war. Soon after hostilities started, it rose to 7,000, reaching 95,000 vehicles in 1918. At Verdun, there were 26 trucks when the war began, 31 in 1915 and 9,000 in 1916.

59. The *7th Reserve Division*, which had suffered heavily at Tahure in October 1915 and in January 1916, was sent to the rear. At the end of May 1916, it arrived at Verdun. It took heavy losses (8,200 men) during the *X Reserve Corps* assaults near Chapitre Woods on 21 June. The division was withdrawn on 1 July since there were few replacements to fill its ranks. The *19th Reserve Division* sustained 79 per cent losses among its infantry in attacks made in April, May and July. The *9th Landwehr Division* remained in the Argonne sector during 1916.

60. Gallwitz was sent to the Somme to command the *1st* and *2nd armies*.

61. The *6th Bavarian Division* came from *III Bavarian Corps*, which was replaced by *I Bavarian Corps* (*5th* and *6th Bavarian divisions*) and sent to the Somme, minus the *6th Bavarian Division*. Höhn, a Bavarian artillery officer, commanded the *2nd Guards Division* before he was assigned to the *6th Bavarian Division*. In mid-October 1916, he took command of *XV Reserve Corps*, designated as a Bavarian formation at the time. The *21st Reserve* and *Guard Ersatz divisions* replaced the depleted *1st* and *103rd divisions*. Their own engagements of 23 June and 11 July resulted in massive casualties.

62. The next day, Italy declared war on Germany, which made little difference to the conflict.

63. The *Alpine Corps* was soon on its way to Siebenburg (Transylvania) for the Rumanian Campaign. Many changes took place including sending three of Mudra's divisions to *XVIII Corps* for a short time to hold the front between Douaumont and Vaux. All these divisions needed rest.

64. The *54th* was a special corps formed under General Kühne in September 1916. It was one of several non-traditional corps-type units and designated as General Command (*Generalkommando*). They formed without organic divisions, but were designed to command from two to six divisions.
65. The Tavannes railway tunnel had been converted into a shelter, headquarters, equipment, ammunition storage area and medical facility. Sanitation was lacking and the place was a health hazard. On 4 September, an accident sparked a fire that lasted for 2 days and killed about 500 men including the commander and staff of the 146th Brigade (73rd Division). Troops from four regiments, regular and territorial, were in the tunnel when the fire broke out. The tunnel continued to serve as a refuge after the fire.
66. The 38th was a sister division to the 37th with similar troops from North Africa.
67. The 400mm howitzers were 14km away at Baleycourt.
68. The remains of the gun turret block were turned into a machine-gun bunker and observation position in 1917.

Chapter 6

1. Hindenburg's orders called for a minimum garrison at the front line and only a few deep dugouts. He prescribed one squad-size dugout every 50m or two dugouts every 100m for two squads each, but nothing larger in the front-line trench. Dugouts were to be no deeper than the required 7m of earth cover and should be built of concrete and steel to achieve minimum depth.
2. Operations continued in the Verdun area, especially in the Argonne where American forces became involved in 1918, but these operations were not part of another battle for Verdun. As the Franco–American forces advanced, at least one of the German Feste of Metz fired off a few rounds. If the Allies had been able to engage any of the German Feste before the war ended, they would have faced the strongest forts built before and during the First World War. The Maginot Line incorporated some of the features of these Feste.

Appendix

1. During the Napoleonic era, this was considered an effective way to employ a massive citizen army with little time to train it in marksmanship. In the twentieth century, there was more time for instruction. However, the French did not think that exchanging rifle fire with the enemy was as effective as facing him with cold steel.
2. Some Lewis guns were mounted on vehicles in 1914.
3. According to most sources, after studying the Russo–Japanese War, the Germans had concluded that grenades would play an important role in any future conflict.
4. The Germans developed flamethrowers before the war and had three specialized battalions for them in 1911.
5. Société de Construction de Batignolles, a civil engineering company in Paris, began producing weapons during the war.
6. In *The World War One Source Book* (London: Arms and Amour Press, 1993), Philip Haythornthwaite gives a weight of 2,080lb, firing a 192lb projectile a maximum of about 1,000m. The projectile created a crater about 10m wide and almost 3m deep.

Bibliography

Publications

Adkin, Mark. *Western Front Companion*. Mechanicsburg, PA: Stackpole, 2013.

Army War College. *Instructions on Wiring (Wire Obstacles)*. Washington, DC: January 1918.

Barnett, Correlli. *The Swordbearers*. Bloomington, IN: Indiana University Press, 1975.

Barton, Peter. *The Somme*. London: Constable & Robinson Ltd, 2011.

The Battle of Verdun 1914–1918. Clermont-Ferrand (France): Michelin & Cie, 1920.

Bérenger, Henri. 'The Iron Key to War and Peace', *Current History*, No. 4 (July 1916), in *The New York Times Current History: The European War*, Vol. VIII (July–September 1916).

Bishop, Chris (ed.). *The Illustrated Encyclopedia of Weapons of World War I*. London: Amber Books, 2014.

Bruce, Anthony. *An Illustrated Companion to the First World War*. London: Penguin, 1989.

Bruce, Robert B. *Pétain: Verdun to Vichy*. Dulles, VA: Potomac Books, 2008.

Bull, Stephen. Trench: *World War I Trench Warfare 1914–1916*. Oxford: Osprey, 2002.

——. *Aspects of War: Trench Warfare*. London: PRC Publishing Ltd, 2003.

——. *A History of Trench Warfare on the Western Front*. Oxford: Osprey, 2010.

Castner, J. 'The Development of Recoil and Counter-recoil Apparatus for Long Recoil Field Guns', *Journal of the United States Field Artillery*, Vol. XXI, 1904, 40–65.

Chasseaud, Peter. *Mapping The First World War*. Glasgow: Harper Collins, 2013.

Chorzepa, Jaroslaw and Antol Wap (eds). *Twiedrze I Dzialania Wojenne na Ziemiach Polskich W Czasie I Wojny Swiatowej (Fortresses and Military Operations on Polish Lands During World War I)*. Bialystok-Przansnysz: Ministry of Culture and Art, 2000.

Cox, Michael and Graham Watson. *Pour la France: A Guide to the Formations and Units of the Land Forces of France 1914–18*. Solihull: Helion & Company, 2012.

Creveld, Martin van. *Supplying War*. New York: Cambridge University Press, 1990.

——. *The Changing Face of War*. New York: Ballantine Books, 2008.

Crivelli, Lieutenant. 'Observation Balloons', *Field Artillery Journal* (January–March 1918), Vol. VIII, 342–8.

Cron, Hermann. *Imperial German Army 1914–18*. repr. Solihull: Helion & Co., 2006.

Delvert, Charles Laurent and Joseph F. Bouchor. *Verdun*. Paris: L. Fournier, 1920.

Donnell, Clayton. *The Fortifications of Verdun 1874–1917*. Oxford: Osprey, 2010.

——. *Breaking the Fortress Line 1914*. Barnsley: Pen & Sword, 2013.

Doughty, Robert A. 'French Strategy in 1914: Joffre's Own', *Journal of Military History*, Vol. 67, No. 2 (April 2003), 427–54.

——. *Pyrrhic Victory: French Strategy and Operations in the Great War*. Cambridge, MA: Belknap Press, 2005.

Drury, Ian. *German Stormtrooper 1914–1918*. London: Osprey, 1995.

Falkenhayn, General Erich von. *General Headquarters 1914 1916*. Repr. Nashville, TN: Battery Press, 2000.

Farmer, Gene (ed.) et al. *The First World War*. Chicago, IL: Time Inc., 1965.

Fleischer, Wolfgang. *Deutsche Artillerie 1914–1918*. Germany: Motorbuch Verlag, 2013.

Fitzsimons, Bernard (ed.). *Tanks & Weapons of World War I*. London: Phoebus, 1973.

Foley, Robert T. *German Strategy and the Path to Verdun*. Cambridge: Cambridge University Press, 2005.

François, Guy, Pierre Touzin and François Vauvillier. *Les Canons de la Victoire 1914–1918*, 3 vols. Paris: Histoire & Collections, 2006–10.

Frijns, Marco, Luc Malchair, Jean-Jacques Moulins and Jean Puelinckx. *Index de la Fortification Française 1874–1914*. Welkenraedt: Auto-édition, 2008.

Gaber, Stéphane. *La Lorraine fortifiée: 1870–1940*. Metz: Editons Serpoenoise, 1979.

General Staff, War Office. *Handbook of the French Army, 1914*. Repr. Nashville, TN: Battery Press, 1995.

Gilbert, Martin. *Atlas of the First World War*. New York: Dorset Press, 1984.

von der Goltz, Colmar. *The Nation in Arms*. London: W.H. Allen and Co., 1887; English translation of Goltz's 1883 *Das Volk in Waffen*.

Grand Quartier Général, 3rd Bureau (Operations Section of General HQ). *Manuel du Chef de Section d'Infanterie* (Edition de Janvier 1918). Paris: Imprimerie National, 1918.

Gray, Randal. *Chronicle of the First World War: Vol. 1, 1914–1916*. New York: Facts on File, 1990.

Greenhalgh, Elizabeth. *The French Army and the First World War*. Cambridge: Cambridge University Press, 2014.

Griffiths, William R. *The Great War: Strategies & Tactics of the First World War*. New York: Square One Publishers, 2003.

Gruszecki, Andrzej (ed.). *Fortyfikacja (Tome IV): Fortyfikacja Rosyjska na Zeimiach Polskich (Russian Fortifications on Polish Territory)*. Warsaw: Ministerstwo Kultury i Sztuki, 1996.

Gudmundsson, Bruce I. *Stormtroop Tactics*. Westport, CT: Praeger, 1989.

——. *On Artillery*. Westport, CT: Praeger, 1993.

Guttman, John. *Nieuport 11/16 Bébé vs. Fokker Eindecker*. Oxford: Osprey, 2014.

Harper's Pictorial Library of the World War, 12 vols. New York: Harper & Brothers Publishers, 1920.

Haythornthwaite, Philip J. *The World War One Source Book*. London: Arms and Amour Press, 1993.

Herbert, William V. *The Defence of Plevna 1877*. London: Longmans, Green & Co., 1895.

Herr, Frederick. 'Field Artillery: Past, Present and Future', *Field Artillery Journal*, Vol. XVII, No. 3 and No. 4 (1927).

Herwig, Holger H. *The First World War: Germany and Austria-Hungary 1914–1918*. New York: Arnold, 1997.

——. *The Marne: 1914*. New York: Random House, 2009.

Hindenburg, Paul von. *The Great War*. London: Greenhill Books, 2006; abridged edn of *Out of My Life*, ed. Charles Messenger, London: Cassell, 1920.

Hogg, Ian V. *Allied Artillery of World War One*. Ramsbury: Crowood Press, 1998.

Hohnadel, Alain and Philippe Bestetti. *La Bataille des Forts (Metz et Verdun de 1865 to 1918)*. Bayeux: Editions Heimdal, 1995.

Holstein, Christina. *Fort Douaumont, Verdun*. Barnsley: Pen & Sword, 2002.

———. *Fort Vaux*. Barnsley: Pen & Sword, 2011.

Horne, Alistair. *The Price of Glory: Verdun 1916*. New York: Penguin, 1978.

Horne, Charles F. (ed.). *Source Records of the Great War*, 7 vols. New York: National Alumni, 1923.

Illustrated Michelin Guides to the Battle-Fields (1914–1918). *Verdun: and the Battles for its Possession*. Repr. Lexington (KY): Michelin Tyre Co. Ltd, 2011.

Idzikowski, Tomasz. *Forty Twierdzy Przemysl*. Przemyśl: Regionalny Osrodek Kultury, Edukacji I Nauki w Przemyślu, 2001.

Jäger, Herbert. *German Artillery of World War One*. Ramsbury: Crowood Press, 2001.

Jankowski, Paul. *Verdun: The Longest Battle of the Great War*. New York: Oxford University Press, 2013.

Joffre, Joseph, Colonel T. Bentley Mott (trans.) and Colonel S.J. Lowe (trans.). *The Personal Memoirs of Joffre*, 2 vols. New York: Harper & Brothers Publishers, 1932.

Johnson, Douglas Wilson. *Topography and Strategy in the War*. New York: Henry Holt & Co., 1917.

Johnson, Hubert C. *Breakthrough!* Novato, CA: Presidio, 1994.

Jollivet, Gaston. *L'epopée de Verdun, 1916*. Paris: Hachette et Cie, 1917.

Jones, Simon. *World War I Gas Warfare Tactics and Equipment*. Oxford: Osprey, 1994.

Jung, Peter. *The Austro-Hungarian Forces in World War I*, 2 vols. Oxford: Osprey, 2005.

La Gorce, Paul-Marie de. *The French Army: A Military-Political History*. New York: George Braziller, Inc. 1963.

Laffargue, André. 'The Attack in Trench Warfare', *Infantry Journal*, Washington, DC: The US Infantry Association, 1916.

Lawson, Eric and Jane. *The First Air Campaign*. Conshohocken, PA: Combined Books, 1996.

Lazard, Lieutenant Colonel. *Cours de fortification. 2me partie. Fortification permanente. 3me section, la fortification permanente pendant la guerre 1914–1918*. France: Ecole Militaire et d'application du Genie, 1931.

Legrand-Girarde, General E. and Colonel H. Plessix. *Manuel Complet de Fortification. A L'Ecole Superieure de Guerre*. Paris: Berger–Levrault, 1909.

Le Hallé, Guy. *Verdun: Les Forts de la Victoire*. Paris: Citédis, 1998.

———. *Le Systèm Séré de Rivières*. Louviers: Ysec Editions, 2001.

von Ludendorff, Erich. 'The Verdun Counter-Attack', in Horne (ed.), *Source Records of the Great War*, 7 vols. New York: National Alumni, 1923, Vol. 4.

McMurray, Frank M. *The Geography of the Great War*. New York: MacMillan Co., 1919.

McNab, Chris. *Verdun 1916: Battle Story*. Stroud: The History Press, 2013.

Madelin, Louis. *Verdun*. Paris: Libraire Felix Alcan, 1920.

Martin, William. *Verdun 1916: They Shall Not Pass*. Oxford: Osprey, 2001.

Mosier, John. *Verdun: The Lost History*. New York: Penguin, 2013.

Moyer, Laurence V. *Victory Must Be Ours*. New York: Hippocrene Books, 1995.

Murray, Nicholas. *The Rocky Road to the Great War*. Washington, DC: Potomac Books, 2013.

Neiberg, Michael. *The Military Atlas of World War I*. London: Amber Books, 2014.

Neiberg, Michael S. and David Jordan. *The Eastern Front 1914–1920*. London: Amber Books, 2012.

Nicou, Paul-Rene. 'Iron Ore Deposits of Eastern and Western France', *The Iron Age*, Vol. CVIII (July–December 1921), New York: Iron Age Publishing Co., 1922.

Oldham, Peter. *Pill Boxes on the Western Front*. London: Leo Cooper, 1995.

Ousby, Ian. *The Road to Verdun*. New York: Random House, 2002.

Palat, General Pierre Lebautcourt. *La grande guerre sur le front occidental*, 3 vols. Paris: Librairie Chapelo, 1917, Vol. 2.

Persons, Lieutenant Colonel William E., Major Joseph Plassmeyer, Captain Paul V. Kellogg and 1st Lieutenant John E. McCammon. *Military Science and Tactics, Junior Course* (ROTC Manual), Vol. 3. Missouri: University of Missouri Co-Operative Store, 1921.

Pétain, Henri Philippe and Margaret MacVeagh (trans.). *Verdun*. Toronto: Dial Press, 1930.

Philpott, William. *War of Attrition*. New York: Overbook Press, 2014.

Prasil, Michal. *Skoda Heavy Guns: 24cm Cannon, 38cm Howitzer, 42cm Howitzer and Gasoline-electrical Trains* (Atglen, PA: Schiffer, 1997).

Racier, Ted S. *Crowns in the Gutter: A Strategic Analysis of World War I*. Bakersfield, CA: Strategy & Tactics Press, 2009.

Recouly, Raymond. *General Joffre and his Battles*. New York: Charles Scribner's Sons, 1916.

Reynolds, Francis J., Allen L. Churchill and Francis T. Miller (eds). *The Story of the Great War: History of the European War from Official Sources*, 8 vols. New York: Collier and Son, 1916, Vol. 4.

Rice, George W. Major. *Critical Analysis of the German Attack at Verdun Beginning February 21, 1916*. Fort Leavenworth, KS: Command and General Staff School, 1933.

Rigg, Bryan Mark. *Hitler's Jewish Soldiers*. Lawrence, KS: University of Kansas Press, 2002.

Rolf, Rudi. *Dictionary on Modern Fortification*. Middelburg: PRAK Publishing, 2004.

Romanych, Mark and Martin Rupp. *42CM 'Big Bertha' and German Siege Artillery of World War I*. Oxford: Osprey, 2014.

Sandusky, Captain Richard M. *Critical analysis of the German attack at Verdun beginning February 21, 1916*. Fort Leavenworth, KS: Command and General Staff School, 1933.

Saunders, Anthony. *Dominating the Enemy*. Stroud: Sutton Publishing, 2000.

——. *Trench Warfare 1850–1950*. Barnsley: Pen & Sword, 2010.

Senior, Ian. *Home Before the Leaves Fall*. Oxford: Osprey, 2012.

Simonds, Frank Herbert. *History of the World War: Verdun and the Somme*. New York: Doubleday, Page & Company, 1919.

Sisemore, Major James D. 'The Russo-Japanese War, Lessons not Learned'. Fort Leavenworth, KS: Command and General Staff School, Master's Thesis, 2003.

de Souza, Count Charles. 'The First Assault on Verdun', in Charles F. Horne (ed.), *Source Records of the Great War*, 7 vols. New York: National Alumni, 1923), Vol. 4.

Strachan, Hew. *The First World War*. New York: Penguin, 2003

Stone, Norman. *The Eastern Front 1914–1917*. New York: Penguin, 1998.

——. *World War One: A Short History*. New York: Basic Books, 2007.

——. *They Shall Not Pass*. Barnsley: Pen & Sword, 2012.

Strong, Paul and Sanders Marble. *Artillery in the Great War*. Barnsley: Pen & Sword, 2011.

Sumner, Ian. *The French Army 1914–18*. Oxford: Osprey, 1995.

Taylor, A.J.P. *History of World War I*. New York: Octopus Books, 1974.

Thompson, Mark. *The White War*. New York: Basic Books, 2008.

*The Times Documentary History of the Great Wa*r. London: Printing House Square, 1919.

Touzin, Pierre and Francois Vaulliller. *Les Canons de la Victoire 1914–1918*, 3 vols. Paris: Historie & Collections, 2009–10.

Tricaud, Captain. *Cours de Fortification: Cuirassements*. Paris: Ecole d' Application de l'Artillerie et du Génie, 1909.

Truttmann, Philippe. *La Barrière der Fer*. Luxembourg: Gerard Klopp, 2000.

United States Army, American Expeditionary Forces, General Staff, G-2. *Histories of two hundred and fifty-one divisions of the German army which participated in the war (1914–1918)*. Washington, DC: G.P.O., 1920.

Verdun: Vision and Comprehension. Barcelona: Editorial Escudo De Oro, 1985.

Weiss, George. 'What the War has done for Steel', *The FORUM*, Vol. LVII (January 1917–June 1917), New York: Forum Publishing Co., 1917.

Wells, Neil J. *Verdun: An Integrated Defence*. Uckfield: Naval & Military Press, 2009.

Westwell, Ian. *Weapons of World War One*. Wigston: Hermes House, 2011.

Westwood, John. *Railways at War*. San Diego, CA: Howell North Books, 1980.

William, Crown Prince of Germany. *My War Experiences*. London: Hurst and Blackett Ltd, 1922.

Winter, J.M. *The Experience of World War I*. New York: Oxford University Press, 1989.

Wolmar, Christian. *Engines of War*. New York: Public Affairs, 2010.

Internet

Boucheré, Jean. *Chemin de Fer Historique de la Voie Sacree*: http://translate.google.com/translate?hl=en&sl=fr&u=http://traintouristique-lasuzanne.fr/index.php/fr/l-histoire-du-meusien/la-guerre&prev=search

Ministère de la défense: http://www.defense.gouv.fr.

Massing, Marcus. 'Fortification Verdun': http://www.douaumont.net/index.htm.

The *Soldier's Burden*: http://www.kaiserscross.com/40029/76401.html.

TIMES History Site: https://archive.org/details/timesdocumentary09londuoft.

Vaubourg, Cédric and Julie. 'La fortification Séré de Rivières': http://www.fortiffsere.fr/.

'Verdun: Les Jours Tragiques': http://chtimiste.com/batailles1418/1916verdun1.htm.

Index